OPERATION DESERT STORM

The Apache helicopters of the 101st Aviation Brigade crossed the border into Iraq on the dark but clear night, with a newly-arrived new moon giving advantage to their night-vision capability. Like the courageous Indian tribe after whom they were named, they were both scouts and killers against overwhelming forces. They had been tapped to spearhead the biggest air assault in world history—and fire the first shots in the Persian Gulf war.

Many miles to the south in Riyadh, General H. Norman Schwarkopf was experiencing what he would later describe as "the most anguished moment of the campaign."

"It was the fact that it was D-Day, H-Hour. A battle was going to start that would result in the loss of human life. We didn't have a pep rally in the War Room. We weren't standing up and cheering. Not by a long shot."

Instead, at 2:30 A.M. Saudi Time, General Schwarkopf assembled his full staff in the War Room. He then asked chief chaplain, Colonel David Peterson, to "say a little prayer for the protection of our troops."
It was January 17, 1991. The war against Iraq had begun.

STORMIN' NORMAN
AN AMERICAN HERO

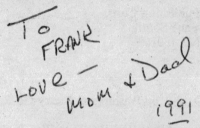

To
FRANK
Love —
Mom & Dad
1991

Jack Anderson
and Dale Van Atta

ZEBRA BOOKS
KENSINGTON PUBLISHING CORP.

ZEBRA BOOKS

are published by

Kensington Publishing Corp.
475 Park Avenue South
New York, NY 10016

First printing: April, 1991

Printed in the United States of America

DEDICATION

This book is dedicated to the spirit and courage of the half a million men and women of Operation Desert Shield and Operation Desert Storm who answered when their country called; to their families who waited at home; and to the valiant few who did not return.

AUTHOR'S NOTE

This book would not have been possible without invaluable reporting and editorial assistance by the staff of the Washington Merry-Go-Round: Associates Dean Boyd, Daryl Gibson, Jim Lynch, Melinda Maas, Scott Sleek and Tim Warner.

Researchers Cindy Gerner and Jonathan Ullman contributed to portions of the book, as did Steve Huettel of *The Tampa Tribune*.

We are also indebted to the countless friends, acquaintances, co-workers and relatives of Gen. Schwarzkopf who gave unselfishly of their time and memories.

Jack Anderson and Dale Van Atta
March 1991 Washington, D.C.

TABLE OF CONTENTS

1.

HANG IN THERE

On the evening of Jan. 16, 1991, Brenda Schwarzkopf heard a snatch of dialogue coming from her television. The bombing of Baghdad was under way. War had begun.

The wife of Gen. H. Norman Schwarzkopf, the supreme U.S. commander in Saudi Arabia, learned of the conflict from the same source as the rest of America—television. Her husband never burdened her with classified information, or extra worry. She had no early word from him that there would even be a war, although her husband had hinted it was likely.

But within minutes after Brenda heard the news on TV, the general called from his high-security basement War Room in downtown Riyadh. It was 4 a.m. Saudi time, 8 p.m. at his modest Tampa home. His timing was unintentionally chilling. Just as he put the call through, air-raid sirens went off in the Saudi capital. Brenda remembers the moment:

"I didn't know that the air war had even started until I turned on the TV. And the first thing I heard was that there were five missiles headed for Riyadh. And I knew that was where my husband was. And I was standing there, in a real panic, thinking about this—and not being able to do anything. At that moment, the telephone rings.

"It was my husband.

"And I said, 'Norm! There are five missiles heading your way!'

"I'm screaming over the telephone like he's going to run somewhere and get out of the way. And, as he always does, there was this calm voice at the other end of the line saying, 'Brenda, it's okay. Everything is all right. I just wanted to call and let you know that the air war has started, but everything is going to be all right.' "

In the same way that he would be able to reassure a nation filled with fathers, mothers, husbands, wives, children, and friends of his troops that all was well, he had gently quieted his wife at the inception of the war. The children quickly joined her on different extensions in the house, and he spoke to each of them.

The general's message, as Brenda remembers it, was simple: "He wanted us to all love one another and take care of one another."

Brenda and the children expressed their love, too, and told him they were his biggest cheering section.

He closed the call with their newly adopted family slogan, "Hang in there."

From the look of him, Norman Schwarzkopf is the personification of the American spirit — tall, burly, big shouldered. His hearty laugh fills a room. But it is his words that jolt, suggesting this is a man worth knowing. Here is a general calling war a profanity. A general who, while he doesn't consider himself dovish, neither considers himself hawkish. He describes himself as owlish — wise enough to avoid war at all costs but, but a believer that there are "still things worth fighting for."

Here is a West Point man who was advised by his own father to stay out of the infantry but, instead, slogged out his career with grunts who stole his heart with their courage in Vietnam.

Here also is a Renaissance man, unusual in higher mili-

10

tary echelons. Someone who speaks French and German, whose musical tastes range from opera and classical to country and western. He devours books from a spectrum that includes military memoirs, philosophers, and the Bible. He considers the great outdoors, from sea to shining sea (and Alaska too), as America's second greatest heritage—second only to freedom.

Norman's conquest has been as much a personal one as a national one. Vietnam was his seminal experience. Back there in the marshes, in some of the bitterness, in some of the agony of lost comrades, Schwarzkopf had lost some of his soul. A mine field full of quiet menace had cost him some of the composure that seemed before like his natural birthright. When he came back, he worked on the experience, he mulled it around in his mind, he probed it for its lessons and became a better man. It was that restorative man who exorcised some of the ghosts of Vietnam and who, for a time in 1991, recalled an America that was once conditioned to happy endings.

Was this fate?

"I can think of no less than five times in my Army career where I came to a 'Y' in the road—and sometimes made a choice about which way to go down, and in other cases was forced to go down one of the routes—and at the time thought it was one of the worst possible things that was happening to me. Looking back, I recognize that I would not be where I am today if I hadn't gone down that path. Now, some people would call that fate. Some would call it destiny. And some people would call it blind, dumb luck. And it's probably a combination of all three."

As with all heroes of history, the character and the caliber of Norman Schwarzkopf were years in the making. He did not spring from the head of Zeus, like Athena, clad in battle-dress and endowed with divine wisdom. The granite-like assurance he exudes was forged in fire and in the blood of past battles. The general who is man enough to cry was nurtured by family, friends, heroes, and experiences which taught him that to be without compassion is to be a worthless human being. The finest endeavor, as native Americans once espoused, is to walk in another person's moccasins . . . or muddy boots.

2.
LIKE FATHER, LIKE SON

Norman Schwarzkopf was born the year Bruno Haupt-mann was arrested for kidnapping and murdering Charles Lindbergh's baby. The two events are linked by more than the calendar. Schwarzkopf's father, Col. Herbert Norman Schwarzkopf, had spent the two years before Norman's birth, on Aug. 22, 1934, trying to track down the most notorious criminal of the decade. As head of the New Jersey State Police, the senior Schwarzkopf led the investigation into the kidnapping. The state's most celebrated cop was also on his way to becoming a major general in the U.S. Army and, like his newborn son, a future Middle East troubleshooter for the U.S. government.

The Schwarzkopfs lived in a big cobblestone house at 2549 Main St. in Lawrenceville, New Jersey, a Norman Rockwellian hamlet, half-way between Trenton and Princeton. Across Main Street from their home stretched acres of sporting grass and the elegant, ivy-clad buildings of the Lawrenceville Prep School. Farther up Main Street was the grocery store and the fish market and not much else. Vines have since claimed the shutters and wrestled parts of the

13

fence to the ground at the Schwarzkopf house. Main Street has edged closer toward the front door.

Norman's father wasted no time telling his son what he was expected to do with his life: You will go to West Point Military Academy someday—just like your father. Few could have looked into their crystal balls and seen pudgy, four-year-old Norman eclipsing the fame of his father.

Norman Sr. was the stout son of a jewelry designer from German stock. His grandfather Christian G. Schwarzkopf had immigrated to America from Germany in 1852. After graduating from West Point in 1917, Schwarzkopf Sr. entered World War I and spent about 50 days at the front. The war was short-lived for Schwarzkopf. He was injured in a mustard gas attack by the Germans on July 15, 1918, and temporarily put out of commission. In the Army of the Occupation after the war, Schwarzkopf was put in charge of the reconstruction of several German farm towns. A series of other assignments followed, until 1920 when his father became ill. Schwarzkopf resigned from the Army to stay close to home in New Jersey.

The brand new New Jersey State Police picked him as its first superintendent in 1921. He was a wizard with a pistol and known for his love of the cavalry. He would badger intimidated new troopers with questions they rarely could answer. His favorite: "What five qualities impress you most about a horse?"

To this day, rookie troopers still must study Schwarzkopf's life and are encouraged to emulate his military demeanor. He was a cop for the moment, but he had started as a military man and forever carried himself as one.

The Schwarzkopf children spent their early years oblivious to the way the Lindbergh kidnapping was sapping the spirits of their parents. The luck of Charles Lindbergh—"Lucky Lindy"—had run out. The handsome American aviator had captured the world's heart when he flew his plane, "The Spirit of St. Louis," across the Atlantic in 1927. When he returned to the United States, he was promoted to colonel and he made a triumphal tour of the country as a beloved hero.

Five years later, on March 1, 1932, Lindbergh and his wife Anne had managed to find some peace and quiet at their Hopewell, New Jersey, home, picked because its isolation screened them from the public adoration. They were relaxing in the house when their nanny climbed the stairs to the nursery to check on 2-year-old Charles Jr. But the baby was gone. A ladder lay in the yard below his bedroom window and a kidnapper's ransom note was taped to the window sill.

The Lindberghs paid the $50,000, but baby Charles was found dead, buried in a wooded lot near the house. The nation was voracious for any news of the hunt for the killer and Schwarzkopf Sr. was at center stage leading the investigation. His men fanned out to chase a seemingly limitless number of dead-end tips before finally catching Bruno Hauptmann, a gravel-voiced German carpenter from the Bronx.

Schwarzkopf pinned the crime, some say too conveniently, on Hauptmann, an ex-convict who had entered the United States illegally. Schwarzkopf never wavered in his belief that Hauptmann was guilty, but the case was subjected to relentless media scrutiny, and questions lingered even after Hauptmann went to the electric chair in 1936. Schwarzkopf's golden image as a sleuth and super-cop was tainted, and, when his term as police superintendent expired, he was not reappointed. His wife Ruth would read books about the kidnapping in the years before her death in 1975 and would note the errors.

It was part of the rites of passage for the Schwarzkopf children that once they were old enough, they were allowed to stay up and listen to their father on the radio. He hosted "Gangbusters," a series of true police adventures. The national audience already knew Schwarzkopf Sr. through the Lindbergh investigation, and the radio show kept him in the limelight. The show went off the air before young Norman was old enough to appreciate it. But its reputation followed him to West Point where his classmates teased him about his father's celebrity.

Norman spent much of his youth surrounded by the Schwarzkopf women. While his father was on overseas assignments, Norman lived with his mother—a cutthroat bridge player and a dynamo of a nurse—and his two older sisters, Ruth Ann and Sally. Closer in age and interests, Norman and the tomboy Sally palled around together and considered Ruth Ann a bit of a priss for learning to play the piano. Norman was an outgoing child who didn't get into much trouble, but he had his moments.

One rainy day in Lawrenceville, restless little Norman griped that he couldn't go outside and play. "Well dear," his mother suggested, "why don't you go upstairs and play Indian?" With the shoot-em-up movie "Geronimo" fresh in his mind, Norman had a different impression of what it meant to play Indian. He scampered upstairs, grabbed a hammer and punched a hole in the forehead of each of his sisters' dolls. Then he tried to scalp them. The massacre stunned his sisters.

As an 8-year-old, Norman watched his hero, his father, leave on a mission to a place he couldn't imagine at the time, but would later play a major role in his life.

The year was 1942 and the United States had just stepped deep into World War II. A crucial allied supply line flowed through the Persian Gulf region into Russia. But the

16

supplies were being waylaid by mountain marauders who stormed down from the windy hills of northern Iran. The Iranian military police were not trained to cope with the bandits. The boyish Shah of Iran asked for help from the United States. President Franklin Delano Roosevelt turned to Schwarzkopf Sr. who accepted the invitation to train Iran's police.

There was already a U.S. military presence in Iran. Schwarzkopf's mission was to work closely and delicately with the Iranian government. He outfitted the Imperial Iranian Gendarmerie with uniforms that sported triangular emblems similar to those worn by the New Jersey State Police.

The job description for the Schwarzkopf-improved Iranian police force included quelling border disputes with the Soviet Union. Sally was stunned to read a headline in the *Trenton Times* about her absentee father: "Schwarzkopf Called Murderer by Soviet Union." Her mother explained that the Soviets were off the mark, not to worry.

The Schwarzkopf clan in New Jersey kept track of Norman Sr. through the letters that arrived at their home every week. He filled their mailbox with the color of Iran—15 to 20 pages at a time rambling about the art, the music, the people and their culture. And, he drew pictures to illustrate his points. The Schwarzkopf children were swept into a Persian odyssey. The letters closed with personal notes for the family and an order for his boy: "Norm, take care of my girls."

At 10, Norm began military school in Bordentown, New Jersey, and escaped the clutches of the Schwarzkopf sisters who had taken to calling him a "sissy." For his class picture one year he had the option of a smiling photograph or a stone-faced one. He picked the dour expression. Why? his mother asked. "Later on, when I'm a general," Norman said. "I want them to know I'm serious."

But life was already becoming a very serious business. At Bordentown, he saw a movie about the dangers of nuclear war. In the film, soldiers being treated after a nuclear blast were carried to a medical tent on the battlefield and sorted, based on whether they were expected to live or die. Group A was the hopeless cases. Group B didn't need immediate help. Group C was treated first. Norm fretted about the image in his daydreams. He would be on a stretcher and someone would condemn him to Group A, the lost causes. "I would spend all day trying to crawl over to Group C, yelling 'I don't want to be over here with Group A! I want to be over there with Group C.' "

When Norm was 12, his father summoned him to Iran. The Schwarzkopf men hunted and toured the countryside, and young Norm joined in on some diplomatic missions as well. The Islamic culture threw him some curves. He accompanied his father to a dignified party where sheeps' eyes were served on a platter. Young Norm looked up at his father for guidance. Norman Sr.'s eyes told the boy he had better eat it with a smile.

The two Normans lived in a huge complex they shared with other members of the U.S. mission. When the Schwarzkopf women arrived six months later, the family moved into a private, palatial residence equipped with a chauffeur, a chef, a butler, a Russian laundress, and a garden boy. The family that had washed its own dishes, shoveled its own coal and taken out its own trash back in New Jersey was now ringing bells to summon the hired help. Norman Sr. saw a problem developing immediately. Less than a week after the family moved in, he gathered his children together. He warned them not to ring a bell or give an order to any servant. They were still middle-class Americans. All of the trappings around them belonged to the job, not them. "You will not develop delusions of graudeur!" was the order of the day. It was an order they would hear again and again, and take to heart. The Schwarzkopf children attended the only English speaking classrooms in Teheran, a Presbyterian missionary school.

While the son learned about the Islamic culture, the father was promoted to brigadier general.

In 1947, the Schwarzkopfs left Teheran for Geneva where the children entered an international school. Norman was a rangy adolescent by then with his hair worn long like the Slavic refugees at the school. He played soccer and tennis and lived freely in the boys' dorm away from his sisters. But he wasn't earning the kind of grades he would need to get into West Point. When his father was transfered to Germany, he pulled Norman out of the boarding school in Geneva and enrolled him in a high school in Heidelberg.

Although the Schwarzkopf household had its rules, Norman Sr. was not a tyrant. Young Norman was a fun-loving teenager and he and his classmates often gravitated to the German pubs.

That was all right with his father as long as Norman was home by midnight. One evening he missed the curfew. The penalty was that he couldn't go out of the house the next weekend.

The weekend came and it was just Norman and his mother. His sisters were at boarding school and his father was away. They lived in a square house with plenty of rooms for a boy to spend his time in, including a music room. Norman retreated there, sat with an accordion and played "Home Sweet Home," all day long. Each time through, he stopped before the final chord. "Be it ever so humble, there's no place like . . ." It drove his mother berserk.

In Germany, Norman blossomed into a determined, ambitious man. He joined the student council and played every school sport he could find.

The 15-year-old Norman Schwarzkopf who returned to the United States in 1950 was far more worldly than his new classmates at Valley Forge Military Academy in hilly Wayne, Pennsylvania. He was also considerably bigger. His 6-foot-3 inch, 200-pound frame towered over the cadets and most of the faculty.

Nobody called him "Stormin Norman" back then, or even "The Bear." Occasionally they ventured to call him "Hugo," when the story went around that the H. in H. Norman Schwarzkopf stood for that. In reality, it simply stands for H. His father detested the name Herbert, so he gave his son only the initial. Schwarzkopf was editor of the class of '52 yearbook, "Cross Sabres," but his classmates somehow managed to sneak by him an insertion in the text by his entry. "Nickname: Hugo."

The class of 1952 was part of the largest enrollment in the school's 24-year history. The 1952 school year was marked with change. The students returned to new sidewalks and freshly-painted buildings. Army Gen. George C. Marshall dedicated the new Chapel of Saint Cornelius the Centurion, its stained-glass windows replete with religious and military imagery. The year also marked the rise of Schwarzkopf as a leader.

Cadets matured quickly in this disciplined world, awakened by the sound of the bugle and ordered to fall into formation in their smart uniforms, their caps pulled low over eyes that did not wander. They learned honor, duty, brotherhood.

Schwarzkopf lived in Wheeler Hall, a simple brick building with large red doors flanked by white pillars. His corner room looked out over the grounds where new cadets learn their drills and walk off their demerits on walking "tours." Even Schwarzkopf walked a tour or two as punishment for misbehaving. His cadet record included this admonition: "It is hoped that you have had time to think this over and understand that we never throw any article of food in the mess hall at Valley Forge."

Maj. Gen. Milton H. Medenbach was the commandant of cadets when Schwarzkopf and his companions walked their tours. Medenbach paced with them and scolded them in their ears. As Schwarzkopf walked one tour Medenbach winked at him. Schwarzkopf sheepishly used the wink as an invitation to admit culpability for his offense. "Yeah, that was pretty stupid," he confessed.

Medenbach liked him and his attitude. "Good enough was not good enough for Norman."

Schwarzkopf excelled at most everything his senior year at Valley Forge. He was the class valedictorian, debate champion and starting lineman on the football team.

His coach Col. L. Maitland Blank never had to yell at him, "never had to rip him." Schwarkopf played better when his temper flared. In fact, the coach quickly figured out that "he'd have to get revved up a little to play the football he was capable of. He needed to be prodded a little to get him going. Any big guy needs to be prodded."

In the cadet hierarchy, Schwarzkopf was the first sergeant, the right hand man to D Troop Cadet Capt. Edward A. Hausberg. He took orders well enough, although sometimes felt compelled to ask why. Hausberg and Schwarzkopf often shared their thoughts. One night near the close of study hall, Hausberg walked two doors down to Schwarzkopf's room. The conversation got around to goals.

"What do you intend to do?" Hausberg asked.

"I want to be a general," Schwarzkopf said. "I'll be very disappointed if I don't make general."

Hausberg "never doubted it for an instant." For him Schwarzkopf was "a man for all seasons. He did more in two years than most do in five or six. He definitely had mind power."

Hausberg saw Schwarzkopf 36 years later when Schwarzkopf received his fourth star in 1988. "He hasn't changed a bit."

Sally was surprised to later find out about how well her brother had done at Valley Forge. "I wasn't in touch with his academic career and he wasn't the kind to talk about it on vacations. He wouldn't sit around and say, "Well, I made valedictorian.' He wouldn't boast."

Schwarzkopf's father was so pleased with what Valley Forge had done with Norman that he donated a portrait of Gen. Dwight D. Eisenhower, which still hangs in the superintendent's office.

In 1989, Schwarzkopf returned to Valley Forge—the academy's first four star general—to deliver the school's commencement speech. "West Point prepared me for the Army," he once wrote in a letter to the academy. "Valley Forge prepared me for life."

Shortly before the Persian Gulf war, when rumors spread about Schwarzkopf's retirement, the academy hoped he would consider returning as the school's superintendent. Even Medenbach sees that was a longshot. "With the four stars he might well be the next (Army) chief of staff." His words were heavy with geniune regret. "There's no hope for him to come back here."

In the fall of 1952, Schwarzkopf entered mystique-laden West Point Military Academy. In four years, it is supposed to mold the cream of the crop into Army officers. The

Academy sits aloft the Hudson Gorge up river from New York City. Stately buildings circle the parade field, known as the "Plain." Off to one side is the National Cemetery where the tombstones of famous military men run to the river bluff. Alongside the cemetery is the cadet chapel, its interior walls covered with plaques honoring generals of the American revolution. One of them, in an out-of-the-way spot, says only, "Major General — — — Born 1740." The name that was once there, Benedict Arnold, has been long since removed from the proud face of West Point.

Class members were grouped by height, and Schwarzkopf went with the other trees. It didn't take long before his classmates latched on to the same nickname his father carried through West Point: "Schwarzie."

It also didn't take long for the upperclassmen to razz him about his famous father. As his class went through the rigors of hazing at "Beast Barracks," the big cadet had to repeat the thematic opening of "Gangbusters" on command. "Schwarzkopf! Give the Gangbusters poop!" He would comply, stomping his feet, mimicking the rat-a-tat of a machine gun and then the wail of sirens. That wasn't all. "Schwarzkopf! How many stones in Cullum Hall?" "Schwarzkopf! Give the definition of discipline!"

Not all the hazing was harmless and some in the class of 1956 cracked, leaving hours after the abuse began. But not H. Norman Schwarzkopf, the son of H. Norman Schwarzkopf. He was ready for it. He expected 100 percent performance from those around him, too. Even those who called themselves his friends always knew he was the man in charge. He saved his scorn for any cadet who did not pull his weight. Classmates now say he was the "same Norm you see on the TV. What you see is what you get."

During Schwarzkopf's second year at West Point in 1953, his father was summoned to the Middle East for another special mission—to protect oil interests. This time Schwarzkopf Sr., who had risen to major general, didn't write his children volumes of details. It is a blank space in his colorful career. The Central Intelligence Agency played a key role in overthrowing Iran's Prime Minister Mohammed Mossadegh and installing the government led by Shah Mohammed Reza Pahlavi. Apparently the CIA thought Schwarzkopf had the right credentials and connections to cope with Mossadegh. At 71, Mossadegh was a frail, wrinkled, banana-nosed man, given to wearing pajamas at official functions and perpetually on the verge of feigned or actual collapse.

In a typical performance, he would be carried to the rostrum on his bed, and from his pillow he would sound laments that would arouse the assembled masses to hysteria. Then he would dissolve into spasms of weeping. The insecure Shah had, to his regret, named Mossadegh his prime minister and Mossadegh soon became too powerful. He nationalized the oil industry, prompting international oil companies to freeze Iran out of the world market.

Mossadegh played a brief and spectacular losing game. The national treasury was quickly emptied, the Shah fled into exile. Then, with the not-so-covert help of the CIA, Mossadegh was overthrown by a street uprising. The Shah was reinstated and Persian Gulf oil interests were once again in the hands of someone who marched to America's beat.

Meanwhile, at West Point, young Schwarzkopf gobbled up his usual overdose of extracurricular activities, including wrestling, football, soccer, tennis, and the German Club. He was commander of his cadet company and led the cadet choir his senior year. The cadets would often sit around and listen to stories of Schwarzkopf's far flung travels as a child.

It was the first time away from home for most of the cadets, but not Schwarzkopf. He flashed his quick wit and was easy to be around. Good grades came easily. He listened to Tchaikovsky's "1812 Overture." He studied the military genius of Grant, Lee, and Alexander the Great. No one pegged him as a future four-star. Instead, they thought he was already equipped with greatness.

When they got time off, Schwarzkopf and his friends went into Manhattan and hit the bars—any place with free snacks. Their favorite spot was the 87th Street Brownhouse. They would eat at Mamma Leone's downstairs and spend the night in the hotel rooms upstairs. The place was packed on weekends. But the well-groomed cadets had no problem cutting to the front of the line if they were in uniform.

On one double date with a classmate, the foursome found a steakhouse—all you can eat for $7.95. Schwarzkopf devoured three steaks and was tempted by a fourth until he saw the waiter's scowl. On graduation night, the same foursome shined themselves up and slipped into a Manhattan restaurant. The same girls who watched Schwarzkopf eat the better part of a cow met more misfortune. The maitre d' seated them next to actress Kim Novak and the two cadets forgot their dates.

Schwarzkopf graduated 42nd out of 485 in the class of 1956. It was a crop of cadets that would come of age as rising military leaders when the United States entered the Vietnam War in 1965. In all, 39 members of the class made general. Schwarzkopf was the first of two to earn four stars.

The same year Norman left West Point his father was retiring from the Army. A glance back at the father's file at West Point reveals a list of extracurricular activities that rivals his son's: "Sharpshooter, football, basketball, polo, boxing, swimming, handball . . ." The class of 1917 yearbook noted that the name Herbert Norman Schwarzkopf "is enough to cause the Secret Service to sit up and take notice." His classmates likened his body shape to a "beer keg." And they poked fun at "Schwarzie's" voracious appetite. "To see Schwarzie attack supper is to sit with wonderment and go starved."

Thirty years after his father's death in 1958, four-star Gen. H. Norman Schwarzkopf spoke at a retirement ceremony for a veteran New Jersey state trooper. He remembered driving with his father through New Jersey and seeing a trooper on the roadside. His father told him to honk. The trooper looked up and waved, probably with no idea of who was waving back. "That's my outfit," his father said.

The similarities between father and son went right down to the toy train sets they insisted on having under their Christmas trees. Both Normans married strong women who ran households while letting their husbands think they were in charge. Both Normans went on from West Point to become generals.

Both Normans put their reputations on the line in the confusing and chaotic Middle East. In 1946, Norman senior met Saudi King Abdul Aziz. More than 40 years later, young Norman strode into the old palace where Abdul Aziz held court and met the current Saudi King Fahd.

During one frustrating stint at the Pentagon, Norman the younger was visited at his home on Fathers' Day by his sister Sally. She brought a gift, a scrapbook that put the two Normans together on paper. There was young Norman in his first military uniform at age 10 on one side of the page and his uniformed father at a similar age on the other side. Then teenage son and teenage father. The matching photos continued to the point where each received his first star. Sally watched her brother study the pictures, his meaty hands turning the pages, slowly and deliberately. Then he finished it, closed the book, crossed the room to his sister and hugged her.

"Thank you," he said.

There were tears in his eyes.

3.

CRYING FOR ALL THE RIGHT REASONS

"I'm going to die! We're all going to die!"

The young private was screaming and flailing around on the ground in terror and pain. Seconds earlier, he had stepped on a land mine, and the blast had hurled him into the air and fractured his leg. A clutch of horrified soldiers stood frozen around him, afraid that his thrashing would trigger another mine. Shaken and slightly injured from the explosion, Lt. Col. Norman Schwarzkopf cautiously stepped across the mine field to reach the private. His artillery liaison officer, Bob Trabbert, was nearby on the radio directing a med-evac helicopter to hurry to the scene.

Schwarzkopf and Trabbert had arrived in a Huey helicopter when they got word that the Bravo Company of the Americal Division's 1st Battalion of the 6th Infantry Brigade was trapped in the mine field on South Vietnam's Batangan Peninsula. Schwarzkopf was their commander, and by the time he got there, Bravo's only two officers had already been wounded by exploding mines. The med-evac helicopter was on the way, but Schwarzkopf ordered the Huey pilot to take off with the two wounded officers while he and Trabbert stayed behind. Schwarzkopf was guiding the rest of the men through the mine field when the private triggered another explosion.

Schwarzkopf reached the screaming man and spread his 6-foot-3-inch frame across him to keep him from moving. Knowing the broken leg would have to be set, the colonel called to Trabbert and three other men to cut a limb from a nearby tree to serve as a splint. One of the soldiers stepped toward the tree and triggered another blast. Three of the men were killed instantly. Trabbert's left leg was blown off, his arm was broken backward and his head was brutally punctured. But he would survive.

Schwarzkopf was awarded his third Silver Star for rescuing the wounded private, but this story, which he told to author C.D.B. Bryan in 1971, as well as the entire Vietnam experience, was a source of a tumultuous inner struggle for the young career military man. It shaped his philosophy on war — and his aversion to it.

Schwarzkopf was more than eager to fight for his country when he volunteered to serve in Vietnam in 1965. To that point, his military career had taken a quiet, conventional route. He attended infantry and airborne schools at Ft. Benning, Georgia, followed by two years with the 101st Airborne Division at Ft. Campbell, Kentucky. He then served two years in Berlin, where parties and an array of fashionable women made the post a bachelor's dream. Next it was Ft. Benning for the career officer course and then a masters degree in mechanical and aerospace engineering in 1963 from the University of Southern California. In 1965, he was ordered back to West Point to teach for three years. Schwarzkopf loved The Point, but he was restless as an instructor during wartime and felt he had a duty to serve in Vietnam. The Army agreed to grant him a transfer request on the condition that he would finish his teaching commitment after a year in Vietnam.

In the summer of 1965, before the war turned completely sour for the soldiers and the people back home, Schwarzkopf became a senior staff advisor to the Airborne Division, U.S. Military Assistance Command in Vietnam. That made him an advisor to Vietnamese airborne forces. The U.S. government for years had been sending such advisers, along with money and hardware, to help the South Vietnamese ward off the Communist insurgency led by the Viet Cong. The time for the advisory role was waning and heavy doses of U.S. combat troops were now being infused into the region.

Serving in Vietnam was a portentous job even then. American advisors were dying. Schwarzkopf arrived when the U.S. troop strength was up to 75,000. Lyndon Johnson had ordered the bombing of North Vietnam. The Marines had landed at Da Nang.

Schwarzkopf called this tour one of the most rewarding years of his life because he was serving a cause he believed in. He slept on the muddy ground with the Vietnamese troops he was guiding and ate rice with chopsticks. He was proud of his unit and of his own service. But even for a young man who had lived all over the world, this jungle-cloaked country was intimidating.

"I got off the airplane and every guy out there in black pajamas, as far as I was concerned, was about to attack me," he said. "It took me two nights to realize that I wasn't in any real danger, and then, they blew up a restaurant right next to where I was staying and I realized that I really was in danger again."

Schwarzkopf won two Silver Stars and two Purple Hearts for his noble acts as a task force advisor on that first tour of Vietman. In one case, he dashed through enemy territory to locate some troops who had become separated from his unit. Along the way he found some injured soldiers, treated them and led them to safety. When his task force assaulted a well-defended Viet Cong position, Schwarzkopf rushed through intensive enemy fire to observe the progress of the attack so he could direct his force's fire. Though wounded four times, he refused to take cover or to be medically evacuated until the mission was accomplished. He earned a Bronze Star early in his tour. In the midst of a mortar attack on a special forces camp, Schwarzkopf organized the unloading of ammunition from a helicopter and saw that some wounded men were placed on board the aircraft and evacuated. And, he earned a commendation medal for directing a successful assault on a heavily-protected Viet Cong position.

But despite his valor and his relentless belief in the cause, Schwarzkopf grumbled about the bureaucratic mismanagement he saw beginning to plague the war operation. Schwarzkopf was especially concerned about the indifference high ranking officers showed toward the men in the field. He was quick to challenge authority when the lives of his men were at stake. When he was three days shy of being promoted to major, he had advised his Vietnamese counterpart not to take his unit into a battle during the 1965 Ia Drang Valley campaign after he learned that commanders hadn't ordered adequate air and artillery support. A few hours later, he was hauled before an array of colonels. "Captain, how dare you say not go?" one of them said. "Who are you to decide what adequate air support is?"

"Sir, in all due respect," Schwarzkopf replied, "When I'm the senior man on the ground, and it's my ass hanging out, adequate air support is about 100 sorties of B-52s circling my head all in direct support of me. I may be willing to accept something less, but that's just barely adequate when it's my butt on the line."

Schwarzkopf attributes the roots of his temper outbreaks to his advisory tour, particularly to a 1965 incident at the Duc Co special forces camp in the Vietnamese highlands. He and the troops he was advising found themselves surrounded by thousands of Viet Cong and North Vietnamese troops, and spent 10 days in a defensive battle. At one point, Schwarzkopf had wounded Vietnamese lying on the ground, desperately needing to be evacuated. Schwarzkopf was on the radio trying to summon a helicopter to carry out the injured men. But the choppers were busy ferrying VIPs. The young officer burned the airwaves with profanity as he angrily called for help.

When a relief unit finally arrived to end the battle, Schwarzkopf had a memorable albeit disheartening encounter with Gen. William Westmoreland, the controversial commander of the U.S. advisory forces in Vietnam from 1965 to 1968. Schwarzkopf, weary and filthy from the fighting, saw helicopters descend with Westmoreland on board. Reporters spilled out of the helicopters, too, and converged on Schwarzkopf for an interview. Westmoreland asked them to give him a moment alone with his officer. Schwarzkopf expected a quiet, soldier-to-soldier pep talk from the general, but Westmoreland instead simply asked him if the mail had gotten through during the fighting. Schwarzkopf was deflated.

He returned home to find few open arms. There were no flags waving, no welcoming committee at the airport. No tickertape. His sister Sally recalled, "After the first tour, he lost his youth when he came back — this light wonderful youth that young men have. He recovered it, but when he first came back he was very serious. It made a deep impression on me. I never discussed it with him. It's not the kind of thing I'd say, 'Gee, you've turned into an old grouch,' which he hadn't. He was just a very serious young man."

Yet his humor wasn't completely buried in the Vietnamese jungle. He continued to let his wit shine at appropriate moments. When a classmate sent him a questionnare to fill out for West Point's Class of '56 10th anniversary book, the bachelor listed his only child as his dog Troll and accompanied his completed form with a poem:

Benning, Campbell, Berlin and California's sunny clime,
At West Point and South Vietnam I've served my
    10 years time.
I've enjoyed every minute of 10 years Army life,
But for the sake of reputation I'd better
    be issued a wife.

As a date, Schwarzkopf was courtly. He made women feel like a million dollars, but none of them got a commitment from him, until he met Brenda Holsinger, a TWA flight attendant from Timberville, Virginia. They met while Schwarzkopf was finishing up his obligation to teach at West Point. Brenda, who lived in New York, had gone with some friends to an Army football game one Saturday in 1967, and in the officers club she bumped into friends she had known years earlier when she dated someone at the Academy. They began telling her about a young man they knew whom they thought she should meet if he came to the club that night. When Norman walked in Brenda said to herself, "I wish it could be that guy."

The two were introduced, and over the course of their conversation, Brenda found him sensitive, calm and gentlemanly. The young officer waited only until Monday to ask Brenda to dinner. They began going to movies and taking walks in Central Park. "I found him a very caring person, a very strong person," Brenda said. "He was a person who liked to tell it like it is and I found it very easy to talk to him."

Two months after their first date, Norman and Brenda were engaged. Norman was 33, and his mother was happy to see his extended bachelorhood coming to an end. She had warned him, "You're going to wind up just like Colonel Joe Schmoe at the Officers' Club every night. What kind of life is that?" But then he met Brenda and his mother was ecstatic: "Oh, I love her! I hope he marries her. She's the one."

Brenda, then 27, had also been listening to her friends fret about her single status. "I think a lot of people were getting worried as to whether or not I was going to make this big step. People would say, 'Why aren't you married at this point?' And I would say, 'I just haven't met that person yet.' And Norm just happened to be that person, so I guess that was what I was looking for."

Norm and Brenda were married July 6, 1968 in the West Point chapel. They honeymooned in Jamaica for eight days. Schwarzkopf was then reassigned from West Point to Ft. Leavenworth, Kansas, to the Command and Staff College. He was promoted to lieutenant colonel ahead of most of his contemporaries. Brenda was a bit skittish about assuming the role of a military wife. "When we first got married, my husband explained to me what this was all about—because I knew nothing about the military. In our first assignment we were going to be with soldiers and a brigade and a company and a battalion. I knew nothing about any of this. So, I had an awful lot to learn and I was a little bit scared about it the first time we went to that assignment. My husband's words were to me then as they are still today, 'Brenda, just be yourself and it will all work out.' "

Schwarzkopf volunteered to return to Vietnam for a second tour, beginning in March, 1969. Brenda stayed in Washington. She only saw him once over the next year, when she met him in Hong Kong for R&R. The war effort that Schwarzkopf joined this time was grim. Dogged by leeches, fever and jungle rot as they trudged through the paddies and villages, the soldiers felt isolated. They were fighting a battle with dwindling support at home and little thanks from their superiors. Men arrived in Vietnam with no concept of jungle warfare and ignorant of both the conditions and the enemy. While the Americans had a fighting chance in the daytime, the Viet Cong were fearsome night warriors. The environment left the soldiers weak and impatient. The unrelenting heat tormented them. The only water on patrol was polluted, and those who drank it developed diarrhea. The men pulled leeches from their necks and legs.

A mixture of racism and mistrust tormented the troops. They began to see any Vietnamese as Viet Cong. Snipers would gun down American troops and then burrow into the jungle, the rice paddies, even the villages. The military pushed officers to produce high enemy body counts. Soldiers coming in from battle would read news accounts of inflated numbers of enemy troops killed. In fact, they were frustrated that their air assaults, artillery barrages, and advanced weaponry were producing few Viet Cong dead.

In the village of My Lai in the coastal Quang Ngai Province, an American infantry company massacred more than 300 Vietnamese peasants—women and children—in cold blood. Soldiers began to suspect that their commanders were covering up other acts of brutality. The peace movement back home was also gaining strength, as Lyndon Johnson, who had been politically decimated by the war, passed the Oval Office to Richard Nixon, who aimed to withdraw from Vietnam without looking like a loser.

Schwarzkopf spent his first five months as a staff officer behind a hated desk at the U.S. Army Vietnam Headquarters, and then was put in command of a batallion, the Americal

Division. He found his men to be poorly trained for fighting, yet they already had been engaged and brutalized in battle. They had suffered numerous casualties, while inflicting few in return. This command was the toughest leadership challenge Schwarzkopf would ever face.

But true to form, he tried to maintain one-on-one contact with his troops. He would visit his company on occasion to talk to the enlisted men. His confidence, intelligence and humor were evident to the men, but these were not brash West Point career men. They found him intimidating. "I remember when we came off a mission and he relieved our company commander for poor leadership," said Bill Savage, an infantryman under Schwarzkopf's command. "A lot of our men had been killed. There was a collective moan from the troops but Schwarkopf's tough talk silenced us."

Like other generals in the Vietnam era, Schwarzkopf left behind him a group of soldiers, scarred both emotionally and physically, who blamed him for the experiences that would haunt them for the rest of their lives. Many thought he was too eager to launch them into battle to get high enemy body counts, which could boost his rank. They became enraged when they were sent into what they regarded as non-strategic areas, looking for Viet Cong, and saw comrades killed and maimed in mine fields and booby traps.

"He didn't care about us," said Martin Culpepper, who served as an infantryman under Schwarzkopf. "I was just a piece of meat without any consideration. As for his character, he was known as 'Buddy Butcher. I never heard anyone call him 'Stormin' Norman' or 'The Bear.' A lot of people got hurt."

The event that brought Schwarzkopf the most criticism occurred on Feb. 18, 1970. Michael Mullen, a 25-year-old sergeant from LaPorte City, Iowa, was killed when an American artillery shell exploded above his fox hole near the village of Tu Chanh. His parents, Gene and Peg Mullen, Iowa farmers, were angered by the Pentagon's apparent indifference to their tragedy and began asking questions about the circumstances surrounding Michael's death. "My son died from friendly fire but my biggest complaint was how his death was handled," Peg Mullen said. "No one would tell me how he died."

35

The original notice from the Army simply said Michael was killed "while at a night defensive position when artillery fire from friendly forces landed in the area." They were told nothing more. They got vague letters signed by Schwarzkopf, which they later discovered he had neither written nor signed. When the Mullens became a nuisance to the Army, Michael's friends in the unit were threatened with court martial if they wrote to his parents. The Pentagon spurned their requests for more information. The Mullens then discovered neither Michael nor another man killed in the incident were listed as casualties, since their deaths weren't battle related. They began to wonder whether the government might be releasing low estimates of American deaths.

Fast becoming anti-war activists, the Mullens spent Michael's death benefit buying an advertisement in the *Des Moines Register* calling for all Iowa parents to speak out against the war. It was filled with 714 small black crosses commemorating Iowa's war dead. A researcher had found that almost one fifth of the Iowa dead weren't included in the Pentagon casualty count. The newspaper ad drew national attention, luring C.D.B. Bryan of the *New Yorker* magazine to the Mullens' home to probe their story.

Bryan's curiosity turned into a book, *Friendly Fire,* followed by a television movie of the same name. He traced the Mullens' efforts to expose the facts surrounding their son's death. The couple became convinced the Army was engaged in a coverup of its mistakes. They discovered another friendly fire incident occurred a month before Michael's death in the same battalion under Schwarzkopf's command.

Bryan spent hours with Schwarzkopf and countless others who helped him recreate the night Michael Mullen died. Bryan concluded Mullen's death was accidental, the result of a careless miscalculation of artillery coordinates. But the Pentagon's cold handling of the case was no accident. Schwarzkopf, while in command, was not on the scene when the artillery fire killed Mullen. Someone above Schwarzkopf had written the terse letters sent out over his signature. The lieutenant colonel had actually been denied permission to write to the Mullens himself.

Mrs. Mullen, now a widow, still blames Schwarzkopf, not for her son's death, but for pursuing the war with such energy. "The thing that really burns me up is when he says he went to Vietnam on a second tour to save lives," she said. "I always believed he went because he wanted to become a general— boost his military rank. You saw it in the way he conducted himself over there. I received countless letters from parents whose sons also served under Schwarzkopf and they all complained of the same thing. Their letters complained of the mine fields and useless death."

Not all of Schwarzkopf's men were naysayers. There was Paul Deer, a platoon sergeant in the Americal division. Although a soldier in Deer's position normally had little contact with a colonel, ugly circumstance brought Deer and Schwarzkopf together. Deer had become agitated over the high ratio of American dead to enemy dead. Morale within the division was low. Deer had graduated from a special Army sniper school near Chu Lai. The Army's best shots were the instructors and 20 men from the Americal Division went through the training. Deer believed sniper warfare like the Viet Cong waged was a way to turn the tables on the enemy. He approached Schwarzkopf and proposed forming a sniper team. Deer was allowed to put together a six-man team and Schwarzkopf gave him complete backing. When Deer requested camouflage fatigues, he got them. When he asked for silencers, they were delivered. The team's needs were always met.

In one instance, Deer's team was looking for the "Phantom 48," a group of Vietnamese women who worked the pastoral fields by day and then turned into warriors at night. Schwarzkopf wanted them found. As the special team searched for the women, Deer bumped into a captain who wouldn't let Deer use his radio to report in to Schwarzkopf. The captain was a bit resentful, Deer thought, because the sniper team had equipment others didn't. The team needed a helicopter, but the captain told them none was available. When Deer finally managed to radio Schwarzkopf, a helicopter was there within

20 minutes. The captain was surprised and embarrassed. Deer felt that without the sniper team, American casualties would have continued to mushroom. "Schwarzkopf wanted to become a general, but he needed more bodies," Deer said. "My sniper team gave him the bodies. He gave us our lives."

If Schwarzkopf was working at earning a star, he didn't plan to do it the way some others did. He showed an aversion to the power struggles he saw in the higher ranks during the war. After the 1970 mine field incident, when he was assigned to the division headquarters in the rear, he was disturbed to find many officers more focused on career promotions than winning the war. The arrogance disgusted him. While his battalion was deployed in the field, the division staff was in the rear eating off white table cloths, being served by soldiers and having tea dances on Sunday afternoons with the Red Cross "Doughnut Dollies."

When Schwarzkopf returned home in July, 1970, the ghosts of his war experience came with him. Joy awaited him in the August birth of his first daughter, Cynthia. Then he entered Walter Reed Army Medical Center a year later for back surgery and met disturbing reminders of his second tour in Vietnam. Friends who visited him said he was easily brought to tears by the sight of the men around him who suffered crippling war wounds. "Norm cries for all the right reasons, mainly in sympathy for someone who gave it his all," said Ward Le Hardy, a West Pointer from the Class of '56 who visited Schwarzkopf in the hospital.

His former artillery liaision officer, Trabbert, was in Walter Reed at the same time — a stinging reminder of the mine field. The nightmare lineup was complete when the Mullens tracked down Schwarzkopf and confronted him in his hospital bed.

It had taken them months to find him. They had come to Washington on an anti-war lobbying mission when they learned through official channels that Schwarzkopf was in Walter Reed. Peg Mullen called Schwarzkopf's room, identified herself as the mother of a boy killed in the friendly fire incident under his command, and said she told him she planned to haul him into federal court. The colonel said he was innocent and asked the Mullens to meet him face to face.

The couple took a cab to Walter Reed and found the hospital to be a devastating experience. It was filthy. Peg was shocked to find even the officers' quarters in poor condition. It was 2 p.m. They found Schwarzkopf in a body cast, and had a brief conversation. The colonel explained his frustration with friendly fire in his battalion and said he was not part of the investigation of the incident in which Michael was killed. "When he saw us, he blubbered like a two year old," Peg Mullen said. "But I didn't feel his tears were real."

Those close to him believed Schwarzkopf was truly grief-stricken over the losses of men he oversaw, but insisted he could not be held responsible for friendly fire deaths. "Mrs. Mullen in particular, was just eating her heart and grinding herself up, and she had to find someone accountable," Sally said. "He just felt very frustrated that they couldn't understand."

Schwarzkopf questioned the whole concept of war and told people he would think long and hard before going into battle again. It was a crushing change of heart for a West Pointer with three Silver Stars. He had difficulty just staying in the military, and was tempted to retreat to a cabin in the wilderness.

"The toughest thing for me to handle was the reaction of the American public to the U.S. military as a result of the Vietnam War. At that time I was young enough and confident of myself enough to know that I could very easily chuck this whole damn military business and go out and make a much better living and get a lot better treatment." When Schwarzkopf went through the painful decision-making process and elected to stay in the Army, he didn't want to have to tread that road in his mind again. When he doubted, he would tell himself, "You've been through this before. Stop and think. Go back and remember what you determined at that time. Remember the rationale from which you determined it and then reevaluate it. Now, do those rules still apply? If the answer is yes, then continue to march."

An event in the spring of 1972 began pulling him out of the emotional pit in which Vietnam had plunged him. Sally, who lived in Washington, had dropped in on her brother's nearby Annandale, Virginia, home one evening carrying a bottle of wine. A war movie was playing on the television as Sally, Norman and Brenda sat and sipped the wine. In the movie, some soldiers came across a mine field, and Schwarzkopf became agitated as he watched the subsequent explosions and fictional-yet-familiar deaths. Sally asked him what he was feeling. Norman tried to explain the horror of the war and lamented the American public's lack of appreciation for the soldiers' efforts. Sally softly pointed out that she believed the anti-war protesters had some valid arguments.

Schwarzkopf burst into tears and told her to get out of his house. When he woke up the next day, he phoned her with an apology. After he hung up the phone, he knew he needed to come to terms with Vietnam before it destroyed him.

4.

THE MAKING OF A GENERAL

When Lt. Col. Schwarzkopf checked into Walter Reed Army Medical Center in the summer of 1971, he was at more than one turning point in his life. Lying in his hospital bed next to soldiers whose bodies had been fragmented by Vietnam, he wrestled with his conscience over the morality of war, the lack of public support, the "baby killer" label tatooed on their efforts. He also worried if he would be medically able to continue his Army career.

An aching back had plagued him since his football days. Leaping in and out of helicopters and parachuting throughout Vietnam hadn't helped. When he had his spine checked, he was told it was fractured, as good as broken. By committing himself to surgery, he had to postpone his invitation into the Army War College in Carlisle, Pennsylvania. The operation came with no guarantees. The surgeons weren't sure it would work. Schwarzkopf gambled that by grafting bone chips from his hip to his backbone, he would regain the powerful spine needed to support his big frame and command troops in the field.

The Army was watching the surgery closely, too. When Schwarzkopf's name didn't appear on the first list of promotion prospects, he worried. The fast-track future of the young Vietnam infantry commander hung in the balance.

West Point classmate George Stapleton was laid up at Walter Reed at the time. Stapleton's back was a mess, too. The reason for his injury was easier to trace. A 122mm rocket broke one of his discs. Stapleton recalls Schwarzkopf's concerns about the surgery. "Norm took a tremendous medical chance to repair his body." Schwarzkopf and Stapleton discussed old times, their dreams at West Point, but mainly the reality of Vietnam and the damage that had been done to the Army.

The operation worked. After shedding his upper-body cast, Schwarzkopf resumed his desk job at the Pentagon. He escaped for a year at the Army War College, but then had to return to the Army's financial management office. He reviewed Army budget proposals and projected the impact of inflation and unemployment on future Army programs—not the sort of work a rugged infantry commander likes to do. Especially if that man is Norman Schwarzkopf.

The paper-pushing, the policy making, the bookkeeping still frustrate Schwarzkopf. His big head hangs lower and he shakes it from side to side. He moans, he groans and he waits, impatient for the open air, and the soldiers. He is no desk jockey. During the period at the financial management office, he yearned to be out in the field accomplishing something— something instead of running in place at the cavernous Pentagon. Even his Virginia apartment seemed too small with two babies, now. Daughter Jessica was born March 12, 1972.

He got his chance for a move in the fall of 1974 when a job opened for a deputy commander of the 172nd Infantry Brigade at Ft. Richardson in Alaska. He jumped at it. Who wanted to go spend an arctic winter near Anchorage? Almost nobody, but Schwarzkopf. That's where he proved to the Army he was a fit and able field officer. He proved it to himself, too.

He took Ft. Richardson by storm, intimidating soldiers with his stern, formidable presence and his stern attention to detail. He ran training exercises with the intensity of a commander on a real battlefield. If one of his batallions was supposed to cross a line at a certain minute they had better be there or the famous Schwarzkopf temper would erupt. He marched his troops out for winter Jack Frost training exercises. Some of the soldiers spent as much as a month running drills and mock battles, surviving in the ice and snow. Schwarzkopf made them build ice bridges over rivers and made it painfully clear they were going to be the best cold weather unit in the Army.

Come Aug. 1, 1975 Schwarzkopf marched his troops 70 miles in three days to Talketna, a tiny town where the Susitna, Chulitna and Talketna rivers collide. His long column of soldiers stretched for miles along the Glen Echo highway. The march was just a prelude to "Ace Car Chulitna," 11 days of simulated battle exercises involving 4,000 soldiers. Ft. Richardson hasn't held the grueling drill since.

Schwarzkopf's burly build and grizzly-like temper spawned the nickname, "Bear." He was part teddy and part grizzly. His temper had become the stuff of lore in the Army. But many of those who have worked beneath and beside him, say he uses it wisely.

"He can eat people alive," said an Army friend that has known him well for 20 years. "But it's brief and after it's over he can turn around, see the guy five minutes later and say, 'How you doing, Walt?' He doesn't hold grudges." Schwarzkopf likes the nickname so much he later named his hunting dog, a black labrador, "Bear." He also bought a Robert Bateman original painting of a polar bear emerging from an ice fog.

Schwarkopf had seen more of the world than most people see in a lifetime but he had seen nothing like the frontier wilds of Alaska. Ft. Richardson rests on the foothills of the Chugach mountain range, a panoramic blast of jagged peaks, chock full of glaciers. A few miles off the post, on a clear day, Mt. McKinley looms 20,300 feet above sea level like a sculpted cloud bank. Tidal shifts roar up the broad Cook Inlet in foot-high mini-tidal waves. Salmon and trout ripple the surface of lakes, rivers and coves. Bear, elk, and moose amble through the forests. Bald eagles glide overhead.

When Schwarzkopf got time off, he disappeared into the

hills, often by himself. One weekend, he had his wife drop him off on the trail head of Resurrection Pass Trail, an old gold mining path through the Chugach Forest. It was Friday and he told Brenda to pick him up on Sunday at about 5 p.m. "I'll just be out alongside the road. You just keep driving and you'll find me." Resurrection Pass Trail was about 38 miles long when Schwarzkopf hiked it. It's the most popular trail in the Chugach, but long enough that a solitary hiker may not see another person for days. The trail is a roller coaster of inclines and declines running along the treeline of spruce and willow and wrapping around lakes. Streams cleave the trail at points and the meadows offer views of the snowy peaks. Some of the world's largest moose feed nearby. Schwarzkopf kissed his wife goodbye and vanished into the greenery.

It rained all weekend. On Sunday evening, Brenda and her two daughters, Jessica and Cindy, hopped into their four-wheel drive GMC Jimmy and went hunting for Norman. They couldn't spot him on the road and started to worry. They turned into a restaurant filling station combo and asked the waitress for help. Where would a man come out if he had just hiked Resurrection?

A couple eating dinner at a nearby table overheard the question. "Are you looking for one man?" the man asked.

"Yes," Brenda said.

"Oh, he's down the road about a mile sitting there alongside the road."

Brenda and the girls drove the mile and found Schwarzkopf, spent, leaning against his backpack, his boots off, his feet bleeding. "He had the biggest smile on his face you've ever seen in your life," Brenda says. "He had a ball. He loves animals and he loves nature. He really got something out of being out there all by himself."

Alaska so enchanted Schwarzkopf that he pestered Sally to make time to visit. He wrote her a letter that said if she arrived at the right time they would go fishing in the wilderness. For Sally, a self-proclaimed workaholic in Washington, D.C., the offer created a dilemma. She discussed it with her mother.

"I'm so essential at work," she told her mother.

Ruth Schwarzkopf bristled. "Sally, You're turning into a turtle!"

Sally listened, then flew to Anchorage and stayed for two weeks. Schwarzkopf rented a camper trailer and he and his wife, sister and two daughters drove off into Mt. McKinley National Park. Sally had never seen such pristine lakes as the ones her brother showed her. He also took her on a classic Alaska fishing trip. A pilot-friend of Norm's flew him and Sally in a tiny plane into the remote terrain. They landed in an Indian village and trekked to a hidden river. Norman caught four salmon and Sally one. The heavy fish slowed their hike back to the plane. Norman, no doubt, recalls the way the salmon tasted that night. Along with rouquefort-stuffed steak, and Breyer's mint chocolate chip ice cream, salmon is his favorite dish.

Schwarzkopf sent a letter to his West Point classmates for their 20th anniversary yearbook in 1976. He raved about Alaska: "We have fallen in love with this state and the many opportunities it offers. This, coupled with my command, has to make this the finest assignment we have yet had. We plan to stay with the Army as long it will have us!"

Alaska satisfied Schwarzkopf's passion for the outdoors. It also put the career he wanted back on track. As deputy commander of the infantry brigade, he got to train and work with soldiers. It's where his reputation as an officer who cared about his soldiers began to grow. It's also where he finally made full colonel. That promotion took seven years. Schwarzkopf would never wait that long again.

In the fall of 1976, Schwarzkopf and his family moved south to Ft. Lewis, near Tacoma, Washington, where Schwarzkopf got his first full command position. The 3,000 infantry soldiers of the 1st Brigade were his. The soldiers soon learned he was tough and demanding. His aggressive demeanor peaked when the troops engaged in simulated combat at the National Training Center at Ft. Irwin, California. One division was pitted against another, and could take prisoners and launch assaults on "the enemy." Umpires graded each brigade. Schwarzkopf barked at his troops. "Do this! You do that! Where's the tank!? Where's the ammunition!?" Another Ft. Lewis brigade commander says that was the day he first heard the nickname "Stormin' Norman."

Schwarzkopf worked his troops into the mud, but he never liked to be too far away from them. And he was loyal. Schwarzkopf's son, Christian was born while the family was posted at Ft. Lewis. Schwarzkopf's blossoming sense of family spilled over into his work. "His brigade was very close," said a colleague. "You see the sense of family in that brigade. Everybody was taken care of." A Fort Lewis awards board soon found out how protective this colonel was of his troops. The board passed out kudos for "best supply room," "best mess hall," and other categories. When Schwarzkopf's men were passed over on award day, he chewed out an old West Point classmate who headed the board. He wanted to make certain it didn't happen again.

After a quick change of command at Ft. Lewis, Schwarzkopf fell under the direction of Gen. Richard E. Cavazos, a likeable Texan with a passion for hunting. Cavazos noticed right off how well Schwarzkopf interacted with his soldiers. He worked them hard. "But more than anything, he was a real maker of military leaders. He wasn't interested in climbing ranks. He was interested in his men." Cavazos and Schwarzkopf would remain friends for many years. When Cavazos retired from the Army, Schwarzkopf was there. "I was crying when I walked out to the plane," Cavazos said. "I noticed he was crying too."

Schwarzkopf also had the pleasure of serving alongside his War College buddy, then-Brig. Gen. Jack Walker. As Walker discovered, Schwarzkopf hunted birds with the same pragmatic foresight he used to draft battle plans. The two Army officers crossed the Cascades into eastern Washington to hunt Chucker, a colorful Middle Eastern bird about the size of a partridge that was imported into the dry Yakima valley. It flies fast and erratically and it's hard to shoot.

Walker and Schwarzkopf spent one grueling day stalking the elusive Chucker. The sun was setting when Walker reached the ridge where Schwarzkopf stood and eyed the valley below. They had been hunting since daybreak, but they hadn't bagged a single bird. Schwarzkopf hadn't even had a chance to fire his shotgun. But it didn't bother him a bit. Instead, as his friend joined him for the view, he bellowed in his gregarious voice: "Great day to be alive in Yakima!"

In 1991, when Walker's son served in the Persian Gulf, he said, "Had my son had to give his life for his country, I can't think of a commander I'd rather have him have to give that ultimate sacrifice for than for Norm."

Every year, Army personnel wizards camp out in a small room and sift through some 4,000 colonels looking for the blue chippers with the right stuff for a star. About 40 colonels make general each year. They need a variety of ingredients. The Army looks for leaders who know how to get the most from their troops—men committed to their soldiers.

In the spring of 1978, Schwarzkopf's name appeared on the promotion list. He and about 40 other stellar colonels were called to Washington for the Army's general orientation school, better known as "Charm School." For six weeks they learned about the changes in the Army, then traveled the country inspecting posts. Even amidst that lofty company, Schwarzkopf stood out. Dallas Brown Jr. went through Charm School with Schwarzkopf and recognized him as a leader among some very ambitious individuals. "The other colonels listened to him when he talked."

Schwarzkopf's next climb toward the Army's summit took him to Hawaii in July of 1978. His new assignment: deputy director of plans for the Pacific Command. It meant developing military, political and economic plans and policy. It meant meeting with Pacific nations and working as a liaison with the Pentagon. Big responsibilities. No soldiers.

Within a month after being assigned to the Pacific Command, Schwarkopf got his first star. He had yet to turn 44-years old. The star was sweet, but the job was a desk. In his spare time, he explored Hawaii's islands. He sent Sally seductive pictures of exotic places and turquoise waters. But he

47

couldn't coax her into a visit. Schwarzkopf played a lot of tennis and learned how to scuba dive. But it wasn't a fulfilling tour. People would say, "Hey, you're in Hawaii. It can't be too bad."

"Yeah," Schwarzkopf would grumble. "But I don't have any soldiers."

Freed from his desk job in the sun, Schwarzkopf welcomed the opportunity to return to the soldiers and the mud. In 1980, he became the assistant division commander for the 8th Infantry Division based in Mainz, West Germany. The Army has had a bevy of strong European commanders. Gen. Paul Gorman was one of the best before he left to head the U.S. Southern Command in Panama. He was succeeded by a string of other fine commanders, including Gen. Carl Vuono, later the Army chief of staff. Schwarzkopf marched into this talented forum an eager one-star ready to learn. He spent two years in his ancestors' stomping grounds and left with his second star.

As another assistant division commander in Europe described it: "Norman had the advantage of being placed in a wonderful learning environment. He had access to some great trainers and military minds." Schwarzkopf also entered the European theatre at a time when revolutionary innovations in simulated warfare became available to Army field units. In the early 1980s the Army introduced the Military Integrated Laser Engagement Simulation (MILES) equipment. For the first time, troops could simulate lifelike combat.

The mix of high-tech equipment, excellent training and brilliant talent revolutionized the 8th Infantry Division. "The 8th was always light years ahead of the others," said Lt. Gen. John Woodmansee Jr., a West Point classmate of Schwarzkopf's and former commander of the Army's V Corps in Europe. "This is where he gained a lot of his experience as 'Norm, the tactician.' He carried all this with him."

Along with his battleground education, Schwarzkopf also gained some entrepreneurial insights from his European tour. While stationed in Mainz, he assumed the role as a community mayor of sorts. His command of German made him an ideal liaison with the local mayor of Mainz. One day the mayor approached the general with a problem. Within a few weeks, Pope John Paul II would visit the city. The mayor needed a place to house the ceremony. He had numerous churches and public buildings to choose from, but none matched the Army post in size. The mayor asked Schwarzkopf if he could host the event. Schwarzkopf jumped at the idea and began prepping for the Pope and the thousands who would, undoubtedly, come to see him. He also struck an agreement with the mayor that the post would handle all the concessions.

Funding was sparse for the day care center and other family support facilites on the post. Commanders are encouraged, if not forced, to keep these services profitable. It's a constant battle to keep them afloat. The Pope's visit was a once-in-a-lifetime opportunity for diplomacy. But, it was also a potential gold mine, a commander's dream fundraiser. Especially if you're Gen. Norman Schwarzkopf, a man driven to improve quality of life for the common soldier.

Schwarzkopf ordered his troops to prepare hot cider and as many ham and cheese sandwiches as humanly possible. By charging about a dollar and a half a sandwich, he figured he would ease the money pinch. But his capitalist scheme didn't take into account the weather. It was miserable. The Pope's robes flapped from side to side in a windy rain storm. Only a handful of visitors arrived for the ceremony. When it was over, the Pope thanked everyone and left, leaving Schwarzkopf with some 2,000 ham and cheese sandwiches.

Months later, a lieutenant from Gen. Woodmansee's post in Kneissen, Germany, stepped into Woodmansee's office. "Sir, you wouldn't believe the deal I've come across. I was offered nearly 2,000 frozen ham and cheese sandwiches for 15 cents a piece!" Woodmansee laughed. He knew they belonged to Schwarzkopf. "They're probably rotting by now. Don't buy them." For weeks, Woodmansee and others teased Schwarzkopf. "Hey Norm, you want to go in on a deal on some sandwiches?" Woodmansee summed it up. "Norm is better suited as a general than an entrepreneur."

* * *

With his second star pinned to his hat, Schwarzkopf returned to Washington, D.C., and the bowels of the Pentagon in August 1982. His new title was director of Army personnel—a policy making job. His duties included developing "policies for active and reserve component promotions," and "policies, procedures and legislation pertaining to: medical, mental, physical, and moral standards for accepting and retaining all military personal" etc. Important work. Big responsibilities. No soldiers.

Luckily for Schwarzkopf's sanity, the job only lasted 10 months. By June 1983, he was Georgia-bound as the incoming commanding general of the 24th Mechanized Infantry Division at Ft. Stewart. It wasn't easy, but West Point classmate Ward Le Hardy convinced Schwarzkopf to take a mini-vacation when the family was driving to their new post. The Le Hardys were lounging on South Carolina's Kiawah Island. Schwarzkopf agreed to drop in and see them.

The Schwarzkopf family pulled up at Le Hardy's beach house in separate cars. Norman wheeled in first in a plush, air-conditioned Mercedes, with Christian beside him. Luciano Pavarotti's tenor belted from the car stereo. Right behind the Mercedes came the family station wagon, loaded down with Brenda, the two girls, a black lab, two parakeets, a gerbil and a cat. Brenda had a bandana around her forehead to keep the sweat out of her eyes. Schwarzkopf stepped out, cool and smiling, into the salty beach air.

"What the hell?" Le Hardy asked. "Why is Brenda in the hot station wagon?"

"How else can I hear classical music?" Schwarzkopf asked, and grinned.

Nothing could dampen the exuberant mood of this two-star general, hellbent for Ft. Stewart and, for the first time in his career, complete command of a post. It meant 14,400 soldiers and a whole lot of mud. It also meant that in four months time he would be called to put all he had learned on the line.

5.

URGENT FURY

On a Sunday afternoon in October 1983, Schwarzkopf first received word of the operation. Weekend afternoons he liked to spend hunting or fishing in the piney woods near Ft. Stewart, Georgia. This Sunday, he chose to go large-mouth bass fishing. He often boasted about catching a 10-pound bass in the waters near the post. This was some of the best bass fishing country in the United States. Only 75 miles south of Ft. Stewart, back in 1932, someone had reeled in the standing world record for largemouth bass — 22 pounds, 4 ounces.

Schwarzkopf didn't know that at this moment his name was one of those being circulated as a potential candidate for a post with Combined Joint Task Force 120 — the command structure which would oversee the invasion of Grenada. Gen. Richard E. Cavazos, Schwarzkopf's former division commander at Ft. Lewis, had since become commanding general of the U.S. Army Forces Command in Atlanta. In this position he would be responsible for providing the Army Rangers and troops from the 82nd Airborne Division for the operation. He would also be responsible for nominating Norman Schwarzkopf for the mission.

In the days leading up to the operation, the Pentagon was searching for an Army liaison officer for the task force. Cavazos didn't have to think for more than a second about whose name he would submit. He knew the operation would require someone well-versed in land warfare. As an

Army man, Schwarzkopf would not be completely welcomed on the Navy ships. But, Cavazos knew Schwarzkopf was flexible enough to deal with a joint operation which included every branch of the military. He had overwhelming confidence in his friend.

As commander of the 1st Brigade, 9th Infantry Division under Cavazos at Ft. Lewis, Schwarzkopf had proved himself again and again. Cavazos knew him as a natural leader who was able to get the most from his men. He had seen how hard Schwarzkopf could be on his troops, and how the men responded positively to that pressure. Schwarzkopf had even talked back to him on occasion, but it was never rude or out of line, "Just airing some things out," Cavazos called it. Cavazos had presided over the ceremony in which Schwarzkopf was given his first star.

The Pentagon was intially reluctant to pull Schwarzkopf out of his command position at Ft. Stewart for the Grenada operation, but Cavazos insisted. "I knew if Norm was there, they wouldn't have to worry about the ground forces. They wouldn't even have to talk to him again. Norm would just rise to the occasion and take over. I really wanted him to become deputy commander for the operation." Gen. John Wickham, the Army chief of staff, agreed to let Schwarzkopf have the job.

The afternoon of fishing in Georgia had yielded a decent catch, and Schwarzkopf returned home to cook up the bass for dinner. The phone rang at 6 p.m. On the other end was Maj. Gen. Richard G. Graves from the Army Forces Command in Atlanta. Schwarzkopf was given few details about the impending military operation for which he had been chosen. All he knew was that he was to be taken to Atlanta at once. He had little idea about what he was getting into. As he walked out the door, Brenda was even more in the dark. She was convinced he was going to Lebanon.

Since March 1979, Grenada had been a growing thorn in the side of Washington. That year saw the overthrow of the conservative government of Sir Eric Gairy, who in 1974 brought independence to the island from Britain. Widespread corruption and Sir Gairy's use of "Mongoose gangs" spawned unrest on the island. The gangs were a private police force instructed by the security men of Chilean dictator Augusto Pinochet, and they did a good job stepping on Sir Gairy's critics. Nonetheless, several opposition parties cropped up, the largest of which was the New Jewel Movement, a socialist-oriented party, led by the enormously popular Maurice Bishop. Bishop's father had been killed by Grenadian police during a human rights demonstration on the island in 1974. Taking advantage of Gairy's temporary absence from the island on March 13, 1979, Bishop took control of the government in a relatively bloodless coup to create the People's Revolutionary Government.

In the years that followed, Grenada reorganized along socialist lines, much to the dismay of Washington. Within months, Grenada began voting with Cuba in the United Nations. Both countries voted against U.N. resolutions condemning the Soviet invasion of Afghanistan.

Before long, Bishop seemed to enjoy sharing a pariah role with Fidel Castro as one of the bad boys of the Caribbean.

The economy of the island did not quite match Bishop's rhetoric. His government created a new state sector, consisting of some 23 enterprises, including hotels and nightclubs, but that only accounted for a third of the economy. The majority of the island's businesses remained in private hands. Bishop's government embarked on literacy and health campaigns and implemented marginal land reforms. In 1981 the World Bank found Grenada's economy one of the few in the Western hemisphere experiencing per capita growth. But in the next few years, the economy became increasingly susceptible to falling commodity prices. Bishop attempted to move away from reliance on the island's traditional exports of nutmeg, cocoa, and bananas, and naturally sought to expand the tourism trade.

Tourists need airports, so Bishop began to build one to replace the dilapidated Pearls Airfield on the northeastern shore of the island. Construction began on a 9,500-foot runway at Point Salines on the southwestern tip of the island, with Cuban funding, construction equipment, and labor. In the eyes of Washington, the work at Salines was nothing less than a potential military base for Soviet and Cuban interests in the eastern Caribbean. In March 1983, President Reagan made public a reconnaissance photograph of the airport, and began to build a case for invading Grenada, arguing that the airport was part of a "rapid buildup unrelated to any conceivable threat" against the small island nation of some 11,000. There were armored fuel storage tanks, and reinforced ammunition storage bunkers near the airport, U.S. officials claimed. It would be a perfect spot for the latest in Soviet-made strike, reconnaissance, and transport aircraft. State Department officials were also concerned because Cuba was paying for the construction of a 75 kilowatt transmitter for Radio Free Grenada, the island's state controlled press.

Cuba and the Soviet Union were also arming and advising the 1,000 soldiers of Grenada's People's Revolutionary Army (PRA), under the command of General Hudson Austin. Bishop, increasingly wary of a violent ouster at the behest of Washington, began ordering Eastern Bloc weaponry as early as October 1979. By the time of the invasion his stockpile had grown to 1,200 AK-47 automatic rifles and another 2,800 small arms of various manufactures. According to a classified Army history of the operation, an inventory after the invasion found that the Soviets had also supplied sixteen 23mm anti-aircraft weapons, five 12.7mm. four-barreled machine guns, 23 heavy machine guns, and nine armored vehicles. Bishop's weapons stockpile was far too big for the number of troops on the island—too ambitious for a banana republic.

Washington watched in alarm as Cubans began arriving on the island in various capacities, although the exact number remained the subject of some dispute. U.S. officials initially estimated there were 1,600 Cubans on Grenada before the invasion, but the number turned out to be no more than 800. Fifty of them were military personnel assigned to advise the PRA, and the rest were construction workers, most of whom had once served in the Cuban army on active duty or as reservists. Though they were few in number, the Cubans would put up a serious fight. Defense intelligence analysts had overestimated their numbers, and then underestimated their abilities, concluding that the "Cuban threat to U.S. insertion of a substantial military force is estimated to be low."

The large stocks of weapons caused most U.S. intelligence analysts to overestimate the number of Grenadian PRA troops on the island as well. The PRA numbered no more than 1,000. U.S. officials were throwing around the number 1,500 in the days before the invasion, and again overestimated numbers and underestimated grit. Washington's read on the PRA was that their combat capability was "minimal against a well-equipped force." As U.S. troops would later find out, the PRA was highly motivated.

In the years leading up to the invasion, Reagan used a number of measures to pressure the left-leaning government. He cut Grenada out of the Caribbean Basin Initiative, blocked aid from the Caribbean Development Bank, and tried to block International Monetary Fund and World Bank loans to the island. He tried to float past Congress a covert destabilization plan against the Bishop government, but the Senate Intelligence Committee refused to approve it.

By 1983 there was active talk of a U.S. military operation against the island. President Reagan in his so-called "Star Wars" speech on March 23 argued that "The Soviet-Cuban militarization of Grenada can only be seen as a power projection into the region." The heated rhetoric prompted Bishop to fly to Washington, where he was largely snubbed, save a 40-minute meeting with National Security Advisor William Clark. Clark refused to talk publicly about the meeting, but Bishop, in an interview months later, indicated that he had "struck a deal." An understanding was secretly reached for Grenada to tone down its anti-U.S. rhetoric and even Marxist policies, in return for improved relations with Washington.

Bishop returned to Grenada, and in the ensuing months, butted heads with his deputy prime minister, Bernard Coard, and other Marxist hardliners in the government. Building on a smoldering inter-party dispute which had raged since 1982, the hardliners felt Bishop was becoming too moderate. On Oct. 12, 1983, Coard had Bishop put under house arrest and charged him with, among other offenses, not being a true revolutionary. Soon, the popular Bishop was freed by a crowd of angry demonstrators. On Oct. 19, Coard and the army responded by shooting into the crowd and recapturing Bishop. Within hours Bishop was executed. The following day, Gen. Hudson Austin proclaimed himself head of Grenada's new 16-man Revolutionary Military Council, which consisted largely of Marxist hardliners. Most Grenadians were devastated by the murder and hostile toward the new military junta. Even Castro was outraged.

Bishop was no favorite in Washington, but the alternative was worse. At the Pentagon, military planners were already in high gear. Planning for a possible evacuation operation of Americans living in Grenada began as early as Oct. 14, before Bishop was killed, according to classified Army documents. As the situation worsened, talk of evacuation turned to talk of invasion.

There were hundreds of U.S. medical students on the island. Reagan had heavily criticized President Jimmy Carter in the 1980 election campaign for the bungled hostage rescue attempt in Iran. He was determined not to let Americans become pawns in his own backyard. But, Reagan still needed some legal pretext for an invasion — an invitation.

He got it on Oct. 21 after a meeting between a senior State Department official and the prime ministers of Dominica, Barbados, Jamaica, Antigua-Barbuda, St. Kitts-Nevis, St. Lucia, St. Vincent, Montserrat and the Grenadines, which—minus Grenada—formed the Organization of Eastern Caribbean States. Out of the meeting came the crucial "urgent invitation" for a U.S. intervention in Grenada.

The message was passed to the White House, and by 9 a.m. the next day, the National Scurity Council received approval for a military plan to restore democracy and eliminate Cuban interference on Grenada. The approval came from the president in Georgia via a secure phone in the Old Executive Office Building. Vice President George Bush instructed that the movement had to be quick, but it "had to be right." There could be no repetition of the failed Iran rescue effort.

By Sunday morning, President Reagan had all the more reason to strike out at someone and prove American military might. That morning in Lebanon, a Mercedes truck drove into the Marine compound and detonated a huge bomb killing 241 American servicemen. Reagan returned angrily to Washington Sunday morning, reconvened the National Security Council and reaffirmed his determination to make a move in Grenada.

Norman Schwarzkopf arrived in Atlanta for a briefing on the operation at 10:15 p.m. on Sunday, Oct. 23. He had not participated in any of the planning up to that point, and was still unsure of what he was getting into. He had no idea that Navy SEAL teams were already in trouble off Grenada. According to a classified Army history, on that Sunday night, 16 Navy SEALs had dropped from helicopters onto two Boston Whaler crafts at sea in an attempt to scope out the new airport at Point Salines. Four of the men were lost in the high seas and none of the Boston Whalers reached Salines. The mission was aborted and rescheduled for the following evening. This was to be the first among many problems encountered by SEAL teams approaching Grenada before the main force.

The next morning, Schwarzkopf got his first look at Vice Admiral Joseph Metcalf III, the task force commander of the Grenada operation with whom he would work elbow to elbow in a small room atop the U.S.S. *Guam* for the next few days. "Schwarzkopf took up half of the room, and I took up 10 percent myself," Metcalf said. With a lieutenant colonel being the only Army liaison on his staff, Metcalf welcomed the addition of a major general. The command structure was virtually invented on the spot and Schwarzkopf was tagged the Army liaison officer for the Joint Task Force.

Although the morning briefing in Atlanta began as a loose, a free-wheeling discussion, the previous night's failure of the SEAL mission gave them pause. There was even a recommendation that the operation be delayed for a day. Everyone left the meeting troubled by the lack of detailed planning. Metcalf's task force was using an old black and white map published by the British Ministry of Overseas Development. Schwarzkopf would grow increasingly perturbed over the lack of good information throughout the rest of Operation Urgent Fury.

Schwarzkopf and Metcalf left for Barbados at 11 a.m Monday and were lifted by helicopter from there to the deck of the USS *Guam* waiting off Grenada. During the trip they used what little time they had to become acquainted. They arrived on the *Guam* minutes before President Reagan formally signed the executive directive authorizing Operation Urgent Fury. The message was relayed to the *Guam*, and invasion was set for 5 a.m. the next day.

After the announcement, Schwarzkopf walked out on the deck of the *Guam*, and stared out at the sea. Just hours before he had been back at home cooking bass. Now he was part of the first major U.S. military operation since Vietnam, and he had had little role in the planning. At the thought of Vietnam, Schwarzkopf began wondering what he was doing here.

58

"I asked myself why on Earth the United States was getting involved in Grenada?" Schwarzkopf told the *Atlanta Constitution* a year later. "Why Grenada?" Ft. Stewart's 285,000 acres of pine woods were three time as large as the island of Grenada. "Then I said, 'Schwarzkopf, just let it sort itself out. You're an instrument of policy. You don't make policy.'"

Later that night, officers on the *Guam* preempted the scheduled feature for a showing of the "Sands of Iwo Jima" starring John Wayne.

The plan for the operation the next morning was fairly simple. Army Rangers were to air drop or land at Point Salines airfield at 5 a.m. and secure the area. Several special operations missions were supposed to inspect the area ahead of time and seize several targets in the town of St. George's, north of Salines. After disarming PRA factions in the southern half of the island the Rangers would be relieved by troops from the 82nd Airborne, ideally in the first day of the operation. Early the same morning, Marine units were to launch an amphibious assault on Pearls Airfield and the town of Grenville. Then they would take the northern half of the island. All in a day's work. But, as often happens in battle, things didn't turn out as planned.

A second SEAL attempt to reconnoiter Point Salines failed Monday night when their Boston Whaler engine flooded, and they drifted out to sea. Another SEAL team going ahead of the Marine assault managed to reach the Grenville area on the northern end of the island. They reported by code that the coast there was unsuitable for the planned amphibious assault by Marine forces. Metcalf decided the Marines would go in by helicopter.

With no human intelligence coming from Point Salines, the Rangers approached the airfield virtually blind. There was Cuban construction equipment all over the runway making a landing impossible. Lt. Col. Wesley B. Taylor, commander of the 1st Army Ranger Battalion, opted for a parachute drop at 5:30 a.m. The pilots, in the rush to leave their bases, had forgotten to install hatch mount devices on their aircraft, and as they tried to relay this message among themselves they were soon plagued with communications problems.

The decision to parachute in immediately caused some changes in the flight patterns of the drop planes. By Schwarzkopf's account, "There's water on both sides of the runway, and in any parachute operation, the higher the jump, the greater the dispersion of troops in the wind. We had no idea what the winds down there were, so to get the maximum number of paratroopers directly onto the airstrip and to keep from getting anybody blown into the sea, we decided to drop them from only 500 feet."

As the Rangers approached Point Salines, they encountered a scene which one pilot likened to a fireworks display on the 4th of July at the Washington Monument. The first of seven aircraft came under heavy fire from at least five anti-aircraft guns and more small arms fire. Luckily the enemy anti-aircraft nests were mounted high in the hills and could not fire at objects lower than 700 feet. "Since they couldn't depress their aim lower than 700 feet, we were flying right under their fire," Schwarzkopf said.

Despite the surprises, the first plane stayed its course, dumping its load of Rangers into a hail of bullets in the early morning twilight. Two more planes aborted their runs after encountering heavy fire. Subsequent drops and strafings were clouded in confusion. Some aircraft had navigational problems. Ranger Specialist William Fedak was dragged in mid-air against the tail of an aircraft after his lines were tangled in the rush to jump.

The Rangers who were floating down to the runway had been advised that the Cuban workers at the airport probably wouldn't resist. But they soon found themselves engaged in a vicious firefight with Cubans and members of the PRA. "We didn't know the exact number of Cubans," one helicopter pilot said later. "The infantry guys just went in there and prepared for the worst. We didn't know who we could count on for assistance. We just expected anything." The badly outnumbered Ranger force set about clearing the airfield of debris and attacking enemy positions until the second major air drop arrived.

The first few hours on the ground were hectic, and cost the Rangers at least five men. But, with reinforcements, the Rangers took on Cuban positions near the runway, and by 7:39 a.m., half the runway was clear, allowing the first C-130s to land, and unload equipment. Three hours after the first jump, the Rangers controlled the runway, and silenced all the anti-aircraft guns nearby. During the course of the fighting, Ranger platoons had started up the hill near the airport, which harbored the True Blue Campus of St. George's University School of Medicine and the U.S. students that the Rangers were supposed to rescue. But the Rangers were in for a surprise.

Instead of finding nearly 600 American students at the True Blue campus as they expected, the Rangers found a shell-shocked resident assistant, and some 138 students who told them that True Blue wasn't even the main campus. There were 224 more students housed at Grand Anse, the main campus. And there were another 202 students located at Lance aux Epines Peninsula. The Rangers realized that the main campus could easily come under enemy control and the students could become hostages. This information was reported back to the *Guam* by ham radio.

For Schwarzkopf, this intelligence gap was inconceivable. Rescuing U.S. citizens on the island was the primary rationale for the invasion, and the Army couldn't find them? In an interview with the PBS show "Frontline," Schwarzkopf later described his first reaction when he was notified that True Blue wasn't the main campus. "If it had been a Hollywood movie, it would have gone like this: the Rangers would have broken through the door and said, 'Ta da, we're here. You're rescued,' and the students would have said, 'Yeah, but what about the rest of us?' And the Rangers would have said, 'What do you mean: the rest of us?' and the students say, 'Oh, we're the small campus. They're all located somewhere else.' I mean, you can imagine the shock."

Metcalf agreed, "We had a terrible time with intelligence. But this thing happened so quickly, Grenada was way down on the list of priorities for intelligence gathering."

Until the Friday before the invasion, U.S. officials thought the entire medical school was at True Blue. Then an employee of the National Security Agency who just happened to have a brother at the school produced some personal snapshots of the Grand Anse campus. The information arrived too late to give the invading forces time to figure out where the students were scattered. And no one knew there were even more students on the Lance aux Pines Peninsula until the Rangers came looking for students at True Blue.

If the events of the morning so far had proved somewhat disturbing for Schwarzkopf, news from the town of St. George's, north of Point Salines, further dampened his spirits. Two Special Operations helicopters had been assigned to rescue Governor General Sir Paul Scoon — a British government official who remained on the island in a largely figurehead capacity. They were supposed to come in under cover of nightfall, but had to abort their mission after coming under heavy fire from the PRA. A subsequent attempt put commandos in the governor's residence at 10:08 a.m. Twenty minutes later, the residence came under attack by armored vehicles and was effectively surrounded. Scoon and the Special Ops force remained pinned down on the estate until they were rescued the next day.

Despite the predicament of the Rangers on the southern end of the island, Schwarzkopf and Metcalf found reason to be pleased with the Marine helicopter assault on Pearls Airfield and Grenville in the north. Led by Col. Ray Smith, commander of the battalion landing team, the Marine units had overcome some faulty intelligence, which would have had them landing in a banana grove. They took the airport by 7:30 a.m. and the nearby town soon after. With the Marines having achieved most of their objectives quite easily, Schwarzkopf and Metcalf soon realized that that they had too much force on the northern half of the island and not enough on the southern half.

At this point, Schwarzkopf came up with an idea which would help turn the tide of the invasion. He suggested making a Marine amphibious assault north of St. George's at Grand Mal Bay to relieve forces at the governor general's estate and secure St. George's. Metcalf ran the idea by his Marine advisors and didn't get a standing ovation. "In the first place, the beach was unsurveyed, they told me," Metcalf said. "I had just said no to a beach that was surveyed, and here I wanted to go in and send them in to an unsurveyed beach." But Metcalf and Schwarzkopf knew the western side of the island was flat and the prevailing winds were blowing from the east. The few photographs they had showed sandy, flat beaches at Grand Mal.

It was a risky maneuver. Metcalf wrestled with Schwarzkopf's idea for a few minutes, then ordered the Marines to do it. By 3 p.m., most the Marines at Pearls Airfield were getting in their helicopters again to head for the other side of the island for the amphibious landing.

Throughout the afternoon, Ranger units in the south continued to encounter resistance from Cubans and PRA. But by 3 p.m., their situation improved somewhat and they captured 150 Cubans at the Castille compound. The 82nd Airborne Division, under the command of Gen. Edward L. Trobaugh, soon began landing at Salines to relieve the Rangers. The landings coincided with a PRA counterattack, prompting Trobaugh to call Ft. Bragg, North Carolina, for reinforcements. "Send battalions until I tell you to stop," he bellowed into the phone. The additional reinforcements would bring the total number of U.S. troops to 6,000 on the island.

Northward, Metcalf ordered an air assault on St. George's, resulting in the loss of two helicopters. Navy A-7 aircraft from the USS *Independence* were soon brought in to take out the PRA headquarters at Ft. Frederick. But, at the same time, they clobbered a mental hospital known locally as "The Crazy House," near Ft. Frederick. Military personnel had been seen entering and leaving the building, but the bombing was, in Metcalf's words, "not one of our sharper hours."

It was a public relations disaster. Metcalf did not know that a mental hospital had been hit, and the joint task force initally denied that it had happened. After that, "It looked like a cover up," Metcalf said. By some estimates, 30 patients were killed. A few survivors went roaming through town until they were rounded up and led to another hospital.

After the air attack, Schwarzkopf and Metcalf put their heads together late that afternoon to review the orders for Day Two. In the course of that meeting, Metcalf decided that Schwarzkopf would be his deputy commander for the rest of the operation. Although some felt the deputy commander should be located on the island, Metcalf was too impressed with Schwarzkopf. He told the others the decision was made. "Schwarzkopf is my deputy commander and you can do whatever you damn want." From that point on Schwarzkopf became the principal advisor for Metcalf on Army operations, and, in effect, in charge of the land component of the operation.

By the next morning, Schwarzkopf's idea to move Marine units from Pearls to St. George's was proving fruitful. During the night, five M-60 tanks and 13 amphibious landing vehicles went ashore at Grand Mal with the Marines. At 3 a.m., they were joined by another Marine company from Pearls. They advanced on St. George's encountering little resistance and secured the governor general's house. Sir Scoon was soon dispatched to the *Guam*. (The next day, Oct

27, a letter signed by Sir Scoon requesting military intervention was delivered to the U.S. Embassy in Bridgetown, Barbados. The letter was purposely back-dated to the day before the invasion, Oct. 24.)

By mid-day the Marines had reached the PRA command center in Ft. Frederick, in the same neighborhood as the unlucky mental hospital. At the same time, the 82nd Airborne and Ranger forces captured a Cuban compound at Calliste and six warehouses full of military equipment and supplies. Nevertheless, by the afternoon of the second day, the Army forces were still several kilometers from the destinations which they had been ordered to reach, and they still hadn't completely secured the area around Salines.

For Schwarzkopf, the performance of the Army units had been courageous. They had a tougher job than the Marines. But they had been bogged down too long at Salines. "That quite frankly pissed Schwarzkopf off," Metcalf said. "He wasn't embarrassed, he was mad. I wasn't so damned pleased either. He got all the guys together and I think he clanged heads." For the next few days, the failure of the Rangers and the 82nd Airborne to move out of Salines continued to rankle Schwarzkopf.

But he was kept busy with the job of securing the American students at Grand Anse. Trobaugh, the commander of the 82nd Airborne, had been ordered to rescue the students before nightfall on the second day. Schwarzkopf and Trobaugh soon began communicating via satellite, although they were constantly interrupted by static whenever the USS *Guam* changed course. The ship's antenna had to be pointing toward the satellite for a connection.

Both were worried that an Army land assault might not reach the students' compound before dark. And they were still not quite sure where the campus was. Schwarzkopf came up with a solution—use Marine helicopters to ferry in Army Rangers to storm the campus while Navy planes covered them from the air. The Marines were less than enthusiastic about the prospect of losing any more helicopters, and were never too happy to have Army personnel along for the ride. But Metcalf ordered it done.

The joint operation only lasted 26 minutes, and went almost perfectly, resulting in the rescue of 223 Americans. One helicopter crashed after its rotor hit a palm tree, and 11 Rangers were left behind in the rush, but no one was injured despite heavy fire at times. The Rangers who were left behind inflated a life raft and rowed to out to a Navy ship that night.

Day Three at Grenada saw fewer pockets of resistance from the enemy and a devastating attack of friendly fire. Stephen Silvasy, commander of the 2nd Batallion of the 82nd Airborne, was pushing northeast with his men. They began crossing paths with other American troops by midmorning. At 4 p.m., some units which had separated from Silvasy's team began receiving small arms fire. They called in an aerial attack on enemy targets ahead of them. The units had been out of contact with each other for hours and shoddy maps didn't help the situation. By many accounts, the troops were using AAA road maps picked up at gas stations and travel shops. After three runs, a Navy A-7 swooped in on its final run looking for the PRA troops that were harassing the Americans. The pilot spotted movement and strafed what turned out to be Silvasy's unit. The pilot had already fired before he heard the word "abort" come across his radio.

Seventeen of Silvasy's troops were wounded, three seriously. Silvasy recalled, "I remember watching two of them have their legs blown off in front of me." One of those soldiers, Sean P. Luketina, later died of gangrene in his legs at Walter Reed Army Medical Center in Washington. A rain storm prevented the wounded soldiers from being evacuated immediately after the incident. One quarter of the airborne combat casualties in Grenada were suffered during this friendly fire incident. But, as Silvasy later surmised, "In war things like this happen. These men did not die in vain."

A second operation marked the afternoon of the third day. Rangers were responsible for securing Ft. Calivagny. According to intelligence figures, there were possibly three hundred Cubans, a Grenadian battalion, and 60 Soviet advisors at the fort. But, these intelligence reports proved wildly inaccurate. Photographs and maps of the fort were similarly outdated. In the assault, three helicopters overshot their landing zone. One helicopter was hit by fire and its rotor blade struck another copter. Both went down. A third, swinging wildly to avoid the wreckage, went down in a ditch. It all transpired in the course of 20 seconds. Despite the problems, the Rangers took the fort handily. The wounded Rangers were brought back to what passed for a field hospital at Salines, and were operated on under flashlights. There were no lights or generators.

In the next few days, resistance all but disappeared on the island. The PRA commander, Hudson Austin, was captured, and the remaining students on the Lance aux Epines Peninsula were rounded up. U.S. forces moved on to the northern island of Carriacou expecting to find PRA members there. The only person to resist was a man who said he had lived in Pittsburgh for 13 years. "We knew then that he had put up a fight because he didn't want to go back to Pittsburgh," dead panned Marine Col. Ray Smith.

Metcalf declared the invasion a success after nine days. Jubilant Grenadians began to come out in droves. One officer thought as he rode through the interior of the island, "I was on a roll. It was like Patton liberating France. People on both sides of the road singing 'God Bless America.' "

For Schwarzkopf, the jubilation of the Grenadians struck home. It was a far cry from the reaction he had received in Vietnam. Schwarzkopf would never forget a helicopter trip he took to St. George's on the second day of the battle. From the air, he saw red graffiti on a wall. "I've seen that sign all over the world—in Berlin and Vietnam, in Tokyo and even on the walls of the Pentagon. It always says something like, 'Long Live Marxism' or 'Down with the United States.' As the helicopter got closer and I could read it, it said, 'God bless America,'" he later told the *Atlanta Constitution*.

As the operation wound down, Metcalf and Schwarzkopf went their separate ways. Metcalf was off to Lebanon and Schwarzkopf went back to Ft. Stewart. Both had learned a great deal. They had presided over the largest military operation since the invasion of the Vietnam War. It was on short notice and they had pulled it off reasonably well.

And Schwarzkopf learned from the mistakes. He particularly learned how not to handle the press. Defense Secretary Caspar Weinberger had ordered that reporters be excluded from the operation. He wanted to make sure the special operations missions on the island were not exposed. Seven journalists chartered a boat to St. George's, on the first day of the operation, but had trouble getting their information out. At one point, Metcalf threatened to shoot at press boats if they continued to come. Public interest in the invasion was an afterthought for the Pentagon.

Schwarzkopf also learned that good intelligence was critical. Lack of it led to deadly confusion.

But because the invasion of Grenada achieved all its objectives, it was a success in the minds of those who were there, including Schwarzkopf. He later said in secret Army documents, "Grenada, once again, proved that even though higher headquarters screws it up every way you can possibly screw it up, it is the initiative and valor on the part of the small units, the small unit of leadership, and the soldiers on the ground that will win it for you every time."

In all, 662 Americans had been rescued. The PRA had been neutralized—146 had been captured and 45 were killed. And the Cuban presence on the island had been entirely removed—25 killed in action, 59 wounded and 602 shipped back to Cuba. Governor Scoon assumed power after the invasion, and served until an election in 1984 brought victory for Herbert Blaize of the New National Party.

Schwarzkopf returned home to find the majority of Americans supportive of the operation. The president and the American public were jubilant that the series of military humiliations — Vietnam, Iran and Lebanon — ended in Grenada. Schwarzkopf got off the plane to find his family, friends, and a military band waiting for him. In an interview with the *New Republic* years later, he said, "Everybody started cheering and my wife and my kids ran up and hugged me, and I didn't understand what was going on. When it finally dawned on me, it was probably one of the greatest thrills I have ever had in my entire life."

6.
LASERS AND SKEET

The America in which Norman Schwarzkopf found himself after returning from Grenada was refreshing. There was an air of confidence among the troops at Ft. Stewart, Georgia, as well as those around the country. No statement more embodied this new sense of pride than the words of Vice Admiral Metcalf when he finished the Grenada assignment: "We blew them away." Grenada wasn't much of a country on which to stake a military reputation, but for U.S. troops it marked a turning point.

"It was good to be involved in an operation that was recognized by everybody as a very successful one, given the recent history of armed forces in Korea, which some people considered a tie, and Vietnam, which others felt was a defeat," Schwarzkopf later relished in an interview.

After a short, but exhausting war, Schwarzkopf came home to resume command of the 24th Mechanized Infantry Division. He had learned a great deal from the Grenada experience, and was more enthusiatic than ever to impress the combat experience on his troops in Georgia. But, Schwarzkopf's singular efforts to improve the 24th were only part and parcel of a much larger movement within the Army which had been bubbling up for years. The result would not be completely realized until Operation Desert Storm eight years later.

The roots of the reform movement within the Army had

taken hold in the wake of Vietnam. As that war wound down, Army strategists began to look toward Europe as the site of the next war in which the United States might participate. They focused their doctrine away from counter-insurgency, jungle warfare to a more conventional strategy that would meet the Soviet Red Army head-on in Europe. The result was the 1976 Army operational handbook.

The book assumed that if Europe was the battleground, U.S. troops would be outmanned and outgunned by the Soviets. American troops stationed permanently in Europe were to hold the line against an attacking army from the Eastern Bloc until reinforcements came. The strategy emphasized massive firepower above maneuverability. "After Vietnam, it was all the Army could afford at the time" recalled military strategist, retired Army Col. Harry G. Summers Jr. "But, this book put the Army on the defensive."

The manual said, "The chief mission of these forces must be to bide time while the defending forces concentrate in front of the [enemy's] main thrust. In mounted warfare, armored and mechanized elements must be set in motion toward the battle positions in the path of the main thrust." A secret flanking attack to sneak up on the enemy's backside was a luxury that the Army could not have afforded back then.

The book emphasized the physical destruction of the enemy piece by piece, in a slow war of attrition. For many, the manual represented no change at all from the tactics of the past. "The 1976 manual was a pile of garbage," said John Boyd, a retired Air Force colonel who assisted in the concept design of the F-15 fighter bomber.

According to Pierre Sprey, a concept designer for the A-10 "Warthog," the Army's close-air support aircraft, "It was the same traditional American approach that we had used since the Civil War. We massed our troops, struck the enemy at one point, and hit them in a sledgehammer-type fashion." Although helicopters had been used in some flanking movements in Vietnam, the ground forces often were instructed or forced by terrain to fight along traditional lines. "Hamburger Hill was a classic example," said Sprey.

71

The overwhelmingly negative reaction to the uninspired 1976 manual sparked a reform movement within the Army, which resulted in a much-improved book in August 1982. For the Army, the 1982 manual was revolutionary. "This edition put the army on the offensive. It focused on the air-land battle. It was a lot more maneuver oriented," Harry Summers said. For the first time, U.S. forces were taught to use extensive maneuvers in addition to heavy fire as a means to fight battles. They didn't just clobber, they could parry too. Several generals had used maneuver warfare in the past, but they were the exception, not the rule. The manual formally adopted maneuver warfare as a weapon in itself.

The 1982 manual also laid out three basic dimensions of warfare. The strategic level defined the objectives of the war — that was the job of the president. The operational level defined the fighting strategies needed to carry out these objectives — the job of the generals. The tactical level defined the nitty gritty for the soldiers. Army strategists began to think of a battlefield in three dimensions, too. There were targets deep behind enemy lines — called the enemy's rear. Then there was the actual battle front, the line of scrimmage. And, finally, the Army's own rear, including logistical operations and supply lines.

The new manuals encouraged U.S. ground forces to strike at enemy strongholds in multiple surges at various points along the front. It was a marked contrast to the old techniques. According to Sprey, "Instead of massing at one point, it made troops to go in via a series of narrow surges. The command positions would watch, and those which proved successful would be followed by heavier stuff."

The maneuver warfare doctrine met some resistance from other branches of the military, but by the mid-1980s, the thinking embodied in the 1982 manual and a slightly revised 1986 version were firmly entrenched among Army troops.

In the early 1980s the Army was also in the process of making hands-on training a priority among its troops. "Prior to

Vietnam, maintenance had been a priority in the Army," according to Summers who felt that keeping things working was not a mission that built good men, just good equipment. "In a sense the Army lost its soul."

In 1981, the Army introduced a revolutionary combat simulation program at the National Training Center in Ft. Irwin, California. This center had, for years, been the place where troops staged large-scale maneuvers in live combat situations. When the Army turned high tech, Ft. Irwin had to do the same. It was among the first locations to use the new Military Integrated Laser Engagement Simulation (MILES) equipment which Schwarzkopf had briefly encountered in Germany. The electronic equipment allowed soldiers to simulate warfare with eye-sensitive laser beams mounted on their weapons. The range of the lasers was the same as the range of the weapons on which they were mounted. The lasers saw what the weapons saw, and went where the ammunition went. They did everything a weapon did except kill.

Each soldier wore a detecting unit on his body. When a beam from a laser hit that unit, the soldier was as good as struck by the weapon that the laser was copying. The device would emit a continuous buzz until the key was removed from the laser firing device. The system could even detect near misses — they set off the buzzer three times.

The laser devices had to be loaded with "amunition," and if a soldier ran out, his laser no longer worked. This predicament forced commanders to implement supply lines which simulated combat conditions. Commanders also were forced to call in replacements, as in live combat. Even the medical teams got a taste of what the battlefield was like. Each soldier was given a card at the beginning of a mock battle, informing him what type of wound he would receive if hit. Medical teams waited on the side, and ran through the motions of treating the soldiers for the wounds spelled out on the cards.

The laser firing devices and detection units were not limited to foot soldiers. Tanks and other weapons possessed the MILES equipment as well. The live firing range at the center was the only one of its kind in the country, equipped with pop-up targets which fired at armored units with laser beams. All mechanized units trained there.

The training center also housed a central command which tracked all casualties and equipment losses sustained during a mock battle. All battles were taped on audio and video cassettes, allowing commanders to review an entire mock war after the fact. And, the center ensured that troops learned the right enemy tactics by pitting them against classic Soviet battle doctrine taught in 33 countries worldwide. The size and remote location of the facilities at Ft. Irwin allowed troops to use riot gas during their battles, so they could prepare for chemical and biological warfare.

In addition to instructing Army personnel on new ways to fight, these centers taught soldiers how to improvise in combat. "They teach you not only how to use high-tech weapons," said retired Army Maj. Gen. Ward Le Hardy. "But they instill in you the idea that once you have the plan, don't wait for specific orders. They instill initiative."

In short, soldiers learned how to think for themselves under fire.

For many Army personnel, including Schwarzkopf, the proving grounds at Ft. Irwin soon exposed the deficiencies of the old Army. Shortly after the combat simulation gadgetry was unveiled in 1981, it began to make waves throughout the Army. Schwarzkopf's predecessor at the 24th Mechanized Infantry Division, Gen. Jack Galvin, was among the many Army commanders who was in for a surprise at Ft. Irwin. Galvin had introduced his own rigorous training program for the 24th based at Ft. Stewart. Shortly after the opening of the center, he took his division to Ft. Irwin for a whirl in laser simulated combat. Galvin fielded the gung-ho 24th against what was supposed to be a Soviet-trained enemy force. His division was soundly beaten several times.

Le Hardy said, "When Galvin saw his forces being demolished, he just tossed out his training program and said we're starting over." For Galvin and the rest of the Army, the tests at Ft. Irwin meant that the training methods of the last 50 years had to be summarily thrown on the trash heap. Galvin returned to Ft. Stewart, and began to rejuvenate his training program.

In the midst of that rejuvenation process, Schwarzkopf replaced Galvin as commander of the 24th Mechanized Infantry Division. He arrived, already proud of the division he was to command, and told his new troops that he would carve a "V" — the symbol of the 24th — on the chest of any enemy that dared challenge them. He then took the lessons Galvin learned and began to train his troops accordingly.

The National Training Center soon became an integral part of Army training. Army units went from losing repeated battles to opposing forces at Ft. Irwin to winning nine out of nine battles during the mock warfare.

In addition to the extensive combat training Army troops were privy to at Ft. Irwin, advanced military schools soon became available to qualified Army personnel. In October 1984, the Army opened the School for Advanced Military Studies (SAMS) at Ft. Leavenworth, Kansas. An elite school for graduates of the Army's Command and General Staff Officer Course, the SAMS course focused on providing the Army with officers specially educated in the art and science of military strategy and operations. "The SAMS school focuses on developing military judgement, instead of just injecting knowledge," said Bill S. Lind, a former defense aide to Sen. Gary Hart, and strategic consultant to the Marines. Integral to this education was the Army's revolutionary 1982 handbook. The graduates of SAMS program all end up in key staff positions.

The combination of improved technology, training, and tactics throughout the 1980s proved to be crucial in creating what many refer to today as "the best army we've ever had." For many, the training system developed by the Army should get much of the credit for the success of Operation Desert Storm. "When books are written about Iraq," said Le Hardy, "the lessons we learned at the National Training Center are what won the ground battle."

Schwarzkopf was at the heart of this resurgence within the

Army. According to retired Gen. Richard E. Cavazos, "Norm certainly put a lot of priority into that operation (Ft. Irwin)." But Cavazos added, "There are a dozen or so Norman Schwarzkopf's in the Army right now. They all went through the National Training Center at Ft. Irwin."

Continued training at Ft. Irwin under the guidance of Schwarzkopf did wonders for the 24th Mechanized Infantry Division. Over the next year and a half Norman "took the 24th into the 21st Century," said West Point classmate, retired Col. George J. Stapleton. Schwarzkopf trained his division harder than ever. Lt. Col. John McNeill, a former public affairs officer at Ft. Stewart recalled Schwarzkopf's techniques: "You'd better salute on post, and you'll get a yelling if you're not cutting the image of a soldier."

Soon the word spread around the Army of the prowess of the 24th, and Schwarzkopf was doing the spreading. Maj. Gen. Stephen Silvasy who had served as a brigade commander for the 82nd Airborne Division in Grenada under Schwarzkopf, remembered one case of braggadocio. Silvasy, who was based nearby at Ft. Bragg, North Carolina, met Schwarzkopf one day in Georgia and, during a break in work, both began rehashing their experiences in Grenada. Schwarzkopf steered the talk around to his incomparable 24th.

"Steve, if we had the 24th in Grenada, it would have been over in a matter of two days," Schwarzkopf boasted.

But Silvasy had been on the ground in Grenada commanding a battalion. He wasn't about to let speculation about what the 24th could have done overshadow what the 82nd did do. "Look Norm. Within 13 hours of receiving notice in the states, we had already set foot in Grenada. In that time you guys couldn't have even found the keys to your motor pool."

Schwarzkopf got up and walked out of the room.

Although Schwarzkopf put his troops at the 24th through hellish training, he was always on the lookout for their well-being. Troops who served under him at Ft. Stewart remembered him as a good soldier's soldier. He always tried to make the quality of life better for them, in one instance making sure they got a new service club and pushing for a new swimming pool. At the same time, Schwarzkopf was able to juggle the needs of his Army and his family at home.

Col. George Stapleton, another class of '56 friend, visited Schwarzkopf one day at the base and remembered Schwarzkopf's excitement during lunch. "The big topic of conversation was his son's first dive into a swimming pool." Schwarzkopf, the commander of an Army division, bent a colleague's ear about his son's dive. "It was really important for him. Despite the fact that he had command of some 15,000 troops there, he still had time for his family," Stapleton said.

After three years at Ft. Stewart, Schwarzkopf reluctantly said goodbye to his 24th and traveled back to Washington, D.C. In July 1985, he went back at the Pentagon for a desk job, or as he put it, "to re-establish my humility." This time he served as assistant deputy chief of staff for operations and plans for nearly a year. In this position he advised the Army Chief of Staff on inter-branch matters, political-military aspects of international affairs, and National Security Council concerns. The Plans and Operations Division in which he worked was primarily responsible for strategy formulation and application. More paperwork, no soldiers. Fortunately for the soul of a wanderer, the assignment only lasted a year.

When Schwarzkopf left the desk this time he was bound for one of his favorite posts, Ft. Lewis, Washington. The timing couldn't have been better. He was stepping out of the stale, humid air of the nation's capital in June, just in time for a mild, breezy Pacific Northwest summer. Back to the trout rivers, the birds of Yakima valley, the skeet range, the soldiers.

Along with the fresh air came Schwarzkopf's third star. A month after he arrived at Ft. Lewis, he became a lieutenant general. He was now in command of the entire Infantry Corps at Ft. Lewis. And everyone knew it. When he introduced himself to his staff he laid out his background, his expectations and a personal touch. "I really don't play golf and all, but I do love to shoot skeet."

For the Ft. Lewis soldiers who had never known Schwarzkopf, there were at least the legendary stories of his last tour. They soon found out what kind of man he was. When it came to "Law Day," in March, he lined up the troops on the parade field before dawn. As the sun began its rise over the glacier fields of Mt. Rainier, Schwarzkopf delivered an inspiring tribute to U.S. soldiers. "We have the best Army today that we've ever had." When he finished, fireworks filled the sky. And then he gave everyone the day off.

Schwarzkopf loved watching soldiers train hard. When the rain storms came and the fields turned muddy, he would greet his fellow officers and his soldiers with the same booming, cheerful voice. "Great day to be a soldier!"

On weekends and occasionally during his Wednesday lunch break, Schwarzkopf drove the five-minute stretch from headquarters to the Northwest Adventure Center skeet range. Since Schwarzkopf was a new face, nobody thought to salute when the three-star general arrived for his first day of shooting in his own car, wearing cut-offs, tennis shoes and his favorite baseball cap. He instantly became pals with Norman Neubert, the man who ran the skeet range. The two Normans even looked alike. The same build, the same receding hairline. As Neubert's wife put it, "Neither of them have a neck."

Skeet shooting sharpens the aim of bird hunters in the off season. The shooter stands at seven stations and shoots clay discs, or "pigeons," as they're catapulted into the sky from two wooden houses. The seven stations provide different angles to master. Schwarzkopf shoots a mean game. He is one of the smoothest shooters Neubert has ever seen. A score of 25 is perfect. Schwarzkopf routinely fires in the 23 to 24 range—good enough to be competitive. The skeet club at Ft. Lewis has a policy that a person who shoots a perfect 25 must then shoot his hat. Schwarzkopf refused. "No way," the three-star said. "Those stars cost too much."

When Ft. Lewis soldiers visited the range and got frustrated with their performance, Schwarzkopf, always the teacher, offered his help, without letting on who he was. "First time you went in the water to swim you didn't swim too well, did you?" Schwarzkopf asked a couple of rookie shooters. "Now come on out here." He walked them through a couple of rounds of shooting, pointing out the nuances, improving their games. The soldiers studied Schwarzkopf's face. They knew they had seen this guy before. Later, back in the club house, they asked Neubert, who is that guy?

"That is General Schwarzkopf," Neubert said. Then he would watch the alarm creep into the young faces.

"Don't worry about it," Neubert told them. "He enjoyed it."

There was no general at the skeet range, Neubert said. "That was Norman Schwarzkopf the shooter. He never used his VIP status. He was just another one of the shooters out here. He didn't want to be anyone else."

There is a story Schwarzkopf tells his skeet shooting buddies. When he arrived at one of his posts, he asked his staff where the skeet shooting range was. He explained that he wanted to shoot a few rounds that day.

"Yes, General. What time would you like?"

Schwarzkopf set a time and was escorted out to the range. He thought it odd that the place was empty, except for the manager who ran it. Schwarzkopf fired a few shots, but grew distracted by the stillness.

"Don't you get many people out here?" he asked.

"Not today. We're closed. They're paying me overtime."

Schwarzkopf's mind fixed on Sen. William Proxmire and his "Golden Fleece" award for government waste. He stopped shooting right then and walked off the range. "If Senator Proxmire gets hold of this," he said, "I'm through."

Neubert and Schwarzkopf had long conversations about the welfare of the soldiers. Schwarzkopf was always exploring ways to improve the quality of life for his troops and their families. Everything from their equipment, to their off duty recreation. The two Norms found ways to make skeet shooting and other activities affordable. They also talked about family. "If you're not a dedicated family man, and if your next concern isn't the soldiers, you'll find out why he's called, The Bear," Neubert said. "He gets angry. You always knew exactly where he was coming from."

At one point, Schwarzkopf tried to convince Neubert he should keep the skeet range open more hours on summer weekends.

"Norm, you should keep this range open a little longer."

"It's open at 10:30 in the morning," Neubert responded.

"Yes. But if I skip church, God might not let me shoot skeet anymore."

Schwarzkopf often arrived at the range with his son, Christian, and his dog, Bear. The dog, like his master, has a knack for leaving a lasting impression on those who meet him. Some politely call the dog "undisciplined." Retired Gen. Richard Cavazos went chucker and pheasant hunting in Yakima with Schwarzkopf. Cavazos thinks Schwarzkopf is an excellent shot. "His only weakness was his dogs. He had poorly trained dogs. They never mind him. I remember him screaming, 'Goddamnit! Come here, Bear!' He was overly sympathetic to his dogs, too nice to them."

Bear often gets too excited and scares the birds out of range of the best shot. But he has personality. Schwarzkopf likes to show off Bear's best trick. "Watch what Bear can do." He opens a can of soda and pours it toward the ground. Bear swallows the stream of liquid without spilling a drop. "That damn dog is something else," Neubert said.

One day, Schwarzkopf came in to the skeet club house and took Neubert into his confidence. He said he was sending Bear to obedience school for a second time. "He didn't learn too well the first time."

As the end of his Ft. Lewis tour neared, Schwarzkopf escaped for a week to go fly-fishing in Oregon. He learned how to tie his own flies and was well on his way to mastering the craft. After the rejuvenating trip, Schwarzkopf, Neubert, Col. Michael Campbell and some other friends sat around chatting. The subject shifted to Schwarzkopf's imminent departure for Washington, D.C. Campbell, a close friend, kidded the general. "Seeing how you're now a qualified fly

80

fishermen, when you get to the Pentagon, where you gonna fish? The Potomac?"

Schwarzkopf's eyebrows rolled up high, the way they later did when he was asked what he thought of Saddam Hussein as a military man.

"You know," Schwarzkopf said. "I got a desk down in the basement of the Pentagon in the dark that might just fit you." Campbell backpedaled, trying to take back his quip. Schwarzkopf warned him, "You mess with the lone ranger, you get the silver bullets."

Schwarzkopf wrote his West Point classmates a letter for their 30 Year anniversary book in which he raved about his tour in the "beautiful Pacific Northwest." He included a humble photo of himself, his son Christian and "Bear" in the foreground. For a background, Schwarzkopf selected Mount Rushmore. By no accident, his head is lined up beside George Washington's. He summarized the last 10 momentous years of his career, then provided an update on his family. "Brenda, my first wife, is still putting up with me and the moves, although I often wonder why. Cindy, our oldest, is a junior in high school, with ambitions to be a psychologist (she considers herself qualified after living with her father). Jessica, our high school freshman, has loftier ambitions. She intends to be a rock star or anything else that will cause her to become filthy rich. The ambitions of Christian, who is now 9, lie somewhere in the nexus of hamster breeder, horny toad trainer, astronaut or GARBAGE PAIL KID! Finally, Bear, the ever-present dog, has just gotten out of jail where I sent him after he attacked the dogs of both the Chief of Staff of the Army and the Chairman of the Joint Chiefs of Staff. Hang in there! The next 30 years are gonna be just as much as fun as the last 30."

At his change of command ceremony, Schwarzkopf praised his soldiers and talked about how much he enjoyed his tour at Ft. Lewis. "I especially want to thank Norman out at the skeet range for the good times we had."

Neubert remembered the kind words. "A man does that and he's touched you in a way you'll never forget." He handed Schwarzkopf a plaque before the general left town. It said, "May all your problems be no larger than a Low House Seven," the easiest shot in skeet.

In August 1987, Schwarzkopf was back in the belly of the Pentagon. Although he grumbled about the paper pushing, the post was widely regarded as a major stepping stone for career officers. He was now deputy chief of staff for operations, one of the top Army posts in the Pentagon. Here, Schwarzkopf was responsible for all Army operations, including training and administration. Although he wasn't thrilled with the desk work, colleagues say he was particularly good at it, prioritizing Army training facilities like the one at Ft. Irwin.

The Pentagon assignment reunited him with an old West Point classmate, Tom Weinstein, who was then the Army's chief of staff for intelligence. Together at the morning briefings they would inject a smidgen of humor while offering solid insight into world events and the state of the Army. "He's got good common sense," Weinstein said. "During a briefing, he can cut through the jargon and nonsense and get right down to the point of what's important."

The post was extremely demanding for Schwarzkopf, keeping him away from his children who were still young. He was holding down one of the most time consuming jobs in the Army. Fifteen-hour days were common, days filled with hours of meetings and mounds of paperwork. But Schwarzkopf had a healthy dose of nonchalance about the Pentagon post. Tony Jezior, his friend from West Point, dropped in on Schwarzkopf one afternoon with a business partner. Schwarzkopf was just on his way out the door for a meeting with his boss, but invited them back into his office for a quick cup of coffee. They chatted for a while, and when Schwarzkopf finally got up to leave he was 20 minutes late for his meeting. Jezior's companion, surprised at the casual encounter, turned to him after Schwarzkopf left and asked, "That's the number two guy for the Army in the Pentagon, and we just walked in without an appointment?"

7.

THE WORST CASE SCENARIO

"I know as well as I know the sun will rise tomorrow that three years from now I'm just going to be Norm Schwarzkopf, U.S. citizen, another retired Army officer."

It was March 1989 and Schwarzkopf was sharing the prediction with a reporter as he completed his fourth full month as chief of U.S. Central Command in Tampa, Florida. The job had its challenges and freed him from the bureaucratic chores he loathed at the Pentagon. He could also focus on his family and his love of sports. He was now fishing and skeet shooting with his son, playing tennis with his daughters and contemplating the thought of being a civilian for the first time in his adult life. The notion that in 17 months he would be leading a battle against a savage dictator wasn't on his agenda as a career closer.

Schwarzkopf officially took over the command in November 1988 in a ceremony laden with military pomp. It was the Pentagon's lavish send-off for Schwarzkopf's predecessor, Gen. George B. Crist. About 300 spectators, including 30 generals and admirals and Defense Secretary Frank Carlucci, were on hand. Two representatives from the Kuwaiti oil ministry also attended. They had a big stake in CentCom.

It was a picture-perfect military affair. Separate formations of Army, Marine, Navy and Air Force personnel from Cent-Com snapped to attention as Crist and Schwarzkopf trooped the line. Flags of the 50 states flapped in the wind. Clad in bright red jackets with black braids, the U.S. Marine Corps band from Washington, known as "The President's Own," played "Ruffles and Flourishes." A battery of Marine artillerymen fired a 19-gun salute in honor of Secretary Carlucci, who hailed CentCom for helping to foster peace in the Persian Gulf. Carlucci said Crist's brilliant leadership directly contributed to CentCom's recent successes.

In his parting remarks, Crist said the U.S. escort of Kuwaiti tankers in the Persian Gulf was viewed as a rare, successful use of U.S. military force and called it a watershed event for the five-year-old command. Indeed, CentCom had come of age. The job Schwarzkopf had taken had traditionally been considered a relatively thankless assignment. Unlike the others, which had headquarters in their areas of responsibility, CentCom was placed at MacDill Air Force Base in Tampa since no Middle Eastern country would host it. Crist once said CentCom was regarded within the military as a "toothless, powerless entity." It was 7,000 miles away from its jurisdiction, and no one thought the command could mobilize fast enough to handle a crisis in the Middle East. It had a staff of less than 700 — not exactly the dream command of a man who loved soldiers. Soon, Schwarzkopf would command more than half a million soldiers, without ever changing jobs.

CentCom had its roots in the Carter administration. With the overthrow of the Shah of Iran and the Soviet invasion of Afghanistan, Carter was worried that the Soviets would take advantage of the instability and try to take over Persian Gulf oil fields. In his 1980 State-Of-The-Union speech, Carter pledged to defend the Gulf region to protect vital U.S. interests. In the event of a conflict, command of more than 400,000 American troops from the four armed services would fall to a new headquarters — the Rapid Deployment Joint Task Force. Its focus was to create a plan to block a Soviet ground invasion of Iran. The Joint Chiefs of Staff decided the task force commander needed a background in land warfare and informally agreed to alternate the assignment between the Marine Corps and the Army.

The task force was established in March 1980 under the command of Marine Lt. Gen. Paul X. Kelley. He commanded only a few U.S. ships in the Persian Gulf and his small headquarters at MacDill. But Kelley had the daunting task of figuring out how to quickly move thousands of troops from bases on the east and west coasts of the United States to the Persian Gulf and keep them supplied once they got there if the Soviets attacked.

When Kelley was named assistant commandant of the Marine Corps in 1981, Army Lt. Gen. Robert Kingston took over command of the task force. Although the Joint Chiefs of Staff argued the headquarters should retain its status as a contingency unit, Defense Secretary Caspar Weinberger redesignated the task force as U.S. Central Command on Jan. 1, 1983.

That made CentCom one of the military's six unified commands. Its responsibility for military operations and security assistance stretched from Southwest Asia to the Arabian Peninsula to the Horn of Africa. Countries within its area of responsiblity were Kuwait, Iraq, Iran, Saudi Arabia, Afghanistan, Bahrain, Djibouti, Egypt, Ethiopia, Jordan, Kenya, Oman, Pakistan, Qatar, Somalia, Sudan, United Arab Emirates and Yemen.

The change brought CentCom on a par with headquarters like European Command and Pacific Command and got Kingston his fourth star the following year. Under Kingston, CentCom kept a low profile. It oversaw exercises in Egypt and California, dispatching AWACS radar planes to Egypt to monitor Libyan air movements or sending helicopters to clear mines from the Red Sea.

That changed when Crist took over in November 1985. CentCom directed the rescue efforts and subsequent investigation after an Iraqi jet hit the American frigate USS *Stark* with an Exocet missile on May 17, 1987—killing 37 sailors. From his office, 7,000 miles away in Tampa, Crist also oversaw the escort of 11 reflagged Kuwaiti oil tankers through the 600-mile-long Persian Gulf at the height of the war between Iran and Iraq. He also had to weather a political firestorm after the USS *Vincennes* accidentally shot down an Iranian airliner in the Gulf on July 3, 1988, killing all 290 people on board.

Between July 24, 1987—when the Kuwaiti supertanker

Bridgeton struck a mine under U.S. escort—and Aug. 20, 1988—when Iran and Iraq declared a cease fire—the Navy engaged in more than a dozen armed clashes with Iranian forces and encounters with Iraqi aircraft. The escort mission was the first ocean convoy the Navy had run since World War II, and it generally got good marks.

When it was time for Crist to retire, Schwarzkopf was sucked into a turf battle. Some Navy brass had criticized CentCom for not having what it took to direct a major naval operation. Arguing that CentCom's mission proved to be primarily sea-borne, the Navy pushed for one of its own—Vice Adm. Henry C. Mustin, the Navy's director of plans, policy and operations—to succeed Crist. That led to, as one congressional staffer called it, a "real pissing match." Army leaders were outraged that the Navy would butt in on the traditional CentCom command arrangement alternating between Marine and Army commanders. They thought the Navy was using tragedies like the attack on the USS *Stark* to grab the Gulf mission. The Army brass pushed hard for Schwarzkopf, who was still deputy chief of staff for operations and plans. The Joint Chiefs of Staff were split between Mustin and Schwarzkopf, forcing the chairman, Adm. William Crowe, to recommend both names to Carlucci. The secretary selected Schwarzkopf in 1988.

He was a sharp contrast from Crist, who was considered dour and would only talk with subordinates when he summoned them to his office. Within his first month at CentCom, Schwarzkopf had walked through virtually every office and shook hands with everyone who worked there. "When you have this big, bear of a man lumbering through in the first couple of weeks, shaking your hand, asking what you do and where you're from, people like that," said a senior CentCom officer. "They like being able to see the boss."

Despite its rising prestige, CentCom perks were limited. The Schwarzkopfs moved into a modest house—at least the 15th home they had lived in since their marriage. They didn't even have a basement for storage. And, because Schwarzkopf had already reached the salary cap of $77,000, there was no pay raise involved in the transfer. The salary limit was a source of irritation for Schwarzkopf. He hadn't seen a pay raise from either of his last two promotions. He was irked when he saw Navy captains and Army colonels earning as much as some of the top brass at the Pentagon. Schwarzkopf himself wasn't earning any more than some of the people working under him.

"People who think we're in this for the money — big-time salaries — that is absolutely ridiculous," he said shortly after assuming the job. "I entertain no illusions about wanting to earn as much money as is being paid in the private sector. But when you have a situation where every one of my subordinate generals in this headquarters makes exactly the same money as I am, it's ludicrous."

Still, after a second frustrating stint at the Pentagon, Schwarzkopf welcomed the chance to spend more time with his family, something the drudgery of the Pentagon had hindered. He and his children would hike and play tennis. They visited Disney World. Schwarzkopf took Cindy kayaking. He took Christian to shoot skeet at the Tampa Sporting Clays, and they would take the dog to the field to keep him in shape for hunting. In addition to Bear, they kept exotic pets: parakeets, a scorpion and a python. Norman and Brenda enjoyed watching western films together. He particularly likes Charles Bronson and Clint Eastwood.

"He doesn't like 15-16 hour a day jobs," said friend Tony Jezior. "That's what he hated about the Pentagon. These guys are working from 6 in the morning to 8 at night. Norm doesn't like that. I wouldn't be surprised if he said, 'Hey, this is an opportunity to do something and still have a decent home life.' "

The general's philosophy on leisure was pleasantly startling to the CentCom staff, which had been used to working obligatory 18-hour days under Crist. Schwarzkopf wanted no workaholics around him. "He believed in folks going out and doing their PT (physical training), and he'd go out and do it too," a senior CentCom official said. "When it wasn't a time of war, he wanted people to be home with their families, so he wouldn't stay in the office as long. It was rare to have a commander with young children. Schwarzkopf had a real reason to get home at a decent hour."

Schwarzkopf was a paradox. His staff found him endearing, yet sometimes demanding and intimidating. He frequently displayed his hot temper when mistakes would arise, or when CentCom would clash with other commands or with the State Department. While Schwarzkopf was particularly demanding with his senior ranking personnel, he showed extraordinary patience with the junior officers when mistakes were made. He was intolerant of high ranking officers who flaunted their rank when dealing with subordinates. Schwarzkopf never denied he had a temper, but he also stressed to his men that his anger was nothing personal. He would boil over on matters of principle, but not over conflicts with individuals.

"I wish I wasn't so quick to anger," he said. "Anytime I anger, I feel terrible afterwards, and if I ever think I have devastated a human being because of my temper, I always make a point to go back to them and apologize." His anger was better received than Crist's had been. "When he blew up," a CentCom official said, "it was always for a good reason and then he was instantly over it. When Crist blew up, it was like he'd lost confidence in you." Although many of Schwarzkopf's subordinates were wary of his ire, they found it productive, too.

"He is, in my judgment, incapable of accepting anything less than the best for himself or anybody who works for him," said Lt. Gen. Joseph Hoar, who was his chief of staff at Cent-Com. "It was difficult to produce that level of work for him. There's the normal problem of human frailty. On the other side of the coin, I never worked for a guy who was more clear on giving guidance on what he wanted." Schwarzkopf was equally lavish with praise, always trying to reward good performance. And he liked to socialize with his staff. He often dined with co-workers at the end of the week.

The CentCom post thrust the Schwarzkopfs into the upper crust of Tampa's social scene, bringing some prominent figures into their lives. When he attended civic events, Schwarzkopf dazzled former New York Yankees owner George Steinbrenner, who also owned a Tampa shipyard. "The general can talk sports, economics, military maneuvers," said Steinbrenner. "He can talk about anything on a par with anybody." The Schwarzkopfs also became friendly with Hugh Culverhouse, owner of the Tampa Bay Buccaneers, and the general became a fan of the team. He was often a guest at home games. During one radio interview during Operation Desert Shield, Schwarzkopf sent the Bucs a message of encouragement. He kept track of their games and knew they had just suffered a 35-14 loss to the Los Angeles Rams. Culverhouse, once a guest in the Schwarzkopf's home, was also impressed by the general's sporting trophies.

Schwarzkopf was as much a perfectionist on social affairs as he was on professional matters. When CentCom began planning its annual family day, the general insisted on casting aside tradition. In past years, CentCom had held an open house where kids could see where their parents worked. Schwarzkopf had children and he knew that wasn't their idea of a good time. He insisted on a half-day picnic on the CentCom grounds, complete with carnival events and door prizes. His staff devised ideas for the event, but he kept sending the plans back for revision, claiming they were too small-scale. "I've got a 12-year-old son," he told his staff. "You've got to have something to keep the kids interested. How are we going to do that?"

The CentCom post also led Schwarzkopf back into a region that had fascinated him since his childhood days in Teheran. He was intrigued by Arab history and society and believed Americans needed to discard stereotypes and learn something about the culture of the region. During a visit to Kuwait in 1989, before a dinner held in his honor, Schwarzkopf's hosts coaxed him into wearing the appropriate dress for the affair, a traditional dishdasha robe. When the robe was delivered to his hotel room, he donned it over his massive frame and stood in front of the mirror. T.E. Lawrence, better known as Lawrence of Arabia, had done the same thing. And, like Lawrence, Schwarzkopf was tempted to do a little waltz in his new threads.

In the three visits he made to the Middle East before the Persian Gulf Crisis, he showed a skill for diplomacy with the leaders of that region. Humility was his tool. "It's important that when I'm meeting with my kings and my prime ministers and my sheiks and my emirs that I just don't get all over-inflated with my own self-importance," he told *Tampa Tribune* reporter Steve Huettel in 1989. "That would be a terrible disservice."

Schwarzkopf's appetite for hunting endeared him to Arab leaders. It was a natural entree in a man's world. In November 1989, while Schwarzkopf was in the United Arab Emirates, Brig. Gen. Mohammed Ben Zayed invited him and his chief of staff Gen. Joe Hoar to learn about falconry. They flew about 45 minutes into the desert via helicopter. Sand dunes surrounded them in every direction when they landed. Men were already stationed there in Range Rovers, and an enormous meal was served. The hunters ate Bedouin style, crouching in the sand and, as tradition dictated, using only their right hand to scoop up the food. That was difficult for Schwarzkopf, who is left handed.

After lunch, the hunt began. The target was a bustard, a large desert bird. The falcons used in the sport are half the size of the prey, but can easily knock a bustard out of the sky or attack it on the ground. "We got in the trucks and started across the sand, looking for bustard tracks," Schwarzkopf later told Frank Sargeant of the *Tampa Tribune*. "When we got close, the handler gave me a falcon, sat it on my arm, and told me to lean out the window. I did, and at that point they saw the bustard and we took off. In nothing flat we were going 60 or 70 miles and hour over the dunes, and the bird and me hanging out the window. When we got close, I pulled the hood off the bird, and launched it after the bustard."

The chase began. Since the falcons can sell for more than $30,000 each, the hunters weren't about to lose sight of their birds. The rovers flew over 10-foot-high sand dunes and dodged camels in gullies trying to keep up with the aerial combat. Gen. Mohammed Ben Zayed's falcon eventually killed the fleeing bustard.

* * *

Schwarzkopf took his role of protecting U.S. interests in the Arab world seriously, but he also wanted to dispell the stereotypes of American military men in the region. "I get to meet a lot of people from other countries and show them the American military is not arch right-wing conservatives wearing jack boots and crew cuts," he said. "We're human beings who believe in democracy, believe in our country, and we're also interested in being true friends of theirs." Schwarzkopf logged an average of 14,000 miles on every trip to the Middle East.

He had always predicted that the United States could easily find itself in a war on Middle East terrain, but he knew it was time to throw out the archaic scenarios that made the Soviets the bad guys. His argument gained new validity as the Berlin Wall fell, U.S.-Soviet relations warmed and the Communist stronghold on Eastern Europe began dissolving. The conflict between the Mid-Eastern states became the biggest menace to U.S. energy interests.

"People looked at the regional conflict as the most likely kind of military activity in the post Cold-War period," Gen. Hoar said. "The volatility of the area was such that it caused everybody to be concerned. Gen. Schwarzkopf used to talk about eight to 10 conflicts going on in his region at one time — like India-Pakistan, Afghanistan, the Iran-Iraq problem, North Yemen-South Yemen, the border problems between Egypt and Libya. He used to say, 'I could give you eight to ten conflicts where people are shooting at each other.' Schwarzkopf also worried that the United States was not treating some Arab nations as friends.

Shortly after taking command, Schwarzkopf and his staff began designing a contingency plan for a war. They theorized that if they prepared for the worst case scenario, they wouldn't be wasting time. "And when you look at the worst case, what was it?" Schwarzkopf said. "Well, they had this huge Iraqi armed forces that had just had a cease fire with Iran. They couldn't put their army back into the civilian world because their economy wouldn't take it. And what kind of threat could they pose? Well, the Saudi Arabian oil fields came to mind immediately. So in looking at everything, we came to the conclusion that probably the major threat we would have to face would be an Iraqi armed forces that tried to take over the Arabian peninsula oil fields. That, therefore, was the one that we really started planning for, because we figured that if we could handle that we could handle anything."

By 1989, CentCom was held in a new esteem. American power and prestige had grown in the Middle East as Soviet economic problems grew and Iran became weaker after its war with Iraq. CentCom was looking so good that it finally saw the possibility of moving the headquarters to its area of operation. An unidentified Persian Gulf country — believed to be Kuwait or Bahrain — invited the United States to establish a base. CentCom officials were elated. They said a new headquarters would make it easier to contact Arab military leaders and demonstrate American resolve in the region.

But Schwarzkopf was skeptical that opening a new base would meet congressional approval. He estimated the price tag could be too high at a time when the Cold War's demise was encouraging Congress to trim the defense budget. Building the headquarters, he said, would also require developing a small city with schools, a commissary and base exchange, swimming pools and gymnasiums.

By early 1990, the Defense Department's attempt to refocus CentCom's attention was in full swing. Word leaked onto the pages of *The New York Times* and *Washington Post* that military leaders saw a Soviet threat in CentCom's region as unlikely and that resources were being centered on a potential conflict between Arab nations. Sen. Sam Nunn, D-Ga., the Senate Armed Services Committee chairman, asked Schwarzkopf to appear at a hearing on changing military strategy to explain the CentCom changes. Schwarzkopf warned about the weapons buildup within the region, raising particular concerns about Iraq's chemical weapons arsenal.

Schwarzkopf would soon find that those weapons and the ominous dictator who created them would place a hurdle between the general and his plans for retirement. But at the time he appeared before Nunn, things were looking as good as they could in the Middle East. It had been only a decade since the

United States had suffered through an OPEC oil embargo, fretted over Soviet threats to secure a warm water port in the gulf area, and been humiliated by a hostile Iranian government holding Americans hostage. The protective actions the nation had taken in the Persian Gulf during the latter 1980s had largely buried those embarrassments. The U.S. had built strong peacetime partnerships with some friendly Arab states, Iranian aggression had been stymied and oil was flowing freely to the West.

"Let me assure you that CentCom is ready to fight and win if we are called on to do so," Schwarzkopf told Nunn.

Schwarzkopf had said the threat would come from Iraq. Saddam Hussein would make a prophet out of Schwarzkopf on Aug. 2, 1990. Less than a week before, CentCom was carrying out a planning exercise for a possible Iraqi invasion of Kuwait. Schwarzkopf had called 350 staff members together in July and told them to draft a strategy for protecting the Gulf's oil fields from Iraq.

8.
BLOOD FOR OIL?

The Persian Gulf war that Norman Schwarzkopf would choreograph started when he was still a gung-ho cadet at West Point. The decisions that shaped it were made when he was dodging mines in Vietnam. By the time he came back from his second tour in Vietnam, a war over oil was a done deal.

In half-a-dozen nations of Islam, along the sunlit curve of the crescent that spans the Middle East, lies 70 percent of the world's oil reserves. The central reality about oil is its abundance. There is just too much of it. Too much in nature. Too much oil-producing capacity. Too much crude that could overflow the market.

In the late 1960s, too much oil meant that the price per barrel could not rise. Discovery always exceeded demand and the price was forced down, down, down. By late 1969, it had sunk below $1.20 a barrel.

The landlords of the desert dreamed of prices more fitting for "black gold," of burgeoning oil wealth, of seizing control from foreigners and freeing themselves from Western exploitation. This dream fired the Muslim radicals in Iran, Iraq, Libya and Syria. It stirred the obstreperous parliamentarians of Kuwait. Even the Saudi princes, though they had been made docile by their wealth, were touched by the dream. It was a Saudi oil minister, Abdullah Tariki, who in 1960 had unfurled the banner: "Arab oil for Arabs."

But it was left to the Americans—specifically Henry Kissinger, the foreign policy virtuoso of the Nixon years—to make the dream come true. Kissinger wanted a regional alliance to defend the U.S. stake in Persian Gulf oil. By 1972, he had settled on the Shah of Iran as the chief protector of U.S. interests there. Kissinger arranged to give the Shah a blank check for whatever weapons he wanted, and that led the Shah to demand higher oil prices to pay for them.

Today Kissinger pleads "not guilty" to being the one who suggested boosting oil prices to finance Iran's arms buildup. But there is no doubt that the Shah had the ear of someone in Washington. Oil prices took a stupendous leap and the administration did nothing to restrain the Shah's price gouging. A secret Central Intelligence Agency summary put it this way in 1974: "The largest oil price increase in history took effect on 1 January 1974, as a result of decisions made at the December meeting of OPEC ministers in Teheran. The increase in the posted price — from $5.04 to $11.65 — came about primarily through efforts of the Shah of Iran."

Awash in oil profits, the single-minded Shah was greedy for more. His greed unnerved the Saudis who feared retribution from the United States. In a secret message to Saudi Crown Prince Fahd, intercepted by U.S. intelligence, the Shah defended the high prices. But the Saudis weren't convinced. They made an offer to Washington to roll back their oil prices.

Nixon's Treasury Secretary William Simon flew quickly to Riyadh and obtained an agreement from the Saudis that they would sell their oil at public auction. That would have prevented from OPEC rigging the prices higher than the market would bear. There was a small caveat: The Saudis, aware of Washington's influence with the Shah, asked only that the Nixon administration intercede with the Shah to reduce his prices too.

Then Gerald Ford replaced Nixon in the White House, and Simon wrote a confidential, six-page memo to the new president saying that Saudi Arabia would press OPEC for lower oil prices, but the United States had to lean on the Shah to cooperate. "They (the Saudis) wonder whether, in fact, we want lower oil prices since we never even raise the subject with the Shah."

Even if the new administration had wanted lower oil prices, it was too late to take the Saudis up on their offer. The new oil economics had taken hold and OPEC was in the driver's seat. The cost of crude peaked at $41 a barrel in 1979. It only came down because some cartel members

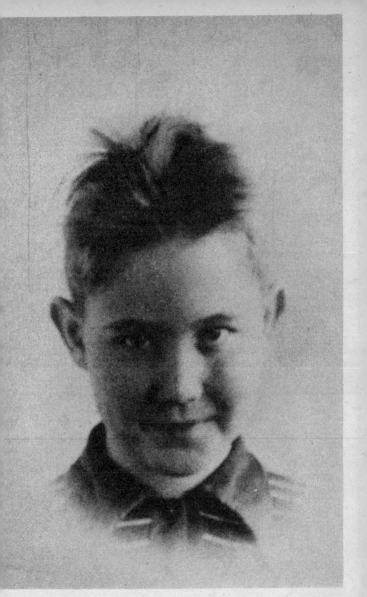

By age 6, Schwarzkopf, pictured here in 1936, was an outgoing, All-American child. *(Visions)*

H. Norman Schwarzkopf's father, Herman Norman Schwarzkopf, pictured here in 1929, three years before he headed the investigation of the Lindbergh baby kidnapping. *(Courtesy New Jersey State Police Museum)*

Pictured with his top commanders in the New Jersey State Police, Schwarzkopf's father is also considered the "father" of the New Jersey State Police. *(Courtesy New Jersey State Police Museum)*

Schwarzkopf's early years were spent in Lawrenceville, New Jersey. Pictured here in front of their Lawrenceville home, Schwarzkopf stands beside his father with his sisters Sally (left) and Ruth Ann (right). Schwarzkopf's father rose to the rank of Brigadier General in the Army. *(Visions)*

Schwarzkopf's first experience in the trenches came as an offensive lineman for the Valley Forge Military Academy. According to his football coach at the time, Schwarzkopf (number 23) was a team player who "played better when he was mad." *(Sygma)*

Schwarzkopf graduated from the Valley Forge Military Academy in 1952 as valedictorian of his class. While at Valley Forge he was also a debate champion, editor of the yearbook, and a member of the honor society. *(Courtesy Department of Defense)*

Sports kept Schwarzkopf fit for action. Pictured here shotputting at Valley Forge Military Academy, Schwarzkopf also enjoys tennis, racquetball, hunting and fishing. *(Sygma)*

Schwarzkopf excelled while studying at West Point. He graduated in 1956, in the top ten percent of his class. *(Sygma)*

Schwarzkopf's greatest supporters are his family. His sister, Sally, pictured here on Schwarzkopf's graduation day at West Point, has been on his side all along. *(Visions)*

In 1956, Schwarzkopf attained the rank of 2nd Lieutenant in the Army. *(Visions)*

In between his two tours in Vietnam, Schwarzkopf married Brenda Holsinger in 1968. He met Brenda at a West Point officer's club party after a football game. *(Courtesy of the Schwarzkopf family/Scott Bolon)*

Schwarzkopf with his first daughter, Cynthia. *(Visions)*

A devoted family man, Schwarzkopf is pictured with his two daughters, Cynthia and Jessica, and his son Christian. *(Courtesy of the Schwarzkopf family/Scott Bolon)*

Schwarzkopf in a 1974 studio photograph with his wife, Brenda and his two daughters, Cynthia (left) and Jessica. *(Visions)*

Pictured here fishing in Alaska, Schwarzkopf is an experienced outdoorsman with extensive training in survival skills. *(Courtesy of the Schwarzkopf family/Scott Bolton)*

Among the many outdoor sports Schwarzkopf enjoys, mountain climbing is one of his favorites. He is pictured here in 1976 in Alaska. *(Courtesy of the Schwarzkopf family)*

Helping an Alaskan squirrel gather its food for the winter, General Schwarzkopf roughs it in the high mountains despite an injured foot that he hurt playing racquetball. *(Courtesy of the Schwarzkopf family/Scott Bolon)*

Pictured here as an Army captain in 1965 during the first of his two tours, Schwarzkopf's first experience of armed conflict came in the Vietnam War. After his marriage in 1968, Schwarzkopf went back to Vietnam for his second tour in 1969. *(Courtesy of the Schwarzkopf family/Scott Bolon)*

Schwarzkopf and a Vietnamese paratrooper help a wounded soldier after a Viet Cong mortar attack at Duc Co where Schwarzkopf was senior advisor to Vietnamese paratroopers. *(AP/Wideworld Photos)*

Schwarzkopf at the 1971 ceremony at which the New Jersey State Police Academy building was dedicated to his father. Accompanying him are his wife Brenda (far left) and his sister Sally Schwarzkopf. *(Courtesy New Jersey State Police Museum)*

Schwarzkopf accepting the Famous Alumnus Award from the Valley Forge Military Academy in 1989. *(Courtesy Department of Defense)*

Schwarzkopf is pictured here in 1988 after he achieved the rank of Four Star General in the U.S. Army and took over the Army's central command in Florida. *(Courtesy Department of Defense)*

In the desert north of Hafr Al Batin, Saudi Arabian King Fahd addresses assembled troops of the Joint Command. From right to left: King Fahd, member of the royal family, Emir of Kuwait, General Schwarzkopf, British General Sir Peter de la Billiere. *(Uniphoto)*

Schwarzkopf accompanies King Fahd on the king's first review of U.S. troops in the field since the invasion of Kuwait. *(AP/Wideworld Photos)*

Conferring with Saudi Arabian Lt. Gen. Khalid Bin Sultan. *(AP/Worldwide Photos)*

Schwarzkopf stands with King Fahd during the king's visit to review U.S. troops. *(AP/Wideworld Photos)*

Schwarzkopf gazes from the window of his aircraft on his way to visit U.S. troops in the desert. *(AP/Wideworld Photos)*

Schwarzkopf disembarks from a helicopter on a visit to U.S. forces. At left is a plainclothes security officer. *(Reuters/Bettmann)*

Addressing troops from the 354th Tactical Air Force Wing. *(Reuters/Bettmann)*

A six-foot-three general stoops to talk with a U.S. Army servicewoman of a smaller stature during a tour of front-line units. *(AP/Worldwide Photos)*

Cadets at Valley Forge Military Academy carry a photograph of Schwarzkopf, in football uniform during his days as a student at the academy, during a "Support the Storm" rally. Autographed by the students, the photograph was sent to Schwarzkopf in Saudi Arabia. *(AP/Wideworld Photos)*

Schwarzkopf and United States Chairman of the Joint Chiefs of Staff General
Colin Powell confer upon arrival at Riyadh airport, February 8, 1991.
(UPI/Bettmann)

(Right) At the Hyatt hotel press conference in Riyadh, February 10, 1991, Schwarzkopf ponders the climactic days of the Persian Gulf War that lie ahead. (Below) With General Powell at the press conference. *(Orban/Sygma)*

Schwarzkopf with General Powell and Secretary of Defense Dick Cheney shortly after the February 10th press conference. *(Reuters/Bettmann)*

When General Schwarzkopf spoke, members of the press listened carefully during the Persian Gulf War. Though the military was criticized for censoring information during the war, Schwarzkopf quickly gained the reputation for telling it like it was. *(Army Times*/Steve Elfers)

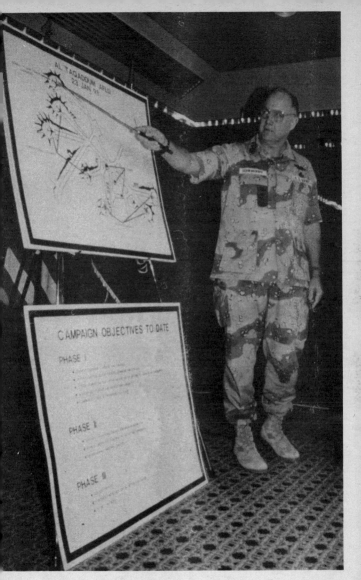

Pictured here during one of the many press briefings during the Persian Gulf War, Schwarzkopf was commended for his ability to translate military language into a language the world could understand. *(Langevin/Sygma)*

"Next question!" From tension to humor, the many faces of General Schwarzkopf's dynamic personality intrigued hundreds of reporters...

...and in turn, millions of television viewers around the world.

Langevin/Sygma

Langevin/Sygma

cheated on their promises to withhold production.

Nixon and Kissinger escaped public censure for the oil catastrophe. They blamed the price explosion on declining supplies and surging demand. Kissinger would later say, "World conditions of supply and demand shifted inexorably against the consumer." But today, instead of an oil shortage, the oil sheikdoms are sitting on millions of barrels a day in unused production capacity and charging prices that are 100 times their production costs.

After two decades of accumulating wealth and buying weapons, the oil monarchies entered the 1990s still helpless — afraid of Israel, afraid of radical Arab neighbors who might grab their oil, and totally dependent on the United States to defend them.

It was only a matter of time before someone made a power grab for their oil riches. Washington strategists even saw him coming.

He was said to be "insane."

That was the only way Americans could explain away the enigma that was Saddam Hussein. One day, few if any in middle America could have named the president of Iraq. The next day, his name was a household word, and he must have been crazy. How else could his brutality be fathomed?

School children took to calling him "Saddam Insane." He was the embodiment of all evil, the next Hitler. Ronald Reagan had told Americans that Libya's Moammar Gadhafi was the "mad dog of the Middle East," that Iran's Ayatollah Khomeini was the bogey man. But Ronald Reagan never told them about Saddam Hussein.

On the night of May 17, 1987, a U.S. Navy Frigate, the USS *Stark,* was on routine patrol in the Persian Gulf, steaming through international waters in the dark. The Iran-Iraq war had turned the gulf into a dangerous place for ships. Some 300 of them, mostly oil tankers, had already been victims of the bitter feud between the Ayatollah Khomeini and Saddam Hussein.

A French-made Iraqi Mirage F-1 jet was about to score the first and only hit on an American naval ship in that war. The jet took off from somewhere in Iraq and sped down the coast of Saudi Arabia toward Bahrain. Ten miles from the *Stark*, the Iraqi pilot launched a single Excocet missile. It skimmed along the top of the sea and found its target in 90 seconds.

The crew of the *Stark* had monitored the flight of the Mirage without much interest. The standard two warnings were radioed to the Iraqi pilot, telling him to keep his distance, but no one panicked. Iranian and Iraqi war planes frequently cruised the Gulf, but they left U.S. ships alone. An Iraqi plane was particularly harmless. After all, the United States maintained a neutral position in the war, but made no secret of its dislike for the glowering Ayatollah Khomeini.

Despite the sophisticated defense system on the *Stark*, the ship's crew never locked on to the Exocet and never knew it was coming. It exploded beneath the ship's bridge and 37 sailors were killed — most of them in their bunks as they slept. Many of the bodies were burned beyond recognition. One was never found.

Saddam Hussein apologized for what he tried to pass off as an unfortunate mistake. "Sorrow and regret are not enough," he wrote in a weepy message to President Reagan. "I hope this unintentional accident will not affect relations." The White House called it an apology, and a month later Reagan blamed Iran as "the real villain in the piece." He reasoned that if Iran had not dragged out the war with Iraq, the "accident" would never have happened. Iraq agreed to pay $27.35 million in damages, and the matter was set aside.

There were more pressing issues in the headlines. The Senate Iran-Contra hearings put the White House at the center of a plot to sell arms to Iran in trade for American hostages, and turn the profits over to the Nicaraguan Contra rebels so they could drag out their civil war. Such was the stuff of American foreign policy in the 1980s. America sells weapons to Iran while befriending Iraq and then blames Iran when Iraq attacks a U.S. ship in the Persian Gulf. And in the meantime, a congressional mandate against funding the Contra war gets trampled on. All in a day's work.

The Central Intelligence Agency, however, did not forget the *Stark*. CIA agents began nosing around. They picked up rumors that Saddam had paid the pilot of the Mirage $35,000 and gave him the use of a Mercedes as thanks for a job well done. There was even talk that a backup plane had been cruising over the Gulf that night just in case the first one missed its target.

A Mirage normally fires one Exocet, but the post mortem on the *Stark* turned up a second, unexploded warhead lodged in the frigate. Was Saddam Hussein festering over the U.S. swap with Iran of arms for hostages? The White House didn't ask.

Things being what they were in the Persian Gulf, America couldn't be too picky about its allies there, if it was to have any allies at all. Saddam looked better than Khomeini, and that was enough.

In retrospect, America should have looked for a friend with a more balanced psyche. Saddam was born in 1935, one year after Norman Schwarzkopf but into a decidedly less nurturing environment.

His father, a farmer, deserted his mother before Saddam was born. Saddam would later say that his father died — an easier story for a boy to live with when his father abandons him. His mother, Subha, had three sons from a previous marriage, and went on the prowl for a third husband. She fixed her sights on Ibrahim Hassan. He was already married, but offered to add her as his second wife, a practice allowed under some circumstances in Islam. But Subha would have none of it. She forced him to divorce his first wife if he wanted to marry her.

Hassan hated young Saddam. Neighbors and early childhood friends of Saddam said that Hassan would awaken the boy in the morning by beating him and yelling, "You son of a dog, I don't want you!" Saddam's native village of Takrit, knew his stepfather as "Hassan the liar." He would send Saddam out to steal chickens and sheep to support the family. At 11, Saddam ran away to his uncle, Khairallah Tulfah, his mother's brother. By that time there was no reforming the child. The CIA files on Saddam say that some to this day claim he committed his first murder at the age of 10. There is no doubt that by 20, he had killed two people. The people of Takrit speak in grotesque, if unbelievable, terms about Saddam—that they could always tell his handiwork if the victim was shot in the back, and that he kept a vat of acid, either in or near his home, to dispose of bodies.

At 22, Saddam turned to politics as an outlet for his aggression. He joined the violent Baath Party and climbed his way to the top over the ruined fortunes and bodies of his predecessors. At 24, the age when most young adults are testing their career paths, Saddam tried to take a short cut to the top. He attempted, but failed to assassinate the ruling despot of Iraq, Abdel Karim Kassem. He had to wait 20 more years until the time was right and enough of his competitors were dead before he took over as supreme ruler of Iraq in 1979.

The first thing he did was weed out any opposition. He made up a story that the Syrians were plotting to kill him, and he badgered one Iraqi official into a blubbering confession of culpability. Then he gathered the cream of the crop in the Iraqi government and replayed a film of the confession. With crocodile tears running down his cheeks, Saddam confided to them that the plot was larger. Then he lit a cigar. Between languid puffs, he read out the names of the "conspirators" in the nonexistent plot. To their horror, they were dragged from the meeting by Saddam's storm troopers and taken to a public place along with some of their family members. Saddam himself joined the firing squad and invited his cabinet members to do the same.

That was enough to establish Saddam as a leader who brooked no dissent, and he continued to reinforce the lesson with tactics borrowed from Hollywood. Saddam loved "The Godfather." He had his own copy of the film and watched it over nd over again. He surrounded himself with family and friends from Takrit and he bonded them to him with blood. When there was killing to be done, he insisted that they do it with him. They were all guilty and thus none were in a position to point a finger at the "Butcher of Baghdad." There were more than enough butchers to go around.

Midway through the Iran-Iraq war, which Iraq was losing largely because of the military ineptness of Saddam, he executed 300 of his top officers for a variety of "crimes" which all boiled down to their inability to win. Saddam, who was rejected by the Iraqi military academy in his youth, finally turned the battle decisions over to his generals in 1986, but not before another round of executions of those who questioned his military prowess.

Legend mixed with fact until it no longer mattered if the stories of his brutality were true. It only mattered that his cowed people believed them. One story finds Saddam near the end of his rope during the eight-year Iran-Iraq war. He calls a cabinet meeting to ask for suggestions. One unfortunate minister takes the invitation seriously and ventures an idea. Since the Ayatollah Khomeini is pursuing the war because of personal hatred for Saddam, perhaps the Iranians could be lulled into a peace if Saddam stepped down temporarily. Saddam asks the cabinet minister to step outside, and shoots him dead.

There is little doubt that Saddam's near-fatal tiff with his son Uday really happened. When Iran and Iraq reached a truce in 1988, Baghdad resounded with the cacaphony of "jubilation bullets" — celebration shots fired into the air. This jubilation over the end of the war may have resulted in the deaths of as many as 300 Iraqis and injury to 2,000 others who learned too late that what goes up must come down. Saddam ordered a stop to the practice, but at a party, his favorite body guard and food taster, a young captain with a few drinks under his belt, began firing his pistol into the air. The hot-tempered Uday reacted by beating the captain to death with a stick.

Uday had more than jubilation bullets on his mind that day. He suspected that the body guard had been the go-between, arranging dangerous liaisons between Saddam and a mistres[s] whom Saddam secretly wanted to take as a second wife. Th[e] woman was already married, but that didn't stop Saddam. H[e] offered her husband, two choices. He could divorce his beauti[-] ful wife and have his pick of assignments anywhere in th[e] world, or he could die. The officer wisely chose divorce.

Uday's mother was shamed and he was carrying a grudge[.] He would soon feel his father's wrath for the murder of the fa[-] vored body guard. Saddam threw Uday in prison and even[ ] considered executing him, but Uday's mother, Sadija, begge[d] for his life. Saddam relented and packed both of them off to Ge[-] neva, out of his sight, to be part of Iraq's mission to the Unite[d] Nations. They were allowed to return after a decent interval.

Uday's banishment to Geneva with his mother was not the[ ] end of the family squabbles over the second Mrs. Hussein[.] Gen. Adnan Khairallah, Saddam's defense minister, was als[o] the brother of the first Mrs. Hussein, and did not like the sligh[t] to his sister. When he complained, he became persona non[ ] grata in Saddam's entourage for a time. Then in May of 1989[,] Khairallah was killed in a helicopter crash. Iraqis had though[t] the two men had reconciled, and Saddam called the crash a[n] accident, but helicopter "accidents" are one of Saddam's signa-tures. After the truce was signed with Iran, several of Saddam's top military officers mysteriously died in helicopter crashes. I[t] became a dark joke in Iraq that Saddam was losing more heli-copters in peace time than in war. When Khairallah's helicop-ter went down, Egyptian President Hosni Mubarak cabled[ ] Saddam and begged him, for the sake of the dignity of all Ar-abs, "Please, no more helicopter crashes."

Killing off his officers for their incompetence may have[ ] made Saddam feel better for botching the Iran-Iraq war. But it[ ] didn't help him pay his $40 billion war debt. He looked around[ ] for help and his eyes fell on Kuwait. The Kuwaiti royal family[ ] was pressing him to repay the money it had loaned him to pros-ecute the war. Saddam felt he had kept Iran at bay for all the[ ] Arab states, not just for himself, and Kuwait wasn't showing[ ] much gratitude. Even the United States—called "The Great

Satan" by the Ayatollah—wasn't grateful enough for what he had done now that the war was over.

It was to keep the Ayatollah from laying his hands on vital oil lands that the United States had quietly aided Saddam during that war. There was no doubt in Washington about what Saddam was—a ruthless tyrant who controlled his people by terror, who had even dumped chemical bombs on his own rebellious citizens for two horrifying days in August of 1988. Secretary of State George Shultz was so personally revolted by the attack, that he dressed down a visiting Iraqi diplomat in very undiplomatic terms.

Yet it seemed nothing could change U.S.-Iraq relations. The White House intervened to stop Congress from voting sanctions against Iraq because of the chemical attack. Ronald Reagan, and then George Bush expected Saddam to be grateful for help they rendered during the Iran-Iraq war. Bush thought he could tame Saddam. American corporations were itching to do business with post-war Iraq and they didn't want politics to stand in the way. In Baghdad, the American Embassy became a virtual branch office for American business interests.

In the 1980s, the United States sold billions of dollars worth of grain and livestock to Iraq every year. The relationship was important to Congress. On a Senate fact-finding mission to the Middle East in April of 1990, five Senators had a chance meeting with Saddam. The five—Robert Dole of Kansas, Howard Metzenbaum of Ohio, Alan Simpson of Wyoming, Frank Murkowski of Alaska and James McClure of Idaho—met with Egyptian President Mubarak and mentioned that they wanted to see Saddam, but were having trouble getting an appointment. Mubarak picked up the phone, called his friend Saddam and wangled an invitation.

The five flew to Baghdad on April 12, but Saddam was not there. He had moved to the northern Iraqi city of Mosul, so the senators were obliged to board an Iraqi plane to join him. They found him in a hotel billeted full of machine-gun toting soldiers. The meeting got off to a bad start. The Iraqi translator was late and arrived breathless, his face ashen and his mind no doubt spinning with the consequences of keeping Saddam waiting. An Iraqi stenographer took verbatim notes.

Metzenbuam, who is Jewish, had not wanted to come to hostile territory, but the others assured him he would be safe. He addressed Saddam: "Mr. President, perhaps you have been given some information on me beforehand. I am a Jew and one of the staunch supporters of Israel. I did have some reservations on whether or not I should come on this visit." Saddam said some soothing words and Metzenbaum continued: "I have been sitting here and listening to you for about an hour, and I am now aware that you are a strong and intelligent man, and that you want peace." Metzenbaum then continued with some advice. If Saddam pursued peace "there would not be a leader to compare with you in the Middle East."

Sen. Simpson chimed in, telling Saddam that "your problems lie with the Western media and not with the U.S. government." The senator urged Saddam not to isolate himself from the press, and added a warning: "It is a haughty and pampered press — they all consider themselves political geniuses."

About an hour into the three-hour meeting Saddam broached the subject of the rebellious Kurds in Iraq — the same people whom he had doused with mustard gas. He offered to take the Senators to any Kurdish village they chose. He would come along. A fleet of five helicopters was waiting in the hotel parking lot. The senators could touch down, mingle among the Kurds and ask them if they loved Saddam. Dole demurred that the senators' time would be better spent talking to Saddam. (Later, when Dole learned of Saddam's poor record with helicopter maintenance, the senator would jest about how wise the decision was to decline Saddam's invitation to be taken for a ride.)

Through the summer of 1990 while Norman Schwarzkopf was trying to read Saddam's mind, the Iraqi leader stewed over Kuwait. He needed money, and Kuwait had it. He needed oil, and there was plenty of it in a disputed border area between the two countries. He secretly began shifting thousands of troops to the border, and then he summoned U.S. Ambassador April Glaspie to his office on July 25. He had a message for President Bush, he said.

Saddam began with one of his windy monologues about the "economic warfare" being waged against Iraq by Kuwait. Glaspie later cabled the State Department that Saddam put on a display of histrionics calculated to bring her to tears. On cue, one of the Iraqi stenographers began to weep. The dry-eyed Glaspie watched as the stenographer was ushered out and replaced by a backup waiting conveniently behind a door. In the conversation that followed, Saddam hinted broadly that he would not tolerate humiliation or "death" for Iraq at the hands of the oil monarchies. And, he made it clear he wanted the United States to stay out of what was to come: "If you use pressure, we will deploy pressure and force. We know that you can harm us although we do not threaten you. But we too can harm you. Everyone can cause harm according to their ability and their size. We cannot come all the way to you in the United States, but individual Arabs may reach you."

Glaspie had her orders from Washington. She was supposed to maintain friendly relations with Saddam. "We have no opinion on the Arab-Arab conflicts, like your border disagreement with Kuwait," she told him.

Two days later — July 27 — the CIA studied satellite photos and noted a massive buildup of Iraqi troops on the border with Kuwait. The White House was informed and passed the warning to Kuwait. The Kuwaitis figured it was probably a bluff — typical Saddam blustering.

9.
A LINE IN THE SAND

Norman Schwarzkopf was on his way to the shower in his Tampa home on the evening of Aug. 1 when a rare event occurred—the hot line phone rang in his bedroom. Sweating from a workout, he picked it up firmly so he wouldn't lose it in his wet hand.

It was the chairman of the Joint Chiefs of Staff Colin Powell. They were personal friends, quite comfortable with each other, having learned long before that both Vietnam veterans were only interested in telling it straight, not doing any kind of diplomatic dance so common in Washington.

"Well, they've crossed," Powell told him tersely. Schwarzkopf knew immediately who "they" were—the Iraqi forces who had been massing across the Kuwaiti border. It was the morning of Aug. 2 in Kuwait.

"I'm not surprised," Schwarzkopf muttered. "Now it's going to be interesting to see what they do."

He was aware that the consensus CIA and Pentagon intelligence reports were now wrong. They had predicted that Saddam was just bluffing. If he wasn't, the intelligence estimates predicted he was only interested in seizing part of the Rumaila oil field that straddled the two countries and/or seizing the disputed Warba and Bubiyan islands in the Persian Gulf. Saddam had long coveted the islands for better Gulf access, and he had accused the Kuwaitis of stealing oil from his side of the Rumaila field.

Powell ordered Schwarzkopf to fly up to Washington in time for a meeting in two days. Schwarzkopf hung up and called his staff for a session to review the intelligence reports on the invasion. And he did a systems check. As CentCom commander in charge of American forces in the Middle East, was he prepared to mass troops to defend Saudi Arabia?

The general was proud that, Cassandra-like, he was more prepared for the event than anyone else in the American government, including anyone in the White House. He already had a draft plan in place for a U.S. response.

Summer was the time for the annual "Command Post Exercise," which was a computer wargame to be based on a hypothetical scenario. The CentCom commander personally selected an exercise which posed a hypothetical Iraqi invasion of Kuwait. Called "Internal Look '90," some 350 members of his staff had participated in the exercise—which had concluded just four days before. "Internal Look '90" quickly evolved into the White House's draft plan for "Desert Shield."

The CentCom commander was alarmed when he began following the intelligence reports of the incursion which happened in the early morning of Aug. 2 Kuwaiti time.

This was no mere seizure of an oil field and a couple of islands. Saddam Hussein was going all out. It was an overwhelming Arab blitzkrieg by the world's fourth largest army into a nearly defenseless smaller country. Tens of thousands of Iraqi soldiers stormed across the border, racing down the six-lane super-highway to Kuwait City, about 80 miles away. They quickly crushed the armed resistance, killing at least 200 Kuwaitis in the assault. That number included the emir of Kuwait's younger brother, Sheik Fahd al-Sabah, who was defending the palace. The emir himself, Sheik Jabir al-Sabah, barely managed to escape, fleeing to Saudi Arabia by plane.

Iraq was claiming, outrageously, that Kuwaiti rebels had overthrown the long-ruling Sabah dynasty and subsequently invited Saddam's troops in to restore order while an interim government was established. But dominance was Saddam's real game. In seizing control of Kuwaiti oil fields, he aimed to turn Iraq into a superpower with an economic choke-hold on the world. Together, Iraq and Kuwait held oil reserves of 195 billion barrels—20 percent of the world supply. The invasion caused a fiscal panic. World oil prices shot

107

up and financial markets plunged into chaos.

The United States immediately condemned the invasion, but Schwarzkopf understood the military sense of it. The one thing he faulted Saddam for—militarily only—was not continuing on to the eastern Saudi oil fields while he could. "On Aug. 2, they could have just driven down the highway and just taken them all," he later reflected. "It would have been that simple. Who was going to stop them?" But, then again, knowing the man as well as Schwarzkopf did, Saddam routinely failed during the Iran-Iraq war to capitalize on one success and push ahead to another.

Worldwide condemnation was swift, and Arab condemnation a little slower. Saddam was promising, with one of many lies, that he would withdraw from Kuwait soon, so some Arab leaders thought it was better to adopt a wait-and-see attitude. But Norman Schwarzkopf was never a wait-and-see guy. When he flew up to Washington, he was prepared not only to advance a defensive U.S. military presence—but an eventual offensive presence.

Even National Security Adviser Brent Scowcroft was somewhat surprised at the Friday Aug. 3 NSC meeting when it became Schwarzkopf's turn to speak. He laid out his plan, based on 'Internal Look '90.' If the United States intended to defend Saudi Arabia, Schwarzkopf said without hesitation, then he would need a swift buildup of 140,000 troops—more than two divisions—a huge naval force and about 700 combat aircraft. One person who was present said the general "blew them away with this." He was talking a massive, Vietnam-style buildup.

President Bush was firming up his own opinion about Saddam's move, and Schwarzkopf's suggestion was not out-of-line with the president's own thinking. There was just one problem: the Saudis hadn't asked for help. Certainly the influential Saudi Ambassador to the United States, Prince Bandar bin Sultan, was pushing for American intervention. But King Fahd was not on board yet, the prince confided to Bush. Maybe he should send a persuasive high-level delegation to Riyadh immediately to lay out the intelligence and military picture personally before the king.

Schwarzkopf stayed in Washington overnight for a second historic meeting on Saturday. This one took place at the president's weekend Camp David retreat in Maryland, and it was time for the general to wow the president with a briefing the same way he would later wow the world. He was up to the task.

Using flip charts and graphs, he carefully took the president through the buildup necessary for a defense of Saudi Arabia. The last chart was a kicker. It showed the buildup needed to boot Saddam's thugs out of Kuwait. The man who, several times before, had thought of leaving the Army, had become the first person to confidently propose to the commander-in-chief that Kuwait could be liberated with a sizeable American offensive force.

George Bush was impressed. Schwarzkopf was his kind of no-nonsense general, but at the same time a man who discussed the prospect of a defensive or offensive engagement in compelling human terms. He was laying out the military options to the president, yet, because he was a soldier who considered war a profanity of sorts, he was not forcefully advocating war.

The president decided it was imperative Schwarzkopf himself brief Saudi King Fahd. But the king was already proving reluctant to approve any American visit. So the president threw Secretary of Defense Dick Cheney into the mix—an envoy of such stature that King Fahd could hardly refuse the visit.

On Monday, Aug. 6, Cheney and Schwarzkopf had an audience with the Custodian of the Two Holy Mosques, as the king liked to be called, in his sumptuous, cooler summer palace at the Red Sea city of Jeddah. Not far from the holy city of Mecca, the King made his decision to invite Western infidel forces in to defend the integrity and sovereignty of his kingdom. He was insistent on one caveat, however. The Americans must leave when they were finished. That's what Schwarzkopf remembered most from the meeting: "We told the Saudis from the outset—when I traveled over here with Secretary Cheney in the very initial invitation to come over here—we said, 'We'll come if we're asked. We will leave when we are asked to leave. We have no intention of having permanent bases in this area.' "

On Thursday, Aug. 9, after his return, Schwarzkopf assembled his staff together. One of those there called it the "fate of the world is in your hands" speech by Schwarzkopf. He told them it was up to CentCom to provide an American deterrent force in Saudi Arabia. Lt. Gen. Chuck Horner, the Central Command Air Force commander, would head up the troops in the field until Schwarzkopf got over to Saudi Arabia. A spokesman for CentCom reported to the press that the general told his staff that "U.S. forces will work together with those of Saudi Arabia and other nations to preserve the integrity of Saudi Arabia and deter further Iraqi aggression through presence, training and exercises that will enhance the overall capability of Saudi armed forces."

On Sunday, Aug. 12, Schwarzkopf got his baptism by press. He held court at his Tampa headquarters office for a "pool" of Washington journalistic hotshots who would then be on their way for the first pool coverage of the American military buildup in Saudi Arabia. Following his president's lead, Schwarzkopf held his cards close to his vest. There was no hint of the enormous numbers of soldiers envisioned if the president went ahead with a military liberation of Kuwait.

Saddam was already playing tough, and Schwarzkopf was mad. Three days earlier, Iraq had closed its borders, and those of its new 19th province, Kuwait, allowing only foreign diplomats to leave. He would soon use Western citizens as hostages and "human shields" against any American-led counter-attack.

Schwarzkopf began the briefing by describing the logistical challenge of transporting U.S. troops and equipment 7,000 miles by air or 12,000 miles by sea from the East Coast. One "heavy" division of tanks would take 1,538 loads aboard a C-141 transport plane, and another 269 loads aboard the largest aircraft in the world, the C-5. "The magnitude of the task, to quote my teenagers, is 'totally awesome.' "

Yet he was confident the United States already had sufficient force to deter Saddam's troops, he indicated. "I would never tell you that the American forces that are there are 100 percent out of harm's way. (But) we have built up a great deal of force over there now, and if they do make an attack, they are going to pay a price for it."

At the time Schwarzkopf was proclaiming this, Saddam had a million-man army, several thousand tanks and many combat aircraft. The mere 2,300 people from the 82nd Airborne Division were not even in place yet. And the 16,500-man Marine amphibious brigade wasn't ready either. There were no tanks to speak of, and few aircraft. He knew his soldiers would be mauled if Saddam chose to attack then. Never before had Schwarzkopf pulled off such a massive bluff while holding next to nothing in his hand.

Schwarzkopf continued the tough stance that implied more strength in the field than he could muster. In his first news conference in Saudi Arabia, on Aug. 31, he boasted about the capabilities of his soldiers: "They're not potted plants. They're not greenhouse shrubs. They're trained for this environment, and they're very, very tough folks."

But privately, he was desperate to get his old division, the 24th Mechanized Infantry Division, and their top-of-the-line 200 plus M-1A1 tanks into the country. By mid-September, they were still not there in significant force. Cargo ships were breaking down, and there weren't enough of them, anyway. For one thing, the Navy had only eight fast sealift vessels. This had always been a sore point with Schwarzkopf: "A lot of us have been testifying for a very long time that we were very concerned about a strategic sealift, and the fact that our Merchant Marine was aging rapidly. I think you're going to see a lot more attention paid to things like the Ready Reserve Fleet."

By late September, Schwarzkopf began to feel just a bit more at ease. Iraq still woefully outnumbered him, but he felt he was moving from a deterrent force — a tripwire — to a truly defensive force. It was the difference between troops able to fight for a few days to a 150,000-man force that could hold out, possibly, for months. "The first forces that came over here were light forces. They were the ones that said to Saddam

111

Hussein, 'If you attack Saudi Arabia now, you're attacking the United States of America.' And that was the deterrent force that we put over here. We've succeeded in our mission to deter and now I'm focusing on the mission to defend and to make darn sure that I can defend against anything that we can defend. We can defend against anything that Saddam Hussein chooses to throw against us. I need to have heavier (armor) forces than I had originally so that's what we're in the process of doing. We're in the process of bringing in more robustness into the defense so that I can be 100 percent confident of success."

Meanwhile, diplomatic efforts were continuing. The United Nations imposed an embargo and economic sanctions. An early September meeting between President Bush and Soviet President Mikhail Gorbachev ended with an agreement that the Soviets would not disagree with America's military deployment to the Middle East. Saddam was finally allowing groups of Westerners to fly home. But he was urging his troops and citizens to prepare for "the mother of all battles."

Schwarzkopf heard the threat, and was busy doing just that. What impressed him the most in the early stage was the professionalism across-the-board of the new all-volunteer Army.

"Gee, we have magnificent young people in our military," he effused. "They really are good. The quality of the individual service members is much, much higher (than the draft Army of the Vietnam war). You have a moral, an ethical, a very, very professional leadership out here. And I think it's a derivative of Vietnam. We came out of Vietnam and those of us who have stuck around are determined that our level of professionalism and our level of ethics and our level of morality will be extremely high. And we don't tolerate people who don't measure up.

"I will tell you, the young lieutenant colonels out there who are commanding battalions today are 10 times better than I was as a battalion commander in their level of professionalism. It's a life thing with them. And they study it, and they work at it, and they talk about it actively and that's very healthy." Schwarzkopf, indeed, had a different caliber of fighting power than he had in Vietnam. The new generation of American soldiers were highly motivated and well trained. They worked 10-hour days, seven days a week, all spread out across the Saudi desert battling boredom as well as heat.

Schwarzkopf was also moved by the incredible difference in American support for him and his troops as compared to Vietnam. He was getting letters, baked goods and other presents. "You get great letters over here. Late at night, the last thing I do before I go to bed is try and answer all the letters." One American family wrote that since he was going to go down in history as a great general he, like Patton, should have a dog with him. They had just the dog, an eight-week-old female puppy they would send along. "I had to write them back and say we all leave loved ones behind, and one of my loved ones is this black male labrador retriever named Bear. And among Bear's many habits is he watches television — particularly when there are dogs on. He'll sit right there. And I said, 'How can I explain to Bear that I've taken up with this female dog over here and left him behind?' So, I graciously declined their offer for the dog." Parenthetically, he added, a young puppy wouldn't be good for all the Persian carpets he was traipsing over in his diplomatic visits to Saudi officials.

The general had to constantly remind himself he was just as much politician as soldier. One reporter from a local Tampa station, Bryan Brewer of WFLA, visited Riyadh and gave him a popular T-shirt with a drawing of Saddam on its front with a screw being driven into his head. "It's just my size," Schwarzkopf laughed, "Extra Large." He posed for photographs with it and had second thoughts later. It would look frivolous and taunting at the same time. Brewer respected his request to keep the photo for his personal collection only.

In October, Schwarzkopf personally developed the flanking plan that would achieve military victory four months later. Built into the plan he presented that fall month was a mid-January launch of a huge bombing campaign to be followed by a late February ground campaign. Schwarzkopf would hop aboard helicopters or planes to visit his units on the front-lines in early October. On one such trip, looking out a plane window into southern Kuwait, Schwarzkopf exlaimed, "If Saddam were to attack, I would want to suck him into the desert as far as I could. Then I'd pound the living hell out of him. Finally, I'd engulf him and police him up. It's that simple."

Gen. Powell flew to Riyadh for a look-see himself — and a special conference with Schwarzkopf on Oct. 21. He asked Schwarzkopf just what he'd need to pull off his war plan. Schwarzkopf said, simply, he'd need to more than double the 180,000 American troops he already had in the field. Powell took it back to other Pentagon officials. In a meeting at the White House on Oct. 30, the timetable and escalation of troops was agreed to.

The next day, on Oct. 31, the president began preparing the people for the announcement of troop escalation. He'd already expressed his outrage on the terrible atrocities the Iraqis were perpetrating as an occupying force on the Kuwaitis — summary executions, rapes, torture, theft of anything not bolted down and even many things that were. To that, Bush added, "The American flag is flying over the Kuwait Embassy and our people inside are being starved by a brutal dictator. And what am I going to do about it? Let's just wait and see, because I have had it with that kind of treatment of Americans." For domestic political considerations, Bush withheld the announcement of the doubling of American troops until two days after the November election — on the 8th.

Though Schwarzkopf had proposed the offensive, there is no question he hoped the sanctions or some miracle would make the war unnecessary. In a late-October interview with Joseph Albright of Cox Newspapers, he said, "Right now, we have people saying, 'Okay, enough of this business, let's get on with it.' Golly, the sanctions have only been in effect about a couple months . . . You don't go out there and say, 'Okay, let's have a nice war today.' God Almighty. That war could last a long, long time and kill an awful lot of people. And so we've just got to be patient." Later, turning more reflective, he added: "War is a profanity because, let's face it, you've got two opposing sides trying to settle their differences by killing as many of each other as they can. That is a profane thing when you get right down to it."

Schwarzkopf was the wiser head who was prevailing. A number of his gung-ho troops wanted to get on with it so they could get out of this place they called "a big beach with no water."

Writing on Nov. 10 to his parents, Army Spec. 4 Mark Nelson rather colorfully described the situation: "(One) problem with border guard(ing) is that we aren't given the bottled water anymore. The army has taken water from somewhere and purified it with chlorine. So now instead of drinking the nasty bottled Haji water, we are drinking the nasty Army pool water. The first time I tasted it, I was reminded of when I got water up my nose during swim practice. It's ironic how just when things seem bad, they get worse. I guess a complaint about having water at all seems a little crazy. We just got spoiled with the bottles . . .

"The flies here are sooo big. How big are they? I'm glad you asked. They're so big when you smack them they laugh at you, go get about 100 of their buddies and buzz your eyes and nose for about six hours. If you happen to kill one, God help you. Another one will find his buddy squished and get a posse to hunt you down. A posse of flies consists of about 200 angry Mack truck flies that are persistent on buzzing in your mouth and up your nose. It doesn't look good. We're outnumbered by about six million."

Nelson complained about what was probably an upcoming visit by Gen. Schwarzkopf himself: "Tomorrow my platoon is putting on a 'dog and pony' show for some four star. All we do is drive from the north in a wedge formation to a hill, park and let the big cheese ask us questions about our job. A real waste of time if you ask me."

Little did Nelson know that Schwarzkopf figured training, training, training would serve two purposes. One was to keep them busy so they would pine less for home. "We're keeping them busy. We're trying to give them something to do with their time, so we keep them very, very busy." A second reason was that the one-time battalion commander knew that incessant, relentless training exercises would later save lives. Schwarzkopf had received a moving letter in Riyadh from one of his men from the Vietnam era who reinforced this lesson:

115

"He said, 'You know, I can remember you giving us hell about wearing our flak jackets and our helmets.' And he said, 'I can think of a thousand times when I really, really didn't like you very much because you forced us to wear our flak jackets and helmets.' He said, 'You may not remember, but I got badly wounded. I wouldn't be alive today if you hadn't made me wear my flak jacket and my helmet.' And he said, 'I see that you're doing the same thing over there now that you did in Vietnam. You're insisting on (the troops) doing the right things rather than the creature comfort things.' He said, 'I just want you to know that you kept me alive and I know that you're going to keep the troops over there under your command alive.' "

Public confidence in the president's Gulf policy—always a separate matter from the near-total support for the troops—was eroding in November. The administration was struggling to articulate the reasons for the deployment. Many Americans were skeptical the initiative was based on anything more than the price at the gas pump. The Bush administration offered several overlapping reasons why troops were risking their lives in the gulf. The president called it an effort to put a stop to Saddam's naked aggression and prompt release of the hostages without negotiation. Vice President Dan Quayle used his sub-bully pulpit to explain America must stop Saddam Hussein from developing nuclear weapons. And Secretary of State James Baker told the troops during an early November visit they they were defending a "new world order."

The tour Baker made to the Gulf, as well as Middle Eastern and European capitals, set the stage for President Bush's own whirlwind tour in late November that culminated with Thanksgiving dinner with the troops.

Asked for his most vivid memories of Schwarzkopf, the President told us, "I remember two instances when I was in Saudi Arabia with Gen. Schwarzkopf for Thanksgiving. The first was a view of the general striding through the air terminal at Jeddah—in command, and totally comfortable with our Saudi allies who were there to meet me. And then, hours later, he was just as comfortable striding through the ranks of his men, enjoying a turkey dinner in the midst of the desert sand."

On that unforgettable trip, President and Mrs. Bush came within 70 miles of the Kuwaiti border in a helicopter escorted by formidable gunships equipped with .50-cal. machine guns. Fighter planes flew high overhead. "Security good?" somebody asked Gen. Schwarzkopf. "It had better be, or I'm in trouble," he replied.

Bush was dressed disarmingly. He wore a blue work shirt, khaki slacks, and floppy camouflaged hat that had become a trademark of the waiting game in the desert. He had a gas mask handy, after learning how to use it aboard *Air Force One*. He walked among the GIs, attempting a bonhomie that was natural. "If push comes to shove, we're going to get Roseanne Barr to go to Iraq and sing the national anthem," he joked, referencing the comedienne's screeching, much-scorned performance at a major league baseball game the previous July.

The president then declared that their sitzkrieg would not last forever. The United States had been patient with Saddam, but its patience was not inexhaustible. His presence and rhetoric overshadowed the other political figures who visited the troops. Bush had shrewdly asked the four top congressional leaders, Sens. George Mitchell and Robert Dole, House Speaker Tom Foley and Minority Leader Robert Michel to join the desert feast. It was an offer that couldn't be refused politically, but it was the president's day in the limelight.

The president had turkey with the Army and Marines on land, and attended Thanksgiving services aboard the Navy's USS *Nassau*, a helicopter landing ship. Schwarzkopf was there, a beaming, sanguine presence. He could see his commander-in-chief was thrilled at the enthusiasm of his troops. "Every day that passes brings Saddam one step closer to realizing his goal of a nuclear weapons arsenal," Bush said at one stop. "And that's another reason, frankly, why more and more our mission is marked by a real sense of urgency." The troops gave a big cheer.

The warrant for war was delivered by the United Nations on Nov. 29.

U.N. Resolution 678 authorized the use of force against Iraq if it did not withdraw from Kuwait by Jan. 15, 1991 — the top-secret planning date Schwarzkopf had already gotten approved earlier as the time for an aerial bombardment to begin. The resolution, approved by the Security Council and hard-won through diplomatic arm-twisting by President Bush, marked only the second time in the U.N.'s 45-year history that it had tacitly provided authority for member states to wage war against another country. (The first was in 1950, at the outset of the Korean War.)

The following day, President Bush proved himself politically dexterous with a surprise offer for a dialogue with Saddam. He still wanted peace, he maintained, but he still wanted Iraq unconditionally out of Kuwait. Dickering over a satisfactory date bogged down the offer, but one result was the unilateral Iraqi release of all its Western hostages in time for Christmas.

Nothing seems to strike home harder for a soldier and his family than to be separated at Christmas time. Back in Tampa, Brenda Schwarzkopf knew that and began working overtime with military and local "support groups." She explained: "It was mainly just making sure that everybody has a place to go. A place to get together and be able to talk over whatever you want to talk about. We have an awful lot of those groups on base, but there are an awful lot of them also in the town, at churches. A lot of them are weekly."

Central Command had its own newsletter and support group for families of the 710 staffers assigned to the command, the bulk of them in Riyadh. The confidential sessions provided detailed pictures of what the staff was doing in Saudi Arabia, and the prognosis for the future. Often, Schwarzkopf would have his people over there send back pictures of his staff—which Brenda and CentCom in Tampa would display on their walls "so that people can try to find their loved one," she explained.

It was also a time "for all of those people to get together and talk." Their name-tags would be color-coded for different Tampa suburbs so a new support group member "can go up to somebody with that color name tag on and say, 'That's where I live. Maybe we can get together and have coffee?' "

Brenda's special support group was a walking group she went out with daily, before Desert Shield had even begun. "I have some very, very dear friends who are other military wives. We have a walking group and we try to walk every day. While we're walking, we talk, and we share our feelings." Normally, they would walk in the morning—usually a set, 4.7 mile course on MacDill Air Force Base where the Schwarzkopfs live.

The Schwarzkopf animal menagerie, less one python, was growing, too. When the general left, there was Bear, a cat, a hamster and two parakeets. But Brenda began attracting every stray cat in the area. "If it comes to my house, it's going to find a loving hand and some food. So, they've just been coming to my door and I've been trying to find some homes for them. Since my husband has been gone, I have found homes for six stray cats and have (more) to go. Are you interested?"

The highlight of her weeks were the calls from her husband. He rarely talked about business. "I've really known that if there's something he wants to tell me about, and can tell me, he will. Otherwise, I'm never even curious. I feel that if I'm not supposed to know, it's best that I don't know." Norm would call about 2:30 a.m. Saudi time if he could, making sure the children would be home from school so he could talk to each of them.

For Christmas, the family sent Schwarzkopf "lots of little Christmas gifts." The big ones were set aside under a little Christmas tree with lights, left standing until he would come home. "We saved the best things for when he comes home."

Schwarzkopf wanted the family's Christmas to be as normal as possible without him there. So Brenda's mother came, and Norm's sister, Sally. He sent some gold cartouches—custom-made Egyptian bracelets spelling out a person's name in hieroglyphics. Ever the general, he sent along with his gifts "a sheet of instructions exactly how to give them out. You know, A, B, C, D. Because he always plays Santa Claus. He's the one who gives out the gifts. I guess he wanted us to follow the order," Brenda said.

The American troops in the desert took their Christmas absence from their family with extraordinary equanimity. But

119

then, the "new Army" was constantly surprising its critics—
especially the Saudi hosts who were once quite wary of having
them in the country.

Never before has America fielded so many abstemious,
clean-shaven, church-going soldiers to a major war. The new
soldier may curse a blue streak, but he was not, in Saudi Arabia, a drunk, a drug addict or a skirt chaser. It was so out of
character for the few, the loud and the unseemly, that they
dubbed this one, even before it started, "the Square War."

Prior to their deployment, the Saudis and other Arabs had
stereotyped Americans as Godless heathen party animals. At
Schwarzkopf's suggestion to King Fahd, concerned and conservative Islamic leaders and scholars were invited to visit any
unit they wanted to. The secret visits were eye openers for
both sides—for the Muslims who were treated with courtesy
and interest, and for the soldiers who got a rare opportunity to
mingle with residents of their host country.

Disciplinary hearings were rare, probably more because of
the lack of liquor than anything else. "What it means is that
we're running the largest detox center in the world here," one
senior Army official observed. "Any of the troops who came
here as alcoholics have been forced to sober up." The soldiers
had to make do with near-beer, which was not quite the same.
Drug use was rare as well. And prostitution was nowhere to be
found. Soldiers could look a long time in the desert before
they caught a glimpse of an ankle. Not only couldn't the men
proposition Saudi women, but they also couldn't talk to them
at all. The GIs came to call the black-veiled Saudi ladies,
"Ninja Women." Most, including the many American women
troops deployed to the front, were proud of being good-will
ambassadors as well as soldiers. "The people of Saudi Arabia
want us here," Air Force Staff Sgt. Dan Gildea wrote his folks.
"We've shown them that we're not a bunch of heathens in the
West. We're here to protect them and their country. They see
Saddam the same as we do, and they want no part of that
United Arab crap he's talking about."

The soldier's general, Schwarzkopf, was equally boastful
about his troop's good behavior. Asked by David Lamb of the
Los Angeles Times about this, the general offered: "The world

predicted, 'Oh my goodness, culturally the Americans are really going to step in it over there. They're going to be drunken soldiers rolling around inside the souk.' It hasn't happened. The fact that we have culturally respected this area cannot be ignored in the Arab world."

No one ignored the Jan. 15 deadline fast approaching, and 11th-hour diplomatic scurrying was the order of the day. But the diplomats were on a doomed course. Baker finally met Iraqi Foreign Minister Tariq Aziz in Geneva, but the Iraqis proved stubborn. And he dared to add insult to intransigence: Aziz refused to take a personal letter written by President Bush back to Saddam Hussein.

Meanwhile, there was plenty of incentive to get on with the war. An unconcerned Saddam didn't seem to believe America had the courage to attack at all. Delays were giving him more time to build power and consolidate his defensive positions, amassing some 530,000 troops in the theater, according to Schwarzkopf's intelligence estimates. And the dreaded high-wind sandstorm season would begin in late March, making it almost impossible to conduct a battle for days at a time.

On Tuesday morning, Jan. 15, President Bush signed the "national security directive" in front of his Oval Office fireplace authorizing Schwarzkopf to implement his plan and begin the bombing of Iraq—unless there was a last-minute change of heart by the Iraqis. There wasn't.

10.
DESERT STORM RISES

The Apache attack helicopters revved up in the early morning hours of Thursday, Jan. 17. The helicopters belonged to the 101st Aviation Brigade — part of the only true air assault division in the world, their commander liked to brag. Gen. Schwarzkopf had tapped them to fire the first shots in the war, to spearhead the biggest air assault in world history.

Only the previous September, the General Accounting Office had criticized the Apache helicopters for their high maintenance needs. The GAO charged that the choppers needed repairs after an average of two and a half hours in the air in peacetime. And they might be totally useless in war.

But Schwarzkopf had confidence in the helicopters. It was not mere jingoism about American manufacturing capability. Experts in helicopter operation and Army mechanics had worked overtime perfecting them at the desert bases, correcting the glitches that caused the poor performance the GAO discovered. The abrasive, fine sand of the desert had caused new problems, particularly the pitting of the helicopter engines, and tremendous wear on the blades. New filters were designed and added on, and the blades were either repainted regularly or wrapped, like athletes, with a special epoxy tape.

Schwarzkopf also had confidence in the men and women who flew the helicopters of the 101st Airborne Division. They were, after all, part of the storied "Screaming Eagles," whose place in history was first cinched during the World War II Battle of the Bulge.

Then acting-commander Brig. Gen. Anthony C. McAuliffe and his 12,000 men were ordered in December 1944 to shore up a front collapsing under a German surprise attack by holding out in the strategic Belgian town of Bastogne. The outnumbered

101st were pounded by the Germans for days. Three days before Christmas, Gen. McAuliffe issued his now-famous reply to the German demand for surrender. "Nuts!" It was Gen. George Patton who then came rushing victoriously to his rescue. When the VII Corps relieved Gen. McAuliffe of the defense of Bastogne in January, their commander presented him with a receipt: "Received from the 101st Airborne Division, the town of Bastogne, Luxembourg Province, Belgium. Condition: Used but serviceable."

That kind of cavalier bravado had been passed down through the ranks and the years in the 101st, and it was a kind of wonderful symmetry to Schwarzkopf that they would have the honor of the first fire in this war Saddam had made inevitable. In Schwarzkopf's mind, this one thing was clear — Saddam had asked for it. A sign in a Saudi hotel would later sum this up for footballer Schwarzkopf: "Iraq has won the toss and has elected to receive."

The Apaches weren't actually first over the border into Iraq. They were preceded on ultra-secret missions by MH-53 Pave Low helicopters carrying Army Special Forces whose job was to locate early-warning radars across the border. It was the job of the heavily-armed Apaches to shoot up the radars, or paint them with lasers so that A-10 Warthog attack bombers could finish the job — if the radars were heavily bunkered.

Schwarzkopf, the infantry veteran from Vietnam, had a knot in his stomach as the Apaches went stealthily on their way. Surrounded by staff in the lower-floor War Room of the Ministry of Defense building in downtown Riyadh, war was a serious business to the general, not a euphoric one. The prevailing mood in these first minutes was almost gloomy.

The Apache helicopters crossed the border into Iraq on the dark but clear night, with a newly-arrived new moon giving advantage to their night-vision capability. Like the courageous Indian tribe after whom they were named, they were both scouts and killers against overwhelming forces. Many miles to the south in Riyadh, Gen. Schwarzkopf was experiencing simultaneously his "most anguished moment" of the campaign. It wasn't the pressure on him as a commander. "It was the fact that it was D-

Day, H-hour. A battle was going to start that would result in the loss of human life. We didn't have a pep rally in the War Room. We weren't standing up and cheering. Not by a long shot."

And so it was that the Apaches of the 101st Airborne Division, defending their flight as they homed in on ground radars, fired the first shots and unleashed the fury that is war. Just 10 minutes before this, at 2:30 a.m. Saudi time, Schwarzkopf assembled his full staff in the War Room. He asked the chief chaplain, Col. David Peterson to say a prayer for the protection of his troops.

Following the prayer, Schwarzkopf ordered the playing of one of his all-time favorite songs, Lee Greenwood's "God Bless the U.S.A." The soaring song filled the room of misty-eyed men and women.

Then Schwarzkopf said, "This is it. Remember, everything you do is going to affect the lives of our troops."

The next group of aircraft into Iraq were the Ravens, the EF-111 electronic warfare planes from the 390th Electronic Combat Squadron. Their job was to jam the enemy radar with sophisticated "electronic countermeasure" (ECM) techniques.

A full half hour before the first attack aircraft went in for the first bombardment, the Ravens of the 390th were on point. One of the lead Ravens was flown by their commanding officer, Lt. Col. Dennis Hardziej and Air Force Capt. Tom Mahoney. Immediately, a "greeting party" of Iraqi MiG-25s and the newer MiG-29s rose to fight the Ravens, which carry no weapons.

Lt. Col. Hardziej, a veteran of the Panama invasion, dove and increased his speed. Terrain-following radar allows the EF-111s to fly as close as 200 feet to the ground. Missiles the Iraqi fighters fired at them hit the ground. "It was kind of scary," Hardziej allowed later. "Terror would be the best word," Mahoney added.

The 390th, as other Raven squadrons that night, did their job of primarily jamming ground-based radars. Navy Lt. Fred Drummond of the 390th explained that the Iraqis watching their radar screens that night and subsequent nights must have been mystified and alarmed. "They might think it is a malfunction to start with—we know that from training with our own people. They see their screen as being whited out. There are large strobes coming across it. By that time, they know that something is coming at them, but they don't know at what altitude or direction it is coming from."

Almost casually, Drummond added that the EF-111 "puts out enough power that we can jam targets from 100 miles away. We have fried crystals (in enemy electronic gear)."

With the Apaches and A-10s knocking out the early-warning radar, the Ravens and Prowlers (the Navy counterpart, or EA-6Bs) hitting the battle radars, it was time for the third wave: the "Wild Weasels." These Vietnam-vintage F-4G aircraft were designed to knock out the greatest anti-aircraft threat to the coalition pilots — the SAM (surface-to-air) missiles the Iraqis were manning.

The trick, often performed by the Ravens and Prowlers, was to get the desperate Iraqis to turn the separate battery-operated SAM radar on after the tactical battle radars were knocked out. The Wild Weasels also act as an inducement for the switch-on. "We use ourselves as bait," explained Maj. Jim Uken of the 81st Tactical Fighter Squadron. "We'll go out and dare these guys and tickle the fringe of their envelope."

Once the Iraqi SAM radar was switched on, the electronic warfare officers on the Wild Weasels — who are nicknamed GIBs, for "Guys in the Back" — acquire it on their systems as a target. Each Wild Weasel carries four High-speed Anti-Radiation Missiles (HARMs) which can ride the radar path down to destroy the SAM radar. Without the radar, the SAMs can't be launched; they're blind. That's why, added Maj. Uken's commander, Lt. Col. Randy Gelwix, "we give a warm fuzzy feeling to the fighter pilots. When their equipment tells them a SAM is looking at them, they feel a lot better knowing we're there to take it out." The Wild Weasels "paint" the ground picture in much the same way, electronically, as the AWACs planes paint the air picture for the fighters.

After these initial attack helicopters and electronic warfare platforms that first night came the most massive air armada ever assembled in history, beginning their launch about 12:50 a.m.

More than 1,000 fighters, bombers and other planes began

taking off from Saudi Arabia and the Gulf states, from ships in the Persian Gulf and Red Sea, and bases elsewhere. They came from seven nations—the United States, the United Kingdom, Saudi Arabia, Kuwait, France, Italy and Canada—and spoke four languages over their intercoms. In the densely-filled skies, lit up like the Fourth of July by anti-aircraft flak and Iraqi jets occasionally coming up to meet them, the coordination between the coalition aircraft was extraordinary. The opposing aircraft were routinely shot down or they fled under fire, and no major "friendly fire" incidents downed the coalition's own.

The lead bombers were the F-117A Stealth fighter-bombers, which had been first used in Panama. Not so long ago, the unusual angular design of the plane, which helps make it invisible to radar, was considered so secret that a toy-maker caused headlines when he produced a model of the classified fighter-bomber. It was a Stealth fighter that dropped the first bomb on Baghdad at about 3 a.m. Iraqi time.

Gen. Schwarzkopf and the architect of the air campaign, Lt. Gen. Charles Horner, commander of the theater air forces, learned of this first successful strike not from their sophisticated intelligence networks, but from American television networks—in particular, CNN. The Western correspondents were reporting from the downtown Baghdad Al Rasheed Hotel, which had been taken off Schwarzkopf's targeting list a few days before. Schwarzkopf believed one room was being used by Saddam for command and control functions, but the general had no intention of harming American journalists.

Chuck Horner was in a basement storage room of the Royal Saudi Air Force headquarters, dubbed the "Black Hole," when the attack began. The room served as the Air Force command post. According to a *Newsweek* account, Horner sent a subordinate to his office upstairs to watch CNN:

"Over a telephone hot line, the supreme air commander called to his scout, 'What are they saying?' Back came the reply: 'Bernie Shaw's under the table and he's got the mike out the window.' Horner checked his watch. At nine minutes past the hour, Saddam's telephone exchange was due to be demolished. CNN needed the exchange to transmit the signal. At nine past, BAR-

RROOM. 'What's Bernard Shaw saying now?' Horner asked. 'He just went off the air.' Much later, Horner recalled: 'You know, some people are mad at CNN. I used it. Did the attack go on time? Did it hit the target? Things like that.' "

Also riveted, with the rest of the nation, to the first minutes of bombing as transmitted by CNN, was the president of the United States. After watching the report for a few minutes, George Bush sent spokesman Marlin Fitzwater out to the White House briefing room at about 7 p.m. (EST) for a short but already obvious announcement: "The liberation of Kuwait has begun."

The operation, he added, was code-named Desert Storm. How appropriate, some of Schwarzkopf's friends felt as they reflected on a twist of his nickname—Desert Stormin' Norman. The nickname begun over his quick but soon-passing temper would now be the term that would give confidence to the troops like victorious American generals of yore—and strike fear in downtown Baghdad, where Saddam Hussein dwelt.

President Bush put some finishing touches on the speech he had been preparing for weeks, and was in time for a 9 p.m. television address in Washington. Among those who tuned in to the commander-in-chief was his commander in the field, Gen. Norman Schwarzkopf.

"Just two hours ago, allied air forces began an attack on military targets in Iraq and Kuwait," Bush began. "These attacks continue as I speak." The President reiterated the unsuccessful efforts he and others had undertaken to induce Saddam Hussein to withdraw from Kuwait. "Now, the 28 countries with forces in the Gulf area have exhausted all reasonable efforts to reach a peaceful resolution, and have no choice but to drive Saddam from Kuwait by force. We will not fail.

"As I report to you, air attacks are under way against military targets in Iraq. We are determined to knock out Saddam Hussein's nuclear bomb potential. We will also destroy his chemical weapons facilities. Much of Saddam's artillery and tanks will be destroyed. Our operations are designed to best protect the lives of all the coalition forces by targeting Saddam's vast military arsenal.

"Initial reports from Gen. Schwarzkopf are that our operations are proceeding according to plan. Our objectives are clear: Saddam Hussein's forces will leave Kuwait. The legitimate government of Kuwait will be restored to its rightful place, and Kuwait will once again be free."

The president talked of patience that the world had exercised for five months, hoping for a peaceful solution, but all to no avail. "While the world waited, Saddam Hussein systematically raped, pillaged and plundered a tiny nation no threat to his own. He subjected the people of Kuwait to unspeakable atrocities, and among those maimed and murdered innocent children.

"While the world waited, Saddam sought to add to the chemical weapons arsenal he now possesses, an infinitely more dangerous weapon of mass destruction — a nuclear weapon. And while the world waited, while the world talked peace and withdrawal, Saddam Hussein dug in and moved massive forces into Kuwait.

"While the world waited, while Saddam stalled, more damage was done to the fragile economies of the Third World, emerging democracies of Eastern Europe, to the entire world, including to our own economy . . . While the world waited, Saddam Hussein met every overture of peace with open contempt. While the world prayed for peace, Saddam prepared for war."

Poised and calming, Bush concluded by talking about Schwarzkopf's troops. "No President can easily commit our sons and daughters to war. They are the nation's finest. Ours is an all-volunteer force, magnificently trained, highly motivated . . . May God bless each and every one of them and the coalition forces at our side in the Gulf, and may He continue to bless our nation, the United States of America."

George Bush, not always a great communicator, had moved his audience — the largest viewing audience in history. Nearly 79 percent of all Americans with televisions in their homes watched, a record only exceeded by the 81 percent who watched John F. Kennedy's 1963 funeral. The audience was larger for Bush because many more Americans now own televisions.

With many others, Schwarzkopf was touched by the president's heartfelt words. He appreciated his president as a leader who had enunciated the clear reasons, Schwarzkopf felt, which justified the risk of some of America's most precious blood on a foreign land so far away. And it didn't fail to pass his attention that the President never once mentioned the word, "oil." Why play into the hands of the counter-demonstrators back home whose rallying cry was, "No blood for oil!"

For the jittery troops in the field in those early white-knuckle hours, the general delivered his own message of confidence and solace. He was a man with command of the English language, and a real sense of history. His audience included pilots listening on their headsets, soldiers throughout the theater with their ears to transistor, ham and short-wave radios, and even some reading the message over fax and teletype machines as it came across at their desert posts. To many, his short message seemed reminiscent of Winston Churchill in some of his finest hours:

"I have seen in your eyes a fire of determination to get this job done quickly," he said, convincingly, "so we all may return to the shores of our great nation. My confidence in you is total. Our cause is just! Now you must be the thunder and lightning of Desert Storm. May God be with you, your loved ones at home and our country."

The bombing of Baghdad and other parts of Iraq and occupied Kuwait continued around the clock in the first 36 hours of the campaign. American and allied airplanes were not invulnerable. Seven were lost during this initial period. The first to disappear was an F/A-18 from the aircraft carrier USS Saratoga, piloted by Lt. Cmdr. Michael Scott Speicher, a 33-year-old father of two from Florida. His plane was hit by a SAM, and he was lost. Of the seven, three were American planes, two British, one Italian and one Kuwaiti. Still, the remarkably low casualties, and ineffectiveness of Saddam's own air force in the first phase produced a cavalier bravado among the pilots who came back reporting many strikes. They dubbed the tracer bullets and small shells indiscriminately spewed at them by the Iraqi "Triple-A" (anti-aircraft artillery) as "Golden BBs." That didn't mean that their guard was down. As one pilot morosely muttered, "It takes only one bullet to ruin your day."

All the hits were from enemy fire, not friendly fire, which was no small feat in Schwarzkopf's mind. "As you can well imagine, coordinating seven different nations and coordinating the air strikes with the type of aircraft that are being used is a rather difficult proposition." His Air Force commander, Lt. Gen. Horner, said it was only possible through the use of computers bringing "together the tens of thousands of minor details — radio frequencies, altitudes, tanker rendezvouses, bomb configurations, who supports who, who's flying escort. There are just thousands and thousands of details, and we work(ed) them together as one group. Put them together in what we call a common Air Tasking Order (ATO). And it provides a sheet of music that everybody sings the same song off."

The daily computerized Air Tasking Order, which could run as many as 500 pages, delineated the targets the planes would strike — so nobody would be wandering around in somebody else's territory getting shot up. The initial targets were important Iraqi air defense and air force facilities; fixed and mobile Scud missile sites; and the chemical, biological and nuclear facilities telegraphed in President Bush's war address. One big difference with this war, was that Schwarzkokpf and Horner would choose the targets, in consultation with their own commanders and, occasionally, their superiors. In the Vietnam days, President Lyndon Johnson himself would sometimes personally choose the targets. Troops ordered to follow-through, in most cases, would have saved more lives or achieved more of a victory if on-scene military commanders had directed such targeting instead of the unschooled Texan in the Oval Office.

Aside from the mercifully low casualties from enemy or friendly fire, the most remarkable aspect of the first hours of the air campaign was the demonstrable accuracy of its bombing. Targeting with the new precision-guided munitions, or so-called "smart bombs," was a far cry from World War II, when bombers were happy to get within a half-mile of their target — or even Vietnam when the accuracy of high-flying bombers averaged within a quarter mile of the target. In this campaign, with 80 percent success in the first 36 hours, pilots were hitting within 20 feet or closer. A commander of a wing of Stealth fighters, Col.

Alton Whitley, put it best: "You pick precisely which target you want, the men's room or the ladies' room."

Schwarzkopf has always been someone who believes you should get what you pay for. He felt that the American taxpayer, at great expense, had coughed up the money (and debt) during the Reagan defense buildup to give him the military strength and equipment he was wielding in the field. So it was only natural that he approved the public showing of a half-dozen actual videos taken by pilots during their bombing runs—which normally are classified "Secret." He reckoned the deterrent value alone was worth it, if Saddam was likely to be one of the television viewers who saw how unerring the technology was.

The videos were unveiled at his first press conference of the war, conducted at 7 a.m. Saudi time (11 p.m. back in Washington), Jan. 18. "Having been at the early hours of the Grenada campaign," he told newsmen and viewers, "I would tell you that we probably have a more accurate picture of what's going on in Operation Desert Storm than I have ever had before in the early hours of a battle." The general properly boasted of the more than 80 percent initial bombing success rate, and "the professionalism that's been exhibited by all of the people (here) in the last 36 hours (which) is nothing short of inspirational. But he cautioned: "It will not be over in a day."

Giving credit to Lt. Gen. Horner as "the architect of the entire air campaign," Schwarzkopf turned over the podium and pointer to him for Chuck Horner's shining moment. Up came the videos: first of F-111s successfully bombing airfields at night, and getting infrared pictures of same; then the unforgettable strike on a Scud storage building in Kuwait where the bomber pilot sent two separate 2,000-pound bombs right through the door; another memorable moment when a bomb is dropped down the shaft of an air defense headquarters in the vicinity of Baghdad, as smoke and debris come out a side door; another bombing of an air-defense building, this time in Western Iraq; and finally, the coup de gras, an airplane dropping a bomb right down through the center of the tall headquarters building of the Iraqi Air Force in Baghdad, blowing off the top floors. "That's my counterpart's headquarters in Baghdad," Horner deadpanned.

After this display, some in America complained that this was going to be a bloodless war, television-wise, and threatened to become a video game. Picking up on this theme a few days after the briefing, ABC News' Cokie Roberts on "This Week With David Brinkley," needled Schwarzkopf about the Nintendo nature of this show-and-tell.

"General, in watching those weapons work, and what we saw those videotapes the other day shown from Riyadh, I must say the reaction here in Washington was one of great excitement," she began. "Hey, look at that! They really blew up the thing! You see a building in a sight — and it looks like a video game more than anything else. Is there any sort of danger that you don't have any sense of the horrors of war here? That it is all just a game?"

Schwarzkopf, the man of the mine field and battles past, took quick umbrage at this. He squared off: "You don't see me treating it like a game. And you don't see me laughing and joking about it going on. There are human lives being lost when that happens. And at this stage of the game, it is not a time for frivolity on the part of anybody."

When the cameras weren't on, though, Schwarzkopf, ever guarded about success, privately confessed to being "up-beat," perhaps even "euphoric" in the first day of the war: "The most euphoria I felt was at the end of the first 24 hours when I recognized the (huge) number of aircraft (which) had been flown and how low the casualty levels were. You don't like to lose a single life. You don't like to lose a single human being, so you don't celebrate by saying, 'Hey, terrific! We only had a hundred people killed!' That's not what you say. What you do say is, 'Thank God that our casualty rate is so low.' Or, 'Thank God it has been so small.' And then you pray that it continues that way. So if that is what you want to describe as euphoria, then I will admit to that."

11.
THE SAND RUNS OUT

For more than 40 days and 40 nights, the coalition warplanes poured millions of tons of fire and steel onto Iraqi facilities and troops from the sky.

Schwarzkopf's first objective, as he later outlined it, "was to disrupt (Iraqi) leadership and control." Some 26 leadership targets — headquarters buildings and bunkers — were struck in the early days, virtually wiping out Saddam's ability to communicate with his troops. One land-line was deliberately left intact because Special Forces units had slipped behind the lines deep inside Iraq, located the cable and tapped into it. Throughout the air war, Schwarzkopf's top intelligence people were using this and other intercepts to anticipate Saddam's moves.

Schwarzkopf wiped out three-quarters of Saddam's command and control facilities by aerial bombardment, which included many of Iraq's power plants, though not all. "We never had any intention of destroying 100 percent of all the Iraqi electrical power — because of our interest in making sure that civilians did not suffer unduly," the general explained during the war. "We have the military power to completely obliterate Iraq if we wanted to. This whole thing could be over with in a couple of days if we were the type of nation that chose to unleash all of our power without regard to the innocent civilians that would be killed. To do this places a certain set of restraints on us. It's always been that way: If you've ever seen the old time cowboy movies, the guys in the black hats, the bad guys, they can do anything they want to. The guys in the white hats have to play by a certain set of rules. And that's what we have here."

The general was in for a big surprise on his second objective, to attack combat aircraft in the air and on the ground to achieve air superiority. The Iraqi Air Force of more than 1,000 combat planes, in Schwarzkopf's words, "didn't choose to fight." He reckoned that one reason was the fact that he had "almost completely taken out their ground control radars. That's the method by which they normally vector their airplanes against their enemy aircraft. As a result, their aircraft have been kept on the ground and in shelters."

The Iraqi planes that did fly up were so outgunned — and so blind and confused because of the array of super-sophisticated electronic warfare thrown at them — that they never scored a kill against coalition planes.

"My biggest danger was running into another U.S. aircraft," Lt. Col. Dick "Snake" White of Arkansas said. The commander of a squadron of Harriers described the huge coalition armada searching for enemy planes and targets as "almost like trying to get to the checkout during a close-out sale on lady's lingerie." That's why Schwarzkopf was able to pull off a political feat early on by giving the Royal Saudi air force their own hero — Capt. Ayed al-Shamrani. The smiling pilot was acclaimed worldwide for his early shootdown of two Iraqi F-1 Mirage fighters. No one talked about how the AWACs plane directing that battle deliberately waved off U.S. and Canadian warplanes that were closer so the Saudis would have someone to brag about.

The swarm of coalition planes and weaponry was so daunting that the Iraqi air force gave up and fled the scene whenever they could get out and had a place to go. So they flew to safer airfields in northern Iraq. But at least 89 top-of-the-line Iraqi aircraft fled across the border into Iran, causing one of the most puzzling moments for Schwarzkopf and his intelligence people: What were they up to? Would they come back?

Many theories were put forward by Pentagon and CIA spooks, but during the war, Schwarzkopf settled on three: "Scenario one, they are flying off to husband them for another day. Number two, they are flying in there to launch an attack against us. Scenario number three, some of those people are defectors. It could be any one of these three things, or a combination of all of them. But it's a very good sign that they don't feel confident where they are. They've got to run some place else to hide. I'm delighted with that outcome." The flight of the enemy's best was a disappointing event, the general acknowledged, to American's own gung-ho flyboys. "If they had their druthers, they'd want those folks to come up and fight them so we could eliminate them much quicker."

On Jan. 23, the best Saddam could do against allied aircraft, Schwarzkopf opined, was use antiquated Triple-A systems to "shoot up in the air in mass numbers — sort of like you shoot a shotgun at a bird, hoping one of the pellets will hit."

On Jan. 30, Schwarzkopf stood up before the world and announced that America and her allies now owned the skies over Iraq and occupied Kuwait. Four days later, the coalition air forces passed the 40,000-sortie mark. Schwarzkopf's fliers had flown 10,000 more missions in a little over two weeks than were flown against Japan in the final 14 months of World War II.

If there is one Schwarzkopf dictum that will go down in the history books, it is this: Never assume away the capabilities of the enemy. He drummed this into his staff and his on-scene commanders so that if they remembered nothing else, it would be that. The lesson was hard learned when he was thrown into the Grenada battle at the last minute and expected to help jump-start it. Others had assumed the Cubans wouldn't fight, but they did, and rather tenaciously. The poor assessment had cost some Americans their lives. And one lost American life in battle was always a tragedy for Schwarzkopf.

Publicly, and in the war room, the commander-in-chief in the theater repeated it so often that his top men spouted it out to their own men throughout the war. The top Marine on the scene, Lt. Gen. Walter Boomer, espoused the Schwarzkopfian dictum time and again to his own men. "I'll tell you this," he lectured them once. "All of my plans assume that every Iraqi up there is going to fight like hell. If that turns out not to be true, that's great. But we've planned for it."

So it wasn't an unexpected answer when the general was asked whether he was worried about Saddam's no-show chemical weapons. "We have planned assuming that chemical weapons will be used," he said. "Once again, you don't assume away capability that the enemy has. As much as we hate the thought

135

of chemical weapons, they are not so terrible that it makes the enemy absolutely invincible if he uses them. We are going to execute a ground campaign with the full expectation that we are going to run into that sort of thing."

Schwarzkopf never saw chemical weapons as the big bogeyman of the war, but he was wary of them. An aide carried his own gas mask nearby whenever he left the sheltered and bunkered Saudi Ministry of Defense building on Prince Abdul Aziz Street. Besides the previous use of gas by Saddam on his own people, there was one key intelligence indicator coming into the war room that suggested the Iraqis might use the ghastly stuff. Spy satellites caught them preparing a half-dozen decontamination sites in southern Iraq. They were not doing this because they feared the U.S. would slime them back, Schwarzkopf reckoned, but because the Iraqis had previously experienced wind shifts that sent toxic clouds back on them.

Schwarzkopf confidently knew after the first few days of bombing that he had at least destroyed supply depots and chemical production facilities at Samarra, Falluja, Salman Pak, Musayyib, Iskandriyah, Baiji and Qaim. But another cardinal rule the general observed in the fog of wartime intelligence-gathering was to take the first BDAs — Bomb Damage Assessments — and divide them by two and that might denote the real destruction which had occurred.

Before the war, Schwarzkopf's intelligence estimates indicated Saddam had built up a stockpile of 2,000 to 4,000 tons of lethal chemicals. Mustard gas formed the bulk of the Iraqi chemical arsenal. It burns the lungs, blisters the skin and can be fatal in high doses. The more dangerous agents are the nerve gases tabun and sarin that Saddam possessed. Sarin, inhaled or absorbed in the skin, can kill a person in two minutes. Tabun takes about 15 minutes.

The chief stigma of the chemical weapons, Maj. Michael Davis, 2nd Armored Calvary Regiment's chemical officer observed, was "fear of the unknown." In some cases, the soldiers opted for an unusual redundant system of gas protection. Experts had lectured them on the near-infallibility of chemical-monitoring equipment to alert them to a gas attack. But the skeptical and enterprising airmen of the 4410th Operations

Wing bought some local chickens to use like canaries were once used in coal mines. Their asphyxiating contortions would warn the airmen before the machines might. The chief chicken was dubbed "Buford," and the base newspaper called "Buford Talks." Declared Col. Bill Van Meter solemnly: "He's a very important bird. As long as Buford talks, we're all in good shape."

Schwarzkopf elected to eradicate much of the fear by issuing each soldier (and himself) two $231 hooded chemical suits complete with gas mask, gloves and galoshes. One drawback was that there was no capacity to store body waste, so using the latrine in a chemical environment was life-threatening. Another was that the suits held heat, adding 10 degrees to the outside temperature, and dehydrating the soldiers training in them because of the charcoal-impregnated aspect of the suits.

Regular rehearsals and training in full chemical gear had the effect, in many cases, of eliminating some of the fear the average foot soldier had of the gas. "I don't think the average Marine worries about it because of our training and suits," said Corporal Jeffery Donders, a driver with the 1st Marine Division.

No one was more grateful than Norman Schwarzkopf—the son of a father who was knocked out of a war by gas—that Saddam's troops never resorted to using the dreaded material. The vaunted Iraqi chemical threat became one of Saddam's biggest dogs of war that barked but never bit.

From the first day on, Saddam Hussein did employ one terror weapon, the long-range Scud missiles. Schwarzkopf had only scorn for the Scud. "I'm not being the least bit facetious when I say this—but saying that Scuds are a danger to your nation is like saying that lightning is a danger to your nation. Because I frankly would be more afraid of standing out in a lightning storm in southern Georgia than I would be standing out in the streets of Riyadh when the Scuds are coming down. If it's going to hit you, it's going to hit you, but the percentages are so much less."

One night, the general was showering when a Scud alert was on. "I didn't bother getting out of the shower," he laughed. "I just went right on with my shower." Another night, Schwarzkopf thought he ought to see just what one of these dreaded missiles looked like. He is the type to kick the tires of a car before he buys it. "I went out and saw the body of one of the Scud missiles," he related. "A Patriot had blown the warhead off and the body fell to the ground here in downtown Riyadh, and I went out and looked at it. It probably is one of the most rudimentary missiles I've ever seen in my life. As I've said from the outset, it is a militarily unimportant, ineffective weapon."

The Bear could bluster about the Scud. He could scoff. But the two leaders of the countries in which they dropped were less sanguine. In fact, Saudi King Fahd summoned Schwarzkopf to his palace early in the conflict to receive assurances from the American commander that Saddam Hussein did not have hundreds of these missiles that he could rain down upon the kingdom.

Schwarzkopf told the king that it didn't matter how many missiles Saddam had. He had to have the launchers to launch them. The best American intelligence estimate at the time was that Saddam had 30 fixed launchers, which were knocked out in the first two days of bombing. The Iraqis had between 20 and 35 mobile launchers, Schwarzkopf confided to the king, and these were more difficult to eliminate. Sixteen had been knocked out by bombing in the first week, so he reassured King Fahd that there weren't many left. (The estimate represented an intelligence failure because eventually more than 150 were located.)

The general concluded with the frank observation, that if Saddam was able to configure the warheads with chemical weapons, it would indeed be a very destructive and worrisome weapon. With that, he left. His Majesty told aides he liked this American general who didn't mince words with him. Who told it like it was.

There was little to soothe the Israelis in that first week, however. As soon as the first Scud was on its way to Tel Aviv, the Israelis were scrambling a dozen jets, ready to punish Iraq. There was a little problem with this: it meant flying over Jordanian and Saudi air space.

Within minutes of the first Scud attack on the evening of Jan.

17, an outraged Moshe Arens, the Israeli defense minister, was demanding to talk to U.S. Defense Secretary Dick Cheney. Code-named "Hammer Rick," the secure hotline had been set up weeks earlier between the Israeli Defense Ministry in Tel Aviv and the Pentagon's crisis center. Arens demanded the IFF codes from Cheney. "Identification Friend or Foe" was the ultra-secret changing code which kept coalition aircraft from firing on each other. Cheney politely refused. Could Arens then have a clear air corridor to attack the Iraqis on their western flank and not accidentally be shot down by U.S. or allied fighters? No, again, Cheney continued. How about a four-hour total call-off of the American-led aerial bombardment so the Israelis could retaliate? Once again, no. Then, Arens added, the Israelis would send in their own Special Forces team to scout and destroy mobile missile launchers known to be at Saddam's western H2 and H3 bases. No, said Cheney. And the issue was closed, at least for the time being.

A special meeting of the National Security Council was convened back in Washington with the purpose of keeping Israel, at all costs, out of the war. The White House planners knew Saddam was trying to taunt Israel into it so America's Arab allies would break up over what they would see as a tacit partnership with Israel. President Bush called Israeli Prime Minister Yitzhak Shamir and promised immediate action.

The orders came down to Schwarzkopf in the field. It was one of the few times politicians back in Washington interfered with his job. They asked him to send a U.S. Special Forces team into western Iraq hunting the Scuds, and give the Scud-busting aerial mission a higher priority. At one point, more than 10 percent of the total allied air assets were diverted to this mission, all to search and destroy missiles Schwarzkopf viewed as militarily ineffective.

He described just how difficult this mission was: "Just the area of western Iraq alone is 29,000 square miles. That's the size of Massachusetts, Vermont and New Hampshire all put together. Then you try and find something the size of a gasoline tank or something smaller that's hidden in that area. It's not an easy challenge. If you find it at night, you send a pilot in there on very short notice. He intercepts that target in the middle of the night—goes screaming in at 600 or 700 miles an hour—to drop his ordnance, and flies away after trying to hit a target the size of a truck." Schwarzkopf noted that the videos of successful hits had given an erroneous impression of overall high performance which "is a mistake. There is an assumption people made that this whole thing is a piece of cake. It's not. It's a very, very difficult problem to go after these mobile launchers. We've known it all along."

But the general was pleased with the success his people had in finding and destroying these pesky missiles. In the first week, Saddam fired 35 Scuds. In the second, 18. And in the third, a half-dozen. The attriting campaign worked well. A total of 81 were eventually launched from the hundreds of missiles Saddam Hussein had stored up against this day. He might have boasted over Baghdad Radio that he had "turned Tel Aviv into a crematorium" but, as Schwarzkopf was wont to say, "Saddam's boasts rarely bore any resemblance to truth."

Schwarzkopf always boasted of having a top staff who supported him in planning for war and during the campaign itself. And he was right. Half the genius of this general is that he knows how to surround himself with bright subordinates, and how to listen to them.

The amazing Patriot missile which turned the Scuds mostly into duds is a case in point: Schwarzkopf would never have bought such Star Wars wizardry, if it were not for a persistent entreaty by the U.S. Army commander in the field, Lt. Gen. John J. Yeosock. It happened during the previous July's wargaming, Schwarzkopf told the *Washington Post*. "John Yeosock deliberately enticed me down to his headquarters in Tampa where he captured me and made me sit through a long briefing on Patriot to tell me how important Patriot was to him and it made sense what he said. Based upon the briefing that he had given me, I decided to raise their priority and get more of them in-country."

The Patriots wound up earning a separate status as the most celebrated weapon system of the war. It was a success story 20 years in the making—and at a cost of hundreds of millions of dollars. The 17 foot 5 inch missile was conceived initially as an anti-aircraft system against aircraft more than 50 miles away, before it was tossed into the 1980s debate over Star Wars programs. President Ronald Reagan directed that it and other weapon systems be modified or built to provide a viable strategic defense against ballistic missiles. So the Patriot was duly altered by 1986 to defend against cruise and tactical missiles that fly at bullet-like speeds. Still, no one was sure how it would work in a real war scenario — until this war.

When the first Iraqi missiles were successfully intercepted by Patriots, the Bear was bullish on them. Always a hands-on manager, Schwarzkopf wanted to know how they worked. The experts explained that a U.S. reconnaissance satellite would first pick up Iraqi activity setting up the launchers and relay that information through an Australian ground station to Schwarzkopf's CentCom headquarters in Riyadh. In the space of this initial 90 seconds, the alert is forwarded to Patriot missile battery crews near the expected place of impact. .

The Scud is soaring above the atmosphere rising to a height of 95 miles before it re-enters, comet-like, at a speed of Mach 8 — about 5,900 miles an hour. The approach lights up screens in the van chock-full of electronics for missile control known as the Engagement Control Station. The missile operators explained that they usually "acquired" the missiles as a target when it was about 50 miles north of their control station. After the human controller places electronic cross-hairs on the blip on the screen, computers take over and gauge the Scud's speed and trajectory and fire two Patriots (an extra one for safety) which break the sound barrier even before their tails leave the launcher tubes. The Patriots reach the speed of Mach 2, or twice the speed of sound, by the time they intercept the Scuds, usually at 35,000 to 100,000 feet above the ground.

Schwarzkopf might marvel at the Patriot's performance, but he was moved and teary-eyed when staffers told him about the particular heroism of one Patriot missile crew in Riyadh. A Scud warning had come late, and its trajectory indicated it was headed directly for their battery site. But the Tactical Control Officer and his NCO assistant chose to stay behind, risking their lives, to make sure the electronic cross-hairs matched the blip, and the missile was launched. The interception was so close to the station that the heat from the fireball of the struck Scud could be felt by Riyadh residents near their battery site. The two men were awarded medals for their valor, at Schwarzkopf's direction.

One Patriot battalion commander, Lt. Col. Leeroy Neel, who watched one of his missiles take out a Scud over Saudi Arabia recalled his experience this way: "I was standing about three kilometers away. I saw the explosion but it didn't register immediately. Then I thought, 'My God, that's one of mine.' "

The Houstonian added simply: "It was there, we reacted properly, and it was gone." He and other Patriot missilemen, soon sported made-to-order T-shirts proclaiming them "Scudbusters." They showed up in children's drawings in Israel, where several batteries were rushed for Israeli protection.

And no less than the president of the United States chose to make one of the most eloquent, patriotic speeches of his career at the birthplace of the Patriot, the Raytheon manufacturing plant in Massachusetts. It was entirely appropriate that the location of Lexington produce the missiles whose controllers became the Minutemen of this modern war.

The four-star general had other stars in his constellation of technology that he singled out for praise. Schwarzkopf had a simple faith in the systems because he believed that "Made in America" meant something. "In the past," he allowed, "there's been a lot of criticism—people who said they aren't going to work. And, of course, you don't know if they are going to work until they do. We've had a lot of firsts in this campaign so far, and all of the firsts have been very successful."

One of those successful firsts was the ship-launched Tomahawk cruise missile, a high-tech wonder on the order of the Patriot. Their use in the opening hours of the war represented the first use of a cruise missile in battle. Like the Patriot, the initial success ratio was remarkable, suggesting Murphy's Law was not operable in this battlefield. More than 85 percent of the first 150 Tomahawk cruise missiles launched in the war struck their intended targets.

Most of the first Tomahawks were fired from the U.S.S. *Wisconsin* from the northern Persian Gulf. "These Tomahawks are the first shots in the opening round of the war," Capt. David S. Bill III declared on the darkened bridge of the warship in the early hours of Jan. 17. Off went the 21-foot long subsonic missiles. Hugging the ground, they were guided by pre-programmed electronics which took them to within 20 yards of targets more than 800 miles away.

American correspondents in Baghdad reported seeing Tomahawks come in at eye-level in their upper-floor hotel rooms and make left or right turns to head unerringly to their target. The success was thanks to Schwarzkopf's insistence the previous August that highly-accurate digital maps of Baghdad and other targets be drawn up for the cruise missiles. The missile uses a video camera that digitally compares the actual images with mapping images in the memory of the Tomahawk.

Though it contributed to the tremendous early success of the missile strikes, a new problem caused a number of failures — and Iraqi civilian casualties — later. So much ordnance had dropped on Baghdad, leveling important buildings and landmarks, that the digital mapping for the cruise missiles was all wrong. If a high military building was used as a guidepost in the digital mapping, and several of its floors had been blown away, then the confused cruise had difficulty locating it and went off in another direction.

Schwarzkopf was as enamored of the "low" technology that worked for his soldiers as the high technology. The best example is the Cinderella story of the war: the amazingly useful but ugly A-10 attack airplane. Only months before, the lumbering wonder — known affectionately by its pilots as the "Warthog" for its appearance — was destined for the Air Force scrap heap. Air Force generals and pilots were against it because they always favor glamorous, fast-flying jets. So Congress was forced to over-ride their resistance over the years and order them to build these slower, heavily-armored planes designed to stick tightly to the ground troops, killing tanks and otherwise defending them. The A-10's armament is a monstrous 30mm, seven-barrel Gatling gun that fires 4,200 rounds a minute and can destroy a tank with a single, well-placed shot. It shoots dense, depleted-uranium ammunition that can penetrate a tank's armor — and rattles around for a while inside doing dam-

143

age to machinery and men. They also carry Maverick missiles, 500-pound Mark 82 iron bombs and Rockeye anti-armor cluster bombs.

In the early stages of the war, the Warthogs became Schwarzkopf's key aerial utility player. They were used to knock out Scud missile sites, artillery supply points, radar installations and surface-to-air missile sites. They even helped rescue a downed Navy pilot. And one engaged in an unexpected dogfight with an Iraqi helicopter. The Warthog won.

One reason the Iraqis had trouble shooting down the Warthogs was that Iraqi anti-aircraft guns usually fire at noise, and the Warthog is relatively quiet, particularly when compared to the other noises of the battlefield. One commander estimated that enemy gunners were able to identify Warthogs by sound in only one of every 100 missions. The sturdy plane is reinforced with titanium, which protects the engines and creates a heavy armor "bathtub" for the pilot. One Warthog took a hit that left a gaping hole in its right wing, destroying a landing gear pod and taking out one of the hydraulic systems. But the plane made it back.

One Air Force intelligence officer, Capt. Jessie Morimoto, standing next to one of the versatile Warthogs (painted with sharks' teeth on its nose), proclaimed proudly: "The A-10s are proving in a war like this that they're just as able to hit the target and get out without being hurt as anybody else — and in some cases, better." One grateful Army intelligence officer at the front wrote, "We would be in serious trouble if they hadn't come. They are THE major weapons between us and the Iraqis and we count on them to take out a huge number of tanks before they get to us."

Schwarzkopf, in this case, was glad that his top Air Force man, Chuck Horner, had relented on bringing the Warthogs over. Sharing his service's disdain for the A-10s, Horner had not included them in the aerial package en route to Saudi Arabia last fall. Several Warthog proponents, including Secretary of Defense Dick Cheney and Schwarzkopf himself, gently interceded, and the Warthog came. After the Warthog's invaluable utility was demonstrated in the first days of the war, Horner manfully offered a mea culpa at a closed-door Air Force command "Battle Staff" meeting on Jan. 19. "I take back all the bad things I've ever said about the A-10s," he offered. "I love them. They're saving our asses!"

Two tactics Saddam Hussein used early on in the campaign sickened the military and ethical soul of Norman Schwarzkopf. One was Saddam's callous television parade of abused American and allied prisoners of war. The sight of the men — particularly Navy Lt. Jeffrey N. Zaun's puffed-up face — and their coerced recantation turned Schwarzkopf's stomach. But he had expected it. Saddam was a thug, Schwarzkopf kept reminding himself, and could never be counted on to do the humane thing, whatever that might be. "I have a gut reaction to anybody that would take someone in that —" the general began, so angry it was difficult for him to continue, "who is so helpless as a POW is, and then go ahead and exploit them by making them a human shield, or beating them up, or intimidating them to the point that they have to appear before television." His voice trailed off, his tremor visible, leaving listeners little doubt what the Bear would do if he could get hold of Saddam at that very moment.

The second unconscionable act was the deliberate fouling of the Persian Gulf by oil spill. The spigots at a marine terminal were opened into the Gulf on Jan. 19, and took some time to form the noticeable spill. "I received the evidence at our headquarters very early in the morning of the 25th of January," Schwarzkopf remembered. "We immediately notified the Saudi Arabians of this." All that day, the general was tied up in meetings with Saudi and American petroleum experts. He had two concerns: the first, since he was running a war, was how much damage would this do to his military operations? And the second was whether there was anything he could do to assist in stopping it.

The experts told Schwarzkopf the first thing would be to set the source of the oil spill on fire. "If we could set it on fire, it would burn off a great deal of pollutants that otherwise would go into the Gulf and continue to flow down." Next, he could take out some key piping that controlled the outflow pressure of the nearby oil fields.

An amused Schwarzkopf recounted that the first objective was accomplished by wartime happenstance. The U.S. Navy that evening was engaging a small Iraqi boat supporting mine-laying operations. The volley set the nearby sea island terminal on fire. Next, the general ordered in F-111 bombers with precision-guided munitions to strike the key pipes, successfully stopping the flow. But the spill, estimated at the time to be 35 miles long and about 10 miles wide, continued to head south in Saudi Arabia. Others would have to worry about that. "War is not a clean business," the general lamented, remembering during World War II "as a very, very small boy, the dirty oil balls rolling up as a result of the type of action that was taking place out in the Atlantic. It's not a desirable thing."

In late January, Saddam Hussein finally chose to meet Schwarzkopf's forces on the ground in a military rather than terrorist engagement. For his battleground, he chose the abandoned Saudi town of Khafji. The Iraqi leader had already been probing Schwarzkopf's defenses south of Kuwait, looking for weaknesses. Schwarzkopf noted: "We've sort of facetiously called one fellow 'Abdul the Rocketeer' because on the very first night, one fellow came down the road on the Iraqi side with his rocket launcher and launched a few rockets over on the Marines. The Marines shot back at him. The next night he came back with a few more of his fellows and lobbed some things over there. And the Marines fired back. And there was sort of this daily escalation."

On Jan. 29, an Iraqi force of about 700 men moved into the unoccupied oil-refining town of Khafji on the Persian Gulf, about eight miles south of the Kuwait border. Saddam proclaimed a great military victory. "From a military standpoint, it's absolutely meaningless," Schwarzkopf pronounced. "It's no more than the irritation of a small mosquito on an elephant — even less than that. Khafji wasn't defended. There weren't any troops there. There was never any intention to defend Khafji. You can't really say they captured Khafji. What they did is they drove into Khafji which is this town that was unoccupied."

Politically, it was a major blunder for Saddam. The Saudis were furious at this intrusion onto their sovereign soil, but the

146

very action justified King Fahd's decision to ask for American help to defend his kingdom. Knowing the political ramifications, Schwarzkopf thought it would be an excellent idea if the Saudis re-captured the town — if they drew first blood.

The Saudis, with critical U.S. Marine and aerial fire support, acquitted themselves fairly well in the two-day engagement. At least 200 Iraqis were killed and 400 taken prisoner by 1:45 p.m. on Jan. 31, when the Saudis re-took their town. Initial Saudi reporting on the battle raised questions about their credibility and war-fighting capability. But Schwarzkopf defended them: "You've got to remember that the Saudis have not fought a major war in literally 1,400 years. We shouldn't expect in their very, very first engagement that they are absolutely sharp and precise in all their reporting."

Eleven Marines died in the Khafji battle, and seven of their deaths brought back an old ghost to Schwarzkopf: "friendly fire." American military investigators concluded the seven had been killed probably by an American pilot firing a heat-guided Maverick missile. Privately, the general was sympathetic to the anguished American who made the mistake. "This is not a surgical business," he told a small gathering soon after the incident. "Even though surgical is a term that's been used quite often, it's a poor word for this type of warfare. There are all sorts of rules in place and had those rules been followed, we would never have had these accidents. Unfortunately, you have to sympathize with a young Air Force pilot who's up in the air, who's in the heat of the battle. He's being shot at, he's shooting, he's flying around at hundreds of miles an hour and he's trying to pick up targets on the ground at night. This is a very, very high stress environment. Mistakes are going to be made. I never accept the loss of a friendly life to our fire, but it's reasonable to expect there are going to be mistakes made out there."

Publicly, he had previously offered as solace an unforgettable personal example during a televised briefing: "These things happen," he said in response to a question about the incident. "I've been bombed by our own Air Force. I don't think they did it intentionally." At this, the newsmen broke out in laughter. Schwarzkopf gently remonstrated: "I really don't mean to make a joke out of this, but you have to understand that bomb racks get hung up and dropped, and I was bombed by B-52s one time in Vietnam in Manyang Pass. They were coming toward us. They did a marvelous job of dropping all their bombs, and then one rack hung up and it released over my position. I certainly never went back and said, 'Why did you do that? I'm angry at you — I know you did it deliberately!' "

The incident sobered up not only Schwarzkopf's staff but Americans watching the war from afar. The 11 Marines symbolized the beginning of major casualties predicted for any ground engagement Schwarzkopf planned.

The general himself was already sobered. He had never taken the low casualties for granted. But even those had caused him a private grief he rarely talked about. When he did, he related it to the widely-acclaimed PBS series on the Civil War, directed by Ken Burns. Colin Powell personally sent tapes of the fall series, and Schwarzkopf watched them avidly in his headquarters.

"One of the great things I saw in the Civil War series was the Grants and the Shermans who — in the minds of other people for a hundred years — were viewed as cold, calculating killers," he recalled. "In the Civil War series, after several battles, they went back to their tents and they cried because of the loss of human life. That's good to know. It's good for me."

The invasion of Saudi territory, the ineffectiveness of the Iraqi troops, the loss of the Marines — all this made Khafji something of a turning point as February rolled around. Chuck Horner, often at Schwarzkopf's right hand, believed the Saddam-planned Khafji operation was the "stupid" act of a "desperate man. He sees that he's getting chewed up. Maybe he sees the sand running out on him."

12.
A DAY IN THE LIFE

Outdoorsman, sun-worshipper and former on-the-scene infantryman, Norman Schwarzkopf rarely saw the sun during the war.

He was forced to be holed up in the Ministry of Defense building on Prince Abdul Aziz Street in Riyadh, Saudi Arabia. He was the supreme commander, and necessarily had to take his place in an upholstered chair in the basement War Room across from maps showing locations of friendly and enemy troops. There was one touch of home on the table, a Christmas present from his sister—a battery-operated baby grizzly bear toy, which emits a growl and shakes its furry head. From the beginning of the war, the bear was firmly ensconced on the table in front of him, next to the red phone which he could use to reach Pentagon superiors or the president.

Schwarzkopf's greatest frustration was not being able to roam free among his beloved troops. The troops loved it when he came. There was an easy banter from the general who proudly wore his infantryman's identification. They loved it when he would shout to them, with great gusto, "I guaran-damn-tee you we're gonna win this war!"

But such visits from the four-star commander often unnecessarily "caused too much disruption," in Schwarzkopf's view. "No matter what I tell them, a visit from the CINC (commander in chief) takes away from the job at hand. Somebody always panics and starts painting the rocks and washing the vehicles and rehearsing briefings."

Schwarzkopf had to resist the temptation to jump right in and do the job himself. "The frustration is realizing as the the-

149

ater commander, you can't get right out there and do whatever is necessary to get this thing over with immediately—do it all yourself. You can't do that. You have to sit back and have great confidence in your subordinates. And I have learned that at every level of command, the higher you get, the less able you are able to influence the action of the minute. You never like it. You always want to say, 'Gosh, I just want to get out there and then I know I could take care of all this.'"

Gen. Schwarzkopf's day would begin with a staff briefing at 0800. "We look at the last 24 hours. Look at the campaign—every incident that occurred from airplanes being shot down to POWs that we have taken. It's an attempt at the beginning of the day to make sure all those necessary actions that need to take place will."

At 1000 hours, a coalition meeting occurred. "We come together and exchange information on what they have been doing, and what we have been doing. We stay well-informed." The two key players at this meeting were Lt. Gen. Khalid bin Sultan, commander of the Saudi and other Arab forces, and British Lt. Gen. Sir Peter de la Billiere. Schwarzkopf won the lasting respect of both. His deference to Gen. Khalid in sovereign Saudi territory over the months had won him major points with the Saudi soldier.

With the British, it took Schwarzkopf's brains and his tactics to win them over. One British commander noted that, at first, "we were taken aback by his gung-ho appearance, but in a very short time we came to realize that here was a highly intelligent soldier—a skilled planner, administrator and battlefield commander." Schwarzkopf and the British commander became particularly close, and Schwarzkopf came to lean on the man, who had previous combat experience in the Middle East and once headed British Special Forces. When asked in Riyadh if he would compare Schwarzkopf to Eisenhower or Patton, Gen. Sir Peter waved aside any comparison and then paid his highest compliment: "He's a bloody good soldier."

The third formal meeting of the day, at 1900 hours, "is when all of my component commanders or their direct representative sit down with me as an update of what happened since the morning." At this meeting, if they could make it, would be

Army commander John Yeosock, Air Force commander Chuck Horner, Navy commander Vice Adm. Stanley Arthur and Marine commander Walter Boomer. "That is where the component commanders and I discuss how we are doing and if there are any modifications that we need to make. It is more of a commanders' conference than it is a staff conference."

"I started out with what I thought was going to be a very orderly schedule," Gen. Schwarzkopf reflected. "A 7 a.m. staff briefing, a 10 a.m. coalition briefing, then a 7 p.m. briefing with the component commanders. Boy, it looked like it was great. But I've got to tell you, more often than not the 7 a.m. meeting has not come off because everybody has been up so late at night."

If Schwarzkopf had the time to venture outside for a look at his troops, or a briefing with reporters at the Hyatt Regency directly across the street, he traveled with a half dozen armed men. To guard against terrorism, a smaller security force was always near him in the headquarters building. The American guards were hand-picked Special Forces troops, sometimes fluent in Arabic. They carried AR-15 automatic weapons fitted with silencers. Usually one would travel in front of him, and two at each side. Saudi guards, who were not relieved for the entire seven months, would complement the American bodyguards, who were rotated in and out of the job.

Schwarzkopf usually put in a minimum 18 hours a day. When the theater work was done, and people were rising in the United States, he would call his friend, the chairman of the Joint Chiefs of Staff, Colin Powell. Sometimes he talked to Powell "three and four and five times a day." Powell usually called about 3 p.m. Saudi time, which was 7 a.m. back in the United States. Schwarzkopf wore two watches to remind him of this, one on Gulf time, and the other set for Washington.

The grueling days, the stress of the job, the frustration of command, and the demand for perfection caused Schwarzkopf occasionally to show his temper. His executive officer, Col. Burwell B. Bell, confirmed that the general "has a full range of emotions. He can get very, very angry, but it's never personal. He's extremely tough on people when it's necessary

151

to get them to do something, but the next minute he'll throw his arm around his shoulders and tell them what a great job they're doing."

The general himself has offered two explanations for his temper. It often erupts, he allows, because he is following his own oft-repeated maxim: "A good leader never walks by a mistake," he told the *Washington Post*. "It's easy to turn your back on something. If I saw a situation that could potentially cost lives and I didn't do something about it and if it did cost lives, I couldn't forgive myself." He added, "My job isn't to go around and say everything is wonderful, everything is marvelous. That's not what I'm here for. That's not what my country expects, or what the families of all those soldiers expect of me, and it certainly isn't what the soldiers expect of me.

He told ABC's Barbara Walters "I have a temper and I'll freely admit to that. I'm not proud of it. I don't like myself when I lose my temper. But I wear my heart squarely on my sleeve, I believe I owe it to everyone to let them know when I don't like something. But I don't carry a grudge. I do not brow-beat my staff. I do not drive people into the ground. I'm not a total martinet."

Norman Schwarzkopf didn't sleep well during the war. "I get enough sleep but I don't get enough rest because I wake up 15, 20, 25 times in the middle of the night," he said during an interview with us that took place in the middle of the war. "My brain is just in turmoil over some of these agonizingly difficult decisions that I have to make." These terrible decisions were the ones "where human life is involved in the decision that you make. Because there are no guarantees in this business. Those are the ones that are hardest for me. It's an intensely personal, emotional thing for me. I agonize over it . . .

"I don't want to make this sound more dramatic than it is — but in every other job that I ever had in the past, I could always kick it upstairs if I wanted." Now "upstairs" was Powell, Cheney or the president. "I don't want you to misunderstand. Colin and I talk about that sort of stuff a lot. But in the final analysis, those kinds of decisions are normally my recommendation to make, or my decision to make."

The general fortuitously picked an ante-room to his office for his bedroom, which allowed him to catch some sleep during the day. "We are napping more during the daytime than we are at night-time. It would be nice to say that I am getting a good eight hours sleep at night. I know I'm not, and I know that no one else on my staff is either. But that is the nature of what my staff and I are involved in."

The bedroom is best described as spartan, and the furnishings sparse. King Fahd had offered him any quarters in Riyadh he wanted, which included Arab palaces. But the pragmatist realized it was easiest to bunk near his workplace. On one bureau was a box of cassettes an American admirer sent who learned he loved classical music. The general was greatly appreciative. Schwarzkopf had a selection of his own including music by artists as diverse as Luciano Pavarotti and Willie Nelson. Another new American friend sent tapes of honking geese, mountain streams and other sounds of nature, like waves on the beach. These, the general said, were the most helpful in putting him to rest on his bed, which was covered with a camouflage poncho liner he used as a blanket. Beside the bed usually rested his favorite double-barreled shotgun. He suggested this comforted him into believing he had a last-ditch defense in case a terrorist or crazy made it past his guards. The truth is that the skeet shooter undoubtedly wanted to be reminded of happier days.

Prominent in the room — on his nightstand and the walls — were photographs of his family. He always carried a dog-eared photo of them in his shirt pocket, as well. Being away from them was the hardest sacrifice the general had to endure: "I dearly love my family and I miss them a lot. I am not that inhuman that I don't miss my family many, many times every single day. But every time I do, I also recognize the fact that there are 500,000 people over here who miss their families too and we're all in this together. And that helps me make it through those times when I miss my family."

Once the war was on, the general could not call Brenda and the children more than twice a week. He treasured each contact with home, asking about their activities, listening to the home-town news. The slices of American life he savored reminded Schwarzkopf of what he was missing—the good and the bad. He could read in the *Tampa Tribune,* which was sent to him sporadically, that several dozen anti-war protesters lined the sides of the Dale Mabry Highway entrance to MacDill Air Force Base that his family called home. A few days later, he would read that thousands of supporters carrying placards drowned them out. He could read about the arguments at Spike's B-29 Bar on Interbay Boulevard where an Air Force and a Navy veteran, shooting pool shot their mouths off about which force was more important in Schwarzkopf's campaign. He could read about servicemen about to be shipped to the Gulf who were having their name and serial number tattooed on their chest, in case their injury was so great that they were otherwise unidentifiable. Or the Army sergeant accused of murdering a prostitute who petitioned to wear his uniform during the trial because of the sympathy that was likely to garner from the jury.

And then there was Super Bowl XXV. He was missing it! Schwarzkopf had never before been stationed in the same city in which it was held and now a war was causing him to give up the 50-yard-line seats appreciative Tampa residents had offered him. The game aside, the event touched him in two ways: Whitney Houston's soul-stirring rendition of the "Star Spangled Banner," and then, instead of the usual endorsement by a winning team member to "go to Disney World," there was the statement of support for the troops.

But none of this compared to two sights of his bride on television. In one instance, a British cameraman was following the general and saw him get an unexpected glimpse of his wife on television attending a military function somewhere in the United States. The big general shed a barely perceptible tear. Out of respect, the British crew never showed the footage.

The second instance much of America watched. His wife had been invited to sit next to Barbara Bush for the President's Jan. 29 State of the Union Address. The applause was continuous when she was introduced. "I was very proud of her," he said. "Anyone who puts up with me for 21 years deserves all the applause they can get. But more importantly, I was proud of what Brenda was representing, and that's the literally half-million military families who have have suffered a lot simply because they've chosen to love a soldier, sailor, airman, Marine or Coast Guard man. That's a pretty wonderful bunch of people. And I was proud that my wife had the opportunity to represent them."

Life was different for the general's men and women out in the field. They were not fond of the incessant desert. Complained Pvt. First Class Kenneth Johns: "This is one big cat box. Nothing more, nothing less."

When many of the soldiers first arrived in Saudi Arabia, soldiers were so fascinated by the sand that they mailed it home in their letters. But it soon lost its luster. Army Maj. Paul Smith could wax eloquent about the stunning Saudi sunsets and the star-studded nights as he drove through the desert. But his tone turned to disgust when the subject changed to sand.

The cinnamon-colored, talcum powder-like stuff got him down, he said, more than anything else except being away from his wife and children. "There's no way to avoid it, even in the tents." Some soldiers paved their tent floors with boards, but puffs of sand came through the cracks anyway. It invaded their sleeping bags and their clothes. Some would wrap scarves around their heads to keep the grit out of their hair, but officers discouraged that look. It was too Vietnam, too Rambo-like for today's Army.

Experts said the sand in northern Saudi Arabia, Iraq and Kuwait is a kind of clay with specks 25 times smaller than the average grain of sand. It doesn't crunch and shift pleasantly underfoot like sand between your toes on a California beach. It puffs and hangs in the air. Sandstorms during the war would begin lightly in the morning and build by early afternoon to gusts of 30 miles per hour, forcing soldiers to hunker down inside their tents or on the leeward side of vehicles.

Soldiers gave up bathing for days at a time. Even if a primitive camp shower was available, the feeling of being clean lasted only a few minutes. "You can smell yourself," Army 2nd Lt. Michael Brumagin wrote home. "You need to shave. Your hair is matted and it's always black under your fingernails. Eventually I bathed, which consisted of pouring water out of bottles over myself. I did laundry. About the same process."

The food had few fans as well. Mostly, the frontline troops got pre-packaged "Meals Ready to Eat," known as MREs. They took to calling them "Meals Rejected by Ethiopians." The ubiquitous MREs could be consumed hot or cold. There were a dozen different entrees, each of which had a little bottle of Tabasco sauce to spice it up. The soldiers got fairly creative with them. Some would add cheese to "Tuna with Noodles," heat it up, crunch some crackers into it and call it casserole. Once "Bean Component" was added to the "Beef Slices" entree, and a dash of Tabasco tossed in, a reasonable chili could be made. Peanut butter fudge could be accomplished with two cocoa packets, four coffee creamers, one envelope of peanut butter and hot water.

Schwarzkopf, who knew armies march on their stomachs, would sometimes eat the MREs back at headquarters. He also knew they marched on their boots — and he was angry that the Army hadn't sent him decent hot-weather boots. The Saudi Shoe Co. factory in Dammam made a killing selling 10,000 to 15,000 pairs of lighter, beige suede boots like high-top Hush Puppies. Some say Schwarzkopf designed a pair himself for the troops on hearing that. It made sense that a general who would order up a custom-made bomb for a special target would also demand a decent boot for his men and women.

The highlight of the soldiers' life, as Schwarzkopf knew, was mail call. Delivering the mail had a high priority, but carting around nearly 300 tons of mail a day got to be more burdensome than a logistics system loaded up with food, water, ammunition and other vitals, could handle. So long delays were coming. One couple estimated it took more than two months between the time a question was asked, answered and followed up. "Writing letters is almost no dialogue at all," one Army major complained to his wife. "It's more like two soliloquies that overlap."

Mostly, it was a tedious, boring wait for the ground war.

Desperate for entertainment, sometimes it would come in the password-response routines. A guard would ask, "Well, sir, read any good *novels* lately?" To which the soldier might reply: "No, just a lot of *rubbish*." To make it more interesting, some were selecting titillating combinations, like the password of "Bedroom" used in a sentence and the response of "Crusade."

The greatest entertainment loss occurred in the first day of the war, when Iraq's own Baghdad Betty went off the air because her station was bombed. Like Tokyo Rose, she was a heavily accented propagandist who lamely tried to get U.S. troops to defect.

How bad was Betty?

She was so bad that she told the soldiers their wives were sleeping with American celebrities — Tom Selleck, Tom Cruise, Kevin Costner and . . . Bart Simpson. Betty was obviously the victim of bad research.

Some diversion was provided by Armed Forces Radio. The local station — known as Wizard 106 because it broadcast from the huge, secret King Khalid Military City (also known as the "Emerald City") — broadcast half news and half music. The station also took requests. After a Scud missile attack, the most in-demand songs were Pat Benatar's "Hit Me With Your Best Shot," or Queen's "Another One Bites the Dust." Mostly they catered to '60s tastes, greeting the day with "Gooooood morning, Saudi Arabia!" in the tradition of Vietnam deejay Adrian Cronauer a la Robin Williams.

"Face it," one private from Boston said. "Rap sound don't make it out here with the scorpions and such. It's okay for punks trying to act bad back on Dot Avenue. But we grunts are the mean green machine that is going to make that King Saddam wish he never was born to breathe. We need real war music from the movies." He meant the soundtracks of "Apocalypse Now," Platoon and other Vietnam-era movies.

Some of the soldiers, like their God-fearing general, got religion. Thousands of special Bibles with desert camouflage covers were dispensed faster than they could be shipped. One had a permanent place on the nightstand next to Schwarzkopf's bed, and it was well-thumbed. His sister, Sally, had said:

"I wouldn't call Norm religious because religious can mean different things to different people. You know, Sunday church going and Sunday school. But I would call him spiritual."

Schwarzkopf himself was more unabashed about his belief. "You know the old adage, 'It gets lonely at the top'? It's awful lonely at the top. If you go back and look at the Civil War series, you will find that an awful lot of those folks—Abe Lincoln himself said he had nobody to turn to but God.

"There is also an old saying, 'There are no atheists in fox-holes.' The chaplains in the field will tell you they are doing a booming business these days. War is an intensely personal, emotional experience for everyone that is involved in it. And you know you have to draw your strength from whatever sources you draw your strength from—more so during war-time than any other time. I have had to." In fact, Schwarzkopf privately offered a number of prayers for his troops.

Otherwise, Schwarzkopf could often find solace in his reading, which varied. For a time, while preparing for the ground war which would include major tank battles, he would page through World War II German Field Marshal Erwin Rommel's *Infantry Attack*. Or it might be William Tecumseh Sherman's memoirs, sent to him by an old friend and West Point classmate. One marked-up passage read: "Some men think that modern armies may be so regulated that a general can sit in an office and play on his several columns as on the keys of a piano; this is a fearful mistake. The directing mind must be at the very head of the army—must be seen there, and the effect of his mind and personal energy must be felt by every officer and man."

He no longer studied the campaigns of Alexander the Great. When he was young, Schwarzkopf said, he indeed idolized the young man who was "the penultimate military leader. His troops literally worshipped him. He could run farther, throw the spear farther. He could do all the things he asked his troops to do. Most of his life, he risked the same perils that his troops risked and suffered the same hardship. He accomplished great things as a pure leader of men." But, contrary to a former West Point classmate's assertion, "I really never thought of myself as one day leading great armies in great bat-

158

tles" like Alexander the Great. The discussions they had were no more than young student fantasies.

Asked about current heroes, the general would usually name his father first, then perhaps Albert Schweitzer or Chief Joseph of the Nez Perce Indian tribe, who never surrendered to U.S. troops and declared finally: "I will fight no more forever."

Legendary World War II tank commander Creighton Abrams, who later generaled troops in Vietnam in 1968, is always high on the list. Abrams was the tank officer who relieved the beleaguered American paratroopers at Bastogne in the Battle of the Bulge, winning Gen. George S. Patton's accolade as "the best tank commander in the Army." Not coincidentally, the chief new tank in Schwarzkopf's desert inventory was the M-1A1 "Abrams" tank. "He was brilliant," Schwarzkopf reflected. He became the number one general in the whole U.S. Army and at the same time he kept his humanity about him and his humility about him. He never got so carried away with pomp and power that he stopped being a human being."

In early February, when asked for a top-of-the-head list of American generals he admired, he named Abrams, Sherman and Ulysses S. Grant. What connected the three?

"Number one, they were all muddy boot soldiers. Number two, none of them ever worried about who got the credit. They just worried about getting the job done. Number three, I think all of them probably intensely hated war. And yet at the same time, when they had to, they waged war ferociously and they didn't enjoy doing it." Besides, the general added, falling back on his renowned humor, another reason to admire "the Grants, the Shermans, the Abrams was that they were just ordinary. They never considered themselves extraordinary. They never, I don't think, considered themselves particularly dashing and handsome and romantic in their uniforms. And perhaps it's my physical characteristics" — patting his belly — "that make me realize that even on my best day, I could not ever be considered dashing!"

Expanding, again, on the subject of war-loving versus peace-loving generals, Schwarzkopf allowed that in Vietnam, there were "a lot who were war lovers there and they scared the living hell out of me. And they are also not very good generals, not from my measurement. Custer loved war, and look what he accomplished."

A real general is compassionate about his troops. He is reluctant to squander their lives. "I guess that's probably more important than anything else. If anybody thinks that this is an enjoyable experience for me, they are dead wrong, dead wrong. If you take nothing away from here but that, that's important. This is not an enjoyable experience. Not fun at all.

"My nightmare is anything that would cause mass casualties among the troops. I don't want my troops to die. I don't want my troops to be maimed. Therefore, every waking and sleeping moment my nightmare is the fact that I will give an order that will cause countless numbers of human beings to lose their life."

13.
IF THIS IS ARMAGEDDON

Gen. Norman Schwarzkopf stared down the enemy for six weeks — and made him blink. A CNN interview with Saddam Hussein proved it. He blinked 40 times a minute compared to less than 25 times in an interview the previous June. For those who believe rapid blinking indicates instability, it was one unscientific indicator that Saddam was coming apart at the seams. Schwarzkopf himself knew that rapid blinking is a symptom common among soldiers who've undergone heavy bombardment.

Schwarzkopf was once accused of trying to intimidate Saddam through his bellicose statements, but the general didn't see it exactly the same way: "I think we have pretty well predicted for Saddam Hussein exactly what would happen if he went to war against us, and he didn't choose to believe it, and I don't know whether he knows what's going on right now. I sincerely hope he knows exactly what's going on. I have no intention of psychologically intimidating him as much as I have of spelling out the simple facts of what's happening and what's going to go on happening."

The reports Schwarzkopf received on his chief enemy throughout this time were mostly anecdotal, he acknowledged. Once, he heard Saddam was totally out of control and doctors had to be rushed in to give him tranquilizers. "Other people have noticed how serenely calm he is at the present time," Gen. Schwarzkopf added, and "others have noted he has taken to pulling out his pistol and shooting some of his people — which isn't necessarily calm, by my definition."

Many, like the seven-year-old son of Capt. Kent Ewing, commander of the carrier USS *America*, wondered why

Schwarzkopf didn't just eliminate Saddam — with the idea this would end the war sooner. "Dad," Capt. Ewing recalled his son telling him, "you don't need to kill a whole bunch of those people over there. You just need to get one of them." He meant the number one bad guy, Saddam Hussein.

Gen. Schwarzkopf explained that "it's never been the American policy to go after a single individual or try to kill anyone." Besides, he added parenthetically, "trying to target one individual person, particularly in a country as large as Iraq — your chances of doing that are far less than finding a needle in a haystack." The general added, "we had a little bit of trouble once before when we were trying to go after one individual (Manuel Antonio Noriega) in a country that's an awful lot smaller — and probably somebody who was an awful lot easier to track. So even if we wanted to go after Saddam, I don't think that's an achievable objective."

The intelligence reports filtering into the War Room were full of sources saying Saddam didn't sleep in the same place every night, that he had dozens of loyal bodyguards around him and had "taken to hiding in buildings and hotels and things of that sort that are deep among innocent civilians, with a lot of innocent people."

German contractors had informed the general that Saddam also had his own luxurious bunker about 60 feet under the presidential palace in Baghdad. The quarters were richly furnished, including a living room with high-quality leather furniture, some of French design. A swimming pool and dressing area were adjacent to the living room. It was filled with enough food for months, and Saddam could hole up in the impregnable fortress built to withstand even a nuclear blast. Fine, one of Schwarzkopf's aides pronounced. "We should go to Baghdad and bulldoze dirt over it and let him rot there for years."

The general shared a similar disgust for Saddam, which he expressed in several different ways. Comparing him to his old Vietnam adversaries, Saddam fell far short in Schwarzkopf's eyes: "Ho Chi Minh and Gen. (Vo Nguyen) Giap didn't live in luxury, didn't have seven different palaces, didn't drive white Mercedes like Saddam Hussein.

Hanoi had an entirely different class of leadership."

And Saddam is no general, Schwarzkopf knew. The American commander had a higher regard for some of Saddam's top generals than he did for the Iraqi president who insisted on meddling in all military decisions even though he is not a gifted general. "Saddam Hussein is not a military man," Schwarzkopf observed during the war. "He thought of this war in tactical terms at the lowest level. He never thought of it in strategic terms. What's happening is that all of a sudden he's finding he's taking a terrible licking strategically and he has no capability to react to that." He miscalculated terribly, Schwarzkopf said. "I will tell you right now that some of the reports we get that are resonating round downtown Iraq are the fact, 'Holy smokes! We've bitten off more than we can chew here!' " The general didn't take any of this for granted. In fact, he concluded: "I don't think we're close to breaking Saddam for awhile. I don't think he's breakable. But I certainly think that we have the capability to break his military."

One of Schwarzkopf's strongest statements about Saddam, during a CNN interview, was also his most impish: "I don't admire Saddam Hussein. I have absolute — I guess I would say I have great disdain for the man. I certainly have no respect for his moral or ethical principles. I have no respect for him as a military leader. He's not a military leader. He's not a military leader by any stretch of the imagination. All he is is a terrorist. He's a terrorist with a military force he's using for terror.

"And do I hate him? No, I don't hate anybody. A very great man one time said, 'Love thy enemies.' And that's not a bad piece of advice. But, you know, you can love them — but by God, that doesn't mean we're not going to fight them!"

Gen. Schwarzkopf found respite in new jokes or jabs at his arch-enemy. One report mentioned that Saddam Hussein had a profound fear of cockroaches. So Orkin Pest Control sent a shipment of "Bug the Thug" bumper stickers to the troops in the Middle East. One personal favorite was the way President Bush would constantly mispronounce Saddam's name, accenting the first syllable and sounding like a rhyme with "Adam." But Schwarzkopf heard that the president's pronunciation was unintentionally insulting Saddam all along. Linguistic experts noted that with the accent properly placed on the second syllable, Saddam means "learned one" or "leader." But on the first syllable, according to a native Egyptian, the word means a boy who fixes or cleans old shoes. "It's the dirtiest possible insult in some parts of the Arab world, but you have to have spent years on the streets of Alexandria or Cairo to know it."

Perhaps the thing Schwarzkopf came to loathe the most about his enemy was Saddam's total disregard for the health and welfare of his troops. The American general, with feeling, would paraphrase Gen. Robert E. Lee: "The military is the only calling I know that demands that you kill those you love the most. To be a good commander, you must love your soldiers. To be a good commander, you must send them out to die." At the same time in Baghdad, the Iraqi dictator would be boasting about the "mother of all battles" in which he would send thousands of his people to die, simply because he wouldn't flinch at the loss of thousands of American soldiers, while the Americans would cave in at the deaths of hundreds.

The troops manning the Iraqi front lines received little in the way of supplies or compassion from their commander. What they did get were racks of bombs from B-52s that shook the ground across the lines in American camps. One large bomb alone from this thunderous pummeling produces a crater 36 feet deep and 50 feet across. Certainly the American soldiers were grateful for the BUFFs—Big Ugly Fat Fellows, according to the more sanitized version—in reducing the ground threat they faced.

But many American G.I.s were still sorrier for the poor Iraqi grunts underneath the carpet-bombing than their own Iraqi supreme commander was. "I feel for them," said Marine Staff Sgt. Percy Smith. "When the B-52s came through, the whole ground was just shaking, just trembling. I feel like I'm glad that I'm on this side and not on their side. I know they're catching hell. I really feel sorry for them." Lance Corporal Gerald Childress said, "They're out there doing the same thing we are. They're doing what they think is right—either that or because they're scared for their families. They've got families at home, children on the way and all that good stuff, just like we have." Cpl. Joey Trecartin noted that "no one talks about 'the enemy.' They talk about Saddam Hussein. 'Hussein did this.' 'Hussein did that.' "

About three miles from the Kuwaiti border, an anonymous Iraqi platoon leader kept a plaintive journal — later discovered by U.S. forces — of his platoon's travails from Jan. 15-28, when he presumably died in a final bombardment. His platoon ran out of food and water at one point. "But God's kindness hasn't left us alone," the lieutenant wrote in painstaking Arabic, "for it started raining heavily, and we collected adequate supplies, which we used to drink, cook and wash." On the 23rd, a strike came uncomfortably close, spreading large shrapnel everywhere. On the 24th, 15 American planes came at dawn and struck throughout the morning. One bomb landed quite close to his bunker: "Thank God, nobody was hit." In the final entry, on the 28th, another of the near-daily intense attacks came and the diarist penned the same refrain: "Thank God, nobody was injured, even though bombing in our area was very heavy." They were his last words.

Schwarzkopf didn't need to find such a diary to know morale in the Iraqi army was suffering. He only had to read the accumulating POW reports piling up on his desk before he launched his ground war. The Iraqis were riddled with lice. They were forced to fight, threatened with being shot in the back if they didn't march to the front. They were starving. Army Sgt. 1st Class Chris Maturich described what happened when he gave four new POWs some MREs: "They ate everything, even the packets of salt and sugar. They swallowed the Chiclets whole. I guess they didn't know it was gum."

Some of the defections and early surrenders were the result of an effective "psychological operations" program conducted by the Army and the CIA — and directed by Schwarzkopf. Millions of leaflets were dropped behind Iraqi lines urging the hungry and tired soldiers to defect. The point of the leaflets was to convince them that their cause was unjust and the resistance to the allies was futile — a message punctuated by round-the-clock bombing that deprived the soldiers of sleep and confidence.

Saddam's response to the leaflets was to send officers out collecting them, and make it a serious offense for anyone else to pick one up. One POW told debriefers that his friend was thrown into the brig and had his head shaved when an officer discovered one of the leaflets in his pocket. The running joke among American troops was that Saddam had newly outfitted his soldiers with green instead of white underwear so they would have nothing to wave. Yet even the indefatigable Apache helicopter pilots of the 101st Airborne were shocked on the evening of Feb. 18 when they captured 400 to 500 stunned Iraqi soldiers out of their bunkers and, from the air, herded them across the border.

Gen. Schwarzkopf's plan to greatly reduce the number of enemy soldiers was working. His experts believed there were 550,000 Iraqi soldiers facing the allies, but with varying levels of competence and training. The front-line troops were "pretty rag-tag and not very good." The second level was better trained. And, at the back, were the best-trained, supplied and fed, the Republican Guard. The ground offensive wouldn't be a go, Schwarzkopf ruled, until half of those men were eliminated through bombing, defection or surrender. "I don't want you to misunderstand to think that the Republican Guard are elite," he once offered. "I have studied their tactics very carefully and I don't think they are elite at all. I think they are unimaginative." Schwarzkopf even doubted their willingness to die for Saddam. "There have been jokes in the past about Kamikaze pilots who had 27 missions. What people claim they are prepared to do, for instance, in the frenzy of a pep rally prior to the football game, the next day they find out they are not capable of pulling it off."

Still, the general reminded himself as well as his staff: "While there is a hope, I don't think that there is a commander out there that's worth a salt who is assuming away the enemy capability. That is a terrible mistake if you do that. What you do is you go into the battle fully expecting to fight that battle just as hard as you have to fight that battle. Then you hope that you will be pleasantly surprised by the action of the enemy. That is the only way to approach this thing."

The general was also fighting — or, rather, jousting — on another front, his own media. The interplay, at first, was generally friendly but serious. "When I saw Norm's first press briefings, he seemed so rigid to me," his sister Sally observed. "Wired. Strained. Frowning. He looked tense. I was shocked because it wasn't the Norman I knew."

The Jan. 30 press briefing, she felt, was the turning point. Her brother invited the journalists to watch a raw video of an F-15 mission destroying a bridge. "I am now going to show you a picture of the luckiest man in Iraq on this particular day," he said. Viewers focused on the cross-hairs of the gunsight as the man's car sped across the bridge in an awful hurry. "Keep your eye on the cross-hairs, right through the cross hairs." The car escaped just as the bridge vanished in an explosion. "And now, in his rear view mirror. . ." the general trailed off, with perfect timing.

"That was the first time I saw him laugh," Sally remembers. "It was the day of 'the luckiest guy in Iraq.' When I saw that, I was so pleased. It was the first time I'd seen his humor come out at one of these briefings. I told reporters, 'It's nice to see him lighten up. It's good for his health.' "

The bantering continued in the same briefing. Someone asked about an American newspaper story which the general responded "contains some inaccuracies. However, reverting to my old style, I would describe that report as bovine scatology — better referred to by the troops as BS." The journalists broke up in laughter.

Credibility with the public was so important to Norm Schwarzkopf that he and his staff underestimated, if anything, the damage they were inflicting on Iraqi men and machinery. "We're trying to be deliberately conservative," he explained. "We don't want to mislead anybody. We don't want to tell you we've done something we haven't done. As a result, we're being deliberately conservative. When we announce something to you that something's happened, you can take it to the bank."

While Schwarzkopf is a clear believer in the role of the press, and the public's right to know, he lost patience with the scribes who prodded him about Iraqi "collateral damage," meaning civilians or civilian facilities destroyed. His pilots, he felt, were going to extraordinary, life-risking lengths to avoid such mistakes. "We are probably endangering our pilots more than they would otherwise be endangered by following this course of action. By requiring that the pilots fly in a certain direction or go to altitudes they normally wouldn't be required to go to, those pilots are at much more risk than they would be otherwise. But we have deliberately decided to do this in order to avoid unnecessary civilian casualties, in order to avoid destroying those religious shrines and that sort of thing."

First, reports from Baghdad began to question whether Schwarzkopf had bombed a biological weapons factory or a baby formula factory. The general testily noted that baby formula is not usually made in heavily guarded facilities, no more than "aspirin" is made in a Libyan building surrounded by anti-aircraft batteries. The whole tone of the query, coupled with the implication that he wasn't "fighting fair" by bombing Iraq for weeks on end profoundly disturbed Schwarzkopf. "You've got to remember that playing by the rules goes both ways. I think you're seeing some sort of contorted morality here that says because the Iraqis are the guys in the black hats, they're allowed to go out and do anything they want to do. They can gas innocent women and children. They can loft Scuds against civilian populations. They can use human shields. All those rules are okay for them because they're the guys in the black hats. But because we're the guys in the white hats, we have to stand up, allow ourselves to be shot at, walk out, take on overwhelming numbers and not use the weaponry we have available. I just don't understand that mentality at all." He was not, he added, going to allow Saddam to taunt him like some Goliath to come out and battle on the ground before he was good and ready.

All along, Norman Schwarzkopf knew it would come down to slogging it out in the trenches and the bunkers.

Air bombardment alone had not accomplished a victory in

168

Vietnam, and would not now. "We had incredible air power in Vietnam," he recalled. "We were totally unopposed in Vietnam. I can remember many times in Vietnam where we sat outside a village, getting ready to go into a village, and we pounded it with both artillery and air ahead of time. And you sat out there and said, 'There is absolutely nothing that could live through that.' And you call off the air strike and went into the village, and they came right out of their holes and fought like devils."

More irritating than the press to Schwarzkopf during this period were many of the hired military analysts on American television shows, a lot of whom were personal friends. But, these Monday — and even Friday — morning quarterbacks, he said, "talked about war as if it was a ballet. They act like this whole thing is choreographed ahead of time. And when the orchestra strikes up and starts playing, everybody goes out there and goes through a set piece. And that set piece results in the ultimate outcome. Yes, it is choreographed. And what happens is the orchestra starts playing and some son of a bitch climbs out of the orchestra pit with a bayonet and starts chasing you around the stage, okay? And the choreography goes right out the window."

Another bad break, still being debated, was the Feb. 13 bombing of a fortified Baghdad air-raid shelter in which nearly 300 civilians were killed. The carnage received widespread television coverage. President Bush and lesser officials maintained their intelligence showed it was a command and control facility. Whether intentional or not, it had the effect of humbling Saddam's leadership. What is not now in doubt is that these were the families of some of the high Baathist Party and military officials. It was an exclusive air-raid shelter with a high fence to keep out the rabble, and room for the Zil limousines that would drive up to deposit VIPs at the facility. It may well have hit Saddam where he would hurt the most. And perhaps it was no coincidence that two days later, Iraq made the first conditional offer to withdraw from Kuwait.

Schwarzkopf kept his mind on the job, no matter what diplomatic efforts were ongoing. He could do nothing about that, and would proceed on the timetable he'd proposed the previous fall — calling for the mid-January air war commencement and a late February ground war beginning.

The general's superiors, Secretary Cheney and Joint Chiefs of Staff Chairman Powell, had flown in on Feb. 9 and met with him for more than eight hours to make sure all was still on track. When Cheney returned two days later, he met with President Bush and advised him Schwarzkopf wanted to set Feb. 21 as the planning date for the ground invasion. Bush agreed. A day or so later, Schwarzkopf relayed a request to change the planning day to Feb. 24, at 4 a.m. Saudi time (8 p.m., Feb. 23, EST).

Schwarzkopf's men and women out in the field were anxious to act. They knew the sooner they launched the invasion, the sooner they could get home. Or, as one lance corporal laconically observed: "If this is Armageddon, let's get on with it."

14.

THE HUNDRED-HOUR WAR

Mikhail Gorbachev picked up the phone that connected him directly to the Oval Office. It was 11:15 a.m. on Saturday, Feb. 23 in Washington. The day before, George Bush had given Saddam Hussein a 24-hour ultimatum to begin the withdrawal from Kuwait by noon Saturday, and be completely out in seven days. The Soviets had negotiated a bottom-line offer from Iraq to withdraw from Kuwait in 21 days, with strings attached. Gorbachev knew it wasn't enough for Bush, but he urged the president not to launch a ground war yet. Their talk was polite. Bush thanked Gorbachev for his efforts. The conversation lasted 28 minutes.

Bush had been publicly courteous and privately unnerved by the eleventh-hour Soviet maneuvering to reach a truce with Iraq. The president wanted to obliterate the Iraqi war machine. That wasn't spelled out in the 12 United Nations resolutions to end the Iraqi occupation, but it was cast in concrete in the minds of more Americans than just George Bush. The latest polls showed that 71 percent of Americans wanted Saddam out of power and 66 percent wanted him stripped of his armaments. Any promised withdrawal now, with half-baked terms, would give Iraq time to resupply its troops and fight on, or at the very least, go home with many of its deadly toys still intact.

If there was any lack of resolve in American minds, the Pentagon and the White House had eliminated it on Friday with the details of Iraqi "scorched earth" treatment of Kuwait. In the last 24 hours, Iraqi troops had set fire to or blown up 200 oil wells in Kuwait. The soldiers were grabbing Kuwaitis and executing them on the streets.

"There seems to be a systematic campaign of execution, particularly people that they may have tortured previously," said Marine Brig. Gen. Richard I. Neal in Riyadh. "They're sort of destroying the evidence, I guess, for lack of a better term."

At the same time, Radio Baghdad was broadcasting Iraq's 59th communique of the war telling its troops to fight on: "Strike, and the whole of Iraq and the faithful will be on your side. Your families are waiting for you to return victorious. We will seek to turn the ground war, which they have wanted, into a hellfire that will sear their scoundrels. Their cohorts will tumble into the great crater of death."

On Saturday, with just 10 minutes left for Iraq to meet Bush's noon ultimatum, Saddam Hussein thumbed his nose at the deadline. A Scud missile sailed from western Iraq into Israel. No one on the ground was injured. In Baghdad, the deadline passed at 8 p.m. local time with the explosion from an allied bomb that told the locals it wasn't over yet. George Bush had done his part. It remained for Norman Schwarzkopf to finish the job.

Schwarzkopf isn't Catholic, but football had taught him the meaning of a "Hail Mary." He would later explain it this way: "I think you recall when the quarterback is desperate for a touchdown at the very end, what he does is he sets up behind the center, and all of a sudden, every single one of his receivers goes way out to one flank, and they all run down the field as fast as they possibly can and into the end zone, and he lobs the ball."

Schwarzkopf had been setting up his "Hail Mary" pass for weeks. With Iraqi troops arrayed behind a nightmare network of booby traps along the Kuwait-Saudi border, the general was taking his football and moving the line of scrimmage.

Tapline Road is what passes for interstate highway in

Saudi Arabia. It runs northwest out of Dhahran to the middle of nowhere, roughly following an oil pipeline and the Saudi-Iraqi border. On a normal day, bedouins drive Tapline Road in their Chevy Suburbans to ply their trade between the wide places in the road that are towns.

But Tapline Road had seen precious few normal days since Schwarzkopf ordered his receivers to prepare for a wide pass to the left of Kuwait. For weeks, the road had been clogged with army transport vehicles moving thousands of troops and supplies west, far from the highest concentration of Iraqi troops in Kuwait. The soldiers renamed the stretch "Suicide Road," and a reported 30 people were killed in traffic accidents during the buildup.

The skies throbbed with the drumbeat of Chinook helicopters with Humvees and howitzers slung beneath them, ferrying the war to a new front. At the top secret base, King Khalid Military City, in north central Saudi Arabia, huge transport planes landed with troops and more supplies— enough supplies to last 60 days if that's what it took to oust the Iraqi army.

Midway through the gargantuan task, the man in charge of Desert Storm logistics, Army Lt. Gen. William G. "Gus" Pagonis, got the third star on his collar. Getting the supplies to the vicinity of Tapline Road was just the first step. Pagonis then had to lay out plans for taking those supplies where the troops would go next—deep into Iraq.

Saddam Hussein didn't know they were coming. With his air force grounded in Iran and his intelligence marginal to begin with, Saddam had no "eyes" in Saudi Arabia. His troops had dug in in Kuwait along the border with Saudi Arabia, and in southern Iraq along the border with Kuwait. They faced forward, little knowing that the allied quarterback was aiming at the backs of their heads.

Elements of the Army's VII Corps and XVIII Airborne Corps along with British Desert Rats and and French Foreign Legionnaires were scattered along 200 miles of Saudi-Iraqi border in camps that—had Saddam been able to see them—would have looked like sand dunes. Out of place sand dunes, as most of the Saudi dunes were in the south. The desert camouflage tents billowed in the cold, gritty wind. That movement was all that differentiated the camps from the rocky and flat surrounding terrain. At night, the GIs drove their vehicles with the lights dimmed as they scurried around making last-minute preparations for G-Day. Instead of using flashlights, the men and women wore night-vision goggles, even for after-dark trips to the latrine.

It was dark when Bush's 8 p.m. deadline came and went. There was a half moon in the sky. High winds and rain had been predicted, but the storm front had passed to the north. Total blackness would have made for better fighting, but that was one logistical detail that Pagonis couldn't change. The troops waited through the night and thought about the job ahead. They had been put on a seven-day countdown to G-Day several times, only to be put on hold because of the shuttle diplomacy between Moscow and Baghdad. Their countdown included reconnaissance flights into Iraq to scout the territory they would claim once Schwarzkopf gave the order. Those flights had told them that enemy troops were lightly peppered throughout southern Iraq with little on their mind except surrender. Iraqis sat unafraid on top of their bunkers and watched the reconnaissance flights like an air show. Hundreds had already surrendered to reconnaissance helicopters. One helicopter crew spotted a military bunker full of sheep. "Don't shoot the sheep," the pilots told each other, and then they savored the irony of war that allowed the killing of people, but not livestock.

The air war had picked off some of Saddam's army in 38 days of ceaseless bombing. His 4,280 tanks had been cut to 1,685. His 2,870 armored personnel carriers now numbered only 925. Forty-eight percent of his artillery was gone and his combat aircraft were either in pieces, in Iran, or unable to take off. The allied pilots hadn't seen anyone else in the skies for days.

But no one on the ground was expecting a cake walk. The U.S. Army's main battle tank, the M-1A1 Abrams—named for Gen. Creighton W. Abrams, one of Schwarzkopf's heroes—had been around for six years. But its 120mm main gun had never been tested in combat. Even its maker, General Dynamics, was not 100 percent sure of what it could do in a real war in the desert. The 25-ton M2/M3 Bradley Fighting Vehicle with guns and TOW missile launchers could carry troops at a speed of 41 miles an hour if the surface was hard enough, and the Bradley could even swim, in the unlikely event that it ran into a lake. But its crews had been complaining about the lack of adequate built-in navigational systems. Some men had taken to climbing out of the Bradleys to get their bearings with crude compasses. In at least one case, a mother in the United States used her credit card to buy her son a small hand-held navigational receiver that took readings from satellites. The Pentagon had bought thousands of similar devices, but there weren't enough to go around.

Up against the Kuwaiti border, the members of the 2nd Armored Cavalry Regiment passed the night thinking about Saddam's deadly maze, the hellish obstacle course between them and Kuwait. The unit, which calls itself "The Merchants of Death," was plucked from U.S. posts in Germany to the front line. Along with Marines and other Army units, they were to be among the first over "The Berm" into Kuwait. Intelligence and Saddam's own boasting prepared them for an obscene array of mines, barbed wire, trenches filled with burning oil, radio-detonated napalm bombs and a 12-foot high wall of sand. Iraq had bought 20 million mines from foreign suppliers and more than half a million of them were assumed to be in place to greet the allied invasion. Some of the mine fields had been cleared, and the berm breached in spots. The first troops to take advantage of the cleared paths were not allies, but Iraqis, carefully picking their way over the lines to surrender.

Out in the Persian Gulf, a 17,000-man Marine amphibious force waited to storm the beaches of Kuwait if it was necessary. It wouldn't be.

Elton John's "Saturday Night's All Right (For Fighting),"

seemed all right for G-Day. And that's what Armed Forces Radio chose to play on Feb. 24. At 4 a.m. Saudi time, Schwarzkopf signaled the beginning of the ground war and handed the reins to his field commanders. Everyone understood his or her orders.

It was 8 p.m. in Washington and President Bush issued a statement: "Saddam Hussein was given one last chance, set forth in very explicit terms, to do what he should have done more than six months ago. I have therefore directed Gen. Norman Schwarzkopf, in conjunction with coalition forces, to use all forces available, including ground forces, to eject the Iraqi army from Kuwait. I ask only that all of you stop what you were doing and say a prayer for all the coalition forces, and especially for our men and women in uniform, who this very moment are risking their lives for their country and for all of us. May God bless and protect each and every one of them and may God bless the United States of America."

The Schwarzkopf battle plan began. The 1st and 2nd Marine Divisions pierced through the Iraqi fortifications and into Kuwait. They wore full chemical protective suits, but Saddam's dreaded chemical attack never came. Within two and a half hours they had broken through the first line of Iraqi defense, and within 22 hours they were on the outskirts of Kuwait. This was the attack that Saddam expected, but the ground troops met minimal resistance. In the first 10 hours of fighting, more than 5,500 Iraqis were taken prisoner.

Farther to the west, Schwarzkopf's "Hail Mary" assault that Saddam didn't expect was meeting even less resistance. The Screaming Eagles of the 101st Airborne Division jumped off from 13 launch points on the Iraqi border and flew 50 miles into Iraq. They claimed an area of 60 square miles and established what amounted to a gas station and staging area manned by 2,000 airborne troops. Chinook helicopters carried in rubber fuel bladders and 100,000 gallons of aviation fuel. They called it The Cobra Zone, and by nightfall, the airborne troops had been joined by 2,000 more soldiers who drove in.

To their right, closer to Kuwait, members of the 24th Mechanized Infantry Division, Schwarzkopf's old unit, the Army VII Armored Corps and the British 1st Armored Division raced into Iraq to sever supply lines to Iraqi soldiers in Kuwait and to meet up with the vaunted Republican Guard for a showdown. To the left of the 101st, French light armored forces and members of the 82nd Airborne Division moved 30 miles into Iraq. Their goal was the Euphrates River in the heart of Iraq, some 150 miles from the Saudi border. At the Pentagon, they were calling it "a Daytona 500 in the sand."

The brass had imposed a press blackout which Defense Secretary Cheney said would last indefinitely. But 12 hours into the offensive, Schwarzkopf walked into the briefing room in his headquarters in Riyadh and gave a 10-minute rundown of events. He was deliberately vague, and cautioned against euphoria, but he could not hide his own satisfaction. In response to questions, the usually loquacious general lapsed into rat-a-tat phrases.

Were the Iraqis retreating, surrendering or simply not fighting?

"All of the above."

Had allied troops encountered the Republican Guard?

"Some."

Were the allies facing the enemy head-on or round-about?

"We're going to go around, over, through, on top, underneath and any other way it takes to beat them."

Will the allies chase the enemy home or stop in Kuwait?

"I'm not going to answer that question. We're going to pursue them in any way it takes to get them to get out of Kuwait."

What the American public didn't know at that point was that the question of whether to pursue the enemy back into Iraq was irrelevant. Several thousand allied forces were already in Iraq lined up to cut off any avenue of retreat.

Saddam Hussein held his own briefing that Sunday over Baghdad Radio. "The enemy attack has failed utterly," he said. "The aggression forces have failed to achieve any of the

177

objectives they have sought and announced. They have suffered heavy losses as a result of the heavy blows by the soldiers of right and faith. Fight them and victory will be yours, so will be dignity, honor and glory. God is greater. God is greater. God is greater. Let the miserable meet their fate. Victory is sweet with the help of God."

On Monday, allied ground troops continued to swarm across the border into Iraq and Kuwait. The number of enemy prisoners rose to nearly 20,000 and the allies were having trouble counting noses. The Saudis had POW camps set up to accommodate 100,000, but the problem was getting them there. The allies were running out of space in a fleet of 500 trucks and buses. Many of the Iraqis had ragged uniforms or wore uniforms taken from Kuwaiti soldiers. Some had no shoes and their feet showed raw sores. A few of the surrendering Iraqis claimed they had walked eight hours to find someone to turn themselves over to. They surrendered to anyone who would take them — medical personnel, circling aircraft, even journalists. One Iraqi officer walked up to a Marine and asked "Where have you guys been? We've been waiting for you guys for two weeks." They received cigarettes, food, water and the promise of a shower and lice-free clothing back at the POW camps.

George Bush had proved himself to be a hands-off commander-in-chief, not one to hover over Schwarzkopf. He could have picked up the phone and reached Schwarzkopf's ear on a whim, but he had no such whims. This day, with the ground war going better than even the optimists had dared to expect, Bush made an exception. He called Schwarzkopf and congratulated him on the "remarkable efficiency" of the campaign.

In Riyadh, the American casualty numbers from the first day of the ground war were announced — four dead and 21 wounded. Then Monday night, Saddam delivered his only significant blow of the entire war. At 8:40 p.m. Saudi time, a Scud missile lobbed from Iraq found its mark by happenstance. A warehouse near the sea front in Al Khobar, a few miles from Dhahran had been converted to barracks for 100 allied troops. Some were eating, some were sleeping when the Scud whined overhead. It broke into lethal pieces and rained down on the building. The explosion ripped the corrugated metal siding from the building and turned the exposed frame into a skeleton resembling the flaming Hindenberg. By the time the fire was put out and the bodies were counted, 28 were dead. All were reservists and some had been in the war zone only a few days. Their families back home thought these sons and daughters were safe. Among the dead were three women—the first to die in the war.

The announcement from Baghdad Radio at 1:30 a.m. Tuesday local time had little to do with Saddam's "sweet" victory: "Orders have been issued to our armed forces to withdraw in an organized manner to the positions held prior to Aug. 1, 1990."

President Bush was playing paddle ball on Capitol Hill with Rep. Sonny Montgomery, D-Miss., when National Security Advisor Brent Scowcroft interrupted the game with the news of the offer from Baghdad. Bush returned to the White House and talked it over with his advisors. Nothing doing, was the response. "The war goes on," announced presidential spokesman Marlin Fitzwater.

Allied troops rolled into Kuwait City Tuesday and took over the U.S. Embassy. An American soldier walked up to the chained gates of the Embassy carrying the stars and stripes. He explained that a Marine had given him the flag during the Tet Offensive in Vietnam in 1968, and then died in his arms. Kuwaitis who had hidden in their houses for nearly seven months, rushed out in the streets to greet the troops. The skies above the city were blackened by the smoke from burning oil wells and pierced by gunfire from the jubilant Kuwaiti resistance.

On the north side of the city, a picture was shaping up that would leave Americans with their most horrific image of the war, which to this point had produced little carnage for the cameras. Iraqi troops were rushing pell-mell toward Basra driving anything they could find that still had a tank of gas in it—tanks, trucks, armored personnel carriers, private cars stolen from Kuwaitis with the trunks full of booty looted from the city. They jockeyed for position on two main highways, driving four abreast in a bumper-to-bumper traffic jam that stretched 25 miles. A Navy pilot summed it up: "It was the road to Daytona Beach at spring break, just bumper to bumper. Spring break's over."

Navy planes along with B-52 bombers and F-15 fighters rained bombs on the convoy. The Navy A-6s from the aircraft carrier USS *Ranger* returned to the site over and over again while the ship's loudspeaker played the "William Tell Overture." There were so many American planes in the sky their pilots feared a mid-air collision. It was, said one pilot, "like shooting fish in a barrel." The 1,500 vehicles could not move. The drivers were cut down as they fled into the desert or as they cowered in their seats. When reporters moved in later with their cameras, Americans would see a highway littered with bodies—the most brutal scene of the war and an uneasy reminder that not all decisions made in the heat of war are black and white.

A fierce battle raged at Kuwait International Airport. In Iraq, the XVIII Airborne Corps reached the Euphrates River to cut off any retreat, and pressed toward Basra to meet the Republican Guards head on. The VII Corps and the 24th Mechanized Infantry Division also met the first Republican Guard divisions near Basra at dusk and battled them through the night in the largest tank battle since World War II.

George Bush and Saddam Hussein engaged in their own verbal battle. Saddam issued a statement over Baghdad Radio saying his troops were withdrawing, victorious. "Shout for victory, Oh brothers; shout for your victory and the victory of all honorable people, Oh Iraqis. You have fought 30 countries, and all the evil and the largest machine of war and destruction in the world that surrounds them. The soldiers of faith have triumphed over the soldiers of wrong." Saddam again ended with the refrain, "Victory is sweet with the help of God."

Bush wasn't about to let that pass. He made a brief statement in the Rose Garden: "Saddam's most recent speech is an outrage. He is not withdrawing. His defeated forces are retreating. He is trying to claim victory in the midst of a rout."

Day Four of the ground war dawned wet and windy with the skies over the battlefield blackened by smoke from the oil fires. "Infantryman's weather," Schwarzkopf called it. "God loves the infantryman, and that's just the kind of weather the infantryman loves to fight in." The two day fight for control of Kuwait International Airport ended with the Marines in control. Enemy prisoners were now beyond counting, but the estimates were 40,000, maybe 50,000. Fifty six Americans had lost their lives in the ground war. On this day, an American A-10 anti-tank plane mistook two British vehicles for the enemy and killed nine British soliders.

The number of Iraqi dead was not so easily determined. Allied commanders refused to discuss it. The British said the subject was "distasteful." The Americans said counting enemy dead served no purpose. Schwarzkopf claimed it had nothing to do with body-count fiascos he had seen in Vietnam: "That's not the point. Number one, it's a totally inaccurate and inappropriate measure and, number two, it, in fact, contributed to the erosion of the integrity within the military, and it also contributed to the erosion of the confidence of the American people in the military because of that lack of integrity. And all of those things, as far as I'm concerned, make body count a lousy way to measure your progress in any military campaign."

The Saudis weren't as worried. Prince Bandar bin Sultan, the Saudi ambassador to the United States, fixed the number of Iraqi dead at anywhere from 60,000 to 100,000.

That afternoon, Dick Cheney told an American Legion audience in Washington that the "mother of all battles" was turning into "the mother of all retreats."

At 1 p.m. EST, Gen. Schwarzkopf emerged from his warren in the Riyadh command center and stepped in front of the TV cameras to deliver the mother of all briefings. "Thank you for being here," he told the press and public, as though the world was doing him a favor by tuning in. And tune in, they did. The hour-long briefing was broadcast live on all major TV networks in the United States, and then rebroadcast later for those who missed it or those who wanted to savor the sweet comfort of victory. *Washington Post* TV critic Tom Shales called it "the most-seen military briefing since George C. Scott's curtain-raiser in the movie 'Patton.' "

America had come through the last six months with its jaws clenched, its brows creased, its hearts afraid to hope that this war would be more honorable than Vietnam, more necessary than Grenada, more principled than Panama. In a few minutes, Schwarzkopf lifted the cloud of national dread.

"What's different about Schwarzkopf," said retired Army Brig. Gen. James Terry, "is that he inspired a high degree of trust in the American public because he was so forthright. He was the first number one commander to be exposed to that much television coverage. Most others in the past have shied away from the press because they were afraid of being misquoted. In being so direct, he gained everyone's trust, and it really worked to his advantage."

Retired Army Col. Harry Summers, once a professor at the War College, summed up the Schwarzkopf that Americans saw. "I tell you, I was so glad to have a big, fat boy in charge. (Servicemen refer to the Pentagon's weight standards as the Fat Boy Program.) He was out of the mold. All these guys they used to have were so well preened, so concerned about how they looked for the press. One thing you can't call Schwarzkopf is a sissy. That really helps the troops as they're looking up to someone. His attitude was, 'Screw the system. I'm going to be invading you.' You can't fake confidence. You have to go in with a no-nonsense attitude and accomplish your mission. Another thing I admired about Schwarzkopf—no one had heard of him. It goes to show you that he is not a grandstander, he was not a brown-noser. He's just a solid soldier."

"He's a leader with a personality," said retired Marine Col.

James A. Donovan. "His TV performance was perfect. I think this will establish a new criteria for the military leaders. They're going to have to be patient, have a good personality, look good, look rugged, and big. I remember some of the military intelligence officials on the television, and they looked like music teachers. Do you see what I mean? They have to at least look like a warrior."

Without trying, Schwarzkopf did all of that. He wore his desert "BDUs"—battle dress uniform—with the sleeves folded, not rolled, to the regulation spot above the elbows. His big head merged with a big neck that blended into big shoulders. His smile was spare as always, from a too-small mouth. A big man should have a bigger smile, but when Schwarzkopf smiles, the effect is of complete control. Generals don't smile too much.

With charts and a pointer, he ticked off the day-by-day maneuvers of the war. His pride over the "Hail Mary" was barely concealed. "I must tell you, I can't recall any time in the annals of military history when this number of forces have moved over this distance to put themselves in a position to be able to attack." He praised his troops. "If I used words like brilliant, it would really be an under-description." He silenced those who thought the allies wanted to take Baghdad. "We were 150 miles from Baghdad and there was nothing between us and Baghdad. If it had been our intention to take Iraq, if it had been our intention to destroy the country, if it had been our intention to overrun the country, we could have done it unopposed."

The chart with casualty numbers was put on the easel and Schwarzkopf explained it with calculated brevity. Seventy nine Americans had died since the war began and 215 had been wounded. The missing numbered 44. "The total being as shown here," he said, and then called for the next chart.

Then he paused, and his face showed the struggle of a man who has something painful he must say. He looked down and rested his pointer on the floor. He swallowed and spoke again. "I would just like to comment briefly about that casualty chart," he began. "The loss of one human life is intolerable to any of us who are in the military. But I would tell you that casualties of that order of magnitude considering the job that's been done and the number of forces that were involved is almost miraculous, as far as the light number of casualties. It will never be . . ." his lips froze for an instant, ". . . miraculous to the famlies of those people, but it is miraculous." There was a minuscule quaver in his voice, and a glint of moisture at the corners of his eyes. Then he moved on.

"This is what happened to date with the Iraqis . . ."—more than 3,000 of their 4,230 tanks destroyed, about 50,000 of their men taken prisoner—". . . we've almost completely destroyed the offensive capability of the Iraqi forces in the Kuwaiti theater of operations."

He invited questions, and the assembled reporters, sensing the impact Schwarzkopf was having on small screens across the United States, were careful not to rock the boat. Schwarzkopf soon reminded them of why they had to be careful when questioning a man who is unaccustomed to being questioned. He listened to questions in his offensive posture—head dipped slightly, neck stretched forward, eyes glowering out from under eyebrows. The effect was of a father waiting with not too much patience while a child explained some misbehavior—even as the father listens, the child knows he isn't buying the story. When the questions were softer, Schwarzkopf relaxed, rocking back on his heels with his hands behind his back.

If 50,000 Iraqis were taken prisoner from among 200,000 troops along the border, where are the rest?

"There were a very, very large number of dead in these units—a very, very large number of dead. There were very heavy desertions. At one point we had reports of desertion rates of more than 30 percent of the units that were along the front here. As you know, we had quite a large number of POWs that came across, so I think it's a combination of desertions, of people that were killed, of the people that we've captured, and of some other people who are just flat still running."

Since the Iraqis are in retreat, what would he say

184

to the public about the purpose of the war now?

"I would say there was a lot more purpose to this war than just get the Iraqis out of Kuwait. The purpose of this war was to enforce the resolutions of the United Nations. But I've got to tell you, that in the business of the military, of a military commander, my job is not to go ahead and at some point say, 'That's great, they've just now pulled out of Kuwait—even though they're still shooting at us, they're moving backward, and therefore, I've accomplished my mission.' That's not the way you fight it, and that's not the way I would ever fight it."

What did he think of Saddam Hussein as a military strategist?

"Hah!" he said, and, with relish, ticked off Saddam's finer qualities. "As far as Saddam Hussein being a great military strategist, he is neither a strategist, nor is he schooled in the operational arts, nor is he a tactician, nor is he a general, nor is he a soldier. Other than that, he's a great military man. I want you to know that."

Were the Iraqi fortifications not as intense or sophisticated as expected?

"Have you ever been in a minefield?"

No.

"All there's got to be is one mine, and that's intense."

How would Schwarzkopf rate the Iraqi army?

"So many people were deserting . . . that the Iraqis brought down execution squads whose job was to shoot people in the front lines. I've got to tell you, a soldier doesn't fight very hard for a leader who is going to shoot him on his own whim. That's not what military leadership is all about. So I attribute a great deal of the failure of the Iraqi army to fight, to their own leadership. They committed them to a cause that they did not believe in."

Will there be a count of the enemy casualties?

"I don't think there's ever been, ever in the history of warfare, been a successful count of the dead . . . So I would say no, there will never be an exact count. Probably in the days to come you're probably going to hear many stories—either over-inflated or under-inflated, depending on who you hear them from. The people who will know best, unfortunately, are the families that won't see their loved ones come home."

Was his strategy accepted by higher ups without change?

"I'm very thankful for the fact that the president of the United States has allowed the United States military and the coalition military to fight this war exactly as it should have been fought, and the president in every case has taken our guidance and our recommendations to heart, and has acted superbly as the commander-in-chief of the United States."

George Bush didn't watch most of the briefing, but half an hour after it ended, at 2:30 p.m. in Washington, he met with Gen. Colin Powell who filled in the blanks. Bush said he was ready to end the war. "I'd like to do it tonight." Powell called Schwarzkopf who agreed it was time.

At 9 p.m., the president went on the air. "Kuwait is liberated. Iraq's army is defeated," he said. "I am pleased to announce that at midnight tonight . . . exactly 100 hours since ground operations commenced and six weeks since the start of Operation Desert Storm, all United States and coalition forces will suspend offensive combat operations."

15.
WHO ARE YOU?

A jet carried Norman Schwarzkopf from Riyadh to Kuwait City on the morning of Sunday, March 3. He transferred to a helicopter and flew over the city to view the destruction of nearly seven months of occupation. It was not the Kuwait City he remembered. "I saw Kuwait many times before the war. I remember it as a beautiful place, full of very nice people, and it's a tragedy to see that somebody could set out to deliberately destroy a country the way the Iraqis have."

The sky was black with smoke still belching from the burning oil wells. "It looked like hell," said Schwarzkopf. He couldn't linger long in Kuwait City, the object of seven months of planning, fighting and dying. Schwarzkopf had an appointment in Iraq, and after seeing what the Iraqis had done to Kuwait, his legendary temper was close to the surface.

His helicopter lifted him to a spot three miles north of the Kuwaiti border to the captured Iraqi airfield at Safwan. He chose it to remind the Iraqis who was in charge in this sector of their country. Schwarzkopf's escort was a fleet of six Apache helicopters, guns loaded in case there was any trouble.

On the ground, eight members of an Iraqi delegation bounced unceremoniously to the meeting place in American Humvees, escorted by Bradley Fighting Vehicles and M-1A1 Abrams tanks. Authorized to speak for Saddam Hussein were Lt. Gen. Sultan Hasheem Ahmed, chief of operations for the Iraqi military, and Lt. Gen. Salah Abud Mahmud: The airfield was heavily guarded by the tanks and armored vehicles of the 1st Infantry Division, "The Big Red One."

Schwarzkopf jumped out of his helicopter and strode toward a tent. The Iraqi generals were out of sight waiting to be searched for weapons. Schwarzkopf ordered an aide to have no pictures taken of the electronic frisking. "I don't want them embarrassed. I don't want them humiliated. I don't want them photographed."

One of the Iraqi generals balked at the search, and then said if he was to be frisked, he wanted it done by the man who was going to negotiate with him. Fine, Schwarzkopf said. He would do it.

The Iraqi general was puzzled. The giant of a man before him was dressed in the same desert camouflage uniform as every other American soldier. Apparently the Iraqi general had missed the four stars on the collar.

"Who are you?" he asked.

"I'm Norman Schwarzkopf."

Apaches and A-10s swarmed overhead. "This is an historic day," Schwarzkopf told a gaggle of reporters. "This isn't a negotiation. I'm not here to give them anything."

Not even a pleasantry. The general who, as a boy, thought generals shouldn't smile, didn't. For two hours he sat across the table from the Iraqi generals. Sitting at his side was Saudi commander Lt. Gen. Khalid bin Sultan. Behind him stood French commander Lt. Gen. Michel Henri Roquejoffre and British commander Lt. Gen. Sir Peter de la Billiere. The allies did most of the talking and the Iraqis did all of the conceding. They agreed to accept all the U.N. resolutions. They agreed to return all prisoners of war. They promised to provide a map of where they had planted land and sea mines. Schwarzkopf and Gen. Hashim Ahmed emerged from the tent and gave each other a crisp salute. The Iraqi smiled. The American did not.

To the reporters Schwarzkopf said, "I am very happy to tell you that we agreed on all matters. I would just say that I think we have made a major step forward in the cause of peace, and I have every expectation that if we continue the open and frank and cooperative dialogue that we had today—

188

and I would say very candidly that the Iraqis came to discuss and to cooperate, with a positive attitude — that we are well on our way to a lasting peace."

Not since 1918 and the term of Woodrow Wilson had a president addressed Congress to announce the end of a war. George Bush broke the dry spell on Tuesday night, March 6.

"From the moment Operation Desert Storm commenced on Jan. 16 until the time the guns fell silent at midnight one week ago, this nation has watched its sons and daughters with pride, watched over them with prayer. As commander-in-chief, I can report to you: Our armed forces fought with honor and valor. As president, I can report to the nation: Aggression is defeated. The war is over."

Bush announced that the first troops would be on their way home that night — appropriately the sentimental favorites of Gen. Schwarzkopf, members of the 24th Mechanized Infantry Division of Ft. Stewart, Georgia.

The president received a dozen standing ovations that night. But the most thunderous applause was saved for the man who had been detained with business in Riyadh. "This military victory also belongs to the one the British call the 'Man of the Match' — the tower of calm in the eye of Desert Storm — Gen. Norman Schwarzkopf."

Calm was what Americans needed in the winter of 1990-91. And they got it from Schwarzkopf — the not-so-old soldier who might have faded away into retirement. Now the nation is on a first-name basis with him — like Sally Schwarzkopf's mail man. Rather than leaving the mail, he knocked on her door and handed it to her. "Are you related to Norm?"

The Persian Gulf war deprived Schwarzkopf of the option to fade away. He hadn't seriously considered it anyway. He wouldn't cash in on his experience to go to work for a defense contractor, he said in 1989. He would rather find a cause. "I love causes. I've served the cause of the defense of our nation for 32 years, and I'd like to find another cause. I don't know if it would be the cause of peace, the cause of education — there are a lot of causes out there. And I would love to find another

189

cause I could serve like I've served the defense of our country."

He keeps in mind a line from the closing scene of the movie "Patton." The story is told of the victorious Roman generals who would come home from their wars to a huge victory parade. A Roman general would always have a slave standing behind him in the chariot holding a golden crown and whispering in the general's ear, "All glory is fleeting."

About The Authors

As America's foremost investigative reporters, JACK ANDERSON and DALE VAN ATTA, together with a team of associates, produce the nationally syndicated column "Washington Merry-Go-Round," which is distributed daily to some 800 newspapers. They are also the Washington editors for *Parade Magazine* and their bi-weekly newsletter, *Jack Anderson Confidential,* shares inside Washington information with thousands of subscribers. A Pulitzer Prize winner, Anderson is the author of a dozen nonfiction books including *The Cambodia File, Fiasco,* and the novels *Zero Time* and *Control.* Van Atta is a frequent contributor to many national publications and co-authored *Prophet of Blood.*

INTRODUCTION

In *Northanger Abbey* Jane Austen reveals her unique, rumbustious sense of humour, which she uses to burlesque certain kinds of popular fiction and to satirise the excess of sentiment prevalent in the society in which she lived. It provides an acute and amusing picture of early nineteenth-century manners and style, but underneath the humour lie some serious and salutary lessons for readers of any age. The novel reveals the absurdity in any slavish adherence to fashionable trends and the insincerity that can underlie social pretensions. Austen demands that we learn to recognise these tendencies in others and guard against them in ourselves. She also illustrates here the human disposition to absorb influences from art; how easy it is to mimic its values and standards of behaviour without being fully aware of doing so. Most pertinently, Austen presents the potentially destabilising repercussions of such behaviour for individuals and society at large. Today, in a society deeply concerned with the possible corruptive influences of film and television, the debate that runs through *Northanger Abbey* holds a good deal of food for thought. Jane Austen offers an opinion on the nature of the moral demands that society should make upon its artists and attempts to provide an example of the standard to which her idea of good art should aspire. She also contends that it is not only art and artists that should come under scrutiny but the consumers of art, particularly those unable to make intelligent, evaluative judgements about what they read and what they see.

Although *Sense and Sensibility* and *Pride and Prejudice* were begun earlier than *Northanger Abbey*, both were substantially revised before publication, and *Northanger Abbey* is generally considered by critics to be Austen's earliest major work. It was written in the years 1798 and 1799 when Austen was twenty-three years old and contains more unrevised material than either of the two previous novels. It was sold to a publisher in 1803 under the title of *Susan* for £10.00 and was advertised but not actually published. Austen bought the manuscript back for the same sum in 1816. The novel was finally published under its present title after Jane Austen's death in 1818. It is not considered to be one of her 'great' works, such a tribute is more likely to be reserved for *Pride and Prejudice* (1813) and *Emma* (1816), but it is, none the less, regarded as a major achievement and is her most explicitly literary work, a novel about novels and the people who read them.

Austen chooses popular fiction and social manners as her targets in *Northanger Abbey* because she fears the artificiality and emotionalism pervasive within both. They were, she believed, undermining the need for self-discipline and emotional restraint she thought essential to the wellbeing of English society at a time when the old aristocratic stronghold was being threatened by powerful forces of change. The French Revolution had brought defeat to the French monarchy in 1789 and had generated a deep insecurity and fear that the revolutionary fervour would spread to England. In addition, the Industrial Revolution was radically altering the structure of society as industrial wealth created a new, powerful and challenging middle class. Jane Austen was born into the upper middle-class, the daughter of a clergyman in Steventon in Hampshire, and staunchly upheld the conservative values of the class into which she was born. This class was comprised of the landowners or the 'gentry' who possessed most of the wealth in an England which was still predominantly an agricultural society. At best, the aristocracy maintained social order through a system of solidarity and deference; at worst it controlled through intimidation and punishment. Although some critics have detected a note of political dissent in her writing, when the revolutionary political climate threatened to destabilise the old order, whatever its shortcomings, Jane Austen rigorously defended it.

Austen's instincts are nostalgically rooted in the eighteenth century, when individual behaviour was governed according to the dictates of reason rather than emotion and the good of society took precedence over individual needs. She shies away from the more progressive ideologies of the nineteenth century and some critics of her work complain that nothing of the revolutionary issues of her time infiltrates her novels. Austen's focus remains on county courtship rituals and only indirectly are political issues significant. Yet Austen was well aware of the consequence of conflict: England was at war for twenty-five of her forty-two years and she had two brothers in the armed forces. Her obvious intelligence could hardly allow her to be blind to political tension and radical social change, but she chooses not to confront these issues directly, rather she focuses on the increasing emphasis on law and order and emotional restraint that were their consequence. As the propertied class did not rule at this time by use of a police force but relied on this system of deferential respect, exemplary behaviour and manners were as much a political necessity as a behavioural code. Out of these forced demands for respect and deference spring Austen's concern that contrived behaviour can breed insincerity and selfishness. One of the major undertakings of all her novels is ruthlessly to strip individuals and society of pretension; she insists that honesty, common morality and genuine concern for others should underlie all forms of human exchange.

As the popular fiction of Austen's time is the butt of many of the jokes in *Northanger Abbey*, a great deal of its fun, and certainly much of the irony, is lost without some knowledge of the popular 'sentimental' and Gothic novels which it burlesques. The novel was a relatively new genre when Jane Austen wrote. It had developed a great deal in the eighteenth century and the work of Defoe, Fielding and Sterne had secured its integrity but, by the end of the century, fiction was acquiring something of a bad name. This was largely because of the excessive emotionalism proliferating in the sentimental novels (such as Mackenzie's *The Man of Feeling*, written in 1771) which some thought could incite immoral behaviour. These novels were hugely popular and easily accessible through the circulating libraries, and were being held responsible for adultery and a laxity in moral standards generally.

Toward the end of the century, Gothic novels had begun to take over from the sentimental novels in popularity. These also reflected many of the ideas of the Romantic movement in their interest in the medieval, heroic quests, dreams and the supernatural, but in the Gothic novel such preoccupations were absurdly over-indulged. The Gothic cult had originated in 1764 with Horace Walpole's *Castle of Otranto* and this spawned such delights as Matthew Lewis's *The Monk* (1796) and Ann Ratcliffe's *The Mysteries of Udolpho* (1794). (In *Northanger Abbey*, the Thorpes, the Tilneys and Catherine have all recently read this.) Gothic novels usually comprised all or some aspects of a prescribed formula. Emphasis was on villainy and magic in remote gloomy castles amid sublime mountain scenery. Castles had dangerous subterranean passages and ghosts, and a mysterious disappearance usually triggered the action. *The Castle of Otranto* sported giant knights, walking portraits and bleeding stones. The principle aim of such devices was, for the most part, nothing more than to evoke a *frisson* in readers but some Gothic literature, it was thought, displayed seditious aspects. *The Castle of Otranto* was interpreted as a subversive challenge to authority because it deals with madness and an unstable ruler (George III, believed to be mad, had come to the English throne in

1760). Ann Radcliffe's *The Mysteries of Udolpho* (1794) stimulated the desire for knowledge of exotic foreign lands and was popular with women, and, it was felt, might stir up longings and fuel growing dissatisfaction with their lives. Through the eighteenth century, women were increasingly forming a larger percentage of the reading public and had access to fiction through the circulating libraries.

Austen approved of neither the over-stimulation of imagination incited by Gothic exoticism nor what she perceived as its threat to the stability of society. She directs her criticism, however, towards over-zealous, gullible readers who exhibit an inability to distinguish art from life rather than towards the novels themselves. Austen invites her readers to compare the way her central characters respond to what they read. Henry Tilney reads Gothic tales with vigour and enjoyment but never for a moment allows his judgement to cross the boundary between fact and fiction. Eleanor Tilney displays good sense in distinguishing between real and imaginative reality in her defence of history books in Chapter 14. But the fact that even she confuses fact and fiction, when Catherine remarks that 'something very shocking indeed will soon come out in London', is Austen's illustration of how easily the boundary between art and life can be confused. Isabella is obviously the most vulnerable to lack of discrimination, ridiculously acting out in life the role of a literary heroine. 'Consult your own understanding, your own sense of the probable, your own observation of what is passing around you,' Henry advises Catherine, who herself falls victim to her own imagination later in the novel. Such sound common sense is Jane Austen's touchstone to reality and antidote to over-zealous imaginations.

Austen thought such down-to-earth, practical common sense needed a voice because she believed that the values of the Romantic movement which were sweeping in from Europe, were manifesting themselves in segments of society in a distorted and morally dangerous form. The demand for sincerity, the belief in instinct as a guide to moral integrity, the love of nature and the sanctifying of innocent childhood which the Romantics passionately advocated were, she felt, progressively being transformed into shallow excuses for self-gratification. Sincerity becomes self-advancement, unrestrained passion is a means of self-assertion and attributing actions to emotional imperatives gives moral absolution to self-indulgence. The obligatory Romantic love for nature and children provides an outlet for sentimentality. Austen was wryly amused and more than a little disturbed by such tendencies and uses her novels as a means of alerting readers to their absurdities and their possibly dangerous consequences.

Such excesses, Austen believes, could result in a state where language fails to relate to true feeling at all, and, consequently, the basis of all human relations, and of society itself, becomes unstable. Misjudgements and painful misunderstandings inevitably result. Isabella Thorpe's comic exaggerations and cruel duplicity reveal both the funniest and most hurtful consequences of such a situation. Isabella's shallowness is intended to be plainly evident to the reader but not to the more gullible Catherine. Austen wants to show how such insincerity causes moral confusion and destabilises the credibility of the most honest. When Catherine ascribes honourable motives to the rakish behaviour of Captain Tilney, his brother Henry (who is the mouthpiece for Austen's values in this novel) is momentarily unsure whether she is being ironic. She defends herself: 'I cannot speak well enough to be unintelligible,' she says, to which Tilney replies, 'Bravo! an excellent satire on modern language.' Later, realising she had again been deceived by false charm, this time by the gushing General Tilney, Henry's father, Catherine wonders how she could possibly have known the truth when he 'should say one thing so positively and mean another all the while . . . How were people, at that rate, to be understood?'

The beautiful but superficial Isabella, whose 'attachments are always excessively strong', is both a parody of the stereotypical heroine of the sentimental novel and a demonstration of how its values infiltrate society. Austen adds a clear indication to the reader of the self-seeking greed and insincerity that can lie beneath faultless social accomplishment and copious sensibility. Isabella's sentiment is an illustration of how it can be no more than a vehicle for self-interest and self-indulgence and Austen reveals how lack of honesty in society aids and abets the proliferation of the least admirable human instincts. Isabella's conversation is without value because it is a vacuous regurgitation of jargon and, even more disturbingly, relates only to her fantasy life and does not engage with the world as it really is. As she sets off in hot pursuit of the two handsome gentlemen who have left the pump rooms she really *believes* that they follow her.

Catherine, on the other hand, is set up as the antithesis of contemporary feminine ideals. The opening pages provide a comic debunking of the obligatory requirements of a heroine as Catherine is revealed as not beautiful but merely 'quite pleasing'. Worse still, she had been a healthy tomboy as a child who was never beaten by her father nor pitifully left bereft by the death of her mother. Most damaging of all, she neither draws nor plays the piano well. In depicting Catherine's ordinariness, Austen flouts literary convention and presents undistinguished normality in place of indulgent fantasy.

Catherine spots Henry Tilney with a woman, and while Isabella would have fainted with grief, Catherine correctly guesses the woman to be his sister, 'thus unthinkingly throwing away a fair opportunity of considering him lost to her forever by being married already'. Because Catherine displays a tendency to sound common sense, when she is so easily fooled by Isabella a menacing and sinister aspect is added to Isabella's duplicity. Misunderstandings occasioned by an over-active imagination provide the fodder for much of the comedy of the novel, but never for a moment are we meant to forget how dangerous and painful they can be.

The novel is divided systematically into two sections: Catherine at Bath with Mr and Mrs Allen and at Northanger Abbey as a guest of the Tilneys. The contrast is contrived to highlight the absurdity of both the Gothic genre and Catherine's behaviour, but many critics feel that the Gothic burlesque section of the novel is rather *too* contrived, and that it sits uneasily alongside the first half. It has to be said that Catherine certainly behaves more stupidly than we have come to expect from her. But Austen does manage to maintain sympathy for her heroine and, after ridiculing her gullibility, redirects criticism toward the reading which has influenced her. Austen ultimately differentiates Catherine from the conventional heroine by her ability to perceive her own faults and learn the wisdom of focusing more sensibly on reality so as to judge others better. Catherine has often been troubled by Isabella, and now she learns the necessity to consider and explore such feelings more deeply. Also, she learns that her perception of General Tilney as a murderous 'Montoni' character had blinded her to the more banal and quite obvious faults of an autocratic, materialistic father. These are the real threats to her happiness and Catherine's embarrassment would have been less had she more fully perceived and understood them. Austen transforms villainy into common human foibles and brings it out of the realms of the fantastic and into the everyday. Life itself, she argues, holds sufficient dangers without importing them from the world of fiction.

Austen's ironic treatment of Catherine's guardian, Mrs Allen, and her trifling preoccupation with the quality and pattern of muslin suggests such triviality was as much an irritant to Jane Austen as it may be to twentieth-century readers. It may also reveal that Austen's distaste is directed as much towards a society that perpetuates such commonplace imbecility as it is towards the women who fail to rise above it. In the eighteenth century the intellect of women was still undervalued, there were few challenging outlets for their talents and Austen's novels reveal much about the pace and quality of life for

women in contemporary society. Without wealth, an unmarried middle-class woman was extremely vulnerable. A good marriage was really
the only way to financial security since the option of a socially
acceptable career was not yet open. Realistically, only two professions
were possible: the stage and teaching, and neither offered any security
or respect. Women were becoming increasingly well educated but
were still regarded with lack of esteem. It was difficult to change the
commonly held belief that they were intellectually inferior to men.
Such attitudes provide Austen with fodder for some of her most comic
lines: ' . . . no one can think more highly of the understanding of
women than I do,' remarks Henry Tilney. 'In my opinion nature has
given them so much, that they never find it necessary to use more than
half.'   Many men feared and felt threatened by women's newly
acquired knowledge and Austen uses Henry Tilney's irony as a vehicle
for ridiculing such attitudes: ' . . . though to the larger and more trifling
part of the sex imbecility in females is a great enhancement of their
personal charms, there is a portion of them too reasonable and too well
informed themselves to desire anything more in a woman than
ignorance.' While the humour is boisterous, the criticism is scathing.
The Law of Entail meant that a woman could not inherit property and
financial concerns were consequently seriously important issues in
male/female relationships. Coming from a modest background and
with such a bevy of brothers and sisters, Catherine Morland represents
a poor matrimonial prospect – hence General Tilney`s rude rejection
on discovering her financial credentials. Eleanor is pathetically powerless to come to Catherine's aid: 'I am but nominal mistress of [this
house] . . . my real power is nothing.' The novel therefore offers a
shrewd insight into the limitations on women's lives. The exploration
of such issues gives the characters a good deal of psychological interest
and in using the novel to explore such dilemmas Jane Austen brought a
new depth and complexity to the English novel. Her portrayal of a
distinct inner life looks forward to the psychological complexity of the
nineteenth-century novel.

In Chapter 5, the complexity of the novel takes the form of self-
reflection on the novel genre itself. Austen holds up the plot and injects
some polemic on its status and function. Her lofty claim that the novel
provides a medium 'in which the greatest powers of the mind are
displayed, in which the most thorough knowledge of human nature,
the happiest delineation of its varieties, the liveliest effusions of wit and
humour are conveyed to the world in the best possible language' is
simultaneously both an ironic comment on the novels she burlesques,
and, stripped of its irony, a revelation of her own vision of what a good

novel should aspire to. Written at such a young age and so soon in her career, *Northanger Abbey* can perhaps be viewed as a working through of Jane Austen's ideas about the demands that literature makes on writers and readers. Here, she attempts to clarify in her own mind what she wants to achieve in her own writing. Austen saw the novel form as worth a lifelong commitment; she realised its potential to enlarge understanding of human psychology, to act as a moral force and practically influence its readers. She also saw its potential to attract consumers such as Isabella and John Thorpe, greedy for entertainment and too indiscriminate to judge its quality. These appear in every generation, and this is why Austen sees the need for strict moral imperatives to be imposed on the author. She fully perceived the dangers that could be wreaked upon society if such moral imperatives were discarded. Austen's ideal reader is one who can intelligently evaluate what he or she reads and recognise the boundaries between fact and fiction. Her ideal vision of literature is not wholly autonomous, but morally accountable to society.

ANNE ROWE
Kingston University

FURTHER READING

Marilyn Butler, *Jane Austen and the War of Ideas*, Clarendon Press 1988

Jan Fergus, *Jane Austen: The Literary Career*, Macmillan 1991

Christopher Gillie, *A Preface to Jane Austen*, Macmillan 1985

Mary Lascelles, *Jane Austen and her Art*, The Athlone Press 1995

Marghanita Laski, *Thames and Hudson Literary Lives: Jane Austen*, Thames and Hudson 1986

Oliver MacDonagh, *Jane Austen: Real and Imagined Worlds*, Yale University Press 1993

David Punter, *The Literature of Terror*, Longman 1980

V. Sage, *The Gothick Novel: A Casebook*, Macmillan 1990

Roger Sales, *Jane Austen and Representations of Regency England*, Routledge 1994

Tony Tanner, *Jane Austen*, Macmillan Press 1966

Ian P. Watt (ed.), *Jane Austen: A Collection of Critical Essays*, Prentice Hall 1985

ADVERTISEMENT

BY THE AUTHORESS

TO

NORTHANGER ABBEY

THIS LITTLE WORK was finished in the year 1803, and intended for immediate publication. It was disposed of to a bookseller, it was even advertised, and why the business proceeded no farther, the author has never been able to learn. That any bookseller should think it worth while to purchase what he did not think it worth while to publish seems extraordinary. But with this, neither the author nor the public have any other concern than as some observation is necessary upon those parts of the work which thirteen years have made comparatively obsolete. The public are entreated to bear in mind that thirteen years have passed since it was finished, many more since it was begun, and that during that period, places, manners, books, and opinions have undergone considerable changes.

Chapter 1

No one who had ever seen Catherine Morland in her infancy, would have supposed her born to be an heroine. Her situation in life, the character of her father and mother, her own person and disposition, were all equally against her. Her father was a clergyman, without being neglected, or poor, and a very respectable man, though his name was Richard[1] – and he had never been handsome. He had a considerable independence, besides two good livings – and he was not in the least addicted to locking up his daughters. Her mother was a woman of useful plain sense, with a good temper, and, what is more remarkable, with a good constitution. She had three sons before Catherine was born; and instead of dying in bringing the latter into the world, as anybody might expect, she still lived on – lived to have six children more – to see them growing up around her, and to enjoy excellent health herself. A family of ten children will be always called a fine family, where there are heads and arms and legs enough for the number; but the Morlands had little other right to the word, for they were in general very plain, and Catherine, for many years of her life, as plain as any. She had a thin awkward figure, a sallow skin without colour, dark lank hair, and strong features; – so much for her person; – and not less unpropitious for heroism seemed her mind. She was fond of all boys' plays, and greatly preferred cricket not merely to dolls, but to the more heroic enjoyments of infancy, nursing a dormouse, feeding a canary-bird, or watering a rose-bush. Indeed she had no taste for a garden; and if she gathered flowers at all, it was chiefly for the pleasure of mischief – at least so it was conjectured from her always preferring those which she was forbidden to take. – Such were her propensities – her abilities were quite as extraordinary. She never could learn or understand anything before she was taught; and sometimes not even then, for she was often inattentive, and occasionally stupid. Her mother was three months in teaching her only to repeat the 'Beggar's Petition';[2] and after all, her next sister, Sally, could say it better than she did. Not that Catherine was always stupid, – by no means; she learnt the fable of 'The Hare and many Friends',[3] as quickly as any girl in England. Her mother wished her to learn music; and Catherine was sure she should like it, for she was very fond of tinkling the keys of the old forlorn spinet; so, at eight years old she began. She learnt a year, and could not bear it; – and Mrs Morland, who did not insist on her daughters being accomplished in spite of incapacity or distaste, allowed her to leave off. The day which dismissed the music-master was one of the happiest of Catherine's life. Her taste for drawing was not superior; though whenever she could obtain the outside of a letter from her mother, or seize upon any other odd piece of paper, she did what she could in that way, by drawing houses and trees, hens and chickens, all very much like one another. – Writing and accounts she was taught by her father; French by her mother: her proficiency in either was not remarkable, and she shirked her lessons in both whenever she could. What a strange, unaccountable character! – for with all these symptoms of profligacy at ten years old, she had neither a bad heart nor a bad temper; was seldom stubborn, scarcely ever quarrelsome, and very kind to the little ones, with few interruptions of tyranny; she was moreover noisy and wild, hated confinement and cleanliness, and loved nothing so well in the world as rolling down the green slope at the back of the house.

Such was Catherine Morland at ten. At fifteen, appearances were mending; she began to curl her hair and long for balls; her complexion improved, her features were softened by plumpness and colour, her eyes gained more animation, and her figure more consequence. Her love of dirt gave way to an inclination for finery, and she grew clean as she grew smart; she had now the pleasure of sometimes hearing her father and mother remark on her personal improvement. 'Catherine grows quite a good-looking girl, – she is almost pretty today,' were words which caught her ears now and then; and how welcome were the sounds! To look *almost* pretty, is an acquisition of higher delight to a girl who has been looking plain the first fifteen years of her life, than a beauty from her cradle can ever receive.

Mrs Morland was a very good woman, and wished to see her children everything they ought to be; but her time was so much occupied in lying-in and teaching the little ones, that her elder daughters were inevitably left to shift for themselves; and it was not very wonderful that Catherine, who had by nature nothing heroic about her, should prefer cricket, baseball, riding on horseback, and running about the country at the age of fourteen, to books – or at least books of information – for, provided that nothing like useful knowledge could be gained from them, provided they were all story and no reflection, she had never any objection to books at all. But from fifteen to seventeen she was in training for a heroine; she read all such works as heroines must read to supply their memories with those quotations which are so serviceable and so soothing in the vicissitudes of their eventful lives.

From Pope,[4] she learnt to censure those who

> bear about the mockery of woe.

From Gray,[5] that

> Many a flower is born to blush unseen,
> And waste its fragrance on the desert air.

From Thompson,[6] that

> – It is a delightful task
> To teach the young idea how to shoot.

And from Shakespeare she gained a great store of information – amongst the rest, that

> – Trifles light as air,
> Are, to the jealous, confirmation strong,
> As proofs of Holy Writ.

That

> The poor beetle, which we tread upon,
> In corporal sufferance feels a pang as great
> As when a giant dies.

And that a young woman in love always looks

> – like Patience on a monument
> Smiling at Grief.[7]

So far her improvement was sufficient – and in many other points she came on exceedingly well; for though she could not write sonnets, she brought herself to read them; and though there seemed no chance of her throwing a whole party into raptures by a prelude on the pianoforte, of her own composition, she could listen to other people's performance with very little fatigue. Her greatest deficiency was in the pencil – she had no notion of drawing – not enough even to attempt a sketch of her lover's profile, that she might be detected in the design. There she fell miserably short of the true heroic height. At present she did not know her own poverty, for she had no lover to portray. She had reached the age of seventeen, without having seen one amiable youth who could call forth her sensibility; without having inspired one real passion, and without having excited even any admiration but what was very moderate and very transient. This was strange indeed! But strange things may be generally accounted for if their cause be fairly searched out. There was not one lord in the neighbourhood; no – not even a baronet. There was not one family among their acquaintance who had reared and supported a boy accidentally found at their door – not one young man whose origin was unknown. Her father had no ward, and the squire of the parish no children.

But when a young lady is to be a heroine, the perverseness of forty surrounding families cannot prevent her. Something must and will happen to throw a hero in her way.

Mr Allen, who owned the chief of the property about Fullerton, the village in Wiltshire where the Morlands lived, was ordered to Bath for the benefit of a gouty constitution; – and his lady, a good-humoured woman, fond of Miss Morland, and probably aware that if adventures will not befall a young lady in her own village, she must seek them abroad, invited her to go with them. Mr and Mrs Morland were all compliance, and Catherine all happiness.

Chapter 2

IN ADDITION TO WHAT has been already said of Catherine Morland's personal and mental endowments, when about to be launched into all the difficulties and dangers of a six weeks' residence in Bath, it may be stated, for the reader's more certain information, lest the following pages should otherwise fail of giving any idea of what her character is meant to be; that her heart was affectionate, her disposition cheerful and open, without conceit or affectation of any kind – her manners just removed from the awkwardness and shyness of a girl; her person pleasing, and, when in good looks, pretty – and her mind about as ignorant and uninformed as the female mind at seventeen usually is.

When the hour of departure drew near, the maternal anxiety of Mrs Morland will be naturally supposed to be most severe. A thousand alarming presentiments of evil to her beloved Catherine from this terrific separation must oppress her heart with sadness, and drown her in tears for the last day or two of their being together; and advice of the most important and applicable nature must of course flow from her wise lips in their parting conference in her closet. Cautions against the

violence of such noblemen and baronets as delight in forcing young
ladies away to some remote farm-house, must, at such a moment,
relieve the fullness of her heart. Who would not think so? But Mrs
Morland knew so little of lords and baronets, that she entertained no
notion of their general mischievousness, and was wholly unsuspicious
of danger to her daughter from their machinations. Her cautions were
confined to the following points. 'I beg, Catherine, you will always
wrap yourself up very warm about the throat, when you come from the
Rooms at night; and I wish you would try to keep some account of the
money you spend; – I will give you this little book on purpose.'

Sally, or rather Sarah, (for what young lady of common gentility will
reach the age of sixteen without altering her name as far as she can?)
must from situation be at this time the intimate friend and confidante
of her sister. It is remarkable, however, that she neither insisted on
Catherine's writing by every post, nor exacted her promise of transmit-
ting the character of every new acquaintance, nor a detail of every
interesting conversation that Bath might produce. Everything indeed
relative to this important journey was done, on the part of the
Morlands, with a degree of moderation and composure, which seemed
rather consistent with the common feelings of common life, than with
the refined susceptibilities, the tender emotions which the first separation of a heroine from her family ought always to excite. Her father,
instead of giving her an unlimited order on his banker, or even putting
an hundred pounds bank-bill into her hands, gave her only ten guineas,
and promised her more when she wanted it.

Under these unpromising auspices, the parting took place, and the
journey began. It was performed with suitable quietness and uneventful
safety. Neither robbers nor tempests befriended them, nor one lucky
overturn to introduce them to the hero. Nothing more alarming
occurred than a fear on Mrs Allen's side, of having once left her clogs
behind her at an inn, and that fortunately proved to be groundless.

They arrived at Bath. Catherine was all eager delight; – her eyes
were here, there, everywhere, as they approached its fine and striking
environs, and afterwards drove through those streets which conducted
them to the hotel. She was come to be happy, and she felt happy
already.

They were soon settled in comfortable lodgings in Pulteney Street.

It is now expedient to give some description of Mrs Allen, that the
reader may be able to judge, in what manner her actions will hereafter
tend to promote the general distress of the work, and how she will,
probably, contribute to reduce poor Catherine to all the desperate
wretchedness of which a last volume is capable – whether by her

imprudence, vulgarity, or jealousy – whether by intercepting her letters, ruining her character, or turning her out of doors.

Mrs Allen was one of that numerous class of females, whose society can raise no other emotion than surprise at there being any men in the world who could like them well enough to marry them. She had neither beauty, genius, accomplishment, nor manner. The air of a gentlewoman, a great deal of quiet, inactive good temper, and a trifling turn of mind, were all that could account for her being the choice of a sensible, intelligent man, like Mr Allen. In one respect she was admirably fitted to introduce a young lady into public, being as fond of going everywhere and seeing everything herself as any young lady could be. Dress was her passion. She had a most harmless delight in being fine; and our heroine's entrée into life could not take place till after three or four days had been spent in learning what was mostly worn, and her chaperon was provided with a dress of the newest fashion. Catherine too made some purchases herself, and when all these matters were arranged, the important evening came which was to usher her into the Upper Rooms. Her hair was cut and dressed by the best hand, her clothes put on with care, and both Mrs Allen and her maid declared she looked quite as she should do. With such encouragement, Catherine hoped at least to pass uncensured through the crowd. As for admiration, it was always very welcome when it came, but she did not depend on it.

Mrs Allen was so long in dressing, that they did not enter the ball-room till late. The season was full, the room crowded, and the two ladies squeezed in as well as they could. As for Mr Allen, he repaired directly to the card-room, and left them to enjoy a mob by themselves. With more care for the safety of her new gown than for the comfort of her protegée, Mrs Allen made her way through the throng of men by the door, as swiftly as the necessary caution would allow; Catherine, however, kept close at her side, and linked her arm too firmly within her friend's to be torn asunder by any common effort of a struggling assembly. But to her utter amazement she found that to proceed along the room was by no means the way to disengage themselves from the crowd; it seemed rather to increase as they went on, whereas she had imagined that when once fairly within the door, they should easily find seats and be able to watch the dances with perfect convenience. But this was far from being the case, and though by unwearied diligence they gained even the top of the room, their situation was just the same; they saw nothing of the dancers but the high feathers of some of the ladies. Still they moved on – something better was yet in view; and by a continued exertion of strength and ingenuity they found themselves at last in the passage behind the highest bench. Here there was something less of a crowd than below; and hence Miss Morland had a comprehensive view of all the company beneath her, and of all the dangers of her late passage through them. It was a splendid sight, and she began, for the first time that evening, to feel herself at a ball: she longed to dance, but she had not an acquaintance in the room. Mrs Allen did all that she could do in such a case by saying very placidly, every now and then, 'I wish you could dance, my dear, – I wish you could get a partner.' For some time her young friend felt obliged to her for these wishes; but they were repeated so often, and proved so totally ineffectual, that Catherine grew tired at last, and would thank her no more.

They were not long able, however, to enjoy the repose of the eminence they had so laboriously gained. – Everybody was shortly in motion for tea, and they must squeeze out like the rest. Catherine began to feel something of disappointment – she was tired of being continually pressed against by people, the generality of whose faces possessed nothing to interest, and with all of whom she was so wholly unacquainted, that she could not relieve the irksomeness of imprisonment by the exchange of a syllable with any of her fellow captives; and when at last arrived in the tea-room, she felt yet more the awkwardness of having no party to join, no acquaintance to claim, no gentleman to assist them. – They saw nothing of Mr Allen; and after looking about them in vain for a more eligible situation, were obliged to sit down at the end of a table, at which a large party were already placed, without having anything to do there, or anybody to speak to, except each other.

Mrs Allen congratulated herself, as soon as they were seated, on having preserved her gown from injury. 'It would have been very shocking to have it torn,' said she, 'would not it? – It is such a delicate muslin. – For my part I have not seen anything I like so well in the whole room, I assure you.'

'How uncomfortable it is,' whispered Catherine, 'not to have a single acquaintance here!'

'Yes, my dear,' replied Mrs Allen, with perfect serenity, 'it is very uncomfortable indeed.'

'What shall we do? – The gentlemen and ladies at this table look as if they wondered why we came here – we seem forcing ourselves into their party.'

'Aye, so we do. – That is very disagreeable. I wish we had a large acquaintance here.'

'I wish we had *any*; – it would be somebody to go to.'

'Very true, my dear; and if we knew anybody we would join them directly. The Skinners were here last year – I wish they were here now.'

'Had not we better go away as it is? – Here are no tea things for us, you see.'

'No more there are, indeed. – How very provoking! But I think we had better sit still, for one gets so tumbled in such a crowd! How is my head, my dear? – Somebody gave me a push that has hurt it I am afraid.'

'No, indeed, it looks very nice. – But, dear Mrs Allen, are you sure there is nobody you know in all this multitude of people? I think you *must* know somebody.'

'I don't upon my word – I wish I did. I wish I had a large acquaintance here with all my heart, and then I should get you a partner. – I should be so glad to have you dance. There goes a strange-looking woman! What an odd gown she has got on! – How old fashioned it is! Look at the back.'

After some time they received an offer of tea from one of their neighbours; it was thankfully accepted, and this introduced a light conversation with the gentleman who offered it, which was the only time that anybody spoke to them during the evening, till they were discovered and joined by Mr Allen when the dance was over.

'Well, Miss Morland,' said he, directly, 'I hope you have had an agreeable ball.'

'Very agreeable indeed,' she replied, vainly endeavouring to hide a great yawn.

'I wish she had been able to dance,' said his wife, 'I wish we could have got a partner for her. – I have been saying how glad I should be if the Skinners were here this winter instead of last; or if the Parrys had come, as they talked of once, she might have danced with George Parry. I am sorry she has not had a partner!'

'We shall do better another evening I hope,' was Mr Allen's consolation.

The company began to disperse when the dancing was over – enough to leave space for the remainder to walk about in some comfort; and now was the time for a heroine, who had not yet played a very distinguished part in the events of the evening, to be noticed and admired. Every five minutes, by removing some of the crowd, gave greater openings for her charms. She was now seen by many young men who had not been near her before. Not one, however, started with rapturous wonder on beholding her, no whisper of eager inquiry ran round the room, nor was she once called a divinity by anybody. Yet Catherine was in very good looks, and had the company only seen her three years before, they would *now* have thought her exceedingly handsome.

She *was* looked at however, and with some admiration; for, in her own hearing, two gentlemen pronounced her to be a pretty girl. Such words had their due effect; she immediately thought the evening pleasanter than she had found it before – her humble vanity was contented – she felt more obliged to the two young men for this simple praise than a true quality heroine would have been for fifteen sonnets in celebration of her charms, and went to her chair in good humour with everybody, and perfectly satisfied with her share of public attention.

Chapter 3

EVERY MORNING now brought its regular duties; – shops were to be visited; some new part of the town to be looked at; and the Pump-room to be attended, where they paraded up and down for an hour, looking at everybody and speaking to no one. The wish of a numerous acquaintance in Bath was still uppermost with Mrs Allen, and she repeated it after every fresh proof, which every morning brought, of her knowing nobody at all.

They made their appearance in the Lower Rooms; and here fortune was more favourable to our heroine. The master of the ceremonies introduced to her a very gentlemanlike young man as a partner: his name was Tilney. He seemed to be about four or five and twenty, was rather tall, had a pleasing countenance, a very intelligent and lively eye, and, if not quite handsome, was very near it. His address was good, and Catherine felt herself in high luck. There was little leisure for speaking while they danced; but when they were seated at tea, she found him as agreeable as she had already given him credit for being. He talked with fluency and spirit – and there was an archness and pleasantry in his manner which interested, though it was hardly understood by her. After chatting some time on such matters as naturally arose from the objects around them, he suddenly addressed her with – 'I have hitherto been very remiss, madam, in the proper attentions of a partner here; I have not yet asked you how long you have been in Bath; whether you were ever here before; whether you have been at the Upper Rooms, the theatre, and the concert; and how you like the place altogether. I have been very negligent – but are you now at leisure to satisfy me in these particulars? If you are I will begin directly.'

'You need not give yourself that trouble, sir.'

'No trouble I assure you, madam.' Then forming his features into a set smile, and affectedly softening his voice, he added, with a simpering air, 'Have you been long in Bath, madam?'

'About a week, sir,' replied Catherine, trying not to laugh.

'Really!' with affected astonishment.

'Why should you be surprised, sir?'

'Why, indeed!' said he, in his natural tone – 'but some emotion must appear to be raised by your reply, and surprise is more easily assumed, and not less reasonable than any other. – Now let us go on. Were you never here before, madam?'

'Never, sir.'

'Indeed! Have you yet honoured the Upper Rooms?'

'Yes, sir, I was there last Monday.'

'Have you been to the theatre?'

'Yes, sir, I was at the play on Tuesday.'

'To the concert?'

'Yes, sir, on Wednesday.'

'And are you altogether pleased with Bath?'

'Yes – I like it very well.'

'Now I must give one smirk, and then we may be rational again.'

Catherine turned away her head, not knowing whether she might venture to laugh.

'I see what you think of me,' said he gravely – 'I shall make but a poor figure in your journal tomorrow.'

'My journal!'

'Yes, I know exactly what you will say: Friday, went to the Lower Rooms; wore my sprigged muslin robe with blue trimmings – plain black shoes – appeared to much advantage; but was strangely harassed by a queer, half-witted man, who would make me dance with him, and distressed me by his nonsense.'

'Indeed I shall say no such thing.'

'Shall I tell you what you ought to say?'

'If you please.'

'I danced with a very agreeable young man, introduced by Mr King; had a great deal of conversation with him – seems a most extraordinary genius – hope I may know more of him. *That*, madam, is what I *wish* you to say.'

'But, perhaps, I keep no journal.'

'Perhaps you are not sitting in this room, and I am not sitting by you. These are points in which a doubt is equally possible. Not keep a journal! How are your absent cousins to understand the tenor of your life in Bath without one? How are the civilities and compliments of every day to be related as they ought to be, unless noted down every evening in a journal? How are your various dresses to be remembered, and the particular state of your complexion, and curl of your hair to be described in all their diversities, without having constant recourse to a journal? – My dear madam, I am not so ignorant of young ladies' ways as you wish to believe me; it is this delightful habit of journalising which largely contributes to form the easy style of writing for which ladies are so generally celebrated. Everybody allows that the talent of writing agreeable letters is peculiarly female. Nature may have done something, but I am sure it must be essentially assisted by the practice of keeping a journal.'

'I have sometimes thought,' said Catherine, doubtingly, 'whether ladies do write so much better letters than gentlemen! That is – I should not think the superiority was always on our side.'

'As far as I have had opportunity of judging, it appears to me that the usual style of letter-writing among women is faultless, except in three particulars.'

'And what are they?'

'A general deficiency of subject, a total inattention to stops, and a very frequent ignorance of grammar.'

'Upon my word! I need not have been afraid of disclaiming the compliment. You do not think too highly of us in that way.'

'I should no more lay it down as a general rule that women write better letters than men, than that they sing better duets, or draw better landscapes. In every power, of which taste is the foundation, excellence is pretty fairly divided between the sexes.'

They were interrupted by Mrs Allen: – 'My dear Catherine,' said she, 'do take this pin out of my sleeve; I am afraid it has torn a hole already; I shall be quite sorry if it has, for this is a favourite gown, though it cost but nine shillings a yard.'

'That is exactly what I should have guessed it, madam,' said Mr Tilney, looking at the muslin.

'Do you understand muslins, sir?'

'Particularly well; I always buy my own cravats, and am allowed to be an excellent judge; and my sister has often trusted me in the choice of a gown. I bought one for her the other day, and it was pronounced to be a prodigious bargain by every lady who saw it. I gave but five shillings a yard for it, and a true Indian muslin.'

Mrs Allen was quite struck by his genius. 'Men commonly take so little notice of those things,' said she: 'I can never get Mr Allen to know one of my gowns from another. You must be a great comfort to your sister, sir.'

'I hope I am, madam.'

'And pray, sir, what do you think of Miss Morland's gown?'

'It is very pretty, madam,' said he, gravely examining it; 'but I do not think it will wash well; I am afraid it will fray.'

'How can you,' said Catherine, laughing, 'be so – ' she had almost said, strange.

'I am quite of your opinion, sir,' replied Mrs Allen; 'and so I told Miss Morland when she bought it.'

'But then you know, madam, muslin always turns to some account or other; Miss Morland will get enough out of it for a handkerchief, or a cap, or a cloak. – Muslin can never be said to be wasted. I have heard my sister say so forty times, when she has been extravagant in buying more than she wanted, or careless in cutting it to pieces.'

'Bath is a charming place, sir; there are so many good shops here. – We are sadly off in the country; not but what we have very good shops in Salisbury, but it is so far to go; – eight miles is a long way; Mr Allen says it is nine, measured nine; but I am sure it cannot be more than eight; and it is such a fag – I come back tired to death. Now here one can step out of doors and get a thing in five minutes.'

Mr Tilney was polite enough to seem interested in what she said; and she kept him on the subject of muslins till the dancing recommenced. Catherine feared, as she listened to their discourse, that he indulged himself a little too much with the foibles of others. – 'What are you thinking of so earnestly?' said he, as they walked back to the ballroom; – 'not of your partner, I hope, for, by that shake of the head, your meditations are not satisfactory.'

Catherine coloured, and said, 'I was not thinking of anything.'

'That is artful and deep, to be sure; but I had rather be told at once that you will not tell me.'

'Well then, I will not.'

'Thank you; for now we shall soon be acquainted, as I am authorised to tease you on this subject whenever we meet, and nothing in the world advances intimacy so much.'

They danced again; and, when the assembly closed, parted, on the lady's side at least, with a strong inclination for continuing the acquaintance. Whether she thought of him so much, while she drank her warm wine and water, and prepared herself for bed, as to dream of him when there, cannot be ascertained; but I hope it was no more than in a slight slumber, or a morning doze at most; for if it be true, as a celebrated writer has maintained, that no young lady can be justified in falling in love before the gentleman's love is declared,* it must be very improper that a young lady should dream of a gentleman before the gentleman is first known to have dreamt of her. How proper Mr Tilney might be as a dreamer or a lover, had not yet perhaps entered

* *Vide* a letter from Mr Richardson, No. 97, Vol. ii, *Rambler*

Mr Allen's head, but that he was not objectionable as a common acquaintance for his young charge he was on inquiry satisfied; for he had early in the evening taken pains to know who her partner was, and had been assured of Mr Tilney's being a clergyman, and of a very respectable family in Gloucestershire.

Chapter 4

WITH MORE THAN USUAL eagerness did Catherine hasten to the Pump-room the next day, secure within herself of seeing Mr Tilney there before the morning were over, and ready to meet him with a smile: – but no smile was demanded – Mr Tilney did not appear. Every creature in Bath, except himself, was to be seen in the room at different periods of the fashionable hours; crowds of people were every moment passing in and out, up the steps and down; people whom nobody cared about, and nobody wanted to see; and he only was absent. 'What a delightful place Bath is,' said Mrs Allen, as they sat down near the great clock, after parading the room till they were tired; 'and how pleasant it would be if we had any acquaintance here.'

This sentiment had been uttered so often in vain, that Mrs Allen had no particular reason to hope it would be followed with more advantage now; but we are told to 'despair of nothing we would attain', as 'unwearied diligence our point would gain';[8] and the unwearied diligence with which she had every day wished for the same thing was at length to have its just reward, for hardly had she been seated ten minutes before a lady of about her own age, who was sitting by her, and had been looking at her attentively for several minutes, addressed her with great complaisance in these words: – 'I think, madam, I cannot be mistaken; it is a long time since I had the pleasure of seeing you, but is not your name Allen?' This question answered, as it readily was, the stranger pronounced hers to be Thorpe; and Mrs Allen immediately recognised the features of a former schoolfellow and intimate, whom she had seen only once since their respective marriages, and that many years ago. Their joy on this meeting was very great, as well it might, since they had been contented to know nothing of each other for the last fifteen years. Compliments on good looks now passed; and, after observing how time had slipped away since they were last together, how little they had thought of meeting in Bath, and what a pleasure it was to see an old friend, they proceeded to make inquiries and give intelligence as to their families, sisters, and cousins, talking both together, far more ready to give than to receive information, and each hearing very little of what the other said. Mrs Thorpe, however, had one great advantage as a talker, over Mrs Allen, in a family of children; and when she expatiated on the talents of her sons, and the beauty of her daughters, – when she related their different situations and views, – that John was at Oxford, Edward at Merchant-Taylors', and William at sea, – and all of them more beloved and respected in their different station than any other three beings ever were, Mrs Allen had no similar information to give, no similar triumphs to press on the unwilling and unbelieving ear of her friend, and was forced to sit and appear to listen to all these maternal effusions, consoling herself, however, with the discovery, which her keen eye soon made, that the lace on Mrs Thorpe's pelisse was not half so handsome as that on her own.

'Here come my dear girls,' cried Mrs Thorpe, pointing at three smart-looking females, who, arm in arm, were then moving towards her. 'My dear Mrs Allen, I long to introduce them; they will be so delighted to see you: the tallest is Isabella, my eldest; is not she a fine young woman? The others are very much admired too, but I believe Isabella is the handsomest.'

The Miss Thorpes were introduced; and Miss Morland, who had been for a short time forgotten, was introduced likewise. The name seemed to strike them all; and, after speaking to her with great civility, the eldest young lady observed aloud to the rest, 'How excessively like her brother Miss Morland is!'

'The very picture of him indeed!' cried the mother – and 'I should have known her anywhere for his sister!' was repeated by them all, two or three times over. For a moment Catherine was surprised; but Mrs Thorpe and her daughters had scarcely begun the history of their acquaintance with Mr James Morland, before she remembered that her eldest brother had lately formed an intimacy with a young man of his own college, of the name of Thorpe; and that he had spent the last week of the Christmas vacation with his family, near London.

The whole being explained, many obliging things were said by the Miss Thorpes of their wish of being better acquainted with her; of being considered as already friends, through the friendship of their brothers, &c. which Catherine heard with pleasure, and answered with all the pretty expressions she could command; and, as the first proof of amity, she was soon invited to accept an arm of the eldest Miss Thorpe, and take a turn with her about the room. Catherine was delighted with this extension of her Bath acquaintance, and almost forgot Mr Tilney while she talked to Miss Thorpe. Friendship is certainly the finest balm for the pangs of disappointed love.

Their conversation turned upon those subjects, of which the free discussion has generally much to do in perfecting a sudden intimacy between two young ladies; such as dress, balls, flirtations, and quizzes.[9] Miss Thorpe, however, being four years older than Miss Morland, and at least four years better informed, had a very decided advantage in discussing such points; she could compare the balls of Bath with those of Tunbridge; its fashions with the fashions of London; could rectify the opinions of her new friend in many articles of tasteful attire; could discover a flirtation between any gentleman and lady who only smiled on each other; and point out a quiz through the thickness of a crowd. These powers received due admiration from Catherine, to whom they were entirely new; and the respect which they naturally inspired might have been too great for familiarity, had not the easy gaiety of Miss Thorpe's manners, and her frequent expressions of delight on this acquaintance with her, softened down every feeling of awe, and left nothing but tender affection. Their increasing attachment was not to be satisfied with half a dozen turns in the Pump-room, but required, when they all quitted it together, that Miss Thorpe should accompany Miss Morland to the very door of Mr Allen's house; and that they should there part with a most affectionate and lengthened shake of hands, after learning, to their mutual relief, that they should see each other across the theatre at night, and say their prayers in the same chapel the next morning. Catherine then ran directly upstairs, and watched Miss Thorpe's progress down the street from the drawing-room window; admired the graceful spirit of her walk, the fashionable air of her figure and dress, and felt grateful, as well she might, for the chance which had procured her such a friend.

Mrs Thorpe was a widow, and not a very rich one; she was a good-humoured, well-meaning woman, and a very indulgent mother. Her eldest daughter had great personal beauty, and the younger ones, by pretending to be as handsome as their sister, imitating her air, and dressing in the same style, did very well.

This brief account of the family is intended to supersede the necessity of a long and minute detail from Mrs Thorpe herself, of her past adventures and sufferings, which might otherwise be expected to occupy the three or four following chapters; in which the worthlessness of lords and attornies might be set forth, and conversations, which had passed twenty years before, be minutely repeated.

Chapter 5

CATHERINE WAS NOT so much engaged at the theatre that evening, in returning the nods and smiles of Miss Thorpe, though they certainly claimed much of her leisure, as to forget to look with an inquiring eye for Mr Tilney in every box which her eye could reach; but she looked in vain. Mr Tilney was no fonder of the play than the Pump-room. She hoped to be more fortunate the next day; and when her wishes for fine weather were answered by seeing a beautiful morning, she hardly felt a doubt about it; for a fine Sunday in Bath empties every house of its inhabitants, and all the world appears on such an occasion to walk about and tell their acquaintance what a charming day it is.

As soon as divine service was over, the Thorpes and Allens eagerly joined each other; and after staying long enough in the Pump-room to discover that the crowd was insupportable, and that there was not a genteel face to be seen, which everybody discovers every Sunday throughout the season, they hastened away to the Crescent, to breathe the fresh air of better company. Here Catherine and Isabella, arm in arm, again tasted the sweets of friendship in an unreserved conversation; – they talked much, and with much enjoyment; but again was Catherine disappointed in her hope of re-seeing her partner. He was nowhere to be met with; every search for him was equally unsuccessful, in morning lounges or evening assemblies; neither at the Upper nor Lower Rooms, at dressed or undressed balls, was he perceivable; nor among the walkers, the horsemen, or the curricle-drivers of the morning. His name was not in the Pump-room book, and curiosity could do no more. He must be gone from Bath. Yet he had not mentioned that his stay would be so short! This sort of mysteriousness, which is always so becoming in a hero, threw a fresh grace in Catherine's imagination around his person and manners, and increased her anxiety to know more of him. From the Thorpes she could learn nothing, for they had been only two days in Bath before they met with Mrs Allen. It was a subject, however, in which she often indulged with her fair friend, from whom she received every possible encouragement to continue to think of him; and his impression on her fancy was not suffered therefore to weaken. Isabella was very sure that he must be a charming young man; and was equally sure that he must have been delighted with her dear Catherine, and would therefore shortly return. She liked him the better for being a clergyman, 'for she must confess herself very partial to the profession;' and something like a sigh escaped her as she said it. Perhaps Catherine was wrong in not demanding the cause of that gentle emotion – but she was not experienced enough in the finesse of love, or the duties of friendship, to know when delicate raillery was properly called for, or when a confidence should be forced.

Mrs Allen was now quite happy – quite satisfied with Bath. She had found some acquaintance, had been so lucky too as to find in them the family of a most worthy old friend; and, as the completion of good fortune, had found these friends by no means so expensively dressed as herself. Her daily expressions were no longer, 'I wish we had some acquaintance in Bath!' They were changed into – 'How glad I am we have met with Mrs Thorpe!' – and she was as eager in promoting the intercourse of the two families, as her young charge and Isabella themselves could be; never satisfied with the day unless she spent the chief of it by the side of Mrs Thorpe, in what they called conversation, but in which there was scarcely ever any exchange of opinion, and not often any resemblance of subject, for Mrs Thorpe talked chiefly of her children, and Mrs Allen of her gowns.

The progress of the friendship between Catherine and Isabella was quick as its beginning had been warm, and they passed so rapidly through every gradation of increasing tenderness, that there was shortly no fresh proof of it to be given to their friends or themselves. They called each other by their Christian name, were always arm in arm when they walked, pinned up each other's train for the dance, and were not to be divided in the set; and if a rainy morning deprived them of other enjoyments, they were still resolute in meeting in defiance of wet and dirt, and shut themselves up, to read novels together. Yes, novels; – for I will not adopt that ungenerous and impolitic custom so common with novel writers, of degrading by their contemptuous censure the very performances, to the number of which they are themselves adding – joining with their greatest enemies in bestowing the harshest epithets on such works, and scarcely ever permitting them to be read by their own heroine, who, if she accidentally take up a novel, is sure to turn over its insipid pages with disgust. Alas! if the heroine of one novel be not patronised by the heroine of another, from whom can she expect protection and regard? I cannot approve of it. Let us leave it to the Reviewers to abuse such effusions of fancy at their leisure, and over every new novel to talk in threadbare strains of the trash with which the press now groans. Let us not desert one another; we are an injured body. Although our productions have afforded more extensive and unaffected pleasure than those of any other literary corporation in the world, no species of composition has been so much decried. From pride, ignorance, or fashion, our foes are almost as many as our readers. And while the abilities of the nine-hundredth abridger of the History of England, or of the man who collects and publishes in a volume some dozen lines of Milton, Pope, and Prior, with a paper from the Spectator, and a chapter from Sterne, are eulogised by a thousand pens, – there seems almost a general wish of decrying the capacity and undervaluing the labour of the novelist, and of slighting the performances which have only genius, wit, and taste to recommend them. 'I am no novel reader – I seldom look into novels – Do not imagine that *I* often read novels – It is really very well for a novel.' – Such is the common cant. – 'And what are you reading, Miss — ?' 'Oh! it is only a novel!' replies the young lady; while she lays down her book with affected indifference, or momentary shame. – 'It is only Cecilia, or Camilla, or Belinda;'[10] or, in short, only some work in which the greatest powers of the mind are displayed, in which the most thorough knowledge of human nature, the happiest delineation of its varieties, the liveliest effusions of wit and humour are conveyed to the world in the best chosen language. Now, had the same young lady been engaged with a volume of the Spectator, instead of such a work, how proudly would she have produced the book, and told its name; though the chances must be against her being occupied by any part of that voluminous publication, of which either the matter or manner would not disgust a young person of taste: the substance of its papers so often consisting in the statement of improbable circumstances, unnatural characters, and topics of conversation, which no longer concern anyone living; and their language, too, frequently so coarse as to give no very favourable idea of the age that could endure it.

Chapter 6

THE FOLLOWING CONVERSATION, which took place between the two friends in the Pump-room one morning, after an acquaintance of eight or nine days, is given as a specimen of their very warm attachment, and of the delicacy, discretion, originality of thought, and literary taste which marked the reasonableness of that attachment.

They met by appointment; and as Isabella had arrived nearly five minutes before her friend, her first address naturally was – 'My dearest creature, what can have made you so late? I have been waiting for you at least this age!'

'Have you, indeed! – I am very sorry for it; but really I thought I was in very good time. It is but just one. I hope you have not been here long?'

'Oh! these ten ages at least. I am sure I have been here this half hour. But now, let us go and sit down at the other end of the room, and enjoy ourselves. I have an hundred things to say to you. In the first place, I was so afraid it would rain this morning, just as I wanted to set off; it looked very showery, and that would have thrown me into agonies! Do you know, I saw the prettiest hat you can imagine, in a shop window in Milsom Street just now – very like yours, only with coquelicot[11] ribbons instead of green; I quite longed for it. But, my dearest Catherine, what have you been doing with yourself all this morning? – Have you gone on with Udolpho?'[12]

'Yes, I have been reading it ever since I woke; and I am got to the black veil.'

'Are you, indeed? How delightful! Oh! I would not tell you what is behind the black veil for the world! Are not you wild to know?'

'Oh! yes, quite; what can it be? – But do not tell me – I would not be told upon any account. I know it must be a skeleton, I am sure it is Laurentina's skeleton. Oh! I am delighted with the book! I should like to spend my whole life in reading it. I assure you, if it had not been to meet you, I would not have come away from it for all the world.'

'Dear creature! how much I am obliged to you; and when you have finished Udolpho, we will read the Italian together; and I have made out a list of ten or twelve more of the same kind for you.'

'Have you, indeed! How glad I am! – What are they all?'

'I will read you their names directly; here they are, in my pocket-book. Castle of Wolfenbach, Clermont, Mysterious Warnings, Necromancer of the Black Forest, Midnight Bell, Orphan of the Rhine, and Horrid Mysteries.[13] Those will last us some time.'

'Yes, pretty well; but are they all horrid, are you sure they are all horrid?'

'Yes, quite sure; for a particular friend of mine, a Miss Andrews, a sweet girl, one of the sweetest creatures in the world, has read every one of them. I wish you knew Miss Andrews, you would be delighted with her. She is netting herself the sweetest cloak you can conceive. I think her as beautiful as an angel, and I am so vexed with the men for not admiring her! – I scold them all amazingly about it.'

'Scold them! Do you scold them for not admiring her?'

'Yes, that I do. There is nothing I would not do for those who are really my friends. I have no notion of loving people by halves, it is not my nature. My attachments are always excessively strong. I told Capt. Hunt at one of our assemblies this winter, that if he was to tease me all night, I would not dance with him, unless he would allow Miss Andrews to be as beautiful as an angel. The men think us incapable of real friendship you know, and I am determined to show them the difference. Now, if I were to hear anybody speak slightingly of you, I should fire up in a moment: – but that is not at all likely, for *you* are just the kind of girl to be a great favourite with the men.'

'Oh! dear,' cried Catherine, colouring, 'how can you say so?'

'I know you very well; you have so much animation, which is exactly what Miss Andrews wants, for I must confess there is something amazingly insipid about her. Oh! I must tell you, that just after we parted yesterday, I saw a young man looking at you so earnestly – I am sure he is in love with you.' Catherine coloured, and disclaimed again. Isabella laughed. 'It is very true, upon my honour, but I see how it is; you are indifferent to everybody's admiration, except that of one gentleman, who shall be nameless. Nay, I cannot blame you – (speaking more seriously) – your feelings are easily understood. Where the heart is really attached, I know very well how little one can be pleased with the attention of anybody else. Everything is so insipid, so uninteresting, that does not relate to the beloved object! I can perfectly comprehend your feelings.'

'But you should not persuade me that I think so very much about Mr Tilney, for perhaps I may never see him again.'

'Not see him again! My dearest creature, do not talk of it. I am sure you would be miserable if you thought so.'

'No, indeed, I should not. I do not pretend to say that I was not very much pleased with him; but while I have Udolpho to read, I feel as if nobody could make me miserable. Oh! the dreadful black veil! My dear Isabella, I am sure there must be Laurentina's skeleton behind it.'

'It is so odd to me, that you should never have read Udolpho before; but I suppose Mrs Morland objects to novels.'

'No, she does not. She very often reads Sir Charles Grandison[14] herself; but new books do not fall in our way.'

'Sir Charles Grandison! That is an amazing horrid book, is it not? – I remember Miss Andrews could not get through the first volume.'

'It is not like Udolpho at all; but yet I think it is very entertaining.'

'Do you indeed! – you surprise me; I thought it had not been readable. But, my dearest Catherine, have you settled what to wear on your head tonight? I am determined at all events to be dressed exactly like you. The men take notice of *that* sometimes you know.'

'But it does not signify if they do;' said Catherine, very innocently.

'Signify! Oh, heavens! I make it a rule never to mind what they say. They are very often amazingly impertinent if you do not treat them with spirit, and make them keep their distance.'

'Are they? – Well, I never observed *that*. They always behave very well to me.'

'Oh! they give themselves such airs. They are the most conceited creatures in the world, and think themselves of so much importance! – By the bye, though I have thought of it a hundred times, I have always forgot to ask you what is your favourite complexion in a man. Do you like them best dark or fair?'

'I hardly know. I never much thought about it. Something between both, I think. Brown – not fair, and not very dark.'

'Very well, Catherine. That is exactly he. I have not forgot your description of Mr Tilney; – "a brown skin, with dark eyes, and rather dark hair." – Well, my taste is different. I prefer light eyes, and as to complexion – do you know – I like a sallow better than any other. You must not betray me, if you should ever meet with one of your acquaintance answering that description.'

'Betray you! – What do you mean?'

'Nay, do not distress me. I believe I have said too much. Let us drop the subject.'

Catherine, in some amazement, complied; and after remaining a few moments silent, was on the point of reverting to what interested her at that time rather more than anything else in the world, Laurentina's skeleton; when her friend prevented her, by saying, – 'For Heaven's sake! let us move away from this end of the room. Do you know, there are two odious young men who have been staring at me this half hour. They really put me quite out of countenance. Let us go and look at the arrivals. They will hardly follow us there.'

Away they walked to the book; and while Isabella examined the names, it was Catherine's employment to watch the proceedings of these alarming young men.

'They are not coming this way, are they? I hope they are not so impertinent as to follow us. Pray let me know if they are coming. I am determined I will not look up.'

In a few moments Catherine, with unaffected pleasure, assured her that she need not be longer uneasy, as the gentlemen had just left the Pump-room.

'And which way are they gone?' said Isabella, turning hastily round. 'One was a very good-looking young man.'

'They went towards the churchyard.'

'Well, I am amazingly glad I have got rid of them! And now, what say you to going to Edgar's Buildings with me, and looking at my new hat? You said you should like to see it.'

Catherine readily agreed. 'Only,' she added, 'perhaps we may overtake the two young men.'

'Oh! never mind that. If we make haste, we shall pass by them presently, and I am dying to show you my hat.'

'But if we only wait a few minutes, there will be no danger of our seeing them at all.'

'I shall not pay them any such compliment, I assure you. I have no notion of treating men with such respect. *That* is the way to spoil them.'

Catherine had nothing to oppose against such reasoning; and therefore, to show the independence of Miss Thorpe, and her resolution of humbling the sex, they set off immediately as fast as they could walk, in pursuit of the two young men.

Chapter 7

HALF A MINUTE conducted them through the Pump Yard to the archway, opposite Union Passage; but here they were stopped. Everybody acquainted with Bath may remember the difficulties of crossing Cheap Street at this point; it is indeed a street of so impertinent a nature, so unfortunately connected with the great London and Oxford roads, and the principal inn of the city, that a day never passes in which parties of ladies, however important their business, whether in quest of pastry, millinery, or even (as in the present case) of young men, are not detained on one side or other by carriages, horsemen, or carts. This evil had been felt and lamented, at least three times a day, by Isabella since her residence in Bath; and she was now fated to feel and lament it once more, for at the very moment of coming opposite to Union Passage, and within view of the two gentlemen who were proceeding through the crowds, and threading the gutters of that interesting alley, they were prevented crossing by the approach of a gig, driven along on bad pavement by a most knowing-looking coachman with all the vehemence that could most fitly endanger the lives of himself, his companion, and his horse.

'Oh, these odious gigs!' said Isabella, looking up, 'how I detest them.' But this detestation, though so just, was of short duration, for she looked again and exclaimed, 'Delightful! Mr Morland and my brother!'

'Good heaven! 'tis James!' was uttered at the same moment by Catherine; and, on catching the young men's eyes, the horse was immediately checked with a violence which almost threw him on his haunches, and the servant having now scampered up, the gentlemen jumped out, and the equipage was delivered to his care.

Catherine, by whom this meeting was wholly unexpected, received her brother with the liveliest pleasure; and he, being of a very amiable disposition, and sincerely attached to her, gave every proof on his side of equal satisfaction, which he could have leisure to do, while the bright eyes of Miss Thorpe were incessantly challenging his notice; and to her his devoirs were speedily paid, with a mixture of joy and embarrassment which might have informed Catherine, had she been more expert in the development of other people's feelings, and less simply engrossed by her own, that her brother thought her friend quite as pretty as she could do herself.

John Thorpe, who in the meantime had been giving orders about the horses, soon joined them, and from him she directly received the amends which were her due; for while he slightly and carelessly touched the hand of Isabella, on her he bestowed a whole scrape and half a short bow. He was a stout young man of middling height, who, with a plain face and ungraceful form, seemed fearful of being too handsome unless he wore the dress of a groom, and too much like a gentleman unless he were easy where he ought to be civil, and impudent where he might be allowed to be easy. He took out his watch: 'How long do you think we have been running it from Tetbury, Miss Morland?'

'I do not know the distance.' Her brother told her that it was twenty-three miles.

'*Three*-and-twenty!' cried Thorpe; 'five-and-twenty if it is an inch.' Morland remonstrated, pleaded the authority of road-books, innkeepers, and milestones; but his friend disregarded them all; he had a surer test of distance. 'I know it must be five-and-twenty,' said he, 'by the time we have been doing it. It is now half after one; we drove out of the inn-yard at Tetbury as the town-clock struck eleven; and I defy any man in England to make my horse go less than ten miles an hour in harness; that makes it exactly twenty-five.'

'You have lost an hour,' said Morland; 'it was only ten o'clock when we came from Tetbury.'

'Ten o'clock! it was eleven, upon my soul! I counted every stroke. This brother of yours would persuade me out of my senses, Miss Morland; do but look at my horse; did you ever see an animal so made for speed in your life?' (The servant had just mounted the carriage and was driving off.) 'Such true blood! Three hours and a half indeed coming only three-and-twenty miles! look at that creature, and suppose it possible if you can.'

'He *does* look very hot to be sure.'

'Hot! he had not turned a hair till we came to Walcot Church: but look at his forehand; look at his loins; only see how he moves; that horse *cannot* go less than ten miles an hour: tie his legs and he will get on. What do you think of my gig, Miss Morland? a neat one, is not it? Well hung; town built; I have not had it a month. It was built for a Christchurch man, a friend of mine, a very good sort of fellow; he ran it a few weeks, till, I believe, it was convenient to have done with it. I happened just then to be looking out for some light thing of the kind, though I had pretty well determined on a curricle too; but I chanced to meet him on Magdalen Bridge, as he was driving into Oxford, last term: "Ah! Thorpe," said he, "do you happen to want such a little thing as this? it is a capital one of the kind, but I am cursed tired of it." "Oh! d—," said I, "I am your man; what do you ask?" And how much do you think he did, Miss Morland?'

'I am sure I cannot guess at all.'

'Curricle-hung you see; seat, trunk, sword-case, splashing-board, lamps, silver moulding, all you see complete; the iron-work as good as new, or better. He asked fifty guineas; I closed with him directly, threw down the money, and the carriage was mine.'

'And I am sure,' said Catherine, 'I know so little of such things that I cannot judge whether it was cheap or dear.'

'Neither one nor t'other; I might have got it for less I dare say; but I hate haggling, and poor Freeman wanted cash.'

'That was very good-natured of you,' said Catherine, quite pleased.

'Oh! d— it, when one has the means of doing a kind thing by a friend, I hate to be pitiful.'

An inquiry now took place into the intended movements of the young ladies; and, on finding whither they were going, it was decided that the gentlemen should accompany them to Edgar's Buildings, and pay their respects to Mrs Thorpe. James and Isabella led the way; and so well satisfied was the latter with her lot, so contentedly was she endeavouring to ensure a pleasant walk to him who brought the double recommendation of being her brother's friend, and her friend's brother, so pure and uncoquettish were her feelings, that, though they overtook and passed the two offending young men in Milsom Street, she was so far from seeking to attract their notice, that she looked back at them only three times.

John Thorpe kept of course with Catherine, and, after a few minutes' silence, renewed the conversation about his gig – 'You will find, however, Miss Morland, it would be reckoned a cheap thing by some people, for I might have sold it for ten guineas more the next day; Jackson, of Oriel, bid me sixty at once; Morland was with me at the time.'

'Yes,' said Morland, who overheard this; 'but you forget that your horse was included.'

'My horse! oh, d— it! I would not sell my horse for a hundred. Are you fond of an open carriage, Miss Morland?'

'Yes, very; I have hardly ever an opportunity of being in one; but I am particularly fond of it.'

'I am glad of it; I will drive you out in mine every day.'

'Thank you,' said Catherine, in some distress, from a doubt of the propriety of accepting such an offer.

'I will drive you up Lansdown Hill tomorrow.'

'Thank you; but will not your horse want rest?'

'Rest! he has only come three-and-twenty miles today; all nonsense; nothing ruins horses so much as rest; nothing knocks them up so soon. No, no; I shall exercise mine at the average of four hours every day while I am here.'

'Shall you indeed!' said Catherine very seriously, 'that will be forty miles a day.'

'Forty! aye fifty, for what I care. Well, I will drive you up Lansdown tomorrow; mind, I am engaged.'

'How delightful that will be!' cried Isabella, turning round; 'my dearest Catherine, I quite envy you; but I am afraid, brother, you will not have room for a third.'

'A third indeed! no, no; I did not come to Bath to drive my sisters about; that would be a good joke, faith! Morland must take care of you.'

This brought on a dialogue of civilities between the other two; but Catherine heard neither the particulars nor the result. Her companion's discourse now sunk from its hitherto animated pitch, to nothing more than a short decisive sentence of praise or condemnation on the face of every woman they met; and Catherine, after listening and agreeing as long as she could, with all the civility and deference of the youthful female mind, fearful of hazarding an opinion of its own in opposition to that of a self-assured man, especially where the beauty of her own sex is concerned, ventured at length to vary the subject by a question which had been long uppermost in her thoughts; it was, 'Have you ever read Udolpho, Mr Thorpe?'

'Udolpho! Oh, Lord! not I; I never read novels; I have something else to do.'

Catherine, humbled and ashamed, was going to apologise for her question, but he prevented her by saying, 'Novels are all so full of nonsense and stuff; there has not been a tolerably decent one come out since Tom Jones,[15] except the Monk; I read that t'other day; but as for all the others, they are the stupidest things in creation.'

'I think you must like Udolpho, if you were to read it; it is so very interesting.'

'Not I, faith! No, if I read any, it shall be Mrs Radcliff's; her novels are amusing enough; they are worth reading; some fun and nature in *them*.'

'Udolpho was written by Mrs Radcliff,' said Catherine, with some hesitation, from the fear of mortifying him.

'No sure; was it? Aye. I remember, so it was; I was thinking of that other stupid book, written by that woman they make such a fuss about, she who married the French emigrant.'

'I suppose you mean Camilla?'

'Yes, that's the book; such unnatural stuff! – An old man playing at see-saw! I took up the first volume once, and looked it over, but I soon found it would not do; indeed I guessed what sort of stuff it must be before I saw it: as soon as I heard she had married an emigrant, I was sure I should never be able to get through it.'

'I have never read it.'

'You had no loss I assure you, it is the horridest nonsense you can imagine; there is nothing in the world in it but an old man's playing at see-saw and learning Latin; upon my soul there is not.'

This critique, the justness of which was unfortunately lost on poor Catherine, brought them to the door of Mrs Thorpe's lodgings, and the feelings of the discerning and unprejudiced reader of Camilla gave way to the feelings of the dutiful and affectionate son, as they met Mrs Thorpe, who had descried them from above, in the passage. 'Ah, mother! how do you do?' said he, giving her a hearty shake of the hand: 'where did you get that quiz of a hat, it makes you look like an old witch? Here is Morland and I come to stay a few days with you, so you must look out for a couple of good beds somewhere near.' And this address seemed to satisfy all the fondest wishes of the mother's heart, for she received him with the most delighted and exulting affection. On his two younger sisters he then bestowed an equal portion of his fraternal tenderness, for he asked each of them how they did, and observed that they both looked very ugly.

These manners did not please Catherine; but he was James's friend and Isabella's brother; and her judgment was further bought off by Isabella's assuring her, when they withdrew to see the new hat, that John thought her the most charming girl in the world, and by John's engaging her before they parted to dance with him that evening. Had she been older or vainer, such attacks might have done little, but, where youth and diffidence are united, it requires uncommon steadiness of reason to resist the attraction of being called the most charming girl in the world, and of being so very early engaged as a partner; and the consequence was, that, when the two Morlands, after sitting an hour with the Thorpes, set off to walk together to Mr Allen's, and James, as the door was closed on them, said, 'Well, Catherine, how do you like my friend Thorpe?' instead of answering, as she probably would have done, had there been no friendship and no flattery in the case, 'I do not like him at all;' she directly replied, 'I like him very much; he seems very agreeable.'

'He is as good-natured a fellow as ever lived; a little of a rattle; but that will recommend him to your sex I believe: and how do you like the rest of the family?'

'Very, very much indeed: Isabella particularly.'

'I am very glad to hear you say so; she is just the kind of young woman I could wish to see you attached to; she has so much good sense, and is so thoroughly unaffected and amiable; I always wanted you to know her; and she seems very fond of you. She said the highest things in your praise that could possibly be; and the praise of such a girl as Miss Thorpe even you, Catherine,' taking her hand with affection, 'may be proud of.'

'Indeed I am,' she replied; 'I love her exceedingly, and am delighted to find that you like her too. You hardly mentioned anything of her, when you wrote to me after your visit there.'

'Because I thought I should soon see you myself. I hope you will be a great deal together while you are in Bath. She is a most amiable girl; such a superior understanding! How fond all the family are of her; she is evidently the general favourite; and how much she must be admired in such a place as this – is not she?'

'Yes, very much indeed, I fancy; Mr Allen thinks her the prettiest girl in Bath.'

'I dare say he does; and I do not know any man who is a better judge of beauty than Mr Allen. I need not ask you whether you are happy here, my dear Catherine; with such a companion and friend as Isabella Thorpe, it would be impossible for you to be otherwise; and the Allens I am sure are very kind to you?'

'Yes, very kind; I never was so happy before; and now you are come it will be more delightful than ever; how good it is of you to come so far on purpose to see *me*.'

James accepted this tribute of gratitude, and qualified his conscience for accepting it too, by saying with perfect sincerity, 'Indeed, Catherine, I love you dearly.'

Inquiries and communications concerning brothers and sisters, the situation of some, the growth of the rest, and other family matters, now passed between them, and continued, with only one small digression on James's part, in praise of Miss Thorpe, till they reached Pulteney Street, where he was welcomed with great kindness by Mr and Mrs Allen, invited by the former to dine with them and summoned by the latter to guess the price and weigh the merits of a new muff and tippet. A pre-engagement in Edgar's Buildings prevented his accepting the invitation of one friend, and obliged him to hurry away as soon as he had satisfied the demands of the other. The time of the two parties uniting in the Octagon Room being correctly adjusted, Catherine was then left to the luxury of a raised, restless, and frightened imagination over the pages of Udolpho, lost from all worldly concerns of dressing and dinner, incapable of soothing Mrs Allen's fears on the delay of an expected dress-maker, and having only one minute in sixty to bestow even on the reflection of her own felicity, in being already engaged for the evening.

Chapter 8

IN SPITE OF UDOLPHO and the dress-maker, however, the party from Pulteney Street reached the Upper Rooms in very good time. The Thorpes and James Morland were there only two minutes before them; and Isabella having gone through the usual ceremonial of meeting her friend with the most smiling and affectionate haste, of admiring the set of her gown, and envying the curl of her hair, they followed their chaperons, arm in arm, into the ballroom, whispering to each other whenever a thought occurred, and supplying the place of many ideas by a squeeze of the hand or a smile of affection.

The dancing began within a few minutes after they were seated; and James, who had been engaged quite as long as his sister, was very importunate with Isabella to stand up; but John was gone into the card-room to speak to a friend, and nothing, she declared, should induce her to join the set before her dear Catherine could join it too: 'I assure you,' said she, 'I would not stand up without your dear sister for all the world; for if I did we should certainly be separated the whole evening.' Catherine accepted this kindness with gratitude, and they continued as they were for three minutes longer, when Isabella, who had been talking to James on the other side of her, turned again to his sister and whispered, 'My dear creature, I am afraid I must leave you, your brother is so amazingly impatient to begin; I know you will not mind my going away, and I dare say John will be back in a moment, and then you may easily find me out.' Catherine, though a little disappointed, had too much good-nature to make any opposition, and the others rising up, Isabella had only time to press her friend's hand and say, 'Good-bye, my dear love,' before they hurried off. The younger Miss Thorpes being also dancing, Catherine was left to the mercy of Mrs Thorpe and Mrs Allen, between whom she now remained. She could not help being vexed at the non-appearance of Mr Thorpe, for she not only longed to be dancing, but was likewise aware that, as the real dignity of her situation could not be known, she was sharing with the scores of other young ladies still sitting down all the discredit of wanting a partner. To be disgraced in the eye of the world, to wear the appearance of infamy while her heart is all purity, her actions all innocence, and the misconduct of another the true source of her debasement, is one of those circumstances which peculiarly belong to the heroine's life, and her fortitude under it what particularly dignifies her character. Catherine had fortitude too; she suffered, but no murmur passed her lips.

From this state of humiliation, she was roused, at the end of ten minutes, to a pleasanter feeling, by seeing, not Mr Thorpe, but Mr Tilney, within three yards of the place where they sat; he seemed to be moving that way, but he did not see her, and therefore the smile and the blush, which his sudden reappearance raised in Catherine, passed away without sullying her heroic importance. He looked as handsome and as lively as ever, and was talking with interest to a fashionable and pleasing-looking young woman, who leant on his arm, and whom Catherine immediately guessed to be his sister; thus unthinkingly throwing away a fair opportunity of considering him lost to her for ever, by being married already. But guided only by what was simple and probable, it had never entered her head that Mr Tilney could be married; he had not behaved, he had not talked, like the married men to whom she had been used; he had never mentioned a wife, and he had acknowledged a sister. From these circumstances sprang the instant conclusion of his sister's now being by his side; and therefore, instead of turning of a death-like paleness, and falling in a fit on Mrs Allen's bosom, Catherine sat erect, in the perfect use of her senses, and with cheeks only a little redder than usual.

Mr Tilney and his companion, who continued, though slowly, to approach, were immediately preceded by a lady, an acquaintance of Mrs Thorpe; and this lady stopping to speak to her, they, as belonging to her, stopped likewise, and Catherine, catching Mr Tilney's eye, instantly received from him the smiling tribute of recognition. She returned it with pleasure, and then advancing still nearer, he spoke both to her and Mrs Allen, by whom he was very civilly acknowledged. 'I am

very happy to see you again, sir, indeed; I was afraid you had left Bath.'
He thanked her for her fears, and said that he had quitted it for a week,
on the very morning after his having had the pleasure of seeing her.

'Well, sir, and I dare say you are not sorry to be back again, for it is
just the place for young people – and indeed for everybody else too. I
tell Mr Allen, when he talks of being sick of it, that I am sure he should
not complain, for it is so very agreeable a place, that it is much better to
be here than at home at this dull time of year. I tell him he is quite in
luck to be sent here for his health.'

'And I hope, madam, that Mr Allen will be obliged to like the place,
from finding it of service to him.'

'Thank you, sir. I have no doubt that he will. – A neighbour of ours,
Dr Skinner, was here for his health last winter, and came away quite
stout.'

'That circumstance must give great encouragement.'

'Yes, sir – and Dr Skinner and his family were here three months; so
I tell Mr Allen he must not be in a hurry to get away.'

Here they were interrupted by a request from Mrs Thorpe to Mrs
Allen, that she would move a little to accommodate Mrs Hughes and
Miss Tilney with seats, as they had agreed to join their party. This was
accordingly done, Mr Tilney still continuing standing before them;
and after a few minutes' consideration, he asked Catherine to dance
with him. This compliment, delightful as it was, produced severe
mortification to the lady; and in giving her denial, she expressed her
sorrow on the occasion so very much as if she really felt it, that had
Thorpe, who joined her just afterwards, been half a minute earlier, he
might have thought her sufferings rather too acute. The very easy
manner in which he then told her that he had kept her waiting, did not
by any means reconcile her more to her lot; nor did the particulars
which he entered into while they were standing up, of the horses and
dogs of the friend whom he had just left, and of a proposed exchange of
terriers between them, interest her so much as to prevent her looking
very often towards that part of the room where she had left Mr Tilney.
Of her dear Isabella, to whom she particularly longed to point out that
gentleman, she could see nothing. They were in different sets. She was
separated from all her party, and away from all her acquaintance; – one
mortification succeeded another, and from the whole she deduced this
useful lesson, that to go previously engaged to a ball, does not
necessarily increase either the dignity or enjoyment of a young lady.
From such a moralising strain as this, she was suddenly roused by a
touch on the shoulder, and turning round, perceived Mrs Hughes
directly behind her, attended by Miss Tilney and a gentleman. 'I beg

your pardon, Miss Morland,' said she, 'for this liberty, – but I cannot anyhow get to Miss Thorpe, and Mrs Thorpe said she was sure you would not have the least objection to letting in this young lady by you.' Mrs Hughes could not have applied to any creature in the room more happy to oblige her than Catherine. The young ladies were introduced to each other, Miss Tilney expressing a proper sense of such goodness, Miss Morland with the real delicacy of a generous mind making light of the obligation; and Mrs Hughes, satisfied with having so respectably settled her young charge, returned to her party.

Miss Tilney had a good figure, a pretty face, and a very agreeable countenance; and her air, though it had not all the decided pretension, the resolute stylishness of Miss Thorpe's, had more real elegance. Her manners showed good sense and good breeding; they were neither shy, nor affectedly open; and she seemed capable of being young, attractive, and at a ball, without wanting to fix the attention of every man near her, and without exaggerated feelings of ecstatic delight or inconceiv- able vexation on every little trifling occurrence. Catherine, interested at once by her appearance and her relationship to Mr Tilney, was desirous of being acquainted with her, and readily talked therefore whenever she could think of anything to say, and had courage and leisure for saying it. But the hindrance thrown in the way of a very speedy intimacy, by the frequent want of one or more of these requisites, prevented their doing more than going through the first rudiments of an acquaintance, by informing themselves how well the other liked Bath, how much she admired its buildings and surrounding country, whether she drew, or played or sang, and whether she was fond of riding on horseback.

The two dances were scarcely concluded before Catherine found her arm gently seized by her faithful Isabella, who in great spirits exclaimed – 'At last I have got you. My dearest creature, I have been looking for you this hour. What could induce you to come into this set, when you knew I was in the other? I have been quite wretched without you.'

'My dear Isabella, how was it possible for me to get at you? I could not even see where you were.'

'So I told your brother all the time – but he would not believe me. Do go and see for her, Mr Morland, said I – but all in vain – he would not stir an inch. Was not it so, Mr Morland? But you men are all so immoderately lazy! I have been scolding him to such a degree, my dear Catherine, you would be quite amazed. – You know I never stand upon ceremony with such people.'

'Look at that young lady with the white beads round her head,' whispered Catherine, detaching her friend from James – 'It is Mr Tilney's sister.'

'Oh! heavens! You don't say so! Let me look at her this moment. What a delightful girl! I never saw anything half so beautiful! But where is her all-conquering brother? Is he in the room? Point him out to me this instant, if he is. I die to see him. Mr Morland, you are not to listen. We are not talking about you.'

'But what is all this whispering about? What is going on?'

'There now, I knew how it would be. You men have such restless curiosity! Talk of the curiosity of women, indeed! – 'tis nothing. But be satisfied, for you are not to know anything at all of the matter.'

'And is that likely to satisfy me, do you think?'

'Well, I declare I never knew anything like you. What can it signify to you, what we are talking of? Perhaps we are talking about you, therefore I would advise you not to listen, or you may happen to hear something not very agreeable.'

In this common-place chatter, which lasted some time, the original subject seemed entirely forgotten; and though Catherine was very well pleased to have it dropped for a while, she could not avoid a little suspicion at the total suspension of all Isabella's impatient desire to see Mr Tilney. When the orchestra struck up a fresh dance, James would have led his fair partner away, but she resisted. 'I tell you, Mr Morland,' she cried, 'I would not do such a thing for all the world. How can you be so teasing; only conceive, my dear Catherine, what your brother wants me to do. He wants me to dance with him again, though I tell him that it is a most improper thing, and entirely against the rules. It would make us the talk of the place, if we were not to change partners.'

'Upon my honour,' said James, 'in these public assemblies, it is as often done as not.'

'Nonsense, how can you say so? But when you men have a point to carry, you never stick at anything. My sweet Catherine, do support me, persuade your brother how impossible it is. Tell him, that it would quite shock you to see me do such a thing; now would not it?'

'No, not at all; but if you think it wrong, you had much better change.'

'There,' cried Isabella, 'you hear what your sister says, and yet you will not mind her. Well, remember that it is not my fault, if we set all the old ladies in Bath in a bustle. Come along, my dearest Catherine, for heaven's sake, and stand by me.' And off they went, to regain their former place. John Thorpe, in the meanwhile, had walked away; and Catherine, ever willing to give Mr Tilney an opportunity of repeating the agreeable request which had already flattered her once, made her way to Mrs Allen and Mrs Thorpe as fast as she could, in the hope of finding him still with them – a hope which, when it proved to be fruitless, she felt to have been highly unreasonable. 'Well, my dear,' said Mrs Thorpe, impatient for praise of her son, 'I hope you have had an agreeable partner.'

'Very agreeable, madam.'

'I am glad of it. John has charming spirits, has not he?'

'Did you meet Mr Tilney, my dear?' said Mrs Allen.

'No, where is he?'

'He was with us just now, and said he was so tired of lounging about, that he was resolved to go and dance; so I thought perhaps he would ask you, if he met with you.'

'Where can he be?' said Catherine, looking round; but she had not looked round long before she saw him leading a young lady to the dance.

'Ah! he has got a partner, I wish he had asked *you*,' said Mrs Allen; and after a short silence, she added, 'he is a very agreeable young man.'

'Indeed he is, Mrs Allen,' said Mrs Thorpe, smiling complacently; 'I must say it, though I *am* his mother, that there is not a more agreeable young man in the world.'

This inapplicable answer might have been too much for the comprehension of many; but it did not puzzle Mrs Allen, for after only a moment's consideration, she said, in a whisper to Catherine, 'I dare say she thought I was speaking of her son.'

Catherine was disappointed and vexed. She seemed to have missed by so little the very object she had had in view; and this persuasion did not incline her to a very gracious reply, when John Thorpe came up to her soon afterwards, and said, 'Well, Miss Morland, I suppose you and I are to stand up and jig it together again.'

'Oh, no; I am much obliged to you, our two dances are over; and, besides, I am tired, and do not mean to dance any more.'

'Do not you? – then let us walk about and quiz people. Come along with me, and I will show you the four greatest quizzers in the room; my two younger sisters and their partners. I have been laughing at them this half hour.'

Again Catherine excused herself; and at last he walked off to quiz his sisters by himself. The rest of the evening she found very dull; Mr Tilney was drawn away from their party at tea, to attend that of his partner; Miss Tilney, though belonging to it, did not sit near her, and James and Isabella were so much engaged in conversing together, that the latter had no leisure to bestow more on her friend than one smile, one squeeze, and one 'dearest Catherine.'

Chapter 9

THE PROGRESS of Catherine's unhappiness from the events of the evening, was as follows. It appeared first in a general dissatisfaction with everybody about her, while she remained in the rooms, which speedily brought on considerable weariness and a violent desire to go home. This, on arriving in Pulteney Street, took the direction of extraordinary hunger, and when that was appeased, changed into an earnest longing to be in bed; such was the extreme point of her distress; for when there she immediately fell into a sound sleep which lasted nine hours, and from which she awoke perfectly revived, in excellent spirits, with fresh hopes and fresh schemes. The first wish of her heart was to improve her acquaintance with Miss Tilney, and almost her first resolution, to seek her for that purpose, in the Pump-room at noon. In the Pump-room, one so newly arrived in Bath must be met with, and that building she had already found so favourable for the discovery of female excellence, and the completion of female intimacy, so admirably adapted for secret discourses and unlimited confidence, that she was most reasonably encouraged to expect another friend from within its walls. Her plan for the morning thus settled, she sat quietly down to her book after breakfast, resolving to remain in the same place and the same employment till the clock struck one; and from habitude very little incommoded by the remarks and ejaculations of Mrs Allen, whose vacancy of mind and incapacity for thinking were such, that as she never talked a great deal, so she could never be entirely silent; and, therefore, while she sat at her work, if she lost her needle or broke her thread, if she heard a carriage in the street, or saw a speck upon her gown, she must observe it aloud, whether there were anyone at leisure to answer her or not. At about half past twelve, a remarkably loud rap drew her in haste to the window, and scarcely had she time to inform Catherine of there being two open carriages at the door, in the first only a servant, her brother driving Miss Thorpe in the second, before John Thorpe came running upstairs, calling out, 'Well, Miss Morland, here I am. Have you been waiting long? We could not come before; the old devil of a coachmaker was such an eternity finding out a thing fit to be got into, and now it is ten thousand to one, but they break down before we are out of the street. How do you do, Mrs Allen? a famous ball last night, was not it? Come, Miss Morland, be quick, for the others are in a confounded hurry to be off. They want to get their tumble over.'

'What do you mean?' said Catherine, 'where are you all going to?'

'Going to? why, you have not forgot our engagement! Did not we agree together to take a drive this morning? What a head you have! We are going up Claverton Down.'

'Something was said about it, I remember,' said Catherine, looking at Mrs Allen for her opinion; 'but really I did not expect you.'

'Not expect me! that's a good one! And what a dust you would have made, if I had not come.'

Catherine's silent appeal to her friend, meanwhile, was entirely thrown away, for Mrs Allen, not being at all in the habit of conveying any expression herself by a look, was not aware of its being ever intended by anybody else; and Catherine, whose desire of seeing Miss Tilney again could at that moment bear a short delay in favour of a drive, and who thought there could be no impropriety in her going with Mr Thorpe, as Isabella was going at the same time with James, was therefore obliged to speak plainer. 'Well, ma'am, what do you say to it? Can you spare me for an hour or two? shall I go?'

'Do just as you please, my dear,' replied Mrs Allen, with the most placid indifference. Catherine took the advice, and ran off to get ready. In a very few minutes she re-appeared, having scarcely allowed the two others time enough to get through a few short sentences in her praise, after Thorpe had procured Mrs Allen's admiration of his gig; and then receiving her friend's parting good wishes, they both hurried downstairs. 'My dearest creature,' cried Isabella, to whom the duty of friendship immediately called her before she could get into the carriage, 'you have been at least three hours getting ready. I was afraid you were ill. What a delightful ball we had last night. I have a thousand things to say to you; but make haste and get in, for I long to be off.'

Catherine followed her orders and turned away, but not too soon to hear her friend exclaim aloud to James, 'What a sweet girl she is! I quite dote on her.'

'You will not be frightened, Miss Morland,' said Thorpe, as he handed her in, 'if my horse should dance about a little at first setting off. He will, most likely, give a plunge or two, and perhaps take the rest for a minute; but he will soon know his master. He is full of spirits, playful as can be, but there is no vice in him.'

Catherine did not think the portrait a very inviting one, but it was too late to retreat, and she was too young to own herself frightened; so, resigning herself to her fate, and trusting to the animal's boasted knowledge of its owner, she sat peaceably down, and saw Thorpe sit down by her. Everything being then arranged, the servant who stood at the horse's head was bid in an important voice 'to let him go,' and off they went in the quietest manner imaginable, without a plunge or a caper, or anything like one. Catherine, delighted at so happy an escape, spoke her pleasure aloud with grateful surprise; and her companion immediately made the matter perfectly simple by assuring her that it was entirely owing to the peculiarly judicious manner in which he had then held the reins, and the singular discernment and dexterity with which he had directed his whip. Catherine, though she could not help wondering that with such perfect command of his horse, he should think it necessary to alarm her with a relation of its tricks, congratulated herself sincerely on being under the care of so excellent a coachman; and perceiving that the animal continued to go on in the same quiet manner, without showing the smallest propensity towards any unpleasant vivacity, and (considering its inevitable pace was ten miles an hour) by no means alarmingly fast, gave herself up to all the enjoyment of air and exercise of the most invigorating kind, in a fine mild day of February, with the consciousness of safety. A silence of several minutes succeeded their first short dialogue; – it was broken by Thorpe's saying very abruptly, 'Old Allen is as rich as a Jew – is not he?' Catherine did not understand him – and he repeated his question, adding in explanation, 'Old Allen, the man you are with.'

'Oh! Mr Allen, you mean. Yes, I believe, he is very rich.'

'And no children at all?'

'No – not any.'

'A famous thing for his next heirs. He is *your* godfather, is not he?'

'My godfather! – no.'

'But you are always very much with them.'

'Yes, very much.'

'Aye, that is what I meant. He seems a good kind of old fellow enough, and has lived very well in his time, I dare say; he is not gouty for nothing. Does he drink his bottle a-day now?'

'His bottle a-day! – no. Why should you think of such a thing? He is a very temperate man, and you could not fancy him in liquor last night?'

'Lord help you! – You women are always thinking of men's being in liquor. Why you do not suppose a man is overset by a bottle? I am sure of *this* – that if everybody was to drink their bottle a-day, there would not be half the disorders in the world there are now. It would be a famous good thing for us all.'

'I cannot believe it.'

'Oh! lord, it would be the saving of thousands. There is not the hundredth part of the wine consumed in this kingdom, that there ought to be. Our foggy climate wants help.'

'And yet I have heard that there is a great deal of wine drank at Oxford.'

'Oxford! There is no drinking at Oxford now, I assure you. Nobody drinks there. You would hardly meet with a man who goes beyond his four pints at the utmost. Now, for instance, it was reckoned a remarkable thing at the last party in my rooms, that upon an average we cleared about five pints a head. It was looked upon as something out of the common way. *Mine* is famous good stuff to be sure. You would not often meet with anything like it in Oxford – and that may account for it. But this will just give you a notion of the general rate of drinking there.'

'Yes, it does give a notion,' said Catherine, warmly, 'and that is, that you all drink a great deal more wine than I thought you did. However, I am sure James does not drink so much.'

This declaration brought on a loud and overpowering reply, of which no part was very distinct, except the frequent exclamations, amounting almost to oaths, which adorned it, and Catherine was left, when it ended, with rather a strengthened belief of there being a great deal of wine drank in Oxford, and the same happy conviction of her brother's comparative sobriety.

Thorpe's ideas then all reverted to the merits of his own equipage, and she was called on to admire the spirit and freedom with which his horse moved along, and the ease which his paces, as well as the excellence of the springs, gave the motion of the carriage. She followed him in all his admiration as well as she could. To go before, or beyond him was impossible. His knowledge and her ignorance of the subject, his rapidity of expression, and her diffidence of herself put that out of her power; she could strike out nothing new in commendation, but she readily echoed whatever he chose to assert, and it was finally settled between them without any difficulty, that his equipage was altogether the most complete of its kind in England, his carriage the neatest, his horse the best goer, and himself the best coachman. – 'You do not really think, Mr Thorpe,' said Catherine, venturing after some time to consider the matter as entirely decided, and to offer some little variation on the subject, 'that James's gig will break down?'

'Break down! Oh! lord! Did you ever see such a little tittuppy thing in your life? There is not a sound piece of iron about it. The wheels have been fairly worn out these ten years at least – and as for the body! Upon my soul, you might shake it to pieces yourself with a touch. It is the most devilish little ricketty business I ever beheld! – Thank God! we have got a better. I would not be bound to go two miles in it for fifty thousand pounds.'

'Good heavens!' cried Catherine, quite frightened, 'then pray let us turn back; they will certainly meet with an accident if we go on. Do let us turn back, Mr Thorpe; stop and speak to my brother, and tell him how very unsafe it is.'

'Unsafe! Oh, lord! what is there in that? they will only get a roll if it does break down; and there is plenty of dirt, it will be excellent falling. Oh, curse it! the carriage is safe enough, if a man knows how to drive it; a thing of that sort in good hands will last above twenty years after it is fairly worn out. Lord bless you! I would undertake for five pounds to drive it to York and back again, without losing a nail.'

Catherine listened with astonishment; she knew not how to reconcile two such very different accounts of the same thing; for she had not been brought up to understand the propensities of a rattle, nor to know to how many idle assertions and impudent falsehoods the excess of vanity will lead. Her own family were plain matter-of-fact people, who seldom aimed at wit of any kind; her father, at the utmost, being contented with a pun, and her mother with a proverb; they were not in the habit therefore of telling lies to increase their importance, or of asserting at one moment what they would contradict the next. She reflected on the affair for some time in much perplexity, and was more than once on the point of requesting from Mr Thorpe a clearer insight into his real opinion on the subject; but she checked herself, because it appeared to her that he did not excel in giving those clearer insights, in making those things plain which he had before made ambiguous; and, joining to this, the consideration that he would not really suffer his sister and his friend to be exposed to a danger from which he might easily preserve them, she concluded at last, that he must know the carriage to be in fact perfectly safe, and therefore would alarm herself no longer. By him the whole matter seemed entirely forgotten; and all the rest of his conversation, or rather talk, began and ended with himself and his own concerns. He told her of horses which he had bought for a trifle and sold for incredible sums; of racing matches in which his judgment had infallibly foretold the winner; of shooting parties, in which he had killed more birds (though without having one good shot) than all his companions together; and described to her some famous day's sport, with the foxhounds, in which his foresight and skill in directing the dogs had repaired the mistakes of the most experienced huntsman, and in which the boldness of his riding, though it had never endangered his own life for a moment, had been constantly leading others into difficulties, which he calmly concluded had broken the necks of many.

Little as Catherine was in the habit of judging for herself, and unfixed as were her general notions of what men ought to be, she could not entirely repress a doubt, while she bore with the effusions of his endless conceit, of his being altogether completely agreeable. It was a bold surmise, for he was Isabella's brother; and she had been assured by James, that his manners would recommend him to all her sex; but in spite of this, the extreme weariness of his company, which crept over her before they had been out an hour, and which continued unceasingly to increase till they stopped in Pulteney Street again, induced her, in some small degree, to resist such high authority, and to distrust his powers of giving universal pleasure.

When they arrived at Mrs Allen's door, the astonishment of Isabella was hardly to be expressed, on finding that it was too late in the day for them to attend her friend into the house: – 'Past three o'clock!' it was inconceivable, incredible, impossible! and she would neither believe her own watch, nor her brother's, nor the servant's; she would believe no assurance of it founded on reason or reality, till Morland produced his watch, and ascertained the fact; to have doubted a moment longer *then*, would have been equally inconceivable, incredible, and impossible; and she could only protest, over and over again, that no two hours and a half had ever gone off so swiftly before, as Catherine was called on to confirm; Catherine could not tell a falsehood even to please Isabella; but the latter was spared the misery of her friend's dissenting voice, by not waiting for her answer. Her own feelings entirely engrossed her; her wretchedness was most acute on finding herself obliged to go directly home. – It was ages since she had had a moment's conversation with her dearest Catherine; and, though she had such thousands of things to say to her, it appeared as if they were never to be together again; so, with smiles of most exquisite misery, and the laughing eye of utter despondency, she bade her friend adieu and went on.

Catherine found Mrs Allen just returned from all the busy idleness of the morning, and was immediately greeted with, 'Well, my dear, here you are;' a truth which she had no greater inclination than power to dispute; 'and I hope you have had a pleasant airing?'

'Yes, ma'am, I thank you; we could not have had a nicer day.'

'So Mrs Thorpe said; she was vastly pleased at your all going.'

'You have seen Mrs Thorpe then?'

'Yes, I went to the Pump-room as soon as you were gone, and there I met her, and we had a great deal of talk together. She says there was hardly any veal to be got at market this morning, it is so uncommonly scarce.'

'Did you see anybody else of our acquaintance?'

'Yes; we agreed to take a turn in the Crescent, and there we met Mrs Hughes, and Mr and Miss Tilney walking with her.'

'Did you indeed? and did they speak to you?'

'Yes, we walked along the Crescent together for half an hour. They seem very agreeable people. Miss Tilney was in a very pretty spotted muslin, and I fancy, by what I can learn, that she always dresses very handsomely. Mrs Hughes talked to me a great deal about the family.'

'And what did she tell you of them?'

'Oh! a vast deal indeed; she hardly talked of anything else.'

'Did she tell you what part of Gloucestershire they come from?'

'Yes, she did; but I cannot recollect now. But they are very good kind of people, and very rich. Mrs Tilney was a Miss Drummond, and she and Mrs Hughes were school-fellows; and Miss Drummond had a very large fortune; and, when she married, her father gave her twenty thousand pounds, and five hundred to buy wedding-clothes. Mrs Hughes saw all the clothes after they came from the warehouse.'

'And are Mr and Mrs Tilney in Bath?'

'Yes, I fancy they are, but I am not quite certain. Upon recollection, however, I have a notion they are both dead; at least the mother is; yes, I am sure Mrs Tilney is dead, because Mrs Hughes told me there was a very beautiful set of pearls that Mr Drummond gave his daughter on her wedding-day and that Miss Tilney has got now, for they were put by for her when her mother died.'

'And is Mr Tilney, my partner, the only son?'

'I cannot be quite positive about that, my dear; I have some idea he is; but, however, he is a very fine young man Mrs Hughes says, and likely to do very well.'

Catherine inquired no further; she had heard enough to feel that Mrs Allen had no real intelligence to give, and that she was most particularly unfortunate herself in having missed such a meeting with both brother and sister. Could she have foreseen such a circumstance, nothing should have persuaded her to go out with the others; and, as it was, she could only lament her ill-luck, and think over what she had lost, till it was clear to her, that the drive had by no means been very pleasant and that John Thorpe himself was quite disagreeable.

Chapter 10

THE ALLENS, Thorpes, and Morlands, all met in the evening at the theatre; and, as Catherine and Isabella sat together, there was then an opportunity for the latter to utter some few of the many thousand things which had been collecting within her for communication, in the immeasurable length of time which had divided them. – 'Oh, heavens!

my beloved Catherine, have I got you at last?' was her address on Catherine's entering the box and sitting by her. 'Now, Mr Morland,' for he was close to her on the other side, 'I shall not speak another word to you all the rest of the evening; so I charge you not to expect it. My sweetest Catherine, how have you been this long age? but I need not ask you, for you look delightfully. You really have done your hair in a more heavenly style than ever: you mischievous creature, do you want to attract everybody? I assure you, my brother is quite in love with you already; and as for Mr Tilney – but that is a settled thing – even *your* modesty cannot doubt his attachment now; his coming back to Bath makes it too plain. Oh! what would not I give to see him! I really am quite wild with impatience. My mother says he is the most delightful young man in the world; she saw him this morning you know: you must introduce him to me. Is he in the house now? – Look about for heaven's sake! I assure you, I can hardly exist till I see him.'

'No,' said Catherine, 'he is not here; I cannot see him anywhere.'

'Oh, horrid! am I never to be acquainted with him? How do you like my gown? I think it does not look amiss; the sleeves were entirely my own thought. Do you know I get so immoderately sick of Bath; your brother and I were agreeing this morning that, though it is vastly well to be here for a few weeks, we would not live here for millions. We soon found out that our tastes were exactly alike in preferring the country to every other place; really, our opinions were so exactly the same, it was quite ridiculous! There was not a single point in which we differed; I would not have had you by for the world; you are such a sly thing, I am sure you would have made some droll remark or other about it.'

'No, indeed I should not.'

'Oh, yes you would indeed; I know you better than you know yourself. You would have told us that we seemed born for each other, or some nonsense of that kind, which would have distressed me beyond conception; my cheeks would have been as red as your roses; I would not have had you by for the world.'

'Indeed you do me injustice; I would not have made so improper a remark upon any account; and besides, I am sure it would never have entered my head.'

Isabella smiled incredulously, and talked the rest of the evening to James.

Catherine's resolution of endeavouring to meet Miss Tilney again continued in full force the next morning; and till the usual moment of going to the Pump-room, she felt some alarm from the dread of a second prevention. But nothing of that kind occurred, no visitors appeared to delay them, and they all three set off in good time for the

Pump-room, where the ordinary course of events and conversation took place; Mr Allen, after drinking his glass of water, joined some gentlemen to talk over the politics of the day and compare the accounts of their newspapers; and the ladies walked about together, noticing every new face, and almost every new bonnet in the room. The female part of the Thorpe family, attended by James Morland, appeared among the crowd in less than a quarter of an hour, and Catherine immediately took her usual place by the side of her friend. James, who was now in constant attendance, maintained a similar position, and separating themselves from the rest of their party, they walked in that manner for some time, till Catherine began to doubt the happiness of a situation which confining her entirely to her friend and brother, gave her very little share in the notice of either. They were always engaged in some sentimental discussion or lively dispute, but their sentiment was conveyed in such whispering voices, and their vivacity attended with so much laughter, that though Catherine's supporting opinion was not unfrequently called for by one or the other, she was never able to give any, from not having heard a word of the subject. At length however she was empowered to disengage herself from her friend, by the avowed necessity of speaking to Miss Tilney, whom she most joyfully saw just entering the room with Mrs Hughes, and whom she instantly joined, with a firmer determination to be acquainted, than she might have had courage to command, had she not been urged by the disappointment of the day before. Miss Tilney met her with great civility, returned her advances with equal good will, and they continued talking together as long as both parties remained in the room; and though in all probability not an observation was made, nor an expression used by either which had not been made and used some thousands of times before, under that roof, in every Bath season, yet the merit of their being spoken with simplicity and truth, and without personal conceit, might be something uncommon. –

'How well your brother dances!' was an artless exclamation of Catherine's towards the close of their conversation, which at once surprised and amused her companion.

'Henry!' she replied with a smile. 'Yes, he does dance very well.'

'He must have thought it very odd to hear me say I was engaged the other evening, when he saw me sitting down. But I really had been engaged the whole day to Mr Thorpe.' Miss Tilney could only bow. 'You cannot think,' added Catherine after a moment's silence, 'how surprised I was to see him again. I felt so sure of his being quite gone away.'

'When Henry had the pleasure of seeing you before, he was in Bath but for a couple of days. He came only to engage lodgings for us.'

'*That* never occurred to me; and of course, not seeing him anywhere, I thought he must be gone. Was not the young lady he danced with on Monday a Miss Smith?'

'Yes, an acquaintance of Mrs Hughes.'

'I dare say she was very glad to dance. Do you think her pretty?'

'Not very.'

'He never comes to the Pump-room, I suppose?'

'Yes, sometimes; but he has rid out this morning with my father.'

Mrs Hughes now joined them, and asked Miss Tilney if she was ready to go. 'I hope I shall have the pleasure of seeing you again soon,' said Catherine. 'Shall you be at the cotillion ball tomorrow?'

'Perhaps we – yes, I think we certainly shall.'

'I am glad of it, for we shall all be there.' – This civility was duly returned; and they parted – on Miss Tilney's side with some knowledge of her new acquaintance's feelings, and on Catherine's, without the smallest consciousness of having explained them.

She went home very happy. The morning had answered all her hopes, and the evening of the following day was now the object of expectation, the future good. What gown and what head-dress she should wear on the occasion became her chief concern. She cannot be justified in it. Dress is at all times a frivolous distinction, and excessive solicitude about it often destroys its own aim. Catherine knew all this very well; her great aunt had read her a lecture on the subject only the Christmas before; and yet she lay awake ten minutes on Wednesday night debating between her spotted and her tamboured [16] muslin, and nothing but the shortness of the time prevented her buying a new one for the evening. This would have been an error in judgment, great though not uncommon, from which one of the other sex rather than her own, a brother rather than a great aunt might have warned her, for man only can be aware of the insensibility of man towards a new gown. It would be mortifying to the feelings of many ladies, could they be made to understand how little the heart of man is affected by what is costly or new in their attire; how little it is biased by the texture of their muslin, and how unsusceptible of peculiar tenderness towards the spotted, the sprigged, the mull or the jackonet. [17] Woman is fine for her own satisfaction alone. No man will admire her the more, no woman will like her the better for it. Neatness and fashion are enough for the former, and a something of shabbiness or impropriety will be most endearing to the latter. – But not one of these grave reflections troubled the tranquillity of Catherine.

She entered the rooms on Thursday evening with feelings very different from what had attended her thither the Monday before. She had then been exulting in her engagement to Thorpe, and was now chiefly anxious to avoid his sight, lest he should engage her again; for though she could not, dared not expect that Mr Tilney should ask her a third time to dance, her wishes, hopes and plans all centred in nothing less. Every young lady may feel for my heroine in this critical moment, for every young lady has at some time or other known the same agitation. All have been, or at least all have believed themselves to be, in danger from the pursuit of someone whom they wished to avoid; and all have been anxious for the attentions of someone whom they wished to please. As soon as they were joined by the Thorpes, Catherine's agony began; she fidgeted about if John Thorpe came towards her, hid herself as much as possible from his view, and when he spoke to her pretended not to hear him. The cotillions were over, the country-dancing beginning, and she saw nothing of the Tilneys. 'Do not be frightened, my dear Catherine,' whispered Isabella, 'but I am really going to dance with your brother again. I declare positively it is quite shocking. I tell him he ought to be ashamed of himself, but you and John must keep us in countenance. Make haste, my dear creature, and come to us. John is just walked off, but he will be back in a moment.'

Catherine had neither time nor inclination to answer. The others walked away, John Thorpe was still in view, and she gave herself up for lost. That she might not appear, however, to observe or expect him, she kept her eyes intently fixed on her fan; and a self-condemnation for her folly, in supposing that among such a crowd they should even meet with the Tilneys in any reasonable time, had just passed through her mind, when she suddenly found herself addressed and again solicited to dance, by Mr Tilney himself. With what sparkling eyes and ready motion she granted his request, and with how pleasing a flutter of heart she went with him to the set, may be easily imagined. To escape, and, as she believed, so narrowly escape John Thorpe, and to be asked, so immediately on his joining her, asked by Mr Tilney, as if he had sought her on purpose! – it did not appear to her that life could supply any greater felicity.

Scarcely had they worked themselves into the quiet possession of a place, however, when her attention was claimed by John Thorpe, who stood behind her. 'Heyday, Miss Morland!' said he, 'what is the meaning of this? – I thought you and I were to dance together.'

'I wonder you should think so, for you never asked me.' 'That is a good one, by Jove! – I asked you as soon as I came into the room, and I was just going to ask you again, but when I turned round, you were gone! – this is a cursed shabby trick! I only came for the sake of dancing with *you*, and I firmly believe you were engaged to me ever since

Monday. Yes; I remember, I asked you while you were waiting in the lobby for your cloak. And here have I been telling all my acquaintance that I was going to dance with the prettiest girl in the room; and when they see you standing up with somebody else, they will quiz me famously.'

'Oh, no; they will never think of me, after such a description as that.'

'By heavens, if they do not, I will kick them out of the room for blockheads. What chap have you there?' Catherine satisfied his curiosity. 'Tilney,' he repeated, 'Hum – I do not know him. A good figure of a man; well put together. – Does he want a horse? – Here is a friend of mine, Sam Fletcher, has got one to sell that would suit anybody. A famous clever animal for the road – only forty guineas. I had fifty minds to buy it myself, for it is one of my maxims always to buy a good horse when I meet with one; but it would not answer my purpose, it would not do for the field. I would give any money for a real good hunter. I have three now, the best that ever were back'd. I would not take eight hundred guineas for them. Fletcher and I mean to get a house in Leicestershire, against the next season. It is so d— uncomfortable, living at an inn.'

This was the last sentence by which he could weary Catherine's attention, for he was just then born off by the resistless pressure of a long string of passing ladies. Her partner now drew near, and said, 'That gentleman would have put me out of patience, had he stayed with you half a minute longer. He has no business to withdraw the attention of my partner from me. We have entered into a contract of mutual agreeableness for the space of an evening, and all our agreeableness belongs solely to each other for that time. Nobody can fasten themselves on the notice of one, without injuring the rights of the other. I consider a country-dance as an emblem of marriage. Fidelity and complaisance are the principal duties of both; and those men who do not choose to dance or marry themselves, have no business with the partners or wives of their neighbours.'

'But they are such very different things! – '

' – That you think they cannot be compared together.'

'To be sure not. People that marry can never part, but must go and keep house together. People that dance, only stand opposite each other in a long room for half an hour.'

'And such is your definition of matrimony and dancing. Taken in that light certainly, their resemblance is not striking; but I think I could place them in such a view. – You will allow, that in both, man has the advantage of choice, woman only the power of refusal; that in both, it is an engagement between man and woman, formed for the advantage of each; and that when once entered into, they belong exclusively to each other till the moment of its dissolution; that it is their duty, each to endeavour to give the other no cause for wishing that he or she had bestowed themselves elsewhere, and their best interest to keep their own imaginations from wandering towards the perfections of their neighbours, or fancying that they should have been better off with anyone else. You will allow all this?'

'Yes, to be sure, as you state it, all this sounds very well; but still they are so very different. – I cannot look upon them at all in the same light, nor think the same duties belong to them.'

'In one respect, there certainly is a difference. In marriage, the man is supposed to provide for the support of the woman; the woman to make the home agreeable to the man; he is to purvey, and she is to smile. But in dancing, their duties are exactly changed; the agreeableness, the compliance are expected from him, while she furnishes the fan and the lavender water. *That*, I suppose, was the difference of duties which struck you, as rendering the conditions incapable of comparison.'

'No, indeed, I never thought of that.'

'Then I am quite at a loss. One thing, however, I must observe. This disposition on your side is rather alarming. You totally disallow any similarity in the obligations; and may I not thence infer, that your notions of the duties of the dancing state are not so strict as your partner might wish? Have I not reason to fear, that if the gentleman who spoke to you just now were to return, or if any other gentleman were to address you, there would be nothing to restrain you from conversing with him as long as you chose?'

'Mr Thorpe is such a very particular friend of my brother's, that if he talks to me, I must talk to him again; but there are hardly three young men in the room besides him, that I have any acquaintance with.'

'And is that to be my only security? alas, alas!'

'Nay, I am sure you cannot have a better; for if I do not know anybody, it is impossible for me to talk to them; and, besides, I do not *want* to talk to anybody.'

'Now you have given me a security worth having; and I shall proceed with courage. Do you find Bath as agreeable as when I had the honour of making the inquiry before?'

'Yes, quite – more so, indeed.'

'More so! – Take care, or you will forget to be tired of it at the proper time. – You ought to be tired at the end of six weeks.'

'I do not think I should be tired, if I were to stay here six months.'

'Bath, compared with London, has little variety, and so everybody finds out every year. "For six weeks, I allow Bath is pleasant enough;

but beyond *that*, it is the most tiresome place in the world." You would be told so by people of all descriptions, who come regularly every winter, lengthen their six weeks into ten or twelve, and go away at last because they can afford to stay no longer.'

'Well, other people must judge for themselves, and those who go to London may think nothing of Bath. But I, who live in a small retired village in the country, can never find greater sameness in such a place as this, than in my own home; for here are a variety of amusements, a variety of things to be seen and done all day long, which I can know nothing of there.'

'You are not fond of the country.'

'Yes, I am. I have always lived there, and always been very happy. But certainly there is much more sameness in a country life than in a Bath life. One day in the country is exactly like another.'

'But then you spend your time so much more rationally in the country.'

'Do I?'

'Do you not?'

'I do not believe there is much difference.'

'Here you are in pursuit only of amusement all day long.'

'And so I am at home – only I do not find so much of it. I walk about here, and so I do there; – but here I see a variety of people in every street, and there I can only go and call on Mrs Allen.'

Mr Tilney was very much amused. 'Only go and call on Mrs Allen!' he repeated. 'What a picture of intellectual poverty! However, when you sink into this abyss again, you will have more to say. You will be able to talk of Bath, and of all that you did here.'

'Oh! yes. I shall never be in want of something to talk of again to Mrs Allen, or anybody else. I really believe I shall always be talking of Bath, when I am at home again – I do like it so very much. If I could but have papa and mamma, and the rest of them here, I suppose I should be too happy! James's coming (my eldest brother) is quite delightful – and especially as it turns out, that the very family we are just got so intimate with, are his intimate friends already. Oh! who can ever be tired of Bath?'

'Not those who bring such fresh feelings of every sort to it, as you do. But papas and mammas, and brothers and intimate friends are a good deal gone by, to most of the frequenters of Bath – and the honest relish of balls and plays, and every-day sights, is past with them.'

Here their conversation closed; the demands of the dance becoming now too importunate for a divided attention.

Soon after their reaching the bottom of the set, Catherine perceived herself to be earnestly regarded by a gentleman who stood among the lookers-on immediately behind her partner. He was a very handsome man, of a commanding aspect, past the bloom, but not past the vigour of life; and with his eye still directed towards her, she saw him presently address Mr Tilney in a familiar whisper. Confused by his notice, and blushing from the fear of its being excited by something wrong in her appearance, she turned away her head. But while she did so, the gentleman retreated, and her partner coming nearer, said, 'I see that you guess what I have just been asked. That gentleman knows your name, and you have a right to know his. It is General Tilney, my father.'

Catherine's answer was only 'Oh!' – but it was an 'Oh!' expressing everything needful; attention to his words, and perfect reliance on their truth. With real interest and strong admiration did her eye now follow the General, as he moved through the crowd, and 'How handsome a family they are!' was her secret remark.

In chatting with Miss Tilney before the evening concluded, a new source of felicity arose to her. She had never taken a country walk since her arrival in Bath. Miss Tilney, to whom all the commonly frequented environs were familiar, spoke of them in terms which made her all eagerness to know them too; and on her openly fearing that she might find nobody to go with her, it was proposed by the brother and sister that they should join in a walk, some morning or other. 'I shall like it,' she cried, 'beyond anything in the world; and do not let us put it off – let us go tomorrow.' This was readily agreed to, with only a proviso of Miss Tilney's, that it did not rain, which Catherine was sure it would not. At twelve o'clock, they were to call for her in Pulteney Street – and 'remember – twelve o'clock,' was her parting speech to her new friend. Of her other, her older, her more established friend, Isabella, of whose fidelity and worth she had enjoyed a fortnight's experience, she scarcely saw anything during the evening. Yet, though longing to make her acquainted with her happiness, she cheerfully submitted to the wish of Mr Allen, which took them rather early away, and her spirits danced within her, as she danced in her chair all the way home.

Chapter 11

THE MORROW BROUGHT a very sober-looking morning; the sun making only a few efforts to appear; and Catherine augured from it, everything most favourable to her wishes. A bright morning, so early in the year, she allowed would generally turn to rain, but a cloudy one foretold improvement as the day advanced. She applied to Mr Allen for confirmation of her hopes, but Mr Allen not having his own skies and barometer about him, declined giving any absolute promise of sunshine. She applied to Mrs Allen, and Mrs Allen's opinion was more positive. 'She had no doubt in the world of its being a very fine day, if the clouds would only go off, and the sun keep out.'

At about eleven o'clock however, a few specks of small rain upon the windows caught Catherine's watchful eye, and 'Oh! dear, I do believe it will be wet,' broke from her in a most desponding tone.

'I thought how it would be,' said Mrs Allen.

'No walk for me today,' sighed Catherine; – 'but perhaps it may come to nothing, or it may hold up before twelve.'

'Perhaps it may, but then, my dear, it will be so dirty.'

'Oh! that will not signify; I never mind dirt.'

'No,' replied her friend very placidly, 'I know you never mind dirt.'

After a short pause, 'It comes on faster and faster!' said Catherine, as she stood watching at a window.

'So it does indeed. If it keeps raining, the streets will be very wet.'

'There are four umbrellas up already. How I hate the sight of an umbrella!'

'They are disagreeable things to carry. I would much rather take a chair at any time.'

'It was such a nice looking morning! I felt so convinced it would be dry!'

'Anybody would have thought so indeed. There will be very few people in the Pump-room, if it rains all the morning. I hope Mr Allen will put on his great coat when he goes, but I dare say he will not, for he had rather do anything in the world than walk out in a great coat; I wonder he should dislike it, it must be so comfortable.'

The rain continued – fast, though not heavy. Catherine went every five minutes to the clock, threatening on each return that, if it still kept on raining another five minutes, she would give up the matter as hopeless. The clock struck twelve, and it still rained. – 'You will not be able to go, my dear.'

'I do not quite despair yet. I shall not give it up till a quarter after twelve. This is just the time of day for it to clear up, and I do think it looks a little lighter. There, it is twenty minutes after twelve, and now I *shall* give it up entirely. Oh! that we had such weather here as they had at Udolpho, or at least in Tuscany and the South of France! – the night that poor St Aubin died! – such beautiful weather!'

At half past twelve, when Catherine's anxious attention to the weather was over, and she could no longer claim any merit from its amendment, the sky began voluntarily to clear. A gleam of sunshine took her quite by surprise; she looked round; the clouds were parting, and she instantly returned to the window to watch over and encourage the happy appearance. Ten minutes more made it certain that a bright afternoon would succeed, and justified the opinion of Mrs Allen, who had 'always thought it would clear up.' But whether Catherine might still expect her friends, whether there had not been too much rain for Miss Tilney to venture, must yet be a question.

It was too dirty for Mrs Allen to accompany her husband to the Pump-room; he accordingly set off by himself, and Catherine had barely watched him down the street, when her notice was claimed by the approach of the same two open carriages, containing the same three people that had surprised her so much a few mornings back.

'Isabella, my brother, and Mr Thorpe, I declare! They are coming for me perhaps – but I shall not go – I cannot go indeed, for you know Miss Tilney may still call.' Mrs Allen agreed to it. John Thorpe was soon with them, and his voice was with them yet sooner, for on the stairs he was calling out to Miss Morland to be quick. 'Make haste! make haste!' as he threw open the door – 'put on your hat this moment – there is no time to be lost – we are going to Bristol. – How d'ye do, Mrs Allen?'

'To Bristol! Is not that a great way off? – But, however, I cannot go with you today, because I am engaged; I expect some friends every moment.' This was of course vehemently talked down as no reason at all; Mrs Allen was called on to second him, and the two others walked in, to give their assistance. 'My sweetest Catherine, is not this delightful? We shall have a most heavenly drive. You are to thank your brother and me for the scheme; it darted into our heads at breakfast-time, I verily believe at the same instant; and we should have been off two hours ago if it had not been for this detestable rain. But it does not signify, the nights are moonlight, and we shall do delightfully. Oh! I am in such ecstasies at the thoughts of a little country air and quiet! – so much better than going to the Lower Rooms. We shall drive directly to Clifton and dine there; and, as soon as dinner is over, if there is time for it, go on to Kingsweston.'

'I doubt our being able to do so much,' said Morland.

'You croaking fellow!' cried Thorpe, 'we shall be able to do ten times more. Kingsweston! aye, and Blaize Castle too, and anything else we can hear of; but here is your sister says she will not go.'

'Blaize Castle!' cried Catherine; 'what is that?'

'The finest place in England – worth going fifty miles at any time to see.'

'What, is it really a castle, an old castle?'

'The oldest in the kingdom.'[18]

'But is it like what one reads of?'

'Exactly – the very same.'

'But now really – are there towers and long galleries?'

'By dozens.'

'Then I should like to see it; but I cannot – I cannot go.'

'Not go! – my beloved creature, what do you mean?'

'I cannot go, because' – (looking down as she spoke, fearful of Isabella's smile) 'I expect Miss Tilney and her brother to call on me to take a country walk. They promised to come at twelve, only it rained; but now, as it is so fine, I dare say they will be here soon.'

'Not they indeed,' cried Thorpe; 'for, as we turned into Broad Street, I saw them – does he not drive a phaeton with bright chesnuts?'

'I do not know indeed.'

'Yes, I know he does; I saw him. You are talking of the man you danced with last night, are not you?'

'Yes.'

'Well, I saw him at that moment turn up the Lansdown Road, – driving a smart-looking girl.'

'Did you indeed?'

'Did upon my soul; knew him again directly, and he seemed to have got some very pretty cattle too.'

'It is very odd! but I suppose they thought it would be too dirty for a walk.'

'And well they might, for I never saw so much dirt in my life. Walk! you could no more walk than you could fly! it has not been so dirty the whole winter; it is ankle-deep everywhere.'

Isabella corroborated it: – 'My dearest Catherine, you cannot form an idea of the dirt; come, you must go; you cannot refuse going now.'

'I should like to see the castle; but may we go all over it? may we go up every staircase, and into every suite of rooms?'

'Yes, yes, every hole and corner.'

'But then, – if they should only be gone out for an hour till it is drier, and call by and bye?'

'Make yourself easy, there is no danger of that, for I heard Tilney hallooing to a man who was just passing by on horseback, that they were going as far as Wick Rocks.'

'Then I will. Shall I go, Mrs Allen?'

'Just as you please, my dear.'

'Mrs Allen, you must persuade her to go,' was the general cry. Mrs Allen was not inattentive to it: – 'Well, my dear,' said she, 'suppose you go.' – And in two minutes they were off.

Catherine's feelings, as she got into the carriage, were in a very unsettled state; divided between regret for the loss of one great pleasure, and the hope of soon enjoying another, almost its equal in degree, however unlike in kind. She could not think the Tilneys had acted quite well by her, in so readily giving up their engagement, without sending her any message of excuse. It was now but an hour later than the time fixed on for the beginning of their walk; and, in spite of what she had heard of the prodigious accumulation of dirt in the course of that hour, she could not from her own observation help thinking, that they might have gone with very little inconvenience. To feel herself slighted by them was very painful. On the other hand, the delight of exploring an edifice like Udolpho, as her fancy represented Blaize Castle to be, was such a counterpoise of good, as might console her for almost anything.

They passed briskly down Pulteney Street, and through Laura Place, without the exchange of many words. Thorpe talked to his horse, and she meditated, by turns, on broken promises and broken arches, phaetons and false hangings, Tilneys and trap-doors. As they entered Argyle Buildings, however, she was roused by this address from her companion, 'Who is that girl who looked at you so hard as she went by?'

'Who? – where?'

'On the right-hand pavement – she must be almost out of sight now.' Catherine looked round and saw Miss Tilney leaning on her brother's arm, walking slowly down the street. She saw them both looking back at her. 'Stop, stop, Mr Thorpe,' she impatiently cried, 'it is Miss Tilney; it is indeed. – How could you tell me they were gone? – Stop, stop, I will get out this moment and go to them.' But to what purpose did she speak? – Thorpe only lashed his horse into a brisker trot; the Tilneys, who had soon ceased to look after her, were in a moment out of sight round the corner of Laura Place, and in another moment she was herself whisked into the Market Place. Still, however, and during the length of another street, she entreated him to stop. 'Pray, pray stop, Mr Thorpe. – I cannot go on. – I will not go on. – I must go back to Miss Tilney.' But Mr Thorpe only laughed, smacked his whip, encouraged his horse, made odd noises, and drove on; and Catherine, angry and vexed as she was, having no power of getting away, was obliged to give up the point and submit. Her reproaches, however, were not spared. 'How could you deceive me so, Mr Thorpe? – How could you say, that you saw them driving up the Lansdown Road? – I would not have had it happen so for the world. – They must think it so strange; so rude of me! to go by them, too, without saying a word! You do not know how vexed I am. – I shall have no pleasure at Clifton, nor in anything else. I had rather, ten thousand times rather get out now, and walk back to them. How could you say, you saw them driving out in a phaeton?' Thorpe defended himself very stoutly, declared he had never seen two men so much alike in his life, and would hardly give up the point of its having been Tilney himself.

Their drive, even when this subject was over, was not likely to be very agreeable. Catherine's complaisance was no longer what it had been in their former airing. She listened reluctantly, and her replies were short. Blaize Castle remained her only comfort; towards *that*, she still looked at intervals with pleasure; though rather than be disappointed of the promised walk, and especially rather than be thought ill of by the Tilneys, she would willingly have given up all the happiness which its walls could supply – the happiness of a progress through a long suite of lofty rooms, exhibiting the remains of magnificent furniture, though now for many years deserted – the happiness of being stopped in their way along narrow, winding vaults, by a low, grated door; or even of having their lamp, their only lamp, extinguished by a sudden gust of wind, and of being left in total darkness. In the meanwhile, they proceeded on their journey without any mischance; and were within view of the town of Keynsham, when a halloo from Morland, who was behind them, made his friend pull up, to know what was the matter. The others then came close enough for conversation, and Morland said, 'We had better go back, Thorpe; it is too late to go on today; your sister thinks so as well as I. We have been exactly an hour coming from Pulteney Street, very little more than seven miles; and, I suppose, we have at least eight more to go. It will never do. We set out a great deal too late. We had much better put it off till another day, and turn round.'

'It is all one to me,' replied Thorpe rather angrily; and instantly turning his horse, they were on their way back to Bath.

'If your brother had not got such a d— beast to drive,' said he soon afterwards, 'we might have done it very well. My horse would have trotted to Clifton within the hour, if left to himself, and I have almost broke my arm with pulling him in to that cursed broken-winded jade's pace. Morland is a fool for not keeping a horse and gig of his own.'

'No, he is not,' said Catherine warmly, 'for I am sure he could not afford it.'

'And why cannot he afford it?'

'Because he has not money enough.'

'And whose fault is that?'

'Nobody's, that I know of.' Thorpe then said something in the loud, incoherent way to which he had often recourse, about its being a d—

thing to be miserly; and that if people who rolled in money could not afford things, he did not know who could; which Catherine did not even endeavour to understand. Disappointed of what was to have been the consolation for her first disappointment, she was less and less disposed either to be agreeable herself, or to find her companion so; and they returned to Pulteney Street without her speaking twenty words.

As she entered the house, the footman told her, that a gentleman and lady had called and inquired for her a few minutes after her setting off; that, when he told them she was gone out with Mr Thorpe, the lady had asked whether any message had been left for her; and on his saying no, had felt for a card, but said she had none about her, and went away. Pondering over these heart-rending tidings, Catherine walked slowly upstairs. At the head of them she was met by Mr Allen, who, on hearing the reason of their speedy return, said, 'I am glad your brother had so much sense; I am glad you are come back. It was a strange, wild scheme.'

They all spent the evening together at Thorpe's. Catherine was disturbed and out of spirits; but Isabella seemed to find a pool of commerce, in the fate of which she shared, by private partnership with Morland, a very good equivalent for the quiet and country air of an inn at Clifton. Her satisfaction, too, in not being at the Lower Rooms, was spoken more than once. 'How I pity the poor creatures that are going there! How glad I am that I am not amongst them! I wonder whether it will be a full ball or not! They have not begun dancing yet. I would not be there for all the world. It is so delightful to have an evening now and then to oneself. I dare say it will not be a very good ball. I know the Mitchells will not be there. I am sure I pity everybody that is. But I dare say, Mr Morland, you long to be at it, do not you? I am sure you do. Well, pray do not let anybody here be a restraint on you. I dare say we could do very well without you; but you men think yourselves of such consequence.'

Catherine could almost have accused Isabella of being wanting in tenderness towards herself and her sorrows; so very little did they appear to dwell on her mind, and so very inadequate was the comfort she offered. 'Do not be so dull, my dearest creature,' she whispered. 'You will quite break my heart. It was amazingly shocking to be sure; but the Tilneys were entirely to blame. Why were not they more punctual? It was dirty, indeed, but what did that signify? I am sure John and I should not have minded it. I never mind going through anything, where a friend is concerned; that is my disposition, and John is just the same; he has amazing strong feelings. Good heavens! what a delightful hand you have got! Kings, I vow! I never was so happy in my life! I would fifty times rather you should have them than myself.'

And now I may dismiss my heroine to the sleepless couch, which is the true heroine's portion; to a pillow strewed with thorns and wet with tears. And lucky may she think herself, if she get another good-night's rest in the course of the next three months.

Chapter 12

'MRS ALLEN,' said Catherine the next morning, 'will there be any harm in my calling on Miss Tilney today? I shall not be easy till I have explained everything.'

'Go by all means, my dear; only put on a white gown; Miss Tilney always wears white.'

Catherine cheerfully complied; and being properly equipped, was more impatient than ever to be at the Pump-room, that she might inform herself of General Tilney's lodgings, for though she believed they were in Milsom Street, she was not certain of the house, and Mrs Allen's wavering convictions only made it more doubtful. To Milsom Street she was directed; and having made herself perfect in the number, hastened away with eager steps and a beating heart to pay her visit, explain her conduct, and be forgiven; tripping lightly through the church-yard, and resolutely turning away her eyes, that she might not be obliged to see her beloved Isabella and her dear family, who, she had reason to believe, were in a shop hard by. She reached the house without any impediment, looked at the number, knocked at the door, and inquired for Miss Tilney. The man believed Miss Tilney to be at home, but was not quite certain. Would she be pleased to send up her name? She gave her card. In a few minutes the servant returned, and with a look which did not quite confirm his words, said he had been mistaken, for that Miss Tilney was walked out. Catherine, with a blush of mortification, left the house. She felt almost persuaded that Miss Tilney *was* at home, and too much offended to admit her; and as she retired down the street, could not withhold one glance at the drawing-room windows, in expectation of seeing her there, but no one appeared at them. At the bottom of the street, however, she looked back again, and then, not at a window, but issuing from the door, she saw Miss Tilney herself. She was followed by a gentleman, whom Catherine believed to be her father, and they turned up towards Edgar's Build-ings. Catherine, in deep mortification, proceeded on her way. She could almost be angry herself at such angry incivility; but she checked the resentful sensation; she remembered her own ignorance. She knew not how such an offence as hers might be classed by the laws of worldly politeness, to what a degree of unforgivingness it might with propriety lead, nor to what rigours of rudeness in return it might justly make her amenable.

Dejected and humbled, she had even some thoughts of not going with the others to the theatre that night; but it must be confessed that they were not of long continuance: for she soon recollected, in the first place, that she was without any excuse for staying at home; and, in the second, that it was a play she wanted very much to see. To the theatre accordingly they all went; no Tilneys appeared to plague or please her; she feared that, amongst the many perfections of the family, a fondness for plays was not to be ranked; but perhaps it was because they were habituated to the finer performances of the London stage, which she knew, on Isabella's authority, rendered everything else of the kind 'quite horrid.' She was not deceived in her own expectation of pleasure; the comedy so well suspended her care, that no one, observing her during the first four acts, would have supposed she had any wretchedness about her. On the beginning of the fifth, however, the sudden view of Mr Henry Tilney and his father, joining a party in the opposite box, recalled her to anxiety and distress. The stage could no longer excite genuine merriment – no longer keep her whole attention. Every other look upon an average was directed towards the opposite box; and, for the space of two entire scenes, did she thus watch Henry Tilney, without being once able to catch his eye. No longer could he be suspected of indifference for a play; his notice was never withdrawn from the stage during two whole scenes. At length, however, he did look towards her, and he bowed – but such a bow! no smile, no continued observance attended it; his eyes were immediately returned to their former direction. Catherine was restlessly miserable; she could almost have run round to the box in which he sat, and forced him to hear her explanation. Feelings rather natural than heroic possessed her; instead of considering her own dignity injured by this ready condemnation – instead of proudly resolving, in conscious innocence, to show her resentment towards him who could harbour a doubt of it, to leave to him all the trouble of seeking an explanation, and to enlighten him on the past only by avoiding his sight, or flirting with somebody else, she took to herself all the shame of misconduct, or at least of its appearance, and was only eager for an opportunity of explaining its cause.

The play concluded – the curtain fell – Henry Tilney was no longer to be seen where he had hitherto sat, but his father remained, and perhaps he might be now coming round to their box. She was right; in a few minutes he appeared, and, making his way through the then thinning rows, spoke with like calm politeness to Mrs Allen and her friend. – Not with such calmness was he answered by the latter: 'Oh! Mr Tilney, I have been quite wild to speak to you, and make my apologies. You must have thought me so rude; but indeed it was not my own fault, – was it, Mrs Allen? Did not they tell me that Mr Tilney and his sister were gone out in a phaeton together? and then what could I do? But I had ten thousand times rather have been with you; now had not I, Mrs Allen?'

'My dear, you tumble my gown,' was Mrs Allen's reply.

Her assurance, however, standing sole as it did, was not thrown away; it brought a more cordial, more natural smile into his countenance, and he replied in a tone which retained only a little affected reserve: – 'We were much obliged to you at any rate for wishing us a pleasant walk after our passing you in Argyle Street: you were so kind as to look back on purpose.'

'But indeed I did not wish you a pleasant walk; I never thought of such a thing; but I begged Mr Thorpe so earnestly to stop; I called out to him as soon as ever I saw you; now, Mrs Allen, did not – Oh! you were not there; but indeed I did; and, if Mr Thorpe would only have stopped, I would have jumped out and run after you.'

Is there a Henry in the world who could be insensible to such a declaration? Henry Tilney at least was not. With a yet sweeter smile, he said everything that need be said of his sister's concern, regret, and dependence on Catherine's honour. – 'Oh! do not say Miss Tilney was not angry,' cried Catherine, 'because I know she was; for she would not see me this morning when I called; I saw her walk out of the house the next minute after my leaving it; I was hurt, but I was not affronted. Perhaps you did not know I had been there.'

'I was not within at the time; but I heard of it from Eleanor, and she has been wishing ever since to see you, to explain the reason of such incivility; but perhaps I can do it as well. It was nothing more than that my father – they were just preparing to walk out, and he being hurried for time, and not caring to have it put off, made a point of her being denied. That was all, I do assure you. She was very much vexed, and meant to make her apology as soon as possible.'

Catherine's mind was greatly eased by this information, yet a something of solicitude remained, from which sprang the following question, thoroughly artless in itself, though rather distressing to the gentleman: – 'But, Mr Tilney, why were *you* less generous than your sister? If she felt such confidence in my good intentions, and could suppose it to be only a mistake, why should *you* be so ready to take offence?'

'Me! – I take offence!'

'Nay, I am sure by your look, when you came into the box, you were angry.'

'I angry! I could have no right.'

'Well, nobody would have thought you had no right who saw your face.' He replied by asking her to make room for him, and talking of the play.

He remained with them some time, and was only too agreeable for Catherine to be contented when he went away. Before they parted, however, it was agreed that the projected walk should be taken as soon as possible; and, setting aside the misery of his quitting their box, she was, upon the whole, left one of the happiest creatures in the world.

While talking to each other, she had observed with some surprise, that John Thorpe, who was never in the same part of the house for ten minutes together, was engaged in conversation with General Tilney; and she felt something more than surprise, when she thought she could perceive herself the object of their attention and discourse. What could they have to say of her? She feared General Tilney did not like her appearance: she found it was implied in his preventing her admittance to his daughter, rather than postpone his own walk a few minutes. 'How came Mr Thorpe to know your father?' was her anxious inquiry, as she pointed them out to her companion. He knew nothing about it; but his father, like every military man, had a very large acquaintance.

When the entertainment was over, Thorpe came to assist them in getting out. Catherine was the immediate object of his gallantry; and, while they waited in the lobby for a chair, he prevented the inquiry which had travelled from her heart almost to the tip of her tongue, by asking, in a consequential manner, whether she had seen him talking with General Tilney: – 'He is a fine old fellow, upon my soul! – stout, active, – looks as young as his son. I have a great regard for him, I assure you: a gentleman-like, good sort of fellow as ever lived.'

'But how came you to know him?'

'Know him! – There are few people much about town that I do not know. I have met him for ever at the Bedford; and I knew his face again today the moment he came into the billiard-room. One of the best players we have, by the bye; and we had a little touch together, though I was almost afraid of him at first: the odds were five to four against me; and, if I had not made one of the cleanest strokes that perhaps ever was made in this world – I took his ball exactly – but I could not make you understand it without a table; – however I *did* beat him. A very fine fellow; as rich as a Jew. I should like to dine with him; I dare say he gives famous dinners. But what do you think we have been talking of? – You.

Yes, by heavens! – and the General thinks you the finest girl in Bath.'

'Oh! nonsense! how can you say so?'

'And what do you think I said?' (lowering his voice) 'Well done, General, said I, I am quite of your mind.'

Here, Catherine, who was much less gratified by his admiration than by General Tilney's, was not sorry to be called away by Mr Allen. Thorpe, however, would see her to her chair, and, till she entered it, continued the same kind of delicate flattery, in spite of her entreating him to have done.

That General Tilney, instead of disliking, should admire her, was very delightful; and she joyfully thought, that there was not one of the family whom she need now fear to meet. – The evening had done more, much more, for her, than could have been expected.

Chapter 13

MONDAY, Tuesday, Wednesday, Thursday, Friday and Saturday have now passed in review before the reader; the events of each day, its hopes and fears, mortifications and pleasures have been separately stated, and the pangs of Sunday only now remain to be described, and close the week. The Clifton scheme had been deferred, not relinquished, and on the afternoon's Crescent of this day, it was brought forward again. In a private consultation between Isabella and James, the former of whom had particularly set her heart upon going, and the latter no less anxiously placed his upon pleasing her, it was agreed that, provided the weather were fair, the party should take place on the following morning; and they were to set off very early, in order to be at home in good time. The affair thus determined, and Thorpe's approbation secured, Catherine only remained to be apprised of it. She had left them for a few minutes to speak to Miss Tilney. In that interval the plan was completed, and as soon as she came again, her agreement was demanded; but instead of the gay acquiescence expected by Isabella, Catherine looked grave, was very sorry, but could not go. The engagement which ought to have kept her from joining in the former attempt, would make it impossible for her to accompany them now. She had that moment settled with Miss Tilney to take their promised walk tomorrow; it was quite determined, and she would not, upon any account, retract. But that she *must* and *should* retract, was instantly the eager cry of both the Thorpes; they must go to Clifton tomorrow, they would not go without her, it would be nothing to put off a mere walk for one day longer, and they would not hear of a refusal. Catherine was distressed, but not subdued. 'Do not urge me, Isabella. I am engaged to Miss Tilney. I cannot go.' This availed nothing. The same arguments assailed her again; she must go, she should go, and they would not hear of a refusal. 'It would be so easy to tell Miss Tilney that you had just been reminded of a prior engagement, and must only beg to put off the walk till Tuesday.'

'No, it would not be easy. I could not do it. There has been no prior engagement.' But Isabella became only more and more urgent; calling on her in the most affectionate manner; addressing her by the most endearing names. She was sure her dearest, sweetest Catherine would not seriously refuse such a trifling request to a friend who loved her so dearly. She knew her beloved Catherine to have so feeling a heart, so sweet a temper, to be so easily persuaded by those she loved. But all in vain; Catherine felt herself to be in the right, and though pained by such tender, such flattering supplication, could not allow it to influence her. Isabella then tried another method. She reproached her with having more affection for Miss Tilney, though she had known her so little a while, than for her best and oldest friends; with being grown cold and indifferent, in short, towards herself. 'I cannot help being jealous, Catherine, when I see myself slighted for strangers, I, who love you so excessively! When once my affections are placed, it is not in the power of anything to change them. But I believe my feelings are stronger than anybody's; I am sure they are too strong for my own peace; and to see myself supplanted in your friendship by strangers, does cut me to the quick, I own. These Tilneys seem to swallow up everything else.'

Catherine thought this reproach equally strange and unkind. Was it the part of a friend thus to expose her feelings to the notice of others? Isabella appeared to her ungenerous and selfish, regardless of everything but her own gratification. These painful ideas crossed her mind, though she said nothing. Isabella, in the meanwhile, had applied her handkerchief to her eyes; and Morland, miserable at such a sight, could not help saying, 'Nay, Catherine. I think you cannot stand out any longer now. The sacrifice is not much; and to oblige such a friend – I shall think you quite unkind, if you still refuse.'

This was the first time of her brother's openly siding against her, and anxious to avoid his displeasure, she proposed a compromise. If they would only put off their scheme till Tuesday, which they might easily do, as it depended only on themselves, she could go with them, and everybody might then be satisfied. But 'No, no, no!' was the immediate answer; 'that could not be, for Thorpe did not know that he might not go to town on Tuesday.' Catherine was sorry, but could do no more; and a short silence ensued, which was broken by Isabella; who in a voice of cold resentment said, 'Very well, then there is an end of the party. If Catherine does not go, I cannot. I cannot be the only woman. I would not, upon any account in the world, do so improper a thing.'

'Catherine, you must go,' said James.

'But why cannot Mr Thorpe drive one of his other sisters? I dare say either of them would like to go.'

'Thank ye,' cried Thorpe, 'but I did not come to Bath to drive my sisters about, and look like a fool. No, if you do not go, d— me if I do. I only go for the sake of driving you.'

'That is a compliment which gives me no pleasure.' But her words were lost on Thorpe, who had turned abruptly away.

The three others still continued together, walking in a most uncomfortable manner to poor Catherine; sometimes not a word was said, sometimes she was again attacked with supplications or reproaches, and her arm was still linked within Isabella's, though their hearts were at war. At one moment she was softened, at another irritated; always distressed, but always steady.

'I did not think you had been so obstinate, Catherine,' said James; 'you were not used to be so hard to persuade; you once were the kindest, best-tempered of my sisters.'

'I hope I am not less so now,' she replied, very feelingly; 'but indeed I cannot go. If I am wrong, I am doing what I believe to be right.'

'I suspect,' said Isabella, in a low voice, 'there is no great struggle.'

Catherine's heart swelled; she drew away her arm, and Isabella made no opposition. Thus passed a long ten minutes, till they were again joined by Thorpe, who coming to them with a gayer look, said, 'Well, I have settled the matter, and now we may all go tomorrow with a safe conscience. I have been to Miss Tilney, and made your excuses.'

'You have not!' cried Catherine.

'I have, upon my soul. Left her this moment. Told her you had sent me to say, that having just recollected a prior engagement of going to Clifton with us tomorrow, you could not have the pleasure of walking with her till Tuesday. She said very well, Tuesday was just as convenient to her; so there is an end of all our difficulties. – A pretty good thought of mine – hey?'

Isabella's countenance was once more all smiles and good-humour, and James too looked happy again.

'A most heavenly thought indeed! Now, my sweet Catherine, all our distresses are over; you are honourably acquitted, and we shall have a most delightful party.'

'This will not do,' said Catherine; 'I cannot submit to this. I must run after Miss Tilney directly and set her right.'

Isabella, however, caught hold of one hand; Thorpe of the other; and remonstrances poured in from all three. Even James was quite angry. When everything was settled, when Miss Tilney herself said that Tuesday would suit her as well, it was quite ridiculous, quite absurd to make any further objection.

'I do not care. Mr Thorpe had no business to invent any such message. If I had thought it right to put it off, I could have spoken to Miss Tilney myself. This is only doing it in a ruder way; and how do I know that Mr Thorpe has – he may be mistaken again perhaps; he led me into one act of rudeness by his mistake on Friday. Let me go, Mr Thorpe; Isabella, do not hold me.'

Thorpe told her it would be in vain to go after the Tilneys; they were turning the corner into Brock Street, when he had overtaken them, and were at home by this time.

'Then I will go after them,' said Catherine; 'wherever they are I will go after them. It does not signify talking. If I could not be persuaded into doing what I thought wrong, I never will be tricked into it.' And with these words she broke away and hurried off. Thorpe would have darted after her, but Morland withheld him. 'Let her go, let her go, if she will go.'

'She is as obstinate as – '

Thorpe never finished the simile, for it could hardly have been a proper one.

Away walked Catherine in great agitation, as fast as the crowd would permit her, fearful of being pursued, yet determined to persevere. As she walked, she reflected on what had passed. It was painful to her to disappoint and displease them, particularly to displease her brother; but she could not repent her resistance. Setting her own inclination apart, to have failed a second time in her engagement to Miss Tilney, to have retracted a promise voluntarily made only five minutes before, and on a false pretence too, must have been wrong. She had not been withstanding them on selfish principles alone, she had not consulted merely her own gratification; *that* might have been ensured in some degree by the excursion itself, by seeing Blaize Castle; no, she had attended to what was due to others, and to her own character in their opinion. Her conviction of being right however was not enough to restore her composure, till she had spoken to Miss Tilney she could not be at ease; and quickening her pace when she got clear of the Crescent, she almost ran over the remaining ground till she gained the top of Milsom Street. So rapid had been her movements, that in spite of the Tilneys' advantage in the outset, they were but just turning into their lodgings as she came within view of them; and the servant still remaining at the open door, she used only the ceremony of saying that she must speak with Miss Tilney that moment, and hurrying by him proceeded upstairs. Then, opening the first door before her, which happened to be the right, she immediately found herself in the drawing-room with General Tilney, his son and daughter. Her explanation, defective only in being – from her irritation of nerves and shortness of breath – no explanation at all, was instantly given. 'I am come in a great hurry – It was all a mistake – I never promised to go – I told them from the first I could not go. – I ran away in a great hurry to explain it. – I did not care what you thought of me. – I would not stay for the servant.'

The business however, though not perfectly elucidated by this speech, soon ceased to be a puzzle. Catherine found that John Thorpe *had* given the message; and Miss Tilney had no scruple in owning herself greatly surprised by it. But whether her brother had still exceeded her in resentment, Catherine, though she instinctively addressed herself as much to one as to the other in her vindication, had no means of knowing. Whatever might have been felt before her arrival, her eager declarations immediately made every look and sentence as friendly as she could desire.

The affair thus happily settled, she was introduced by Miss Tilney to her father, and received by him with such ready, such solicitous politeness as recalled Thorpe's information to her mind, and made her think with pleasure that he might be sometimes depended on. To such anxious attention was the general's civility carried, that not aware of her extraordinary swiftness in entering the house, he was quite angry with the servant whose neglect had reduced her to open the door of the apartment herself. 'What did William mean by it? He should make a point of inquiring into the matter.' And if Catherine had not most warmly asserted his innocence, it seemed likely that William would lose the favour of his master for ever, if not his place, by her rapidity.

After sitting with them a quarter of an hour, she rose to take leave, and was then most agreeably surprised by General Tilney's asking her if she would do his daughter the honour of dining and spending the rest of the day with her. Miss Tilney added her own wishes. Catherine was greatly obliged; but it was quite out of her power. Mr and Mrs Allen would expect her back every moment. The general declared he could say no more; the claims of Mr and Mrs Allen were not to be superseded; but on some other day he trusted, when longer notice could be given, they would not refuse to spare her to her friend. 'Oh, no; Catherine was sure they would not have the least objection, and she should have great pleasure in coming.' The general attended her himself to the street-door, saying everything gallant as they went downstairs, admiring the elasticity of her walk, which corresponded exactly with the spirit of her dancing, and making her one of the most graceful bows she had ever beheld, when they parted.

Catherine, delighted by all that had passed, proceeded gaily to Pulteney Street; walking, as she concluded, with great elasticity, though she had never thought of it before. She reached home without seeing anything more of the offended party; and now that she had been triumphant throughout, had carried her point and was secure of her walk, she began (as the flutter of her spirits subsided) to doubt whether she had been perfectly right. A sacrifice was always noble; and if she had given way to their entreaties, she would have been spared the distressing idea of a friend displeased, a brother angry, and a scheme of great happiness to both destroyed, perhaps through her means. To ease her mind, and ascertain by the opinion of an unprejudiced person what her own conduct had really been, she took occasion to mention before Mr Allen the half-settled scheme of her brother and the Thorpes for the following day. Mr Allen caught at it directly. 'Well,' said he, 'and do you think of going too?'

'No; I had just engaged myself to walk with Miss Tilney before they told me of it; and therefore you know I could not go with them, could I?'

'No, certainly not; and I am glad you do not think of it. These schemes are not at all the thing. Young men and women driving about the country in open carriages! Now and then it is very well; but going to inns and public places together! It is not right; and I wonder Mrs Thorpe should allow it. I am glad you do not think of going; I am sure Mrs Morland would not be pleased. Mrs Allen, are not you of my way of thinking? Do not you think these kind of projects objectionable?'

'Yes, very much so indeed. Open carriages are nasty things. A clean gown is not five minutes wear in them. You are splashed getting in and getting out; and the wind takes your hair and your bonnet in every direction. I hate an open carriage myself.'

'I know you do; but that is not the question. Do not you think it has an odd appearance, if young ladies are frequently driven about in them by young men, to whom they are not even related?'

'Yes, my dear, a very odd appearance indeed. I cannot bear to see it.'

'Dear madam,' cried Catherine, 'then why did not you tell me so before? I am sure if I had known it to be improper, I would not have gone with Mr Thorpe at all; but I always hoped you would tell me, if you thought I was doing wrong.'

'And so I should, my dear, you may depend on it; for as I told Mrs

Morland at parting, I would always do the best for you in my power. But one must not be over particular. Young people *will* be young people, as your good mother says herself. You know I wanted you, when we first came, not to buy that sprigged muslin, but you would. Young people do not like to be always thwarted.'

'But this was something of real consequence; and I do not think you would have found me hard to persuade.'

'As far as it has gone hitherto, there is no harm done,' said Mr Allen; 'and I would only advise you, my dear, not to go out with Mr Thorpe any more.'

'That is just what I was going to say,' added his wife.

Catherine, relieved for herself, felt uneasy for Isabella; and after a moment's thought, asked Mr Allen whether it would not be both proper and kind in her to write to Miss Thorpe, and explain the indecorum of which she must be as insensible as herself; for she considered that Isabella might otherwise perhaps be going to Clifton the next day, in spite of what had passed. Mr Allen however discouraged her from doing any such thing. 'You had better leave her alone, my dear, she is old enough to know what she is about; and if not, has a mother to advise her. Mrs Thorpe is too indulgent beyond a doubt; but however you had better not interfere. She and your brother choose to go, and you will be only getting ill-will.'

Catherine submitted; and though sorry to think that Isabella should be doing wrong, felt greatly relieved by Mr Allen's approbation of her own conduct, and truly rejoiced to be preserved by his advice from the danger of falling into such an error herself. Her escape from being one of the party to Clifton was now an escape indeed; for what would the Tilneys have thought of her, if she had broken her promise to them in order to do what was wrong in itself? if she had been guilty of one breach of propriety, only to enable her to be guilty of another?

Chapter 14

THE NEXT MORNING was fair, and Catherine almost expected another attack from the assembled party. With Mr Allen to support her, she felt no dread of the event: but she would gladly be spared a contest, where victory itself was painful; and was heartily rejoiced therefore at neither seeing nor hearing anything of them. The Tilneys called for her at the appointed time; and no new difficulty arising, no sudden recollection, no unexpected summons, no impertinent intrusion to disconcert their measures, my heroine was most unnaturally able to fulfil her engagement, though it was made with the hero himself. They determined on walking round Beechen Cliff, that noble hill, whose beautiful verdure and hanging coppice render it so striking an object from almost every opening in Bath.

'I never look at it,' said Catherine, as they walked along the side of the river, 'without thinking of the south of France.'

'You have been abroad then?' said Henry, a little surprised.

'Oh! no, I only mean what I have read about. It always puts me in mind of the country that Emily and her father travelled through, in the "Mysteries of Udolpho." But you never read novels, I dare say?'

'Why not?'

'Because they are not clever enough for you – gentlemen read better books.'

'The person, be it gentleman or lady, who has not pleasure in a good novel, must be intolerably stupid. I have read all Mrs Radcliffe's works, and most of them with great pleasure. The Mysteries of Udolpho, when I had once begun it, I could not lay down again; – I remember finishing it in two days – my hair standing on end the whole time.'

'Yes,' added Miss Tilney, 'and I remember that you undertook to read it aloud to me, and that when I was called away for only five minutes to answer a note, instead of waiting for me, you took the volume into the Hermitage Walk, and I was obliged to stay till you had finished it.'

'Thank you, Eleanor; – a most honourable testimony. You see, Miss Morland, the injustice of your suspicions. Here was I, in my eagerness to get on, refusing to wait only five minutes for my sister; breaking the promise I had made of reading it aloud, and keeping her in suspense at a most interesting part, by running away with the volume, which, you are to observe, was her own, particularly her own. I am proud when I reflect on it, and I think it must establish me in your good opinion.'

'I am very glad to hear it indeed, and now I shall never be ashamed of liking Udolpho myself. But I really thought before, young men despised novels amazingly.'

'It is *amazingly*; it may well suggest *amazement* if they do – for they read nearly as many as women. I myself have read hundreds and hundreds. Do not imagine that you can cope with me in a knowledge of Julias and Louisas. If we proceed to particulars, and engage in the never-ceasing inquiry of "Have you read this?" and "Have you read that?" I shall soon leave you as far behind me as – what shall I say? – I want an appropriate simile; – as far as your friend Emily herself left poor Valancourt when she went with her aunt into Italy. Consider how many years I have had the start of you. I had entered on my studies at Oxford, while you were a good little girl working your sampler at home!'

'Not very good I am afraid. But now really, do not you think Udolpho the nicest book in the world?'

'The nicest; – by which I suppose you mean the neatest. That must depend upon the binding.'

'Henry,' said Miss Tilney, 'you are very impertinent. Miss Morland, he is treating you exactly as he does his sister. He is for ever finding fault with me, for some incorrectness of language, and now he is taking the same liberty with you. The word "nicest," as you used it, did not suit him; and you had better change it as soon as you can, or we shall be overpowered with Johnson and Blair[19] all the rest of the way.'

'I am sure,' cried Catherine, 'I did not mean to say anything wrong; but it *is* a nice book, and why should not I call it so?'

'Very true,' said Henry, 'and this is a very nice day, and we are taking a very nice walk, and you are two very nice young ladies. Oh! it is a very nice word indeed! – it does for everything. Originally perhaps it was applied only to express neatness, propriety, delicacy, or refinement; – people were nice in their dress, in their sentiments, or their choice. But now every commendation on every subject is comprised in that one word.'

'While, in fact,' cried his sister, 'it ought only to be applied to you, without any commendation at all. You are more nice than wise. Come, Miss Morland, let us leave him to meditate over our faults in the utmost propriety of diction, while we praise Udolpho in whatever terms we like best. It is a most interesting work. You are fond of that kind of reading?'

'To say the truth, I do not much like any other.'

'Indeed!'

'That is, I can read poetry and plays, and things of that sort, and do not dislike travels. But history, real solemn history, I cannot be interested in. Can you?'

'Yes, I am fond of history.'

'I wish I were too. I read it a little as a duty, but it tells me nothing that does not either vex or weary me. The quarrels of popes and kings, with wars or pestilences, in every page; the men all so good for nothing, and hardly any women at all – it is very tiresome: and yet I often think it odd that it should be so dull, for a great deal of it must be invention. The speeches that are put into the heroes' mouths, their thoughts and designs – the chief of all this must be invention, and invention is what delights me in other books.'

'Historians, you think,' said Miss Tilney, 'are not happy in their flights of fancy. They display imagination without raising interest. I am fond of history – and am very well contented to take the false with the true. In the principal facts they have sources of intelligence in former histories and records, which may be as much depended on, I conclude, as anything that does not actually pass under one's own observation; and as for the little embellishments you speak of, they are embellishments, and I like them as such. If a speech be well drawn up, I read it with pleasure, by whomsoever it may be made – and probably with much greater, if the production of Mr Hume or Mr Robertson, than if the genuine words of Caractacus, Agricola, or Alfred the Great.'

'You are fond of history! – and so are Mr Allen and my father; and I have two brothers who do not dislike it. So many instances within my small circle of friends is remarkable! At this rate, I shall not pity the writers of history any longer. If people like to read their books, it is all very well, but to be at so much trouble in filling great volumes, which, as I used to think, nobody would willingly ever look into, to be labouring only for the torment of little boys and girls, always struck me as a hard fate; and though I know it is all very right and necessary, I have often wondered at the person's courage that could sit down on purpose to do it.'

'That little boys and girls should be tormented,' said Henry, 'is what no one at all acquainted with human nature in a civilised state can deny; but in behalf of our most distinguished historians, I must observe, that they might well be offended at being supposed to have no higher aim; and that by their method and style, they are perfectly well qualified to torment readers of the most advanced reason and mature time of life. I use the verb "to torment," as I observed to be your own method, instead of "to instruct," supposing them to be now admitted as synonymous.'

'You think me foolish to call instruction a torment, but if you had been as much used as myself to hear poor little children first learning their letters and then learning to spell, if you had ever seen how stupid they can be for a whole morning together, and how tired my poor mother is at the end of it, as I am in the habit of seeing almost every day of my life at home, you would allow that to *torment* and to *instruct* might sometimes be used as synonymous words.'

'Very probably. But historians are not accountable for the difficulty of learning to read; and even you yourself, who do not altogether seem particularly friendly to very severe, very intense application, may perhaps be brought to acknowledge that it is very well worth while to be tormented for two or three years of one's life, for the sake of being able to read all the rest of it. Consider – if reading had not been taught, Mrs Radcliffe would have written in vain – or perhaps might not have written at all.'

Catherine assented – and a very warm panegyric from her on that lady's merits, closed the subject. – The Tilneys were soon engaged in another on which she had nothing to say. They were viewing the country with the eyes of persons accustomed to drawing, and decided on its capability of being formed into pictures, with all the eagerness of real taste. Here Catherine was quite lost. She knew nothing of drawing – nothing of taste: – and she listened to them with an attention which brought her little profit, for they talked in phrases which conveyed scarcely any idea to her. The little which she could understand however appeared to contradict the very few notions she had entertained on the matter before. It seemed as if a good view were no longer to be taken from the top of an high hill, and that a clear blue sky was no longer a proof of a fine day. She was heartily ashamed of her ignorance. A misplaced shame. Where people wish to attach, they should always be ignorant. To come with a well-informed mind, is to come with an inability of administering to the vanity of others, which a sensible person would always wish to avoid. A woman especially, if she have the misfortune of knowing anything, should conceal it as well as she can.

The advantages of natural folly in a beautiful girl have been already set forth by the capital pen of a sister author, – and to her treatment of the subject I will only add in justice to men, that though to the larger and more trifling part of the sex, imbecility in females is a great enhancement of their personal charms, there is a portion of them too reasonable and too well informed themselves to desire anything more in woman than ignorance. But Catherine did not know her own advantages – did not know that a good-looking girl, with an affectionate heart and a very ignorant mind, cannot fail of attracting a clever young man, unless circumstances are particularly untoward. In the present instance, she confessed and lamented her want of knowledge; declared that she would give anything in the world to be able to draw; and a lecture on the picturesque immediately followed, in which his instructions were so clear that she soon began to see beauty in everything admired by him, and her attention was so earnest, that he became perfectly satisfied of her having a great deal of natural taste. He talked of fore-grounds, distances, and second distances – side-screens and perspectives – lights and shades; – and Catherine was so hopeful a scholar, that when they gained the top of Beechen Cliff, she voluntarily rejected the whole city of Bath, as unworthy to make part of a landscape. Delighted with her progress, and fearful of wearying her with too much wisdom at once, Henry suffered the subject to decline, and by an easy transition from a piece of rocky fragment and the withered oak which he had placed near its summit, to oaks in general, to forests, the inclosure of them, waste lands, crown lands and government, he shortly found himself arrived at politics; and from politics, it was an easy step to silence. The general pause which succeeded his short disquisition on the state of the nation, was put an end to by Catherine, who, in rather a solemn tone of voice, uttered these words, 'I have heard that something very shocking indeed, will soon come out in London.'

Miss Tilney, to whom this was chiefly addressed, was startled, and hastily replied, 'Indeed! – and of what nature?'

'That I do not know, nor who is the author. I have only heard that it is to be more horrible than anything we have met with yet.'

'Good heaven! – Where could you hear of such a thing?'

'A particular friend of mine had an account of it in a letter from London yesterday. It is to be uncommonly dreadful. I shall expect murder and everything of the kind.'

'You speak with astonishing composure! But I hope your friend's accounts have been exaggerated; – and if such a design is known beforehand, proper measures will undoubtedly be taken by government to prevent its coming to effect.'

'Government,' said Henry, endeavouring not to smile, 'neither desires nor dares to interfere in such matters. There must be murder; and government cares not how much.'

The ladies stared. He laughed, and added, 'Come, shall I make you understand each other, or leave you to puzzle out an explanation as you can? No – I will be noble. I will prove myself a man, no less by the generosity of my soul than the clearness of my head. I have no patience with such of my sex as disdain to let themselves sometimes down to the comprehension of yours. Perhaps the abilities of women are neither sound not acute – neither vigorous nor keen. Perhaps they may want observation, discernment, judgment, fire, genius, and wit.'

'Miss Morland, do not mind what he says; – but have the goodness to satisfy me as to this dreadful riot.'

'Riot! – what riot?'

'My dear Eleanor, the riot is only in your own brain. The confusion there is scandalous. Miss Morland has been talking of nothing more dreadful than a new publication which is shortly to come out, in three duodecimo volumes, two hundred and seventy-six pages in each, with a frontispiece to the first, of two tombstones and a lantern – do you understand? – And you, Miss Morland – my stupid sister has mistaken all your clearest expressions. You talked of expected horrors in London – and instead of instantly conceiving, as any rational creature would have done, that such words could relate only to a circulating library, she immediately pictured to herself a mob of three thousand men assembling in St George's Fields; the Bank attacked, the Tower threatened, the streets of London flowing with blood, a detachment of the 12th Light Dragoons, (the hopes of the nation,) called up from Northampton to quell the insurgents, and the gallant Capt. Frederick Tilney, in the moment of charging at the head of his troop, knocked off his horse by a brickbat from an upper window. Forgive her stupidity. The fears of the sister have added to the weakness of the woman; but she is by no means a simpleton in general.'

Catherine looked grave. 'And now, Henry,' said Miss Tilney, 'that you have made us understand each other, you may as well make Miss Morland understand yourself – unless you mean to have her think you intolerably rude to your sister, and a great brute in your opinion of women in general. Miss Morland is not used to your odd ways.'

'I shall be most happy to make her better acquainted with them.'

'No doubt; – but that is no explanation of the present.'

'What am I to do?'

'You know what you ought to do. Clear your character handsomely before her. Tell her that you think very highly of the understanding of women.'

'Miss Morland, I think very highly of the understanding of all the women in the world – especially of those – whoever they may be – with whom I happen to be in company.'

'That is not enough. Be more serious.'

'Miss Morland, no one can think more highly of the understanding of women than I do. In my opinion, nature has given them so much, that they never find it necessary to use more than half.'

'We shall get nothing more serious from him now, Miss Morland. He is not in a sober mood. But I do assure you that he must be entirely misunderstood, if he can ever appear to say an unjust thing of any woman at all, or an unkind one of me.'

It was no effort to Catherine to believe that Henry Tilney could never be wrong. His manner might sometimes surprise, but his meaning must always be just: – and what she did not understand, she was almost as ready to admire, as what she did. The whole walk was delightful, and though it ended too soon, its conclusion was delightful too; – her friends attended her into the house, and Miss Tilney, before they parted, addressing herself with respectful form, as much to Mrs Allen as to Catherine, petitioned for the pleasure of her company to dinner on the day after the next. No difficulty was made on Mrs Allen's side – and the only difficulty on Catherine's was in concealing the excess of her pleasure.

The morning had passed away so charmingly as to banish all her friendship and natural affection; for no thought of Isabella or James had crossed her during their walk. When the Tilneys were gone, she became amiable again, but she was amiable for some time to little effect; Mrs Allen had no intelligence to give that could relieve her anxiety, she had heard nothing of any of them. Towards the end of the morning however, Catherine having occasion for some indispensable yard of ribbon which must be bought without a moment's delay, walked out into the town, and in Bond Street overtook the second Miss Thorpe, as she was loitering towards Edgar's Buildings between two of the sweetest girls in the world, who had been her dear friends all the morning. From her, she soon learned that the party to Clifton had taken place. 'They set off at eight this morning,' said Miss Anne, 'and I am sure I do not envy them their drive. I think you and I are very well off to be out of the scrape. – It must be the dullest thing in the world, for there is not a soul at Clifton at this time of year. Belle went with your brother, and John drove Maria.'

Catherine spoke the pleasure she really felt on hearing this part of the arrangement.

'Oh! yes,' rejoined the other, 'Maria is gone. She was quite wild to go. She thought it would be something very fine. I cannot say I admire her taste; and for my part I was determined from the first not to go, if they pressed me ever so much.'

Catherine, a little doubtful of this, could not help answering, 'I wish you could have gone too. It is a pity you could not all go.'

'Thank you; but it is quite a matter of indifference to me. Indeed, I would not have gone on any account. I was saying so to Emily and Sophia when you overtook us.'

Catherine was still unconvinced; but glad that Anne should have the friendship of an Emily and a Sophia to console her, she bade her adieu without much uneasiness, and returned home, pleased that the party had not been prevented by her refusing to join it, and very heartily wishing that it might be too pleasant to allow either James or Isabella to resent her resistance any longer.

Chapter 15

EARLY THE NEXT DAY, a note from Isabella, speaking peace and tenderness in every line, and entreating the immediate presence of her friend on a matter of the utmost importance, hastened Catherine, in the happiest state of confidence and curiosity, to Edgar's Buildings. – The two youngest Miss Thorpes were by themselves in the parlour; and, on Anne's quitting it to call her sister, Catherine took the opportunity of asking the other for some particulars of their yesterday's party. Maria desired no greater pleasure than to speak of it; and Catherine immediately learnt that it had been altogether the most delightful scheme in the world; that nobody could imagine how charming it had been, and that it had been more delightful than anybody could conceive. Such was the information of the first five minutes; the second unfolded thus much in detail, – that they had driven directly to the York Hotel, ate some soup, and bespoke an early dinner, walked down to the Pump-room, tasted the water, and laid out some shillings in purses and spars; thence adjourned to eat ice at a pastry-cook's, and hurrying back to the Hotel, swallowed their dinner in haste, to prevent being in the dark; and then had a delightful drive back, only the moon was not up, and it rained a little, and Mr Morland's horse was so tired he could hardly get along.

Catherine listened with heartfelt satisfaction. It appeared that Blaize Castle had never been thought of; and, as for all the rest, there was nothing to regret for half an instant. – Maria's intelligence concluded with a tender effusion of pity for her sister Anne, whom she represented as insupportably cross, from being excluded the party.

'She will never forgive me, I am sure; but, you know, how could I help it? John would have me go, for he vowed he would not drive her, because she had such thick ankles. I dare say she will not be in good humour again this month; but I am determined I will not be cross; it is not a little matter that puts me out of temper.'

Isabella now entered the room with so eager a step, and a look of such happy importance, as engaged all her friend's notice. Maria was without ceremony sent away, and Isabella, embracing Catherine, thus began: – 'Yes, my dear Catherine, it is so indeed; your penetration has not deceived you. – Oh! that arch eye of yours! – It sees through everything.'

Catherine replied only by a look of wondering ignorance.

'Nay, my beloved, sweetest friend,' continued the other, 'compose yourself. – I am amazingly agitated, as you perceive. Let us sit down and talk in comfort. Well, and so you guessed it the moment you had my note? – Sly creature! – Oh! my dear Catherine, you alone who know my heart can judge of my present happiness. Your brother is the most charming of men. I only wish I were more worthy of him. – But what will your excellent father and mother say? – Oh! heavens! when I think of them I am so agitated!'

Catherine's understanding began to wake: an idea of the truth suddenly darted into her mind; and, with the natural blush of so new an emotion, she cried out, 'Good heaven! – my dear Isabella, what do you mean? Can you – can you really be in love with James?'

This bold surmise, however, she soon learnt comprehended but half the fact. The anxious affection, which she was accused of having continually watched in Isabella's every look and action, had, in the course of their yesterday's party, received the delightful confession of an equal love. Her heart and faith were alike engaged to James. – Never had Catherine listened to anything so full of interest, wonder, and joy. Her brother and her friend engaged! – New to such circumstances, the importance of it appeared unspeakably great, and she contemplated it as one of those grand events, of which the ordinary course of life can hardly afford a return. The strength of her feelings she could not express; the nature of them, however, contented her friend. The happiness of having such a sister was their first effusion, and the fair ladies mingled in embraces and tears of joy.

Delighting, however, as Catherine sincerely did in the prospect of the connection, it must be acknowledged that Isabella far surpassed her in tender anticipations. – 'You will be so infinitely dearer to me, my Catherine, than either Anne or Maria: I feel that I shall be so much more attached to my dear Morland's family than to my own.'

This was a pitch of friendship beyond Catherine.

'You are so like your dear brother,' continued Isabella, 'that I quite doted on you the first moment I saw you. But so it always is with me; the first moment settles everything. The very first day that Morland came to us last Christmas – the very first moment I beheld him – my heart was irrecoverably gone. I remember I wore my yellow gown, with my hair done up in braids; and when I came into the drawing-room, and John introduced him, I thought I never saw anybody so handsome before.'

Here Catherine secretly acknowledged the power of love; for, though exceedingly fond of her brother, and partial to all his endowments, she had never in her life thought him handsome.

'I remember too, Miss Andrews drank tea with us that evening, and wore her puce-coloured sarsenet; and she looked so heavenly, that I thought your brother must certainly fall in love with her; I could not sleep a wink all night for thinking of it. Oh! Catherine, the many sleepless nights I have had on your brother's account! – I would not have you suffer half what I have done! I am grown wretchedly thin I know; but I will not pain you by describing my anxiety; you have seen enough of it. I feel that I have betrayed myself perpetually; – so unguarded in speaking of my partiality for the church! – But my secret I was always sure would be safe with *you*.'

Catherine felt that nothing could have been safer; but ashamed of an ignorance little expected, she dared no longer contest the point, nor refuse to have been as full of arch penetration and affectionate sympathy as Isabella chose to consider her. Her brother she found was preparing to set off with all speed to Fullerton, to make known his situation and ask consent; and here was a source of some real agitation to the mind of Isabella. Catherine endeavoured to persuade her, as she was herself persuaded, that her father and mother would never oppose their son's wishes. – 'It is impossible,' said she, 'for parents to be more kind, or more desirous of their children's happiness; I have no doubt of their consenting immediately.'

'Morland says exactly the same,' replied Isabella; 'and yet I dare not expect it; my fortune will be so small; they never can consent to it. Your brother, who might marry anybody!'

Here Catherine again discerned the force of love.

'Indeed, Isabella, you are too humble. – The difference of fortune can be nothing to signify.'

'Oh! my sweet Catherine, in *your* generous heart I know it would signify nothing; but we must not expect such disinterestedness in many. As for myself, I am sure I only wish our situations were reversed. Had I the command of millions, were I mistress of the whole world, your brother would be my only choice.'

This charming sentiment, recommended as much by sense as novelty, gave Catherine a most pleasing remembrance of all the heroines of her acquaintance; and she thought her friend never looked more lovely than in uttering the grand idea. – 'I am sure they will consent,' was her frequent declaration; 'I am sure they will be delighted with you.'

'For my own part,' said Isabella, 'my wishes are so moderate, that the smallest income in nature would be enough for me. Where people are really attached, poverty itself is wealth: grandeur I detest: I would not settle in London for the universe. A cottage in some retired village would be ecstasy. There are some charming little villas about Richmond.'

'Richmond!' cried Catherine. – 'You must settle near Fullerton. You must be near us.'

'I am sure I shall be miserable if we do not. If I can but be near *you*, I shall be satisfied. But this is idle talking! I will not allow myself to think of such things, till we have your father's answer. Morland says that by sending it tonight to Salisbury, we may have it tomorrow. – Tomorrow? – I know I shall never have courage to open the letter. I know it will be the death of me.'

A reverie succeeded this conviction – and when Isabella spoke again, it was to resolve on the quality of her wedding-gown.

Their conference was put an end to by the anxious young lover himself, who came to breathe his parting sigh before he set off for Wiltshire. Catherine wished to congratulate him, but knew not what to say, and her eloquence was only in her eyes. From them however the eight parts of speech shone out most expressively, and James could combine them with ease. Impatient for the realisation of all that he hoped at home, his adieus were not long; and they would have been yet shorter, had he not been frequently detained by the urgent entreaties of his fair one that he would go. Twice was he called almost from the door by her eagerness to have him gone. 'Indeed, Morland, I must drive you away. Consider how far you have to ride. I cannot bear to see you linger so. For Heaven's sake, waste no more time. There, go, go – I insist on it.'

The two friends, with hearts now more united than ever, were inseparable for the day; and in schemes of sisterly happiness the hours flew along. Mrs Thorpe and her son, who were acquainted with everything, and who seemed only to want Mr Morland's consent, to consider Isabella's engagement as the most fortunate circumstance imaginable for their family, were allowed to join their counsels, and add their quota of significant looks and mysterious expressions to fill up the measure of curiosity to be raised in the unprivileged younger sisters. To Catherine's simple feelings, this odd sort of reserve seemed neither kindly meant, nor consistently supported; and its unkindness she would hardly have forborn pointing out, had its inconsistency been less their friend, – but Anne and Maria soon set her heart at ease by the sagacity of their 'I know what;' and the evening was spent in a sort of war of wit, a display of family ingenuity; on one side in the mystery of an affected secret, on the other of undefined discovery, all equally acute.

Catherine was with her friend again the next day, endeavouring to support her spirits, and while away the many tedious hours before the delivery of the letters; a needful exertion, for as the time of reasonable expectation drew near, Isabella became more and more desponding, and before the letter arrived, had worked herself into a state of real distress. But when it did come, where could distress be found? 'I have had no difficulty in gaining the consent of my kind parents, and am promised that everything in their power shall be done to forward my happiness,' were the first three lines, and in one moment all was joyful security. The brightest glow was instantly spread over Isabella's features, all care and anxiety seemed removed, her spirits became almost too high for control, and she called herself without scruple the happiest of mortals.

Mrs Thorpe, with tears of joy, embraced her daughter, her son, her visitor, and could have embraced half the inhabitants of Bath with satisfaction. Her heart was overflowing with tenderness. It was 'dear John,' and 'dear Catherine' at every word; – 'dear Anne and dear Maria' must immediately be made sharers in their felicity; and two 'dears' at once before the name of Isabella were not more than that beloved child had now well earned. John himself was no skulker in joy. He not only bestowed on Mr Morland the high commendation of being one of the finest fellows in the world, but swore off many sentences in his praise.

The letter, whence sprang all this felicity, was short, containing little more than this assurance of success; and every particular was deferred till James could write again. But for particulars Isabella could well afford to wait. The needful was comprised in Mr Morland's promise; his honour was pledged to make everything easy; and by what means their income was to be formed, whether landed property were to be resigned, or funded money made over, was a matter in which her disinterested spirit took no concern. She knew enough to feel secure of an honourable and speedy establishment, and her imagination took a rapid flight over its attendant felicities. She saw herself at the end of a few weeks, the gaze and admiration of every new acquaintance at Fullerton, the envy of every valued old friend in Putney, with a carriage at her command, a new name on her tickets, and a brilliant exhibition of hoop rings on her finger.

When the contents of the letter were ascertained, John Thorpe, who had only waited its arrival to begin his journey to London, prepared to set off. 'Well, Miss Morland,' said he, on finding her alone in the parlour, 'I am come to bid you good-bye.' Catherine wished him a good journey. Without appearing to hear her, he walked to the window, fidgeted about, hummed a tune, and seemed wholly self-occupied.

'Shall not you be late at Devizes?' said Catherine. He made no answer; but after a minute's silence burst out with, 'A famous good thing this marrying scheme upon my soul! A clever fancy of Morland's and Belle's. What do you think of it, Miss Morland? *I* say it is no bad notion.'

'I am sure I think it a very good one.'

'Do you? – that's honest, by heavens! I am glad you are no enemy to matrimony however. Did you ever hear the old song, "Going to one wedding brings on another?" I say, you will come to Belle's wedding, I hope.'

'Yes; I have promised your sister to be with her, if possible.'

'And then you know' – twisting himself about and forcing a foolish laugh – 'I say, then you know, we may try the truth of this same old song.'

'May we? – but I never sing. Well, I wish you a good journey. I dine with Miss Tilney today, and must now be going home.'

'Nay, but there is no such confounded hurry. – Who knows when we may be together again? – Not but that I shall be down again by the end of a fortnight, and a devilish long fortnight it will appear to me.'

'Then why do you stay away so long?' replied Catherine – finding that he waited for an answer.

'That is kind of you, however – kind and good-natured. – I shall not forget it in a hurry. – But you have more good-nature and all that, than anybody living I believe. A monstrous deal of good-nature, and it is not only good-nature, but you have so much, so much of everything; and then you have such – upon my soul I do not know anybody like you.'

'Oh! dear, there are a great many people like me, I dare say, only a good deal better. Good-morning to you.'

'But I say, Miss Morland, I shall come and pay my respects at Fullerton before it is long, if not disagreeable.'

'Pray do. – My father and mother will be very glad to see you.'

'And I hope – I hope, Miss Morland, *you* will not be sorry to see me.'

'Oh! dear, not at all. There are very few people I am sorry to see. Company is always cheerful.'

'That is just my way of thinking. Give me but a little cheerful company, let me only have the company of the people I love, let me only be where I like and with whom I like, and the devil take the rest, say I. – And I am heartily glad to hear you say the same. But I have a notion, Miss Morland, you and I think pretty much alike upon most matters.'

'Perhaps we may; but it is more than I ever thought of. And as to *most matters*, to say the truth, there are not many that I know my own mind about.'

'By Jove, no more do I. It is not my way to bother my brains with what does not concern me. My notion of things is simple enough. Let me only have the girl I like, say I, with a comfortable house over my head, and what care I for all the rest? Fortune is nothing. I am sure of a good income of my own; and if she had not a penny, why so much the better.'

'Very true. I think like you there. If there is a good fortune on one side, there can be no occasion for any on the other. No matter which has it, so that there is enough. I hate the idea of one great fortune looking out for another. And to marry for money I think the wickedest thing in existence. – Good day. – We shall be very glad to see you at Fullerton, whenever it is convenient.' And away she went. It was not in the power of all his gallantry to detain her longer. With such news to communicate, and such a visit to prepare for, her departure was not to be delayed by anything in his nature to urge; and she hurried away, leaving him to the undivided consciousness of his own happy address, and her explicit encouragement.

The agitation which she had herself experienced on first learning her brother's engagement, made her expect to raise no inconsiderable emotion in Mr and Mrs Allen, by the communication of the wonderful event. How great was her disappointment! The important affair, which many words of preparation ushered in, had been foreseen by them both ever since her brother's arrival; and all that they felt on the occasion was comprehended in a wish for the young people's happiness, with a remark, on the gentleman's side, in favour of Isabella's beauty, and on the lady's, of her great good luck. It was to Catherine the most surprising insensibility. The disclosure however of the great secret of James's going to Fullerton the day before, did raise some emotion in Mrs Allen. She could not listen to that with perfect calmness; but repeatedly regretted the necessity of its concealment, wished she could have known his intention, wished she could have seen him before he went, as she should certainly have troubled him with her best regards to his father and mother, and her kind compliments to all the Skinners.

Chapter 16

CATHERINE'S EXPECTATIONS of pleasure from her visit in Milsom Street were so very high, that disappointment was inevitable; and accordingly, though she was most politely received by General Tilney, and kindly welcomed by his daughter, though Henry was at home, and no one else of the party, she found, on her return, without spending many hours in the examination of her feelings, that she had gone to her appointment preparing for happiness which it had not afforded. Instead of finding herself improved in acquaintance with Miss Tilney, from the intercourse of the day, she seemed hardly so intimate with her as before; instead of seeing Henry Tilney to greater advantage than ever, in the ease of a family party, he had never said so little, nor been so little agreeable; and, in spite of their father's great civilities to her – in spite of his thanks, invitations, and compliments – it had been a release to get away from him. It puzzled her to account for all this. It could not be General Tilney's fault. That he was perfectly agreeable and good-natured, and altogether a very charming man, did not admit of a doubt, for he was tall and handsome, and Henry's father. *He* could not be accountable for his children's want of spirits, or for her want of enjoyment in his company. The former she hoped at last might have been accidental, and the latter she could only attribute to her own stupidity. Isabella, on hearing the particulars of the visit, gave a different explanation: 'It was all pride, pride, insufferable haughtiness and pride! She had long suspected the family to be very high, and this made it certain. Such insolence of behaviour as Miss Tilney's she had never heard of in her life! Not to do the honours of her house with common good-breeding! – To behave to her guest with such supercili-ousness! – Hardly even to speak to her!'

'But it was not so bad as that, Isabella; there was no superciliousness; she was very civil.'

'Oh! don't defend her! And then the brother, he, who had appeared so attached to you! Good heavens! well, some people's feelings are incomprehensible. And so he hardly looked once at you the whole day?'

'I do not say so; but he did not seem in good spirits.'

'How contemptible! Of all things in the world inconstancy is my aversion. Let me entreat you never to think of him again, my dear Catherine; indeed he is unworthy of you.'

'Unworthy! I do not suppose he ever thinks of me.'

'That is exactly what I say; he never thinks of you. – Such fickleness! Oh! how different to your brother and to mine! I really believe John has the most constant heart.'

'But as for General Tilney, I assure you it would be impossible for anybody to behave to me with greater civility and attention; it seemed to be his only care to entertain and make me happy.'

'Oh! I know no harm of him; I do not suspect him of pride. I believe he is a very gentleman-like man. John thinks very well of him, and John's judgment –'

'Well, I shall see how they behave to me this evening; we shall meet them at the rooms.'

'And must I go?'

'Do not you intend it? I thought it was all settled.'

'Nay, since you make such a point of it, I can refuse you nothing. But do not insist upon my being very agreeable, for my heart, you know, will be some forty miles off. And as for dancing, do not mention it I beg; *that* is quite out of the question. Charles Hodges will plague me to death I dare say; but I shall cut him very short. Ten to one but he guesses the reason, and that is exactly what I want to avoid, so I shall insist on his keeping his conjecture to himself.'

Isabella's opinion of the Tilneys did not influence her friend; she was sure there had been no insolence in the manners either of brother or sister; and she did not credit there being any pride in their hearts. The evening rewarded her confidence; she was met by one with the same kindness, and by the other with the same attention as heretofore: Miss Tilney took pains to be near her, and Henry asked her to dance.

Having heard the day before in Milsom Street, that their elder brother, Captain Tilney, was expected almost every hour, she was at no loss for the name of a very fashionable-looking, handsome young man, whom she had never seen before, and who now evidently belonged to their party. She looked at him with great admiration, and even supposed it possible, that some people might think him handsomer than his brother, though, in her eyes, his air was more assuming, and his countenance less prepossessing. His taste and manners were beyond a doubt decidedly inferior; for, within her hearing, he not only protested against every thought of dancing himself, but even laughed openly at Henry for finding it possible. From the latter circumstance it may be presumed, that, whatever might be our heroine's opinion of him, his admiration of her was not of a very dangerous kind; not likely to produce animosities between the brothers, nor persecutions to the lady. *He* cannot be the instigator of the three villains in horsemen's great coats, by whom she will hereafter be forced into a travelling chaise and four, which will drive off with incredible speed. Catherine, meanwhile, undisturbed by presentiments of such an evil, or of any evil at all, except that of having but a short set to dance down, enjoyed her usual happiness with Henry Tilney, listening with sparkling eyes to everything he said; and, in finding him irresistible, becoming so herself.

At the end of the first dance, Captain Tilney came towards them again, and, much to Catherine's dissatisfaction, pulled his brother away. They retired whispering together; and, though her delicate sensibility did not take immediate alarm, and lay it down as fact, that Captain Tilney must have heard some malevolent misrepresentation of her, which he now hastened to communicate to his brother, in the hope of separating them for ever, she could not have her partner conveyed from her sight without very uneasy sensations. Her suspense was of full five minutes' duration; and she was beginning to think it a very long quarter of an hour, when they both returned, and an explanation was given, by Henry's requesting to know, if she thought her friend, Miss Thorpe, would have any objection to dancing, as his brother would be most happy to be introduced to her. Catherine, without hesitation, replied, that she was very sure Miss Thorpe did not mean to dance at all. The cruel reply was passed on to the other, and he immediately walked away.

'Your brother will not mind it I know,' said she, 'because I heard him say before, that he hated dancing; but it was very good-natured in him to think of it. I suppose he saw Isabella sitting down, and fancied she might wish for a partner; but he is quite mistaken, for she would not dance upon any account in the world.'

Henry smiled, and said, 'How very little trouble it can give you to understand the motive of other people's actions.'

'Why? – What do you mean?'

'With you, it is not, How is such a one likely to be influenced? What is the inducement most likely to act upon such a person's feelings, age, situation, and probable habits of life considered? – but, how should *I* be influenced, what would be *my* inducement in acting so and so?'

'I do not understand you.'

'Then we are on very unequal terms, for I understand you perfectly well.'

'Me? – yes; I cannot speak well enough to be unintelligible.'

'Bravo! – an excellent satire on modern language.'

'But pray tell me what you mean.'

'Shall I indeed? – Do you really desire it? – But you are not aware of the consequences; it will involve you in a very cruel embarrassment, and certainly bring on a disagreement between us.'

'No, no; it shall not do either; I am not afraid.'

'Well then, I only meant that your attributing my brother's wish of dancing with Miss Thorpe to good-nature alone, convinced me of your being superior in good-nature yourself to all the rest of the world.'

Catherine blushed and disclaimed, and the gentleman's predictions were verified. There was a something, however, in his words which repaid her for the pain of confusion; and that something occupied her mind so much, that she drew back for some time, forgetting to speak or to listen, and almost forgetting where she was; till, roused by the voice of Isabella, she looked up and saw her with Captain Tilney preparing to give them hands across.

Isabella shrugged her shoulders and smiled, the only explanation of this extraordinary change which could at that time be given; but as it was not quite enough for Catherine's comprehension, she spoke her astonishment in very plain terms to her partner.

'I cannot think how it could happen! Isabella was so determined not to dance.'

'And did Isabella never change her mind before?'

'Oh! but, because – and your brother! – After what you told him from me, how could he think of going to ask her?'

'I cannot take surprise to myself on that head. You bid me be surprised on your friend's account, and therefore I am; but as for my brother, his conduct in the business, I must own, has been no more than I believed him perfectly equal to. The fairness of your friend was an open attraction; her firmness, you know, could only be understood by yourself.'

'You are laughing; but, I assure you, Isabella is very firm in general.'

'It is as much as should be said of anyone. To be always firm must be to be often obstinate. When properly to relax is the trial of judgment; and, without reference to my brother, I really think Miss Thorpe has by no means chosen ill in fixing on the present hour.'

The friends were not able to get together for any confidential discourse till all the dancing was over; but then, as they walked about the room arm in arm, Isabella thus explained herself: – 'I do not wonder at your surprise; and I am really fatigued to death. He is such a rattle! – Amusing enough, if my mind had been disengaged; but I would have given the world to sit still.'

'Then why did not you?'

'Oh! my dear! it would have looked so particular; and you know how I abhor doing that. I refused him as long as I possibly could, but he would take no denial. You have no idea how he pressed me. I begged him to excuse me, and get some other partner – but no, not he; after aspiring to my hand, there was nobody else in the room he could bear to think of; and it was not that he wanted merely to dance, he wanted to be with *me*. Oh! such nonsense! – I told him he had taken a very unlikely way to prevail upon me; for, of all things in the world, I hated fine speeches and compliments; – and so – and so then I found there would be no peace if I did not stand up. Besides, I thought Mrs Hughes, who introduced him, might take it ill if I did not: and your dear brother, I am sure he would have been miserable if I had sat down the whole evening. I am so glad it is over! My spirits are quite jaded with listening to his nonsense: and then, – being such a smart young fellow, I saw every eye was upon us.'

'He is very handsome indeed.'

'Handsome! – Yes, I suppose he may. I dare say people would admire him in general; but he is not at all in my style of beauty. I hate a florid complexion and dark eyes in a man. However, he is very well. Amazingly conceited, I am sure. I took him down several times you know in my way.'

When the young ladies next met, they had a far more interesting subject to discuss. James Morland's second letter was then received, and the kind intentions of his father fully explained. A living, of which Mr Morland was himself patron and incumbent, of about four hundred pounds yearly value, was to be resigned to his son as soon as he should be old enough to take it; no trifling deduction from the family income, no niggardly assignment to one of ten children. An estate of at least equal value, moreover, was assured as his future inheritance.

James expressed himself on the occasion with becoming gratitude; and the necessity of waiting between two and three years before they could marry, being, however unwelcome, no more than he had expected, was born by him without discontent. Catherine, whose expectations had been as unfixed as her ideas of her father's income, and whose judgment was now entirely led by her brother, felt equally well satisfied, and heartily congratulated Isabella on having everything so pleasantly settled.

'It is very charming indeed,' said Isabella, with a grave face. 'Mr Morland has behaved vastly handsome indeed,' said the gentle Mrs Thorpe, looking anxiously at her daughter. 'I only wish I could do as much. One could not expect more from him you know. If he finds he *can* do more by and bye, I dare say he will, for I am sure he must be an excellent good-hearted man. Four hundred is but a small income to begin on indeed, but your wishes, my dear Isabella, are so moderate, you do not consider how little you ever want, my dear.'

'It is not on my own account I wish for more; but I cannot bear to be the means of injuring my dear Morland, making him sit down upon an income hardly enough to find one in the common necessaries of life. For myself, it is nothing; I never think of myself.'

'I know you never do, my dear; and you will always find your reward in the affection it makes everybody feel for you. There never was a young woman so beloved as you are by everybody that knows you; and I dare say when Mr Morland sees you, my dear child – but do not let us distress our dear Catherine by talking of such things. Mr Morland has behaved so very handsome you know. I always heard he was a most excellent man; and you know, my dear, we are not to suppose but what, if you had had a suitable fortune, he would have come down with something more, for I am sure he must be a most liberal-minded man.'

'Nobody can think better of Mr Morland than I do, I am sure. But everybody has their failing you know, and everybody has a right to do what they like with their own money.' Catherine was hurt by these insinuations. 'I am very sure,' said she, 'that my father has promised to do as much as he can afford.'

Isabella recollected herself. 'As to that, my sweet Catherine, there cannot be a doubt, and you know me well enough to be sure that a much smaller income would satisfy me. It is not the want of more money that makes me just at present a little out of spirits; I hate money; and if our union could take place now upon only fifty pounds a year, I should not have a wish unsatisfied. Ah! my Catherine, you have found me out. There's the sting. The long, long, endless two years and half that are to pass before your brother can hold the living.'

'Yes, yes, my darling Isabella,' said Mrs Thorpe, 'we perfectly see into your heart. You have no disguise. We perfectly understand the present vexation; and everybody must love you the better for such a noble honest affection.'

Catherine's uncomfortable feelings began to lessen. She endeavoured to believe that the delay of the marriage was the only source of Isabella's regret; and when she saw her at their next interview as cheerful and amiable as ever, endeavoured to forget that she had for a minute thought otherwise. James soon followed his letter, and was received with the most gratifying kindness.

Chapter 17

THE ALLENS had now entered on the sixth week of their stay in Bath; and whether it should be the last, was for some time a question, to which Catherine listened with a beating heart. To have her acquaintance with the Tilneys end so soon, was an evil which nothing could counterbalance. Her whole happiness seemed at stake, while the affair was in suspense, and everything secured when it was determined that the lodgings should be taken for another fortnight. What this additional fortnight was to produce to her beyond the pleasure of sometimes seeing Henry Tilney, made but a small part of Catherine's speculation. Once or twice indeed, since James's engagement had taught her what *could* be done, she had got so far as to indulge in a secret 'perhaps,' but in general the felicity of being with him for the present bounded her views; the present was now comprised in another three weeks, and her happiness being certain for that period, the rest of her life was at such a distance as to excite but little interest. In the course of the morning which saw this business arranged, she visited

Miss Tilney, and poured forth her joyful feelings. It was doomed to be a day of trial. No sooner had she expressed her delight in Mr Allen's lengthened stay, than Miss Tilney told her of her father's having just determined upon quitting Bath by the end of another week. Here was a blow! The past suspense of the morning had been ease and quiet to the present disappointment. Catherine's countenance fell, and in a voice of most sincere concern she echoed Miss Tilney's concluding words, 'By the end of another week!'

'Yes, my father can seldom be prevailed on to give the waters what I think a fair trial. He has been disappointed of some friends' arrival whom he expected to meet here, and as he is now pretty well, is in a hurry to get home.'

'I am very sorry for it,' said Catherine dejectedly, 'if I had known this before – '

'Perhaps,' said Miss Tilney in an embarrassed manner, 'you would be so good – it would make me very happy if – '

The entrance of her father put a stop to the civility, which Catherine was beginning to hope might introduce a desire of their corresponding. After addressing her with his usual politeness, he turned to his daughter and said, 'Well, Eleanor, may I congratulate you on being successful in your application to your fair friend?'

'I was just beginning to make the request, sir, as you came in.'

'Well, proceed by all means. I know how much your heart is in it. My daughter. Miss Morland,' he continued, without leaving his daughter time to speak, 'has been forming a very bold wish. We leave Bath, as she has perhaps told you, on Saturday se'nnight. A letter from my steward tells me that my presence is wanted at home; and being disappointed in my hope of seeing the Marquis of Longtown and General Courteney here, some of my very old friends, there is nothing to detain me longer in Bath. And could we carry our selfish point with you, we should leave it without a single regret. Can you, in short, be prevailed on to quit this scene of public triumph and oblige your friend Eleanor with your company in Gloucestershire? I am almost ashamed to make the request, though its presumption would certainly appear greater to every creature in Bath than yourself. Modesty such as yours – but not for the world would I pain it by open praise. If you can be induced to honour us with a visit, you will make us happy beyond expression. 'Tis true, we can offer you nothing like the gaieties of this lively place; we can tempt you neither by amusement nor splendour, for our mode of living, as you see, is plain and unpretending; yet no endeavours shall be wanting on our side to make Northanger Abbey not wholly disagreeable.'

Northanger Abbey! – These were thrilling words, and wound up

Catherine's feelings to the highest point of ecstasy. Her grateful and gratified heart could hardly restrain its expressions within the language of tolerable calmness. To receive so flattering an invitation! To have her company so warmly solicited! Everything honourable and soothing, every present enjoyment, and every future hope was contained in it; and her acceptance, with only the saving clause of papa and mamma's approbation, was eagerly given. – 'I will write home directly,' said she, 'and if they do not object, as I dare say they will not' –

General Tilney was not less sanguine, having already waited on her excellent friends of Pulteney Street, and obtained their sanction of his wishes. 'Since they can consent to part with you,' said he, 'we may expect philosophy from all the world.'

Miss Tilney was earnest, though gentle, in her secondary civilities, and the affair became in a few minutes as nearly settled, as this necessary reference to Fullerton would allow.

The circumstance of the morning had led Catherine's feelings through the varieties of suspense, security, and disappointment; but they were now safely lodged in perfect bliss; and with spirits elated to rapture, with Henry at her heart, and Northanger Abbey on her lips, she hurried home to write her letter. Mr and Mrs Morland, relying on the discretion of the friends to whom they had already entrusted their daughter, felt no doubt of the propriety of an acquaintance which had been formed under their eye, and sent therefore by return of post their ready consent to her visit in Gloucestershire. This indulgence, though not more than Catherine had hoped for, completed her conviction of being favoured beyond every other human creature, in friends and fortune, circumstance and chance. Everything seemed to co-operate for her advantage. By the kindness of her first friends the Allens, she had been introduced into scenes, where pleasures of every kind had met her. Her feelings, her preferences had each known the happiness of a return. Wherever she felt attachment, she had been able to create it. The affection of Isabella was to be secured to her in a sister. The Tilneys, they, by whom above all, she desired to be favourably thought of, outstripped even her wishes in the flattering measures by which their intimacy was to be continued. She was to be their chosen visitor, she was to be for weeks under the same roof with the person whose society she mostly prized – and, in addition to all the rest, this roof was to be the roof of an abbey! – Her passion for ancient edifices was next in degree to her passion for Henry Tilney – and castles and abbeys made usually the charm of those reveries which his image did not fill. To see and explore either the ramparts and keep of the one, or the cloisters of the other, had been for many weeks a darling wish, though to be more than the visitor of an hour, had seemed too nearly impossible for desire. And yet, this was to happen. With all the chances against her of house, hall, place, park, court, and cottage, Northanger turned up an abbey, and she was to be its inhabitant. Its long, damp passages, its narrow cells and ruined chapel, were to be within her daily reach, and she could not entirely subdue the hope of some traditional legends, some awful memorials of an injured and ill-fated nun.

It was wonderful that her friends should seem so little elated by the possession of such a home; that the consciousness of it should be so meekly born. The power of early habit only could account for it. A distinction to which they had been born gave no pride. Their superiority of abode was no more to them than their superiority of person.

Many were the inquiries she was eager to make of Miss Tilney; but so active were her thoughts, that when these inquiries were answered, she was hardly more assured than before, of Northanger Abbey having been a richly-endowed convent at the time of the Reformation, of its having fallen into the hands of an ancestor of the Tilneys on its dissolution, of a large portion of the ancient building still making a part of the present dwelling although the rest was decayed, or of its standing low in a valley, sheltered from the north and east by rising woods of oak.

Chapter 18

WITH A MIND thus full of happiness, Catherine was hardly aware that two or three days had passed away, without her seeing Isabella for more than a few minutes together. She began first to be sensible of this, and to sigh for her conversation, as she walked along the Pump-room one morning, by Mrs Allen's side, without anything to say or to hear; and scarcely had she felt a five minutes' longing of friendship, before the object of it appeared, and inviting her to a secret conference, led the way to a seat. 'This is my favourite place,' said she, as they sat down on a bench between the doors, which commanded a tolerable view of everybody entering at either, 'it is so out of the way.'

Catherine, observing that Isabella's eyes were continually bent towards one door or the other, as in eager expectation, and remembering how often she had been falsely accused of being arch, thought the present a fine opportunity for being really so; and therefore gaily said, 'Do not be uneasy, Isabella. James will soon be here.'

'Psha! my dear creature,' she replied, 'do not think me such a simpleton as to be always wanting to confine him to my elbow. It would be hideous to be always together; we should be the jest of the place. And so you are going to Northanger! – I am amazingly glad of it. It is one of the finest old places in England, I understand. I shall depend upon a most particular description of it.'

'You shall certainly have the best in my power to give. But who are you looking for? Are your sisters coming?'

'I am not looking for anybody. One's eyes must be somewhere, and you know what a foolish trick I have of fixing mine, when my thoughts are an hundred miles off. I am amazingly absent; I believe I am the most absent creature in the world. Tilney says it is always the case with minds of a certain stamp.'

'But I thought, Isabella, you had something in particular to tell me?'

'Oh! yes, and so I have. But here is a proof of what I was saying. My poor head! I had quite forgot it. Well, the thing is this, I have just had a letter from John; – you can guess the contents.'

'No, indeed, I cannot.'

'My sweet love, do not be so abominably affected. What can he write about, but yourself? You know he is over head and ears in love with you.'

'With *me*, dear Isabella!'

'Nay, my sweetest Catherine, this is being quite absurd! Modesty, and all that, is very well in its way, but really a little common honesty is sometimes quite as becoming. I have no idea of being so overstrained! It is fishing for compliments. His attentions were such as a child must have noticed. And it was but half an hour before he left Bath, that you gave him the most positive encouragement. He says so in this letter, says that he as good as made you an offer, and that you received his advances in the kindest way; and now he wants me to urge his suit, and say all manner of pretty things to you. So it is in vain to affect ignorance.'

Catherine, with all the earnestness of truth, expressed her astonishment at such a charge, protesting her innocence of every thought of Mr Thorpe's being in love with her, and the consequent impossibility of her having ever intended to encourage him. 'As to any attentions on his side, I do declare, upon my honour, I never was sensible of them for a moment – except just his asking me to dance the first day of his coming. And as to making me an offer, or anything like it, there must be some unaccountable mistake. I could not have misunderstood a thing of that kind, you know! – and, as I ever wish to be believed, I solemnly protest that no syllable of such a nature ever passed between us. The last half hour before he went away! – It must be all and completely a mistake – for I did not see him once that whole morning.'

'But *that* you certainly did, for you spent the whole morning in

Edgar's Buildings – it was the day your father's consent came – and I am pretty sure that you and John were alone in the parlour, some time before you left the house.'

'Are you? – Well, if you say it, it was so, I dare say – but for the life of me, I cannot recollect it. – I *do* remember now being with you, and seeing him as well as the rest – but that we were ever alone for five minutes – However, it is not worth arguing about, for whatever might pass on his side, you must be convinced, by my having no recollection of it, that I never thought, nor expected, nor wished for anything of the kind from him. I am excessively concerned that he should have any regard for me – but indeed it has been quite unintentional on my side, I never had the smallest idea of it. Pray undeceive him as soon as you can, and tell him I beg his pardon – that is – I do not know what I ought to say – but make him understand what I mean, in the properest way. I would not speak disrespectfully of a brother of yours, Isabella, I am sure; but you know very well that if I could think of one man more than another – *he* is not the person.' Isabella was silent. 'My dear friend, you must not be angry with me. I cannot suppose your brother cares so very much about me. And, you know, we shall still be sisters.'

'Yes, yes,' (with a blush) 'there are more ways than one of our being sisters. – But where am I wandering to? – Well, my dear Catherine, the case seems to be, that you are determined against poor John – is not it so?'

'I certainly cannot return his affection, and as certainly never meant to encourage it.'

'Since that is the case, I am sure I shall not tease you any further. John desired me to speak to you on the subject, and therefore I have. But I confess, as soon as I read his letter, I thought it a very foolish, imprudent business, and not likely to promote the good of either; for what were you to live upon, supposing you came together? You have both of you something to be sure, but it is not a trifle that will support a family now-a-days; and after all that romancers may say, there is no doing without money. I only wonder John could think of it; he could not have received my last.'

'You *do* acquit me then of anything wrong? – You are convinced that I never meant to deceive your brother, never suspected him of liking me till this moment?'

'Oh! as to that,' answered Isabella laughingly, 'I do not pretend to determine what your thoughts and designs in time past may have been. All that is best known to yourself. A little harmless flirtation or so will occur, and one is often drawn on to give more encouragement than one wishes to stand by. But you may be assured that I am the last person in the world to judge you severely. All those things should be allowed for in youth and high spirits. What one means one day, you know, one may not mean the next. Circumstances change, opinions alter.'

'But my opinion of your brother never did alter; it was always the same. You are describing what never happened.'

'My dearest Catherine,' continued the other without at all listening to her, 'I would not for all the world be the means of hurrying you into an engagement before you knew what you were about. I do not think anything would justify me in wishing you to sacrifice all your happiness merely to oblige my brother, because he is my brother, and who perhaps after all, you know, might be just as happy without you, for people seldom know what they would be at, young men especially, they are so amazingly changeable and inconstant. What I say is, why should a brother's happiness be dearer to me than a friend's? You know I carry my notions of friendship pretty high. But, above all things, my dear Catherine, do not be in a hurry. Take my word for it, that if you are in too great a hurry, you will certainly live to repent it. Tilney says, there is nothing people are so often deceived in, as the state of their own affections, and I believe he is very right. Ah! here he comes; never mind, he will not see us, I am sure.'

Catherine, looking up, perceived Captain Tilney; and Isabella, earnestly fixing her eye on him as she spoke, soon caught his notice. He approached immediately, and took the seat to which her movements invited him. His first address made Catherine start. Though spoken low, she could distinguish, 'What! always to be watched, in person or by proxy!'

'Psha, nonsense!' was Isabella's answer in the same half whisper. 'Why do you put such things into my head? If I could believe it – my spirit, you know, is pretty independent.'

'I wish your heart were independent. That would be enough for me.'

'My heart, indeed! What can you have to do with hearts? You men have none of you any hearts.'

'If we have not hearts, we have eyes; and they give us torment enough.'

'Do they? I am sorry for it; I am sorry they find anything so disagreeable in me. I will look another way. I hope this pleases you, (turning her back on him,) I hope your eyes are not tormented now.'

'Never more so; for the edge of a blooming cheek is still in view – at once too much and too little.'

Catherine heard all this, and quite out of countenance could listen no longer. Amazed that Isabella could endure it, and jealous for her brother, she rose up, and saying she should join Mrs Allen, proposed their walking. But for this Isabella showed no inclination. She was so amazingly tired, and it was so odious to parade about the Pump-room, and if she moved from her seat she should miss her sisters, she was expecting her sisters every moment; so that her dearest Catherine must excuse her, and must sit quietly down again. But Catherine could be stubborn too; and Mrs Allen just then coming up to propose their returning home, she joined her and walked out of the Pump-room, leaving Isabella still sitting with Captain Tilney. With much uneasiness did she thus leave them. It seemed to her that Captain Tilney was falling in love with Isabella, and Isabella unconsciously encouraging him; unconsciously it must be, for Isabella's attachment to James was as certain and well acknowledged as her engagement. To doubt her truth or good intentions was impossible; and yet, during the whole of their conversation her manner had been odd. She wished Isabella had talked more like her usual self, and not so much about money; and had not looked so well pleased at the sight of Captain Tilney. How strange that she should not perceive his admiration! Catherine longed to give her a hint of it, to put her on her guard, and prevent all the pain which her too lively behaviour might otherwise create both for him and her brother.

The compliment of John Thorpe's affection did not make amends for this thoughtlessness in his sister. She was almost as far from believing as from wishing it to be sincere; for she had not forgotten that he could mistake, and his assertion of the offer and of her encouragement convinced her that his mistakes could sometimes be very egregious. In vanity therefore she gained but little, her chief profit was in wonder. That he should think it worth his while to fancy himself in love with her, was a matter of lively astonishment. Isabella talked of his attentions; *she* had never been sensible of any; but Isabella had said many things which she hoped had been spoken in haste, and would never be said again; and upon this she was glad to rest altogether for present ease and comfort.

Chapter 19

A FEW DAYS passed away, and Catherine, though not allowing herself to suspect her friend, could not help watching her closely. The result of her observations was not agreeable. Isabella seemed an altered creature. When she saw her indeed surrounded only by their immediate friends in Edgar's Buildings or Pulteney Street, her change of manners was so trifling that, had it gone no farther, it might have passed unnoticed. A something of languid indifference, or of that boasted absence of mind which Catherine had never heard of before, would occasionally come across her; but had nothing worse appeared, *that* might only have spread a new grace and inspired a warmer interest. But when Catherine saw her in public, admitting Captain Tilney's attentions as readily as they were offered, and allowing him almost an equal share with James in her notice and smiles, the alteration became too positive to be passed over. What could be meant by such unsteady conduct, what her friend could be at, was beyond her comprehension. Isabella could not be aware of the pain she was inflicting; but it was a degree of wilful thoughtlessness which Catherine could not but resent. James was the sufferer. She saw him grave and uneasy; and however careless of his present comfort the woman might be who had given him her heart, to *her* it was always an object. For poor Captain Tilney too she was greatly concerned. Though his looks did not please her, his name was a passport to her good will, and she thought with sincere compassion of his approaching disappointment; for, in spite of what she had believed herself to overhear in the Pump-room, his behaviour was so incompatible with a knowledge of Isabella's engagement, that she could not, upon reflection, imagine him aware of it. He might be jealous of her brother as a rival, but if more had seemed implied, the fault must have been in her misapprehension. She wished, by a gentle remonstrance, to remind Isabella of her situation, and make her aware of this double unkindness; but for remonstrance, either opportunity or comprehension was always against her. If able to suggest a hint, Isabella could never understand it. In this distress, the intended departure of the Tilney family became her chief consolation; their journey into Gloucestershire was to take place within a few days, and Captain Tilney's removal would at least restore peace to every heart but his own. But Captain Tilney had at present no intention of removing; he was not to be of the party to Northanger, he was to continue at Bath. When Catherine knew this, her resolution was directly made. She spoke to Henry Tilney on the subject, regretting his brother's evident partiality for Miss Thorpe, and entreating him to make known her prior engagement.

'My brother does know it,' was Henry's answer.

'Does he? – then why does he stay here?'

He made no reply, and was beginning to talk of something else; but she eagerly continued, 'Why do not you persuade him to go away? The longer he stays, the worse it will be for him at last. Pray advise him for his own sake, and for everybody's sake, to leave Bath directly. Absence will in time make him comfortable again; but he can have no hope here, and it is only staying to be miserable.' Henry smiled and said, 'I am sure my brother would not wish to do that.'

'Then you will persuade him to go away?'

'Persuasion is not at command; but pardon me, if I cannot even endeavour to persuade him. I have myself told him that Miss Thorpe is engaged. He knows what he is about, and must be his own master.'

'No, he does not know what he is about,' cried Catherine; 'he does not know the pain he is giving my brother. Not that James has ever told me so, but I am sure he is very uncomfortable.'

'And are you sure it is my brother's doing?'

'Yes, very sure.'

'Is it my brother's attentions to Miss Thorpe, or Miss Thorpe's admission of them, that gives the pain?'

'Is not it the same thing?'

'I think Mr Morland would acknowledge a difference. No man is offended by another man's admiration of the woman he loves; it is the woman only who can make it a torment.'

Catherine blushed for her friend, and said, 'Isabella is wrong. But I am sure she cannot mean to torment, for she is very much attached to my brother. She has been in love with him ever since they first met, and while my father's consent was uncertain, she fretted herself almost into a fever. You know she must be attached to him.'

'I understand: she is in love with James, and flirts with Frederick.'

'Oh! no, not flirts. A woman in love with one man cannot flirt with another.'

'It is probable that she will neither love so well, nor flirt so well, as she might do either singly. The gentlemen must each give up a little.'

After a short pause, Catherine resumed with 'Then you do not believe Isabella so very much attached to my brother?'

'I can have no opinion on that subject.'

'But what can your brother mean? If he knows her engagement, what can he mean by his behaviour?'

'You are a very close questioner.'

'Am I? – I only ask what I want to be told.'

'But do you only ask what I can be expected to tell?'

'Yes, I think so; for you must know your brother's heart.'

'My brother's heart, as you term it, on the present occasion, I assure you I can only guess at.'

'Well?'

'Well! – Nay, if it is to be guess-work, let us all guess for ourselves. To be guided by second-hand conjecture is pitiful. The premises are before you. My brother is a lively, and perhaps sometimes a thought-less young man; he has had about a week's acquaintance with your friend, and he has known her engagement almost as long as he has known her.'

'Well,' said Catherine, after some moments' consideration, '*you* may be able to guess at your brother's intentions from all this; but I am sure I cannot. But is not your father uncomfortable about it? – Does not he want Captain Tilney to go away? – Sure, if your father were to speak to him, he would go.'

'My dear Miss Morland,' said Henry, 'in this amiable solicitude for your brother's comfort, may you not be a little mistaken? Are you not carried a little too far? Would he thank you, either on his own account or Miss Thorpe's, for supposing that her affection, or at least her good-behaviour, is only to be secured by her seeing nothing of Captain Tilney? Is he safe only in solitude? – or, is her heart constant to him only when unsolicited by anyone else? – He cannot think this – and you may be sure that he would not have you think it. I will not say, "Do not be uneasy," because I know that you are so, at this moment; but be as little uneasy as you can. You have no doubt of the mutual attachment of your brother and your friend; depend upon it therefore, that real jealousy never can exist between them; depend upon it that no disagreement between them can be of any duration. Their hearts are open to each other, as neither heart can be to you; they know exactly what is required and what can be borne; and you may be certain, that one will never tease the other beyond what is known to be pleasant.'

Perceiving her still to look doubtful and grave, he added, 'Though Frederick does not leave Bath with us, he will probably remain but a very short time, perhaps only a few days behind us. His leave of absence will soon expire, and he must return to his regiment. – And what will then be their acquaintance? – The mess-room will drink Isabella Thorpe for a fortnight, and she will laugh with your brother over poor Tilney's passion for a month.'

Catherine would contend no longer against comfort. She had resisted its approaches during the whole length of a speech, but it now carried her captive. Henry Tilney must know best. She blamed herself for the extent of her fears, and resolved never to think so seriously on the subject again.

Her resolution was supported by Isabella's behaviour in their parting interview. The Thorpes spent the last evening of Catherine's stay in Pulteney Street, and nothing passed between the lovers to excite her uneasiness, or make her quit them in apprehension. James was in excellent spirits, and Isabella most engagingly placid. Her tenderness for her friend seemed rather the first feeling of her heart; but that at such a moment was allowable; and once she gave her lover a flat contradiction, and once she drew back her hand; but Catherine remembered Henry's instructions, and placed it all to judicious affection. The embraces, tears, and promises of the parting fair ones may be fancied.

Chapter 20

MR AND MRS ALLEN were sorry to lose their young friend, whose good-humour and cheerfulness had made her a valuable companion, and in the promotion of whose enjoyment their own had been gently increased. Her happiness in going with Miss Tilney, however, prevented their wishing it otherwise; and, as they were to remain only one more week in Bath themselves, her quitting them now would not long be felt. Mr Allen attended her to Milsom Street, where she was to breakfast, and saw her seated with the kindest welcome among her new friends; but so great was her agitation in finding herself as one of the family, and so fearful was she of not doing exactly what was right, and of not being able to preserve their good opinion, that, in the embarrassment of the first five minutes, she could almost have wished to return with him to Pulteney Street.

Miss Tilney's manners and Henry's smile soon did away some of her unpleasant feelings; but still she was far from being at ease; nor could the incessant attentions of the General himself entirely reassure her. Nay, perverse as it seemed, she doubted whether she might not have felt less, had she been less attended to. His anxiety for her comfort – his continual solicitations that she would eat, and his often-expressed fears of her seeing nothing to her taste – though never in her life before had she beheld half such variety on a breakfast-table – made it impossible for her to forget for a moment that she was a visitor. She felt utterly unworthy of such respect, and knew not how to reply to it. Her tranquillity was not improved by the General's impatience for the appearance of his eldest son, nor by the displeasure he expressed at his laziness when Captain Tilney at last came down. She was quite pained by the severity of his father's reproof, which seemed disproportionate to the offence; and much was her concern increased, when she found herself the principal cause of the lecture; and that his tardiness was chiefly resented from being disrespectful to her. This was placing her in a very uncomfortable situation, and she felt great compassion for

Captain Tilney, without being able to hope for his good-will.

He listened to his father in silence, and attempted not any defence, which confirmed her in fearing, that the inquietude of his mind, on Isabella's account, might, by keeping him long sleepless, have been the real cause of his rising late. – It was the first time of her being decidedly in his company, and she had hoped to be now able to form her opinion of him; but she scarcely heard his voice while his father remained in the room; and even afterwards, so much were his spirits affected, she could distinguish nothing but these words, in a whisper to Eleanor, 'How glad I shall be when you are all off.'

The bustle of going was not pleasant. – The clock struck ten while the trunks were carrying down, and the General had fixed to be out of Milsom Street by that hour. His great coat, instead of being brought for him to put on directly, was spread out in the curricle in which he was to accompany his son. The middle seat of the chaise was not drawn out, though there were three people to go in it, and his daughter's maid had so crowded it with parcels, that Miss Morland would not have room to sit; and, so much was he influenced by this apprehension when he handed her in, that she had some difficulty in saving her own new writing-desk from being thrown out into the street. – At last, however, the door was closed upon the three females, and they set off at the sober pace in which the handsome, highly-fed four horses of a gentleman usually perform a journey of thirty miles: such was the distance of Northanger from Bath, to be now divided into two equal stages. Catherine's spirits revived as they drove from the door; for with Miss Tilney she felt no restraint; and, with the interest of a road entirely new to her, of an abbey before, and a curricle behind, she caught the last view of Bath without any regret, and met with every mile-stone before she expected it. The tediousness of a two hours' bait at Petty-France, in which there was nothing to be done but to eat without being hungry, and loiter about without anything to see, next followed – and her admiration of the style in which they travelled, of the fashionable chaise-and-four – postilions handsomely liveried, rising so regularly in their stirrups, and numerous out-riders properly mounted, sunk a little under this consequent inconvenience. Had their party been perfectly agreeable, the delay would have been nothing; but General Tilney, though so charming a man, seemed always a check upon his children's spirits, and scarcely anything was said but by himself; the observation of which, with his discontent at whatever the inn afforded, and his angry impatience at the waiters, made Catherine grow every moment more in awe of him, and appeared to lengthen the two hours into four. – At last, however, the order of release was given; and much was Catherine then surprised by the General's proposal of her taking his place in his son's curricle for the rest of the journey: – 'the day was fine, and he was anxious for her seeing as much of the country as possible.'

The remembrance of Mr Allen's opinion, respecting young men's open carriages, made her blush at the mention of such a plan, and her first thought was to decline it; but her second was of greater deference for General Tilney's judgment; he could not propose anything improper for her; and, in the course of a few minutes, she found herself with Henry in the curricle, as happy a being as ever existed. A very short trial convinced her that a curricle was the prettiest equipage in the world; the chaise-and-four wheeled off with some grandeur, to be sure, but it was a heavy and troublesome business, and she could not easily forget its having stopped two hours at Petty-France. Half the time would have been enough for the curricle, and so nimbly were the light horses disposed to move, that, had not the General chosen to have his own carriage lead the way, they could have passed it with ease in half a minute. But the merit of the curricle did not all belong to the horses; – Henry drove so well, – so quietly – without making any disturbance, without parading to her, or swearing at them; so different from the only gentleman-coachman whom it was in her power to compare him with! – And then his hat sat so well, and the innumerable capes of his great coat looked so becomingly important! – To be driven by him, next to being dancing with him, was certainly the greatest happiness in the world. In addition to every other delight, she had now that of listening to her own praise; of being thanked at least, on his sister's account, for her kindness in thus becoming her visitor; of hearing it ranked as real friendship, and described as creating real gratitude. His sister, he said, was uncomfortably circumstanced – she had no female companion – and, in the frequent absence of her father, was sometimes without any companion at all.

'But how can that be?' said Catherine, 'are not you with her?'

'Northanger is not more than half my home; I have an establishment at my own house in Woodston, which is nearly twenty miles from my father's, and some of my time is necessarily spent there.'

'How sorry you must be for that!'

'I am always sorry to leave Eleanor.'

'Yes; but besides your affection for her, you must be so fond of the abbey! – After being used to such a home as the abbey, an ordinary parsonage-house must be very disagreeable.'

He smiled, and said, 'You have formed a very favourable idea of the abbey.'

'To be sure I have. Is not it a fine old place, just like what one reads about?'

'And are you prepared to encounter all the horrors that a building such as "what one reads about" may produce? – Have you a stout heart? – Nerves fit for sliding panels and tapestry?'

'Oh! yes – I do not think I should be easily frightened, because there would be so many people in the house – and besides, it has never been uninhabited and left deserted for years, and then the family come back to it unawares, without giving any notice, as generally happens.'

'No, certainly. – We shall not have to explore our way into a hall dimly lighted by the expiring embers of a wood fire – nor be obliged to spread our beds on the floor of a room without windows, doors, or furniture. But you must be aware that when a young lady is (by whatever means) introduced into a dwelling of this kind, she is always lodged apart from the rest of the family. While they snugly repair to their own end of the house, she is formally conducted by Dorothy the ancient house-keeper up a different staircase, and along many gloomy passages, into an apartment never used since some cousin or kin died in it about twenty years before. Can you stand such a ceremony as this? Will not your mind misgive you, when you find yourself in this gloomy chamber – too lofty and extensive for you, with only the feeble rays of a single lamp to take in its size – its walls hung with tapestry exhibiting figures as large as life, and the bed, of dark green stuff or purple velvet, presenting even a funeral appearance. Will not your heart sink within you?'

'Oh! but this will not happen to me, I am sure.'

'How fearfully will you examine the furniture of your apartment! – And what will you discern? – Not tables, toilettes, wardrobes, or drawers, but on one side perhaps the remains of a broken lute, on the other a ponderous chest which no efforts can open, and over the fire-place the portrait of some handsome warrior, whose features will so incomprehensibly strike you, that you will not be able to withdraw your eyes from it. Dorothy meanwhile, no less struck by your appear-ance, gazes on you in great agitation, and drops a few unintelligible hints. To raise your spirits, moreover, she gives you reason to suppose that the part of the abbey you inhabit is undoubtedly haunted, and informs you that you will not have a single domestic within call. With this parting cordial she curtseys off – you listen to the sound of her receding footsteps as long as the last echo can reach you – and when, with fainting spirits, you attempt to fasten your door, you discover, with increased alarm, that it has no lock.'

'Oh! Mr Tilney, how frightful! – This is just like a book! – But it cannot really happen to me. I am sure your housekeeper is not really

Dorothy. – Well, what then?'

'Nothing further to alarm perhaps may occur the first night. After surmounting your *unconquerable* horror of the bed, you will retire to rest, and get a few hours' unquiet slumber. But on the second, or at farthest the *third* night after your arrival, you will probably have a violent storm. Peals of thunder so loud as to seem to shake the edifice to its foundation will roll round the neighbouring mountains – and during the frightful gusts of wind which accompany it, you will probably think you discern (for your lamp is not extinguished) one part of the hanging more violently agitated than the rest. Unable of course to repress your curiosity in so favourable a moment for indulging it, you will instantly arise, and throwing your dressing-gown around you, proceed to examine this mystery. After a very short search, you will discover a division in the tapestry so artfully constructed as to defy the minutest inspection, and on opening it, a door will immediately appear – which door being only secured by massy bars and a padlock, you will, after a few efforts, succeed in opening, – and, with your lamp in your hand, will pass through it into a small vaulted room.'

'No, indeed; I should be too much frightened to do any such thing.'

'What! not when Dorothy has given you to understand that there is a secret subterraneous communication between your apartment and the chapel of St Anthony, scarcely two miles off – Could you shrink from so simple an adventure? No, no, you will proceed into this small vaulted room, and through this into several others, without perceiving anything very remarkable in either. In one perhaps there may be a dagger, in another a few drops of blood, and in a third the remains of some instrument of torture; but there being nothing in all this out of the common way, and your lamp being nearly exhausted, you will return towards your own apartment. In repassing through the small vaulted room, however, your eyes will be attracted towards a large, old-fashioned cabinet of ebony and gold, which, though narrowly examining the furniture before, you had passed unnoticed. Impelled by an irresistible presentiment, you will eagerly advance to it, unlock its folding doors, and search into every drawer; – but for some time without discovering anything of importance – perhaps nothing but a considerable hoard of diamonds. At last, however, by touching a secret spring, an inner compartment will open – a roll of paper appears: – you seize it – it contains many sheets of manuscript – you hasten with the precious treasure into your own chamber, but scarcely have you been able to decipher "Oh! thou – whomsoever thou mayst be, into whose hands these memoirs of the wretched Matilda may fall" – when your lamp suddenly expires in the socket, and leaves you in total darkness.'

'Oh! no, no – do not say so. Well, go on.'

But Henry was too much amused by the interest he had raised, to be able to carry it farther; he could no longer command solemnity either of subject or voice, and was obliged to entreat her to use her own fancy in the perusal of Matilda's woes. Catherine, recollecting herself, grew ashamed of her eagerness, and began earnestly to assure him that her attention had been fixed without the smallest apprehension of really meeting with what he related. 'Miss Tilney, she was sure, would never put her into such a chamber as he had described! – She was not at all afraid.'

As they drew near the end of their journey, her impatience for a sight of the abbey – for some time suspended by his conversation on subjects very different – returned in full force, and every bend in the road was expected with solemn awe to afford a glimpse of its massy walls of grey stone, rising amidst a grove of ancient oaks, with the last beams of the sun playing in beautiful splendour on its high Gothic windows. But so low did the building stand, that she found herself passing through the great gates of the lodge into the very grounds of Northanger, without having discerned even an antique chimney.

She knew not that she had any right to be surprised, but there was a something in this mode of approach which she certainly had not expected. To pass between lodges of a modern appearance, to find herself with such ease in the very precincts of the abbey, and driven so rapidly along a smooth, level road of fine gravel, without obstacle, alarm or solemnity of any kind, struck her as odd and inconsistent. She was not long at leisure however for such considerations. A sudden scud of rain driving full in her face, made it impossible for her to observe anything further, and fixed all her thoughts on the welfare of her new straw bonnet: – and she was actually under the Abbey walls, was springing, with Henry's assistance, from the carriage, was beneath the shelter of the old porch, and had even passed on to the hall, where her friend and the General were waiting to welcome her, without feeling one aweful foreboding of future misery to herself, or one moment's suspicion of any past scenes of horror being acted within the solemn edifice. The breeze had not seemed to waft the sighs of the murdered to her; it had wafted nothing worse than a thick mizzling rain; and having given a good shake to her habit, she was ready to be shown into the common drawing-room, and capable of considering where she was.

An abbey! – yes, it was delightful to be really in an abbey! – but she doubted, as she looked round the room, whether anything within her observation, would have given her the consciousness. The furniture was in all the profusion and elegance of modern taste. The fire-place, where she had expected the ample width and ponderous carving of former times, was contracted to a Rumford,[20] with slabs of plain though handsome marble, and ornaments over it of the prettiest English china. The windows, to which she looked with peculiar dependence, from having heard the General talk of his preserving them in their Gothic form with reverential care, were yet less what her fancy had portrayed. To be sure, the pointed arch was preserved – the form of them was Gothic – they might be even casements – but every pane was so large, so clear, so light! To an imagination which had hoped for the smallest divisions, and the heaviest stonework, for painted glass, dirt and cobwebs, the difference was very distressing.

The General, perceiving how her eye was employed, began to talk of the smallness of the room and simplicity of the furniture, where everything being for daily use, pretended only to comfort, &c.; flattering himself however that there were some apartments in the Abbey not unworthy her notice – and was proceeding to mention the costly gilding of one in particular, when taking out his watch, he stopped short to pronounce it with surprise within twenty minutes of five! This seemed the word of separation, and Catherine found herself hurried away by Miss Tilney in such a manner as convinced her that the strictest punctuality to the family hours would be expected at Northanger.

Returning through the large and lofty hall, they ascended a broad staircase of shining oak, which, after many flights and many landing-places, brought them upon a long wide gallery. On one side it had a range of doors, and it was lighted on the other by windows which Catherine had only time to discover looked into a quadrangle, before Miss Tilney led the way into a chamber, and scarcely staying to hope she would find it comfortable, left her with an anxious entreaty that she would make as little alteration as possible in her dress.

Chapter 21

A MOMENT'S GLANCE was enough to satisfy Catherine that her apartment was very unlike the one which Henry had endeavoured to alarm her by the description of. – It was by no means unreasonably large, and contained neither tapestry nor velvet. – The walls were papered, the floor was carpeted; the windows were neither less perfect, nor more dim than those of the drawing-room below; the furniture, though not of the latest fashion, was handsome and comfortable, and the air of the room altogether far from uncheerful. Her heart instantaneously at ease on this point, she resolved to lose no time in particular examination of anything, as she greatly dreaded disobliging the General by any delay. Her habit therefore was thrown off with all possible haste, and she was preparing to unpin the linen package, which the chaise-seat had conveyed for her immediate accommodation, when her eye suddenly fell on a large high chest, standing back in a deep recess on one side of the fire-place. The sight of it made her start; and, forgetting everything else, she stood gazing on it in motionless wonder, while these thoughts crossed her:

'This is strange indeed! I did not expect such a sight as this! – An immense heavy chest! – What can it hold? – Why should it be placed here? – Pushed back too, as if meant to be out of sight! – I will look into it – cost me what it may, I will look into it – and directly too – by day-light. – If I stay till evening my candle may go out.' She advanced and examined it closely: it was of cedar, curiously inlaid with some darker wood, and raised, about a foot from the ground, on a carved stand of the same. The lock was silver, though tarnished from age; at each end were the imperfect remains of handles also of silver, broken perhaps prematurely by some strange violence; and, on the centre of the lid, was a mysterious cypher, in the same metal. Catherine bent over it intently, but without being able to distinguish anything with certainty. She could not, in whatever direction she took it, believe the last letter to be a *T*; and yet that it should be anything else in that house was a circumstance to raise no common degree of astonishment. If not originally theirs, by what strange events could it have fallen into the Tilney family?

Her fearful curiosity was every moment growing greater; and seizing, with trembling hands, the hasp of the lock, she resolved at all hazards to satisfy herself at least as to its contents. With difficulty, for something seemed to resist her efforts, she raised the lid a few inches; but at that moment a sudden knocking at the door of the room made her, starting, quit her hold, and the lid closed with alarming violence. This ill-timed intruder was Miss Tilney's maid, sent by her mistress to be of use to Miss Morland; and though Catherine immediately dismissed her, it recalled her to the sense of what she ought to be doing, and forced her, in spite of her anxious desire to penetrate this mystery, to proceed in her dressing without further delay. Her progress was not quick, for her thoughts and her eyes were still bent on the object so well calculated to interest and alarm; and though she dared not waste a moment upon a second attempt, she could not remain many paces from the chest. At length, however, having slipped one arm into her gown, her toilette seemed so nearly finished, that the impatience of her curiosity might safely be indulged. One moment surely might be spared; and, so desperate should be the exertion of her strength, that, unless secured by supernatural means, the lid in one moment should be thrown back. With this spirit she sprang forward, and her confidence did not deceive her. Her resolute effort threw back the lid, and gave to her astonished eyes the view of a white cotton counterpane, properly folded, reposing at one end of the chest in undisputed possession!

She was gazing on it with the first blush of surprise, when Miss Tilney, anxious for her friend's being ready, entered the room, and to the rising shame of having harboured for some minutes an absurd expectation, was then added the shame of being caught in so idle a search. 'That is a curious old chest, is not it?' said Miss Tilney, as Catherine hastily closed it and turned away to the glass. 'It is impossible to say how many generations it has been here. How it came to be first put in this room I know not, but I have not had it moved, because I thought it might sometimes be of use in holding hats and bonnets. The worst of it is that its weight makes it difficult to open. In that corner, however, it is at least out of the way.'

Catherine had no leisure for speech, being at once blushing, tying her gown, and forming wise resolutions with the most violent dispatch. Miss Tilney gently hinted her fear of being late; and in half a minute they ran downstairs together, in an alarm not wholly unfounded, for General Tilney was pacing the drawing-room, his watch in his hand, and having, on the very instant of their entering, pulled the bell with violence, ordered 'Dinner to be on table *directly!*'

Catherine trembled at the emphasis with which he spoke, and sat pale and breathless, in a most humble mood, concerned for his children, and detesting old chests; and the General recovering his politeness as he looked at her, spent the rest of his time in scolding his daughter, for so foolishly hurrying her fair friend, who was absolutely out of breath from haste, when there was not the least occasion for hurry in the world: but Catherine could not at all get over the double distress of having involved her friend in a lecture and been a great simpleton herself, till they were happily seated at the dinner-table, when the General's complacent smiles, and a good appetite of her own, restored her to peace. The dining-parlour was a noble room, suitable in its dimensions to a much larger drawing-room than the one in common use, and fitted up in a style of luxury and expense which was almost lost on the unpractised eye of Catherine, who saw little more than its spaciousness and the number of their attendants. Of the former, she spoke aloud her admiration, and the General, with a very gracious countenance, acknowledged that it was by no means an ill-sized room; and further confessed, that, though as careless on such subjects as most people, he did look upon a tolerably large eating-room as one of the necessaries of life; he supposed, however, 'that she must have been used to much better sized apartments at Mr Allen's?'

'No, indeed,' was Catherine's honest assurance; 'Mr Allen's dining-parlour was not more than half as large:' and she had never seen so large a room as this in her life. The General's good-humour increased. – Why, as he *had* such rooms, he thought it would be simple not to make use of them; but, upon his honour, he believed there might be more comfort in rooms of only half their size. Mr Allen's house, he was sure, must be exactly of the true size for rational happiness.

The evening passed without any further disturbance, and, in the occasional absence of General Tilney, with much positive cheerfulness. It was only in his presence that Catherine felt the smallest fatigue from her journey; and even then, even in moments of languor or restraint, a sense of general happiness preponderated, and she could think of her friends in Bath without one wish of being with them.

The night was stormy; the wind had been rising at intervals the whole afternoon; and by the time the party broke up, it blew and rained violently. Catherine, as she crossed the hall, listened to the tempest with sensations of awe; and, when she heard it rage round a corner of the ancient building and close with sudden fury a distant door, felt for the first time that she was really in an Abbey. – Yes, these were characteristic sounds; – they brought to her recollection a countless variety of dreadful situations and horrid scenes, which such buildings had witnessed, and such storms ushered in; and most heartily did she rejoice in the happier circumstances attending her entrance within walls so solemn! – *She* had nothing to dread from midnight assassins or drunken gallants. Henry had certainly been only in jest in what he had told her that morning. In a house so furnished, and so guarded, she could have nothing to explore or to suffer; and might go to her bedroom as securely as if it had been her own chamber at Fullerton. Thus wisely fortifying her mind, as she proceeded upstairs, she was enabled, especially on perceiving that Miss Tilney slept only two doors from her, to enter her room with a tolerably stout heart; and her spirits were immediately assisted by the cheerful blaze of a wood fire. 'How much better is this,' said she, as she walked to the fender – 'how much better to find a fire ready lit, than to have to wait shivering in the cold till all the family are in bed, as so many poor girls have been obliged to do, and then to have a faithful old servant frightening one by coming in with a faggot! How glad I am that Northanger is what it is! If it had been like some other places, I do not know that, in such a night as this, I could have answered for my courage: – but now, to be sure, there is nothing to alarm one.'

She looked round the room. The window curtains seemed in motion. It could be nothing but the violence of the wind penetrating through the divisions of the shutters; and she stepped boldly forward, carelessly humming a tune, to assure herself of its being so, peeped courageously behind each curtain, saw nothing on either low window seat to scare her, and on placing a hand against the shutter, felt the strongest conviction of the wind's force. A glance at the old chest, as she turned away from this examination, was not without its use; she scorned the causeless fears of an idle fancy, and began with a most happy indifference to prepare herself for bed. 'She should take her time; she should not hurry herself; she did not care if she were the last person up in the house. But she would not make up her fire; *that* would seem cowardly, as if she wished for the protection of light after she were in bed.' The fire therefore died away, and Catherine, having spent the best part of an hour in her arrangements, was beginning to think of stepping into bed, when, on giving a parting glance round the room, she was struck by the appearance of a high, old-fashioned black cabinet, which, though in a situation conspicuous enough, had never caught her notice before. Henry's words, his description of the ebony cabinet which was to escape her observation at first, immediately rushed across her; and though there could be nothing really in it, there was something whimsical, it was certainly a very remarkable coincidence! She took her candle and looked closely at the cabinet. It was not absolutely ebony and gold; but it was Japan, black and yellow Japan of the handsomest kind; and as she held her candle, the yellow had very much the effect of gold. The key was in the door, and she had a strange fancy to look into it; not however with the smallest expectation of finding anything, but it was so very odd, after what Henry had said. In short, she could not sleep till she had examined it. So, placing the candle with great caution on a chair, she seized the key with a very tremulous hand and tried to turn it; but it resisted her utmost strength. Alarmed, but not discouraged, she tried it another way; a bolt flew, and she believed herself successful; but how strangely mysterious! – the door was still immoveable. She paused a moment in breathless wonder. The wind roared down the chimney, the rain beat in torrents against the windows, and everything seemed to speak the awfulness of her situation. To retire to bed, however, unsatisfied on such a point, would be vain, since sleep must be impossible with the consciousness of a cabinet so mysteriously closed in her immediate vicinity. Again therefore she applied herself to the key, and after moving it in every possible way for some instants with the determined celerity of hope's last effort, the door suddenly yielded to her hand: her heart leaped with exultation at such a victory, and having thrown open each folding door, the second being secured only by bolts of less wonderful construction than the lock, though in that her eye could not discern anything unusual, a double range of small drawers appeared in view, with some larger drawers above and below them; and in the centre, a small door, closed also with a lock and key, secured in all probability a cavity of importance.

Catherine's heart beat quick, but her courage did not fail her. With a cheek flushed by hope, and an eye straining with curiosity, her fingers grasped the handle of a drawer and drew it forth. It was entirely empty. With less alarm and greater eagerness she seized a second, a third, a fourth; each was equally empty. Not one was left unsearched, and in not one was anything found. Well read in the art of concealing a treasure, the possibility of false linings to the drawers did not escape her, and she felt round each with anxious acuteness in vain. The place in the middle alone remained now unexplored; and though she had 'never from the first had the smallest idea of finding anything in any part of the cabinet, and was not in the least disappointed at her ill success thus far, it would be foolish not to examine it thoroughly while she was about it.' It was some time however before she could unfasten the door, the same difficulty occurring in the management of this inner lock as of the outer; but at length it did open; and not vain, as hitherto, was her search; her quick eyes directly fell on a roll of paper pushed back into the further part of the cavity, apparently for concealment, and her feelings at that moment were indescribable. Her heart fluttered, her knees trembled, and her cheeks grew pale. She seized, with an unsteady hand, the precious manuscript, for half a glance sufficed to ascertain written characters; and while she acknowledged with awful sensations this striking exemplification of what Henry had foretold, resolved instantly to peruse every line before she attempted to rest.

The dimness of the light her candle emitted made her turn to it with alarm; but there was no danger of its sudden extinction, it had yet some hours to burn; and that she might not have any greater difficulty in distinguishing the writing than what its ancient date might occasion, she hastily snuffed it. Alas! it was snuffed and extinguished in one. A lamp could not have expired with more awful effect. Catherine, for a few moments, was motionless with horror. It was done completely; not a remnant of light in the wick could give hope to the rekindling breath. Darkness impenetrable and immoveable filled the room. A violent gust of wind, rising with sudden fury, added fresh horror to the moment.

Catherine trembled from head to foot. In the pause which succeeded, a sound like receding footsteps and the closing of a distant door struck on her affrighted ear. Human nature could support no more. A cold sweat stood on her forehead, the manuscript fell from her hand, and groping her way to the bed, she jumped hastily in, and sought some suspension of agony by creeping far underneath the clothes. To close her eyes in sleep that night, she felt must be entirely out of the question. With a curiosity so justly awakened, and feelings in every way so agitated, repose must be absolutely impossible. The storm too abroad so dreadful! – she had not been used to feel alarm from wind, but now every blast seemed fraught with awful intelligence. The manuscript so wonderfully found, so wonderfully accomplishing the morning's prediction, how was it to be accounted for? – What could it contain? – to whom could it relate? – by what means could it have been so long concealed? – and how singularly strange that it should fall to her lot to discover it! Till she had made herself mistress of its contents, however, she could have neither repose nor comfort; and with the sun's first rays she was determined to peruse it. But many were the tedious hours which must yet intervene. She shuddered, tossed about in her bed, and envied every quiet sleeper. The storm still raged, and various were the noises, more terrific even than the wind, which struck at intervals on her startled ear. The very curtains of her bed seemed at one moment in motion, and at another the lock of her door was agitated, as if by the attempt of somebody to enter. Hollow murmurs seemed to creep along the gallery, and more than once her blood was chilled by the sound of distant moans. Hour after hour passed away, and the wearied Catherine had heard three proclaimed by all the clocks in the house, before the tempest subsided, or she unknowingly fell fast asleep.

Chapter 22

THE HOUSEMAID'S FOLDING BACK her window-shutters at eight o'clock the next day, was the sound which first roused Catherine; and she opened her eyes, wondering that they could ever have been closed, on objects of cheerfulness; her fire was already burning, and a bright morning had succeeded the tempest of the night. Instantaneously with the consciousness of existence, returned her recollection of the manuscript; and springing from the bed in the very moment of the maid's going away, she eagerly collected every scattered sheet which had burst from the roll on its falling to the ground, and flew back to enjoy the luxury of their perusal on her pillow. She now plainly saw that she must not expect a manuscript of equal length with the generality of what she had shuddered over in books, for the roll, seeming to consist entirely of small disjointed sheets, was altogether but of trifling size, and much less than she had supposed it to be at first.

Her greedy eye glanced rapidly over a page. She started at its import. Could it be possible, or did not her senses play her false? – An inventory of linen, in coarse and modern characters, seemed all that was before her! If the evidence of sight might be trusted, she held a washing-bill in her hand. She seized another sheet, and saw the same articles with little variation; a third, a fourth, and a fifth presented nothing new. Shirts, stockings, cravats and waistcoats faced her in each. Two others, penned by the same hand, marked an expenditure scarcely more interesting, in letters, hair-powder, shoe-string and breeches-ball. And the larger sheet, which had enclosed the rest, seemed by its first cramp line, 'To poultice chesnut mare,' – a farrier's bill! Such was the collection of papers (left perhaps, as she could then suppose, by the negligence of a servant in the place whence she had taken them) which had filled her with expectation and alarm, and robbed her of half her night's rest! She felt humbled to the dust. Could not the adventure of the chest have taught her wisdom? A corner of it catching her eye as she lay, seemed to rise up in judgment against her. Nothing could now be clearer than the absurdity of her recent fancies. To suppose that a manuscript of many generations back could have remained undiscovered in a room such as that, so modern, so habitable! – or that she should be the first to possess the skill of unlocking a cabinet, the key of which was open to all!

How could she have so imposed on herself? – Heaven forbid that Henry Tilney should ever know her folly! And it was in a great measure his own doing, for had not the cabinet appeared so exactly to agree with his description of her adventures, she should never have felt the smallest curiosity about it. This was the only comfort that occurred. Impatient to get rid of those hateful evidences of her folly, those detestable papers then scattered over the bed, she rose directly, and folding them up as nearly as possible in the same shape as before, returned them to the same spot within the cabinet, with a very hearty wish that no untoward accident might ever bring them forward again, to disgrace her even with herself.

Why the locks should have been so difficult to open however, was still something remarkable, for she could now manage them with perfect ease. In this there was surely something mysterious, and she indulged in the flattering suggestion for half a minute, till the possibility of the door's having been at first unlocked, and of being herself its fastener, darted into her head, and cost her another blush.

She got away as soon as she could from a room in which her conduct produced such unpleasant reflections, and found her way with all speed to the breakfast-parlour, as it had been pointed out to her by Miss Tilney the evening before. Henry was alone in it; and his immediate hope of her having been undisturbed by the tempest, with an arch reference to the character of the building they inhabited, was rather distressing. For the world would she not have her weakness suspected; and yet, unequal to an absolute falsehood, was constrained to acknowledge that the wind had kept her awake a little. 'But we have a charming morning after it,' she added, desiring to get rid of the subject; 'and storms and sleeplessness are nothing when they are over. What beautiful hyacinths! – I have just learnt to love a hyacinth.'

'And how might you learn? – By accident or argument?'

'Your sister taught me; I cannot tell how. Mrs Allen used to take pains, year after year, to make me like them; but I never could, till I saw them the other day in Milsom Street; I am naturally indifferent about flowers.'

'But now you love a hyacinth. So much the better. You have gained a new source of enjoyment, and it is well to have as many holds upon happiness as possible. Besides, a taste for flowers is always desirable in your sex, as a means of getting you out of doors, and tempting you to more frequent exercise than you would otherwise take. And though the love of a hyacinth may be rather domestic, who can tell, the sentiment once raised, but you may in time come to love a rose?'

'But I do not want any such pursuit to get me out of doors. The pleasure of walking and breathing fresh air is enough for me, and in fine weather I am out more than half my time. – Mamma says, I am never within.'

'At any rate, however, I am pleased that you have learnt to love a hyacinth. The mere habit of learning to love is the thing; and a teachableness of disposition in a young lady is a great blessing. – Has my sister a pleasant mode of instruction?'

Catherine was saved the embarrassment of attempting an answer, by the entrance of the General, whose smiling compliments announced a happy state of mind, but whose gentle hint of sympathetic early rising did not advance her composure.

The elegance of the breakfast set forced itself on Catherine's notice when they were seated at table; and, luckily, it had been the General's choice. He was enchanted by her approbation of his taste, confessed it to be neat and simple, thought it right to encourage the manufacture of his country; and for his part, to his uncritical palate, the tea was as well flavoured from the clay of Staffordshire, as from that of Dresden or Sève. But this was quite an old set, purchased two years ago. The manufacture was much improved since that time; he had seen some beautiful specimens when last in town, and had he not been perfectly without vanity of that kind, might have been tempted to order a new set. He trusted, however, that an opportunity might ere long occur of selecting one – though not for himself. Catherine was probably the only one of the party who did not understand him.

Shortly after breakfast Henry left them for Woodston, where business required and would keep him two or three days. They all attended in the hall to see him mount his horse, and immediately on re-entering the breakfast room, Catherine walked to a window in the hope of catching another glimpse of his figure. 'This is a somewhat heavy call upon your brother's fortitude,' observed the General to Eleanor. 'Woodston will make but a sombre appearance today.'

'Is it a pretty place?' asked Catherine.

'What say you, Eleanor? – speak your opinion, for ladies can best tell the taste of ladies in regard to places as well as men. I think it would be acknowledged by the most impartial eye to have many recommendations. The house stands among fine meadows facing the south-east, with an excellent kitchen-garden in the same aspect; the walls surrounding which I built and stocked myself about ten years ago, for the benefit of my son. It is a family living, Miss Morland; and the property in the place being chiefly my own, you may believe I take care that it shall not be a bad one. Did Henry's income depend solely on this living, he would not be ill provided for. Perhaps it may seem odd, that with only two younger children, I should think any profession necessary for him; and certainly there are moments when we could all wish him disengaged from every tie of business. But though I may not exactly make converts of you young ladies, I am sure your father, Miss Morland, would agree with me in thinking it expedient to give every young man some employment. The money is nothing, it is not an object, but employment is the thing. Even Frederick, my eldest son, you see, who will perhaps inherit as considerable a landed property as any private man in the county, has his profession.'

The imposing effect of this last argument was equal to his wishes. The silence of the lady proved it to be unanswerable.

Something had been said the evening before of her being shown over the house, and he now offered himself as her conductor; and though Catherine had hoped to explore it accompanied only by his daughter, it was a proposal of too much happiness in itself, under any circumstances, not to be gladly accepted; for she had been already eighteen hours in the Abbey, and had seen only a few of its rooms. The netting-box, just leisurely drawn forth, was closed with joyful haste, and she was ready to attend him in a moment. 'And when they had gone over the house, he promised himself moreover the pleasure of accompanying her into the shrubberies and garden.' She curtsied her acquiescence. 'But perhaps it might be more agreeable to her to make those her first object. The weather was at present favourable, and at this time of year the uncertainty was very great of its continuing so. – Which would she prefer? He was equally at her service. – Which did his daughter think would most accord with her fair friend's wishes? – But he thought he could discern. – Yes, he certainly read in Miss Morland's eyes a judicious desire of making use of the present smiling weather. – But when did she judge amiss? – The Abbey would be always safe and dry. – He yielded implicitly, and would fetch his hat and attend them in a moment.' He left the room, and Catherine, with a disappointed, anxious face, began to speak of her unwillingness that he should be taking them out of doors against his own inclination, under a mistaken idea of pleasing her; but she was stopped by Miss Tilney's saying, with a little confusion, 'I believe it will be wisest to take the morning while it is so fine; and do not be uneasy on my father's account, he always walks out at this time of day.'

Catherine did not exactly know how this was to be understood. Why was Miss Tilney embarrassed? Could there be any unwillingness on the General's side to show her over the Abbey? The proposal was his own. And was not it odd that he should *always* take his walk so early? Neither her father nor Mr Allen did so. It was certainly very provoking. She was all impatience to see the house, and had scarcely any curiosity about the grounds. If Henry had been with them indeed! – but now she should not know what was picturesque when she saw it. Such were her thoughts, but she kept them to herself, and put on her bonnet in patient discontent.

She was struck however, beyond her expectation, by the grandeur of the Abbey, as she saw it for the first time from the lawn. The whole building enclosed a large court; and two sides of the quadrangle, rich in Gothic ornaments, stood forward for admiration. The remainder was shut off by knolls of old trees, or luxuriant plantations, and the steep woody hills rising behind to give it shelter, were beautiful even in the leafless month of March. Catherine had seen nothing to compare with it; and her feelings of delight were so strong, that without waiting for any better authority, she boldly burst forth in wonder and praise. The General listened with assenting gratitude; and it seemed as if his own estimation of Northanger had waited unfixed till that hour.

The kitchen-garden was to be next admired, and he led the way to it across a small portion of the park.

The number of acres contained in this garden was such as Catherine could not listen to without dismay, being more than double the extent of all Mr Allen's, as well as her father's including church-yard and orchard. The walls seemed countless in number, endless in length; a village of hot-houses seemed to rise among them, and a whole parish to be at work within the enclosure. The General was flattered by her looks of surprise, which told him almost as plainly, as he soon forced her to tell him in words, that she had never seen any gardens at all equal to them before; – and he then modestly owned that, 'without any ambition of that sort himself – without any solicitude about it, – he did not believe them to be unrivalled in the kingdom. If he had a hobby-horse, it was *that*. He loved a garden. Though careless enough in most matters of eating, he loved good fruit – or if he did not, his friends and children did. There were great vexations however attending such a garden as his. The utmost care could not always secure the most valuable fruits. The pinery had yielded only one hundred in the last year. Mr Allen, he supposed, must feel these inconveniences as well as himself.'

'No, not at all. Mr Allen did not care about the garden, and never went into it.'

With a triumphant smile of self-satisfaction, the General wished he could do the same, for he never entered his, without being vexed in some way or other, by its falling short of his plan.

'How were Mr Allen's succession-houses worked?' describing the nature of his own as they entered them.

'Mr Allen had only one small hot-house, which Mrs Allen had the use of for her plants in winter, and there was a fire in it now and then.'

'He is a happy man!' said the General, with a look of very happy contempt.

Having taken her into every division, and led her under every wall, till she was heartily weary of seeing and wondering, he suffered the girls at last to seize the advantage of an outer door, and then expressing his wish to examine the effect of some recent alterations about the tea-house, proposed it as no unpleasant extension of their walk, if Miss Morland were not tired. 'But where are you going, Eleanor? – Why do you choose that cold, damp path to it? Miss Morland will get wet. Our best way is across the park.'

'This is so favourite a walk of mine,' said Miss Tilney, 'that I always think it the best and nearest way. But perhaps it may be damp.'

It was a narrow winding path through a thick grove of old Scotch firs; and Catherine, struck by its gloomy aspect, and eager to enter it, could not, even by the General's disapprobation, be kept from stepping forward. He perceived her inclination, and having again urged the plea of health in vain, was too polite to make further opposition. He excused himself however from attending them: – 'The rays of the sun were not too cheerful for him, and he would meet them by another course.' He turned away; and Catherine was shocked to find how much her spirits were relieved by the separation. The shock however being less real than the relief, offered it no injury; and she began to talk with easy gaiety of the delightful melancholy which such a grove inspired.

'I am particularly fond of this spot,' said her companion, with a sigh. 'It was my mother's favourite walk.'

Catherine had never heard Mrs Tilney mentioned in the family before, and the interest excited by this tender remembrance, showed itself directly in her altered countenance, and in the attentive pause with which she waited for something more.

'I used to walk here so often with her!' added Eleanor; 'though I never loved it then, as I have loved it since. At that time indeed I used to wonder at her choice. But her memory endears it now.'

'And ought it not,' reflected Catherine, 'to endear it to her husband? Yet the General would not enter it.' Miss Tilney continuing silent, she ventured to say, 'Her death must have been a great affliction!'

'A great and increasing one,' replied the other, in a low voice. 'I was only thirteen when it happened; and though I felt my loss perhaps as strongly as one so young could feel it, I did not, I could not then know what a loss it was.' She stopped for a moment, and then added, with great firmness, 'I have no sister, you know – and though Henry – though my brothers are very affectionate, and Henry is a great deal here, which I am most thankful for, it is impossible for me not to be often solitary.'

'To be sure you must miss him very much.'

'A mother would have been always present. A mother would have been a constant friend; her influence would have been beyond all other.'

'Was she a very charming woman? Was she handsome? Was there any picture of her in the Abbey? And why had she been so partial to that grove? Was it from dejection of spirits?' – were questions now eagerly poured forth; – the first three received a ready affirmative, the two others were passed by; and Catherine's interest in the deceased Mrs Tilney augmented with every question, whether answered or not. Of her unhappiness in marriage, she felt persuaded. The General certainly had been an unkind husband. He did not love her walk: – could he therefore have loved her? And besides, handsome as he was, there was a something in the turn of his features which spoke his not having behaved well to her.

'Her picture, I suppose,' blushing at the consummate art of her own question, 'hangs in your father's room?'

'No; – it was intended for the drawing-room; but my father was dissatisfied with the painting, and for some time it had no place. Soon after her death I obtained it for my own, and hung it in my bed-chamber – where I shall be happy to show it you; – it is very like.' – Here was another proof. A portrait – very like – of a departed wife, not valued by the husband! – He must have been dreadfully cruel to her!

Catherine attempted no longer to hide from herself the nature of the feelings which, in spite of all his attentions, he had previously excited; and what had been terror and dislike before, was now absolute aversion. Yes, aversion! His cruelty to such a charming woman made him odious to her. She had often read of such characters; characters which Mr Allen had been used to call unnatural and overdrawn; but here was proof positive of the contrary.

She had just settled this point, when the end of the path brought them directly upon the General; and in spite of all her virtuous indignation, she found herself again obliged to walk with him, listen to him, and even to smile when he smiled. Being no longer able however to receive pleasure from the surrounding objects, she soon began to walk with lassitude; the General perceived it, and with a concern for her health, which seemed to reproach her for her opinion of him, was most urgent for returning with his daughter to the house. He would follow them in a quarter of an hour. Again they parted – but Eleanor was called back in half a minute to receive a strict charge against taking her friend round the Abbey till his return. This second instance of his anxiety to delay what she so much wished for, struck Catherine as very remarkable.

Chapter 23

AN HOUR PASSED AWAY before the General came in, spent, on the part of his young guest, in no very favourable consideration of his character. – 'This lengthened absence, these solitary rambles, did not speak a mind of ease, or a conscience void of reproach.' – At length he appeared; and, whatever might have been the gloom of his meditations, he could still smile with *them*. Miss Tilney, understanding in part her friend's curiosity to see the house, soon revived the subject; and her father being, contrary to Catherine's expectations, unprovided with any pretence for further delay, beyond that of stopping five minutes to order refreshments to be in the room by their return, was at last ready to escort them.

They set forward; and, with a grandeur of air, a dignified step, which caught the eye, but could not shake the doubts of the well-read Catherine, he led the way across the hall, through the common drawing-room and one useless anti-chamber, into a room magnificent both in size and furniture – the real drawing-room, used only with company of consequence. – It was very noble – very grand – very charming! – was all that Catherine had to say, for her indiscriminating eye scarcely discerned the colour of the satin; and all minuteness of praise, all praise that had much meaning, was supplied by the General: the costliness or elegance of any room's fitting-up could be nothing to her; she cared for no furniture of a more modern date than the fifteenth century. When the General had satisfied his own curiosity, in a close examination of every well-known ornament, they proceeded into the library, an apartment, in its way, of equal magnificence, exhibiting a collection of books, on which an humble man might have looked with pride. – Catherine heard, admired, and wondered with more genuine feeling than before – gathered all that she could from this store-house of knowledge, by running over the titles of half a shelf, and was ready to proceed. But suites of apartments did not spring up with her wishes. – Large as was the building, she had already visited the greatest part; though, on being told that, with the addition of the kitchen, the six or seven rooms she had now seen surrounded three sides of the court, she could scarcely believe it, or overcome the suspicion of there being many chambers secreted. It was some relief, however, that they were to return to the rooms in common use, by passing through a few of less importance, looking into the court, which, with occasional passages, not wholly unintricate, connected the different sides; – and she was further soothed in her progress, by being told, that she was treading what had once been a cloister, having traces of cells pointed out, and observing several doors, that were neither opened nor explained to her; – by finding herself successively in a billiard-room, and in the General's private apartment, without comprehending their connection, or being able to turn aright when she left them; and lastly, by passing through a dark little room, owning Henry's authority, and strewed with his litter of books, guns, and great coats.

From the dining-room of which, though already seen, and always to be seen at five o'clock, the General could not forego the pleasure of pacing out the length, for the more certain information of Miss Morland, as to what she neither doubted nor cared for, they proceeded by quick communication to the kitchen – the ancient kitchen of the convent, rich in the massy walls and smoke of former days, and in the stoves and hot closets of the present. The General's improving hand had not loitered here: every modern invention to facilitate the labour of the cooks, had been adopted within this, their spacious theatre; and, when the genius of others had failed, his own had often produced the perfection wanted. His endowments of this spot alone might at any time have placed him high among the benefactors of the convent.

With the walls of the kitchen ended all the antiquity of the Abbey; the fourth side of the quadrangle having, on account of its decaying state, been removed by the General's father, and the present erected in its place. All that was venerable ceased here. The new building was not only new, but declared itself to be so; intended only for offices, and enclosed behind by stable-yards, no uniformity of architecture had been thought necessary. Catherine could have raved at the hand which had swept away what must have been beyond the value of all the rest, for the purposes of mere domestic economy; and would willingly have been spared the mortification of a walk through scenes so fallen, had the General allowed it; but if he had a vanity, it was in the arrangement of his offices; and as he was convinced, that, to a mind like Miss Morland's, a view of the accommodations and comforts, by which the labours of her inferiors were softened, must always be gratifying, he should make no apology for leading her on. They took a slight survey of all; and Catherine was impressed, beyond her expectation, by their multiplicity and their convenience. The purposes for which a few shapeless pantries and a comfortless scullery were deemed sufficient at Fullerton, were here carried on in appropriate divisions, commodious and roomy. The number of servants continually appearing, did not strike her less than the number of their offices. Wherever they went, some pattened girl stopped to curtsey, or some footman in dishabille sneaked off. Yet this was an Abbey! – How inexpressibly different in these domestic arrangements from such as she had read about – from abbeys and castles, in which, though certainly larger than Northanger, all the dirty work of the house was to be done by two pair of female hands at the utmost. How they could get through it all, had often amazed Mrs Allen; and, when Catherine saw what was necessary here, she began to be amazed herself.

They returned to the hall, that the chief staircase might be ascended, and the beauty of its wood, and ornaments of rich carving might be pointed out: having gained the top, they turned in an opposite direction from the gallery in which her room lay, and shortly entered one on the same plan, but superior in length and breadth. She was here shown successively into three large bed-chambers, with their dressing-rooms, most completely and handsomely fitted up; everything that money and taste could do, to give comfort and elegance to apartments, had been bestowed on these; and, being furnished within the last five years, they were perfect in all that would be generally pleasing, and wanting in all that could give pleasure to Catherine. As they were surveying the last, the General, after slightly naming a few of the distinguished characters, by whom they had at times been honoured, turned with a smiling countenance to Catherine, and ventured to hope, that henceforward some of their earliest tenants might be 'our friends from Fullerton.' She felt the unexpected compliment, and deeply regretted the impossibility of thinking well of a man so kindly disposed towards herself, and so full of civility to all her family.

The gallery was terminated by folding doors, which Miss Tilney, advancing, had thrown open, and passed through, and seemed on the point of doing the same by the first door to the left, in another long reach of gallery, when the General, coming forwards, called her hastily, and, as Catherine thought, rather angrily back, demanding whither she were going? – And what was there more to be seen? – Had not Miss Morland already seen all that could be worth her notice? – And did she not suppose her friend might be glad of some refreshment after so much exercise? Miss Tilney drew back directly, and the heavy doors were closed upon the mortified Catherine, who, having seen, in a momentary glance beyond them, a narrower passage, more numerous openings, and symptoms of a winding staircase, believed herself at last within the reach of something worth her notice; and felt, as she unwillingly paced back the gallery, that she would rather be allowed to examine that end of the house, than see all the finery of all the rest. – The General's evident desire of preventing such an examination was an additional stimulant. Something was certainly to be concealed; her fancy, though it had trespassed lately once or twice, could not mislead her here; and what that something was, a short sentence of Miss Tilney's, as they followed the General at some distance downstairs, seemed to point out: – 'I was going to take you into what was my mother's room – the room in which she died – ' were all her words; but few as they were, they conveyed pages of intelligence to Catherine. It was no wonder that the General should shrink from the sight of such objects as that room must contain; a room in all probability never entered by him since the dreadful scene had passed, which released his suffering wife, and left him to the stings of conscience.

She ventured, when next alone with Eleanor, to express her wish of being permitted to see it, as well as all the rest of that side of the house; and Eleanor promised to attend her there, whenever they should have a convenient hour. Catherine understood her: – the General must be watched from home, before that room could be entered. 'It remains as it was, I suppose?' said she, in a tone of feeling.

'Yes, entirely.'

'And how long ago may it be that your mother died?'

'She has been dead these nine years.' And nine years, Catherine knew was a trifle of time, compared with what generally elapsed after the death of an injured wife, before her room was put to rights.

'You were with her, I suppose, to the last?'

'No,' said Miss Tilney, sighing; 'I was unfortunately from home. – Her illness was sudden and short; and, before I arrived it was all over.'

Catherine's blood ran cold with the horrid suggestions which naturally sprang from these words. Could it be possible? – Could Henry's father? – And yet how many were the examples to justify even the blackest suspicions! – And, when she saw him in the evening, while she worked with her friend, slowly pacing the drawing-room for an hour together in silent thoughtfulness, with downcast eyes and contracted brow, she felt secure from all possibility of wronging him. It was the air and attitude of a Montoni! – What could more plainly speak the gloomy workings of a mind not wholly dead to every sense of humanity, in its fearful review of past scenes of guilt? Unhappy man! – And the anxiousness of her spirits directed her eyes towards his figure so repeatedly, as to catch Miss Tilney's notice. 'My father,' she whispered, 'often walks about the room in this way; it is nothing unusual.'

'So much the worse!' thought Catherine; such ill-timed exercise was of a piece with the strange unseasonableness of his morning walks, and boded nothing good.

After an evening, the little variety and seeming length of which made her peculiarly sensible of Henry's importance among them, she was heartily glad to be dismissed; though it was a look from the General not designed for her observation which sent his daughter to the bell. When the butler would have lit his master's candle, however, he was forbidden. The latter was not going to retire. 'I have many pamphlets to finish,' said he to Catherine, 'before I can close my eyes; and perhaps may be poring over the affairs of the nation for hours after you are asleep. Can either of us be more meetly employed? My eyes will be blinding for the good of others; and *yours* preparing by rest for future mischief.'

But neither the business alleged, not the magnificent compliment, could win Catherine from thinking, that some very different object must occasion so serious a delay of proper repose. To be kept up for hours, after the family were in bed, by stupid pamphlets, was not very likely. There must be some deeper cause: something was to be done which could be done only while the household slept; and the probability that Mrs Tilney yet lived, shut up for causes unknown, and receiving from the pitiless hands of her husband a nightly supply of coarse food, was the conclusion which necessarily followed. Shocking as was the idea, it was at least better than a death unfairly hastened, as, in the natural course of things, she must ere long be released. The suddenness of her reputed illness; the absence of her daughter, and probably of her other children, at the time – all favoured the supposition of her imprisonment. – Its origin – jealousy perhaps, or wanton cruelty – was yet to be unravelled.

In revolving these matters, while she undressed, it suddenly struck her as not unlikely, that she might that morning have passed near the very spot of this unfortunate woman's confinement – might have been within a few paces of the cell in which she languished out her days; for what part of the Abbey could be more fitted for the purpose than that which yet bore the traces of monastic division? In the high-arched passage, paved with stone, which already she had trodden with peculiar awe, she well remembered the doors of which the General had given no account. To what might not those doors lead? In support of the plausibility of this conjecture, it further occurred to her, that the forbidden gallery, in which lay the apartments of the unfortunate Mrs Tilney, must be, as certainly as her memory could guide her, exactly over this suspected range of cells, and the staircase by the side of those apartments of which she had caught a transient glimpse, communicating by some secret means with those cells, might well have favoured the barbarous proceedings of her husband. Down that staircase she had perhaps been conveyed in a state of well-prepared insensibility!

Catherine sometimes started at the boldness of her own surmises, and sometimes hoped or feared that she had gone too far; but they were supported by such appearances as made their dismissal impossible.

The side of the quadrangle, in which she supposed the guilty scene to be acting, being, according to her belief, just opposite her own, it struck her that, if judiciously watched, some rays of light from the General's lamp might glimmer through the lower windows, as he passed to the prison of his wife; and, twice before she stepped into bed, she stole gently from her room to the corresponding window in the gallery, to see if it appeared; but all abroad was dark, and it must yet be too early. The various ascending noises convinced her that the servants must still be up. Till midnight, she supposed it would be in vain to watch; but then, when the clock had struck twelve, and all was quiet, she would, if not quite appalled by darkness, steal out and look once more. The clock struck twelve – and Catherine had been half an hour asleep.

Chapter 24

THE NEXT DAY afforded no opportunity for the proposed examination of the mysterious apartments. It was Sunday, and the whole time between morning and afternoon service was required by the General in exercise abroad or eating cold meat at home; and great as was Catherine's curiosity, her courage was not equal to a wish of exploring them after dinner, either by the fading light of the sky between six and seven o'clock, or by the yet more partial though stronger illumination of a treacherous lamp. The day was unmarked therefore by anything to interest her imagination beyond the sight of a very elegant monument to the memory of Mrs Tilney, which immediately fronted the family pew. By that her eye was instantly caught and long retained; and the perusal of the highly-strained epitaph, in which every virtue was ascribed to her by the inconsolable husband, who must have been in some way or other her destroyer, affected her even to tears.

That the General, having erected such a monument, should be able to face it, was not perhaps very strange, and yet that he could sit so boldly collected within its view, maintain so elevated an air, look so fearlessly around, nay, that he should even enter the church, seemed wonderful to Catherine. Not however that many instances of beings equally hardened in guilt might not be produced. She could remember dozens who had persevered in every possible vice, going on from crime to crime, murdering whomsoever they chose, without any feeling of humanity or remorse; till a violent death or a religious retirement closed their black career. The erection of the monument itself could not in the smallest degree affect her doubts of Mrs Tilney's actual decease. Were she even to descend into the family vault where her ashes were supposed to slumber, were she to behold the coffin in which they were said to be enclosed – what could it avail in such a case? Catherine had read too much not to be perfectly aware of the ease with which a waxen figure might be introduced, and a supposititious funeral carried on.

The succeeding morning promised something better. The General's early walk, ill-timed as it was in every other view, was favourable here; and when she knew him to be out of the house, she directly proposed to Miss Tilney the accomplishment of her promise. Eleanor was ready to oblige her; and Catherine reminding her as they went of another promise, their first visit in consequence was to the portrait in her bedchamber. It represented a very lovely woman, with a mild and pensive countenance, justifying, so far, the expectations of its new observer; but they were not in every respect answered, for Catherine had depended upon meeting with features, air, complexion that should be the very counterpart, the very image, if not of Henry's, of Eleanor's; – the only portraits of which she had been in the habit of thinking, bearing always an equal resemblance of mother and child. A face once taken was taken for generations. But here she was obliged to look and consider and study for a likeness. She contemplated it, however, in spite of this drawback, with much emotion; and, but for a yet stronger interest, would have left it unwillingly.

Her agitation as they entered the great gallery was too much for any endeavour at discourse; she could only look at her companion. Eleanor's countenance was dejected, yet sedate; and its composure spoke her enured to all the gloomy objects to which they were advancing. Again she passed through the folding-doors, again her hand was upon the important lock, and Catherine, hardly able to breathe, was turning to close the former with fearful caution, when the figure, the dreaded figure of the General himself at the further end of the gallery, stood before her! The name of 'Eleanor' at the same moment, in his loudest tone, resounded through the building, giving to his daughter the first intimation of his presence, and to Catherine terror upon terror. An attempt at concealment had been her first instinctive movement on perceiving him, yet she could scarcely hope to have escaped his eye; and when her friend, who with an apologising look darted hastily by her, had joined and disappeared with him, she ran for safety to her own room, and, locking herself in, believed that she should never have courage to go down again. She remained there at least an hour, in the greatest agitation, deeply commiserating the state of her poor friend, and expecting a summons herself from the angry General to attend him in his own apartment. No summons however arrived; and at last, on seeing a carriage drive up to the Abbey, she was emboldened to descend and meet him under the protection of visitors. The breakfast-room was gay with company; and she was named to them by the General, as the friend of his daughter, in a complimentary style, which so well concealed his resentful ire, as to make her feel secure at least of life for the present. And Eleanor, with a command of countenance which did honour to her concern for his character, taking an early occasion of saying to her, 'My father only wanted me to answer a note,' she began to hope that she had either been unseen by the General, or that from some consideration of policy she should be allowed to suppose herself so. Upon this trust she dared still to remain in his presence, after the company left them, and nothing occurred to disturb it.

In the course of this morning's reflections, she came to a resolution of making her next attempt on the forbidden door alone. It would be much better in every respect that Eleanor should know nothing of the matter. To involve her in the danger of a second detection, to court her into an apartment which must wring her heart, could not be the office of a friend. The General's utmost anger could not be to herself what it might be to a daughter; and, besides, she thought the examination itself would be more satisfactory if made without any companion. It would be impossible to explain to Eleanor the suspicions, from which the other had, in all likelihood, been hitherto happily exempt; nor could she therefore, in *her* presence, search for those proofs of the General's cruelty, which however they might yet have escaped discovery, she felt confident of somewhere drawing forth, in the shape of some fragmented journal, continued to the last gasp. Of the way to the apartment she was now perfectly mistress; and as she wished to get it over before Henry's return, who was expected on the morrow, there was no time to be lost. The day was bright, her courage high; at four o'clock, the sun was now two hours above the horizon, and it would be only her retiring to dress half an hour earlier than usual.

It was done; and Catherine found herself alone in the gallery before the clocks had ceased to strike. It was no time for thought; she hurried on, slipped with the least possible noise through the folding doors, and without stopping to look or breathe, rushed forward to the one in question. The lock yielded to her hands and, luckily, with no sullen sound that could alarm a human being. On tip-toe she entered; the room was before her; but it was some minutes before she could advance another step. She beheld what fixed her to the spot and agitated every feature. – She saw a large, well-proportioned apartment, an handsome dimity bed,[21] arranged as unoccupied with an housemaid's care, a bright Bath stove, mahogany wardrobes and neatly-painted chairs, on which the warm beams of a western sun gaily poured through two sash windows! Catherine had expected to have her feelings worked, and worked they were. Astonishment and doubt first seized them; and a shortly succeeding ray of common sense added some bitter emotions of shame. She could not be mistaken as to the room; but how grossly mistaken in everything else! – in Miss Tilney's meaning, in her own calculation! This apartment, to which she had given a date so ancient, a position so awful, proved to be one end of what the General's father had built. There were two other doors in the chamber, leading probably into dressing-closets; but she had no inclination to open either. Would the veil in which Mrs Tilney had last walked, or the volume in which she had last read, remain to tell what nothing else was allowed to whisper? No: whatever might have been the General's crimes, he had certainly too much wit to let them sue for detection. She was sick of exploring, and desired but to be safe in her own room, with her own heart only privy to its folly; and she was on the point of retreating as softly as she had entered, when the sound of footsteps, she could hardly tell where, made her pause and tremble. To be found there, even by a servant, would be unpleasant; but by the General, (and he seemed always at hand when least wanted,) much worse! – She listened – the sound had ceased; and resolving not to lose a moment, she passed through and closed the door. At that instant a door underneath was hastily opened; someone seemed with swift steps to ascend the stairs, by the head of which she had yet to pass before she could gain the gallery. She had no power to move. With a feeling of terror not very definable, she fixed her eyes on the staircase, and in a few moments it gave Henry to her view. 'Mr Tilney!' she exclaimed in a voice of more than common astonishment. He looked astonished too. 'Good God!' she continued, not attending to his address, 'how came you here? – how came you up that staircase?'

'How came I up that staircase!' he replied, greatly surprised. 'Because it is my nearest way from the stable-yard to my own chamber; and why should I not come up it?'

Catherine recollected herself, blushed deeply, and could say no more. He seemed to be looking in her countenance for that explanation which her lips did not afford. She moved on towards the gallery. 'And may I not, in my turn,' said he, as he pushed back the folding doors, 'ask how *you* came here? – This passage is at least as extraordinary a road from the breakfast-parlour to your apartment, as that staircase can be from the stables to mine.'

'I have been,' said Catherine, looking down, 'to see your mother's room.'

'My mother's room! – Is there anything extraordinary to be seen there?'

'No, nothing at all. – I thought you did not mean to come back till tomorrow.'

'I did not expect to be able to return sooner, when I went away; but three hours ago I had the pleasure of finding nothing to detain me. – You look pale. – I am afraid I alarmed you by running so fast up those stairs. Perhaps you did not know – you were not aware of their leading from the offices in common use?'

'No, I was not. – You have had a very fine day for your ride.'

'Very; – and does Eleanor leave you to find your way into all the rooms in the house by yourself?'

'Oh! no; she showed me over the greatest part on Saturday – and we were coming here to these rooms – but only – (dropping her voice) – your father was with us.'

'And that prevented you;' said Henry, earnestly regarding her. – 'Have you looked into all the rooms in that passage?'

'No, I only wanted to see – Is not it very late? I must go and dress.'

'It is only a quarter past four, (showing his watch) and you are not now in Bath. No theatre, no rooms to prepare for. Half an hour at Northanger must be enough.'

She could not contradict it, and therefore suffered herself to be detained, though her dread of further questions made her, for the first time in their acquaintance, wish to leave him. They walked slowly up the gallery. 'Have you had any letter from Bath since I saw you?'

'No, and I am very much surprised. Isabella promised so faithfully to write directly.'

'Promised so faithfully! – A faithful promise! – That puzzles me. – I have heard of a faithful performance. But a faithful promise – the fidelity of promising! It is a power little worth knowing however, since it can deceive and pain you. My mother's room is very commodious, is it not? Large and cheerful-looking, and the dressing closets so well disposed! It always strikes me as the most comfortable apartment in the house, and I rather wonder that Eleanor should not take it for her own. She sent you to look at it, I suppose?'

'No.'

'It has been your own doing entirely' – Catherine said nothing – After a short silence, during which he had closely observed her, he added, 'As there is nothing in the room in itself to raise curiosity, this must have proceeded from a sentiment of respect for my mother's character, as described by Eleanor, which does honour to her memory. The world, I believe, never saw a better woman. But it is not often that virtue can boast an interest such as this. The domestic, unpretending merits of a person never known, do not often create that kind of fervent, venerating tenderness which would prompt a visit like yours. Eleanor, I suppose, has talked of her a great deal?'

'Yes, a great deal. That is – no, not much, but what she did say, was very interesting. Her dying so suddenly,' (slowly, and with hesitation it was spoken,) 'and you – none of you being at home – and your father, I thought – perhaps had not been very fond of her.'

'And from these circumstances,' he replied, (his quick eye fixed on hers,) 'you infer perhaps the probability of some negligence – some – (involuntarily she shook her head) – or it may be – of something still less pardonable.' She raised her eyes towards him more fully than she had ever done before. 'My mother's illness,' he continued, 'the seizure which ended in her death *was* sudden. The malady itself, one from which she had often suffered, a bilious fever – its cause therefore constitutional. On the third day, in short as soon as she could be prevailed on, a physician attended her, a very respectable man, and one in whom she had always placed great confidence. Upon his opinion of her danger, two others were called in the next day, and remained in almost constant attendance for four-and-twenty hours. On the fifth day she died. During the progress of her disorder, Frederick and I *(we* were both at home) saw her repeatedly; and from our own observation can bear witness of her having received every possible attention which could spring from the affection of those about her, or which her situation in life could command. Poor Eleanor *was* absent, and at such a distance as to return only to see her mother in her coffin.'

'But your father,' said Catherine, 'was *he* afflicted?'

'For a time, greatly so. You have erred in supposing him not attached to her. He loved her, I am persuaded, as well as it was possible for him to – We have not all, you know, the same tenderness of disposition – and I will not pretend to say that while she lived, she might not often have had much to bear, but though his temper injured her, his judgment never did. His value of her was sincere; and, if not permanently, he was truly afflicted by her death.'

'I am very glad of it,' said Catherine, 'it would have been very shocking!' –

'If I understand you rightly, you have formed a surmise of such horror as I have hardly words to – Dear Miss Morland, consider the dreadful nature of the suspicions you have entertained. What have you been judging from? Remember the country and the age in which we live. Remember that we are English, that we are Christians. Consult your own understanding, your own sense of the probable, your own observation of what is passing around you – Does our education prepare us for such atrocities? Do our laws connive at them? Could they be perpetrated without being known, in a country like this, where social and literary intercourse is on such a footing; where every man is surrounded by a neighbourhood of voluntary spies, and where roads and newspapers lay everything open? Dearest Miss Morland, what ideas have you been admitting?'

They had reached the end of the gallery; and with tears of shame she ran off to her own room.

Chapter 25

THE VISIONS OF ROMANCE were over. Catherine was completely awakened. Henry's address, short as it had been, had more thoroughly opened her eyes to the extravagance of her late fancies than all their several disappointments had done. Most grievously was she humbled. Most bitterly did she cry. It was not only with herself that she was sunk – but with Henry. Her folly, which now seemed even criminal, was all exposed to him, and he must despise her for ever. The liberty which her imagination had dared to take with the character of his father, could he ever forgive it? The absurdity of her curiosity and her fears, could they ever be forgotten? She hated herself more than she could express. He had – she thought he had, once or twice before this fatal morning, shown something like affection for her. – But now – in short, she made herself as miserable as possible for about half an hour, went down when the clock struck five, with a broken heart, and could scarcely give an intelligible answer to Eleanor's inquiry, if she was well. The formidable Henry soon followed her into the room, and the only difference in his behaviour to her, was that he paid her rather more attention than usual. Catherine had never wanted comfort more and he looked as if he was aware of it.

The evening wore away with no abatement of this soothing politeness; and her spirits were gradually raised to a modest tranquillity. She did not learn either to forget or defend the past; but she learned to hope that it would never transpire farther, and that it might not cost her Henry's entire regard. Her thoughts being still chiefly fixed on what she had with such causeless terror felt and done, nothing could shortly be clearer, than that it had been all a voluntary, self-created delusion, each trifling circumstance receiving importance from an imagination resolved on alarm, and everything forced to bend to one purpose by a mind which, before she entered the Abbey, had been craving to be frightened. She remembered with what feelings she had prepared for a knowledge of Northanger. She saw that the infatuation had been created, the mischief settled long before her quitting Bath, and it seemed as if the whole might be traced to the influence of that sort of reading which she had there indulged.

Charming as were all Mrs Radcliffe's works, and charming even as were the works of all her imitators, it was not in them perhaps that human nature, at least in the midland counties of England, was to be looked for. Of the Alps and Pyrenees, with their pine forests and their vices, they might give a faithful delineation; and Italy, Switzerland, and the South of France, might be as fruitful in horrors as they were there represented. Catherine dared not doubt beyond her own country, and even of that, if hard pressed, would have yielded the northern and western extremities. But in the central part of England there was surely some security for the existence even of a wife not beloved, in the laws of the land, and the manners of the age. Murder was not tolerated, servants were not slaves, and neither poison nor sleeping potions to be procured, like rhubarb, from every druggist. Among the Alps and Pyrenees, perhaps, there were no mixed characters. There, such as were not as spotless as an angel, might have the dispositions of a fiend. But in England it was not so; among the English, she believed, in their hearts and habits, there was a general though unequal mixture of good and bad. Upon this conviction, she would not be surprised if even in Henry and Eleanor Tilney, some slight imperfection might hereafter appear; and upon this conviction she need not fear to acknowledge some actual specks in the character of their father, who, though cleared from the grossly injurious suspicions which she must ever blush to have entertained, she did believe, upon serious consideration, to be not perfectly amiable.

Her mind made up on these several points, and her resolution formed, of always judging and acting in future with the greatest good sense, she had nothing to do but to forgive herself and be happier than ever; and the lenient hand of time did much for her by insensible gradations in the course of another day. Henry's astonishing generosity and nobleness of conduct, in never alluding in the slightest way to what had passed, was of the greatest assistance to her; and sooner than she could have supposed it possible in the beginning of her distress, her spirits became absolutely comfortable, and capable, as heretofore, of continual improvement by anything he said. There were still some subjects indeed, under which she believed they must always tremble; – the mention of a chest or a cabinet, for instance – and she did not love the sight of japan in any shape: but even *she* could allow, that an occasional memento of past folly, however painful, might not be without use.

The anxieties of common life began soon to succeed to the alarms of romance. Her desire of hearing from Isabella grew every day greater. She was quite impatient to know how the Bath world went on, and how the Rooms were attended; and especially was she anxious to be assured of Isabella's having matched some fine netting-cotton, on which she had left her intent; and of her continuing on the best terms with James.

Her only dependence for information of any kind was on Isabella. James had protested against writing to her till his return to Oxford; and Mrs Allen had given her no hopes of a letter till she had got back to Fullerton. – But Isabella had promised and promised again; and when she promised a thing, she was so scrupulous in performing it! this made it so particularly strange!

For nine successive mornings, Catherine wondered over the repetition of a disappointment, which each morning became more severe: but, on the tenth, when she entered the breakfast-room, her first object was a letter, held out by Henry's willing hand. She thanked him as heartily as if he had written it himself. ' 'Tis only from James, however,' as she looked at the direction. She opened it; it was from Oxford; and to this purpose:

DEAR CATHERINE,

Though, God knows, with little inclination for writing, I think it my duty to tell you, that everything is at an end between Miss Thorpe and me. – I left her and Bath yesterday, never to see either again. I shall not enter into particulars, they would only pain you more. You will soon hear enough from another quarter to know where lies the blame; and I hope will acquit your brother of everything but the folly of too easily thinking his affection returned. Thank God! I am undeceived in time! But it is a heavy blow! – After my father's consent had been so kindly given – but no more of this. She has made me miserable for ever! Let me soon hear from you, dear Catherine; you are my only friend; *your* love I do build upon. I wish your visit at Northanger may be over before Captain Tilney makes his engagement known, or you will be uncomfortably circumstanced. – Poor Thorpe is in town: I dread the sight of him; his honest heart would feel so much. I have written to him and my father. Her duplicity hurts me more than all; till the very last, if I reasoned with her, she declared herself as much attached to me as ever, and laughed at my fears. I am ashamed to think how long I bore with it; but if ever man had reason to believe himself loved, I was that man. I cannot understand even now what she would be at, for there could be no need of my being played off to make her secure of Tilney. We parted at last by mutual consent – happy for me had we never met! I can never expect to know such another woman! Dearest Catherine, beware how you give your heart.

Believe me, &c.

Catherine had not read three lines before her sudden change of countenance, and short exclamations of sorrowing wonder, declared her to be receiving unpleasant news; and Henry, earnestly watching her through the whole letter, saw plainly that it ended no better than it began. He was prevented, however, from even looking his surprise by his father's entrance. They went to breakfast directly; but Catherine could hardly eat anything. Tears filled her eyes, and even ran down her cheeks as she sat. The letter was one moment in her hand, then in her lap, and then in her pocket; and she looked as if she knew not what she did. The General, between his cocoa and his newspaper, had luckily no leisure for noticing her; but to the other two her distress was equally visible. As soon as she dared leave the table she hurried away to her own room; but the house-maids were busy in it, and she was obliged to come down again. She turned into the drawing-room for privacy, but Henry and Eleanor had likewise retreated thither, and were at that moment deep in consultation about her. She drew back, trying to beg their pardon, but was, with gentle violence, forced to return; and the others withdrew, after Eleanor had affectionately expressed a wish of being of use or comfort to her.

After half an hour's free indulgence of grief and reflection, Catherine felt equal to encountering her friends; but whether she should make her distress known to them was another consideration. Perhaps, if particularly questioned, she might just give an idea – just distantly hint at it – but not more. To expose a friend, such a friend as Isabella had been to her – and then her own brother so closely concerned in it! – She believed she must waive the subject altogether. Henry and Eleanor were by themselves in the breakfast-room; and each, as she entered it, looked at her anxiously. Catherine took her place at the table, and, after a short silence, Eleanor said, 'No bad news from Fullerton, I hope? Mr and Mrs Morland – your brothers and sisters – I hope they are none of them ill?'

'No, I thank you,' (sighing as she spoke,) 'they are all very well. My letter was from my brother at Oxford.'

Nothing further was said for a few minutes; and then speaking through her tears, she added, 'I do not think I shall ever wish for a letter again!'

'I am sorry,' said Henry, closing the book he had just opened; 'if I had suspected the letter of containing anything unwelcome, I should have given it with very different feelings.'

'It contained something worse than anybody could suppose! – Poor James is so unhappy! – You will soon know why.'

'To have so kind-hearted, so affectionate a sister,' replied Henry, warmly, 'must be a comfort to him under any distress.'

'I have one favour to beg,' said Catherine, shortly afterwards, in an agitated manner, 'that, if your brother should be coming here, you will give me notice of it, that I may go away.'

'Our brother! – Frederick!'

'Yes; I am sure I should be very sorry to leave you so soon, but something has happened that would make it very dreadful for me to be in the same house with Captain Tilney.'

Eleanor's work was suspended while she gazed with increasing astonishment; but Henry began to suspect the truth, and something, in which Miss Thorpe's name was included, passed his lips.

'How quick you are!' cried Catherine: 'you have guessed it, I declare! – And yet, when we talked about it in Bath, you little thought of its ending so. Isabella – no wonder *now* I have not heard from her – Isabella has deserted my brother, and is to marry yours! Could you have believed there had been such inconstancy and fickleness, and everything that is bad in the world?'

'I hope, so far as concerns my brother, you are misinformed. I hope he has not had any material share in bringing on Mr Morland's disappointment. His marrying Miss Thorpe is not probable. I think you must be deceived so far. I am very sorry for Mr Morland – sorry that anyone you love should be unhappy; but my surprise would be greater at Frederick's marrying her, than at any other part of the story.'

'It is very true, however; you shall read James's letter yourself. – Stay – there is one part – ' recollecting with a blush the last line.

'Will you take the trouble of reading to us the passages which concern my brother?'

'No, read it yourself,' cried Catherine, whose second thoughts were clearer. 'I do not know what I was thinking of' (blushing again that she had blushed before,) – 'James only means to give me good advice.' He gladly received the letter; and, having read it through, with close attention, returned it saying, 'Well, if it is to be so, I can only say that I am sorry for it. Frederick will not be the first man who has chosen a wife with less sense than his family expected. I do not envy his situation, either as a lover or a son.'

Miss Tilney, at Catherine's invitation, now read the letter likewise; and, having expressed also her concern and surprise, began to inquire into Miss Thorpe's connections and fortune.

'Her mother is a very good sort of woman,' was Catherine's answer.

'What was her father?'

'A lawyer, I believe. – They live at Putney.'

'Are they a wealthy family?'

'No, not very. I do not believe Isabella has any fortune at all: but that will not signify in your family. – Your father is so very liberal! He told me the other day, that he only valued money as it allowed him to promote the happiness of his children.' The brother and sister looked at each other. 'But,' said Eleanor, after a short pause, 'would it be to promote his happiness to enable him to marry such a girl? – She must be an unprincipled one, or she could not have used your brother so. – And how strange an infatuation on Frederick's side! A girl who, before his eyes, is violating an engagement voluntarily entered into with another man! Is not it inconceivable, Henry? Frederick too, who always wore his heart so proudly! who found no woman good enough to be loved!'

'That is the most unpromising circumstance, the strongest presumption against him. When I think of his past declarations, I give him up. – Moreover, I have too good an opinion of Miss Thorpe's prudence, to suppose that she would part with one gentleman before the other was secured. It is all over with Frederick indeed! He is a deceased man – defunct in understanding. Prepare for your sister-in-law, Eleanor, and such a sister-in-law as you must delight in! – Open, candid, artless, guileless, with affections strong but simple, forming no pretensions and knowing no disguise.'

'Such a sister-in-law, Henry, I should delight in,' said Eleanor, with a smile.

'But perhaps,' observed Catherine, 'though she has behaved so ill by our family, she may behave better by yours. Now she has really got the man she likes, she may be constant.'

'Indeed I am afraid she will,' replied Henry; 'I am afraid she will be very constant, unless a baronet should come in her way; that is Frederick's only chance. – I will get the Bath paper, and look over the arrivals.'

'You think it is all for ambition then? – And, upon my word, there are some things that seem very like it. I cannot forget, that, when she first knew what my father would do for them, she seemed quite disappointed that it was not more. I never was so deceived in anyone's character in my life before.'

'Among all the great variety that you have known and studied.'

'My own disappointment and loss in her is very great; but, as for poor James, I suppose he will hardly ever recover it.'

'Your brother is certainly very much to be pitied at present; but we must not, in our concern for his sufferings, undervalue yours. You feel, I suppose, that, in losing Isabella, you lose half yourself: you feel a void in your heart which nothing else can occupy. Society is becoming irksome; and as for the amusements in which you were wont to share at Bath, the very idea of them without her is abhorrent. You would not, for instance, now go to a ball for the world. You feel that you have no longer any friend to whom you can speak with unreserve; on whose regard you can place dependence; or whose counsel, in any difficulty, you could rely on. You feel all this?'

'No,' said Catherine, after a few moments' reflection, 'I do not – ought I? To say the truth, though I am hurt and grieved, that I cannot still love her, that I am never to hear from her, perhaps never to see her again, I do not feel so very, very much afflicted as one would have thought.'

'You feel, as you always do, what is most to the credit of human nature. – Such feelings ought to be investigated, that they may know themselves.'

Catherine, by some chance or other, found her spirits so very much relieved by this conversation, that she could not regret her being led on, though so unaccountably, to mention the circumstance which had produced it.

Chapter 26

FROM THIS TIME, the subject was frequently canvassed by the three young people; and Catherine found, with some surprise, that her two young friends were perfectly agreed in considering Isabella's want of consequence and fortune as likely to throw great difficulties in the way of her marrying their brother. Their persuasion that the General would, upon this ground alone, independent of the objection that might be raised against her character, oppose the connection, turned her feelings moreover with some alarm towards herself. She was as insignificant, and perhaps as portionless as Isabella; and if the heir of the Tilney property had not grandeur and wealth enough in himself, at what point of interest were the demands of his younger brother to rest? The very painful reflections to which this thought led, could only be dispersed by a dependence on the effect of that particular partiality, which, as she was given to understand by his words as well as his actions, she had from the first been so fortunate as to excite in the General; and by a recollection of some most generous and disinterested sentiments on the subject of money, which she had more than once heard him utter, and which tempted her to think his disposition in such matters misunderstood by his children.

They were so fully convinced, however, that their brother would not have the courage to apply in person for his father's consent, and so repeatedly assured her that he had never in his life been less likely to come to Northanger than at the present time, that she suffered her mind to be at ease as to the necessity of any sudden removal of her own. But as it was not to be supposed that Captain Tilney, whenever he made his application, would give his father any just idea of Isabella's conduct, it occurred to her as highly expedient that Henry should lay the whole business before him as it really was, enabling the General by that means to form a cool and impartial opinion, and prepare his objections on a fairer ground than inequality of situations. She proposed it to him accordingly; but he did not catch at the measure so eagerly as she had expected. 'No,' said he, 'my father's hands need not be strengthened, and Frederick's confession of folly need not be forestalled. He must tell his own story.'

'But he will tell only half of it.'

'A quarter would be enough.'

A day or two passed away and brought no tidings of Captain Tilney. His brother and sister knew not what to think. Sometimes it appeared to them as if his silence would be the natural result of the suspected engagement, and at others that it was wholly incompatible with it. The General, meanwhile, though offended every morning by Frederick's remissness in writing, was free from any real anxiety about him; and had no more pressing solicitude than that of making Miss Morland's time at Northanger pass pleasantly. He often expressed his uneasiness on this head, feared the sameness of every day's society and employments would disgust her with the place, wished the Lady Frasers had been in the country, talked every now and then of having a large party to dinner, and once or twice began even to calculate the number of young dancing people in the neighbourhood. But then it was such a dead time of year, no wild-fowl, no game, and the Lady Frasers were not in the country. And it all ended, at last, in his telling Henry one morning, that when he next went to Woodston, they would take him by surprise there some day or other, and eat their mutton with him. Henry was greatly honoured and very happy, and Catherine was quite delighted with the scheme. 'And when do you think, sir, I may look forward to this pleasure? – I must be at Woodston on Monday to attend the parish meeting, and shall probably be obliged to stay two or three days.'

'Well, well, we will take our chance some one of those days. There is no need to fix. You are not to put yourself at all out of your way. Whatever you may happen to have in the house will be enough. I think I can answer for the young ladies making allowance for a bachelor's table. Let me see; Monday will be a busy day with you, we will not come on Monday; and Tuesday will be a busy one with me. I expect my surveyor from Brockham with his report in the morning; and afterwards I cannot in decency fail attending the club. I really could not face my acquaintance if I stayed away now; for, as I am known to be in the country, it would be taken exceedingly amiss; and it is a rule with me, Miss Morland, never to give offence to any of my neighbours, if a small sacrifice of time and attention can prevent it. They are a set of very worthy men. They have half a buck from Northanger twice a year; and I dine with them whenever I can. Tuesday, therefore, we may say is out of the question. But on Wednesday, I think, Henry, you may expect us; and we shall be with you early, that we may have time to look about us. Two hours and three quarters will carry us to Woodston, I suppose; we shall be in the carriage by ten; so, about a quarter before one on Wednesday, you may look for us.'

A ball itself could not have been more welcome to Catherine than this little excursion, so strong was her desire to be acquainted with Woodston; and her heart was still bounding with joy, when Henry, about an hour afterwards, came booted and great coated into the room where she and Eleanor were sitting, and said, 'I am come, young ladies, in a very moralising strain, to observe that our pleasures in this world are always to be paid for, and that we often purchase them at a great disadvantage, giving ready-monied actual happiness for a draft on the future, that may not be honoured. Witness myself, at this present hour. Because I am to hope for the satisfaction of seeing you at Woodston on Wednesday, which bad weather, or twenty other causes may prevent, I must go away directly, two days before I intended it.'

'Go away!' said Catherine, with a very long face; 'and why?'

'Why! – How can you ask the question? – Because no time is to be lost in frightening my old housekeeper out of her wits, – because I must go and prepare a dinner for you to be sure.'

'Oh! not seriously!'

'Aye, and sadly too – for I had much rather stay.'

'But how can you think of such a thing, after what the General said? when he so particularly desired you not to give yourself any trouble, because *anything* would do.'

Henry only smiled. 'I am sure it is quite unnecessary upon your sister's account and mine. You must know it to be so; and the General made such a point of your providing nothing extraordinary: – besides, if he had not said half so much as he did, he has always such an excellent dinner at home, that sitting down to a middling one for one day could not signify.'

'I wish I could reason like you, for his sake and my own. Good-bye. As tomorrow is Sunday, Eleanor. I shall not return.'

He went; and, it being at any time a much simpler operation to Catherine to doubt her own judgment than Henry's, she was very soon obliged to give him credit for being right, however disagreeable to her his going. But the inexplicability of the General's conduct dwelt much on her thoughts. That he was very particular in his eating, she had, by her own unassisted observation, already discovered; but why he should say one thing so positively, and mean another all the while, was most unaccountable! How were people, at that rate, to be understood? Who but Henry could have been aware of what his father was at?

From Saturday to Wednesday, however, they were now to be without Henry. This was the sad finale of every reflection: – and Captain Tilney's letter would certainly come in his absence; and Wednesday she was very sure would be wet. The past, present, and future, were all equally in gloom. Her brother so unhappy, and her loss in Isabella so great; and Eleanor's spirits always affected by Henry's absence! What was there to interest or amuse her? She was tired of the woods and the shrubberies – always so smooth and so dry; and the Abbey in itself was no more to her now than any other house. The painful remembrance of the folly it had helped to nourish and perfect, was the only emotion which could spring from a consideration of the building. What a revolution in her ideas! she, who had so longed to be in an abbey! Now, there was nothing so charming to her imagination as the unpretending comfort of a well-connected Parsonage, something like Fullerton, but better: Fullerton had its faults, but Woodston probably had none. – If Wednesday should ever come!

It did come, and exactly when it might be reasonably looked for. It came – it was fine – and Catherine trod on air. By ten o'clock, the chaise-and-four conveyed the trio from the Abbey; and, after an agreeable drive of almost twenty miles, they entered Woodston, a large and populous village, in a situation not unpleasant. Catherine was ashamed to say how pretty she thought it, as the General seemed to think an apology necessary for the flatness of the country, and the size of the village; but in her heart she preferred it to any place she had ever been at, and looked with great admiration at every neat house above the rank of a cottage, and at all the little chandler's shops which they passed. At the further end of the village, and tolerably disengaged from the rest of it, stood the Parsonage, a new-built substantial stone house, with its semi-circular sweep and green gates; and, as they drove up to the door, Henry, with the friends of his solitude, a large Newfoundland puppy and two or three terriers, was ready to receive and make much of them.

Catherine's mind was too full, as she entered the house, for her either to observe or to say a great deal; and, till called on by the General for her opinion of it, she had very little idea of the room in which she was sitting. Upon looking round it then, she perceived in a moment that it was the most comfortable room in the world; but she was too guarded to say so, and the coldness of her praise disappointed him.

'We are not calling it a good house,' said he. – 'We are not comparing it with Fullerton and Northanger – We are considering it as a mere Parsonage, small and confined, we allow, but decent perhaps, and habitable; and altogether not inferior to the generality, – or, in other words, I believe there are few country parsonages in England half so good. It may admit of improvement, however. Far be it from me to say otherwise; and anything in reason – a bow thrown out, perhaps – though, between ourselves, if there is one thing more than another my aversion, it is a patched-on bow.'

Catherine did not hear enough of this speech to understand or be pained by it; and other subjects being studiously brought forward and supported by Henry, at the same time that a tray full of refreshments was introduced by his servant, the General was shortly restored to his complacency, and Catherine to all her usual ease of spirits.

The room in question was of a commodious, well proportioned size, and handsomely fitted up as a dining parlour; and on their quitting it to walk round the grounds, she was shown, first into a smaller apartment, belonging peculiarly to the master of the house, and made unusually tidy on the occasion; and afterwards into what was to be the drawing-room, with the appearance of which, though unfurnished, Catherine was delighted enough even to satisfy the General. It was a prettily-shaped room, the windows reaching to the ground, and the view from them pleasant, though only over green meadows; and she expressed her admiration at the moment with all the honest simplicity with which she felt it. 'Oh! why do not you fit up this room, Mr Tilney? What a pity not to have it fitted up! It is the prettiest room I ever saw; – it is the prettiest room in the world!'

'I trust,' said the General, with a most satisfied smile, 'that it will very speedily be furnished: it waits only for a lady's taste!'

'Well, if it was my house, I should never sit anywhere else. Oh! what a sweet little cottage there is among the trees – apple trees too! It is the prettiest cottage!' –

'You like it – you approve it as an object; – it is enough. Henry, remember that Robinson is spoken to about it. The cottage remains.'

Such a compliment recalled all Catherine's consciousness, and silenced her directly; and, though pointedly applied to by the General for her choice of the prevailing colour of the paper and hangings, nothing like an opinion on the subject could be drawn from her. The influence of fresh objects and fresh air, however, was of great use in dissipating these embarrassing associations; and, having reached the ornamental part of the premises, consisting of a walk round two sides of a meadow, on which Henry's genius had begun to act about half a year ago, she was sufficiently recovered to think it prettier than any pleasure-ground she had ever been in before, though there was not a shrub in it higher than the green bench in the corner.

A saunter into other meadows, and through part of the village, with a visit to the stables to examine some improvements, and a charming game of play with a litter of puppies just able to roll about, brought them to four o'clock, when Catherine scarcely thought it could be three. At four they were to dine, and at six to set off on their return. Never had any day passed so quickly!

She could not but observe that the abundance of the dinner did not seem to create the smallest astonishment in the General; nay, that he was even looking at the side-table for cold meat which was not there. His son and daughter's observations were of a different kind. They had seldom seen him eat so heartily at any table but his own; and never before known him so little disconcerted by the melted butter's being oiled.

At six o'clock, the General having taken his coffee, the carriage again received them; and so gratifying had been the tenor of his conduct throughout the whole visit, so well assured was her mind on the subject of his expectations, that, could she have felt equally confident of the wishes of his son, Catherine would have quitted Woodston with little anxiety as to the How or the When she might return to it.

Chapter 27

THE NEXT MORNING brought the following very unexpected letter from Isabella:

Bath, April —

MY DEAREST CATHERINE,

I received your two kind letters with the greatest delight, and have a thousand apologies to make for not answering them sooner. I really am quite ashamed of my idleness; but in this horrid place one can find time for nothing. I have had my pen in my hand to begin a letter to you almost every day since you left Bath, but have always been prevented by some silly trifler or other. Pray write to me soon, and direct to my own home. Thank God! we leave this vile place tomorrow. Since you went away, I have had no pleasure in it – the dust is beyond anything; and everybody one cares for is gone. I believe if I could see you I should not mind the rest, for you are dearer to me than anybody can conceive. I am quite uneasy about your dear brother, not having heard from him since he went to Oxford; and am fearful of some misunderstanding. Your kind offices will set all right: – he is the only man I ever did or could love, and I trust you will convince him of it. The spring fashions are partly down; and the hats the most frightful you can imagine. I hope you spend your time pleasantly, but am afraid you never think of me. I will not say all that I could of the family you are with, because I would not be ungenerous, or set you against those you esteem; but it is very difficult to know whom to trust, and young men never know their minds two days together. I rejoice to say, that the young man whom, of all others, I particularly abhor, has left Bath. You will know, from this description, I must mean Captain Tilney, who, as you may remember, was amazingly disposed to follow and tease me, before you went away. Afterwards he got worse, and became quite my shadow. Many girls might have been taken in, for never were such attentions; but I knew the fickle sex too well. He went away to his regiment two days ago, and I trust I shall never be plagued with him again. He is the greatest coxcomb I ever saw, and amazingly disagreeable. The last two days he was always by the side of Charlotte Davis: I pitied his taste, but took no notice of him. The last time we met was in Bath Street, and I turned directly into a shop that he might not speak to me, – I would not even look at him. He went into the Pump-room afterwards; but I would not have followed him for all the world. Such a contrast between him and your brother! – pray send me some news of the latter – I am quite unhappy about him, he seemed so uncomfortable when he went away, with a cold, or something that affected his spirits. I would write to him myself; but have mislaid his direction; and, as I hinted above, am afraid he took something in my conduct amiss. Pray explain everything to his satisfaction; or, if he still harbours any doubt, a line from himself to me, or a call at Putney when next in town, might set all to rights. I have not been to the Rooms this age, nor to the Play, except going in last night with the Hodges's, for a frolic, at half-price: they teased me into it; and I was determined they should not say I shut myself up because Tilney was gone. We happened to sit by the Mitchells, and they pretended to be quite surprised to see me out. I knew their spite: – at one time they could not be civil to me, but now they are all friendship; but I am not such a fool as to be taken in by them. You know I have a pretty good spirit of my own. Anne Mitchell had tried to put on a turban like mine, as I wore it the week before at the Concert, but made wretched work of it – it happened to become my odd face I believe, at least Tilney told me so at the time, and said every eye was upon me; but he is the last man whose word I would take. I wear nothing but purple now: I know I look hideous in it, but no matter – it is your dear brother's favourite colour. Lose no time, my dearest, sweetest Catherine, in writing to him and to me,

Who ever am, &c.

Such a strain of shallow artifice could not impose even upon Catherine. Its inconsistencies, contradictions, and falsehood, struck her from the very first. She was ashamed of Isabella, and ashamed of having ever loved her. Her professions of attachment were now as disgusting as her excuses were empty, and her demands impudent. 'Write to James on her behalf! – No, James should never hear Isabella's name mentioned by her again.'

On Henry's arrival from Woodston, she made known to him and Eleanor their brother's safety, congratulating them with sincerity on it, and reading aloud the most material passages of her letter with strong indignation. When she had finished it, – 'So much for Isabella,' she cried, 'and for all her intimacy! She must think me an idiot, or she could not have written so; but perhaps this has served to make her character better known to me than mine is to her. I see what she has been about. She is a vain coquette, and her tricks have not answered. I do not believe she had ever any regard either for James or for me, and I wish I had never known her.'

'It will soon be as if you never had,' said Henry.

'There is but one thing that I cannot understand. I see that she has had designs on Captain Tilney, which have not succeeded; but I do not understand what Captain Tilney has been about all this time. Why should he pay her such attentions as to make her quarrel with my brother, and then fly off himself?'

'I have very little to say for Frederick's motives, such as I believe them to have been. He has his vanities as well as Miss Thorpe, and the chief difference is, that, having a stronger head, they have not yet injured himself. If the *effect* of his behaviour does not justify him with you, we had better not seek after the cause.'

'Then you do not suppose he ever really cared about her?'

'I am persuaded that he never did.'

'And only made believe to do so for mischief's sake?'

Henry bowed his assent.

'Well, then, I must say that I do not like him at all. Though it has turned out so well for us, I do not like him at all. As it happens, there is no great harm done, because I do not think Isabella has any heart to lose. But, suppose he had made her very much in love with him?'

'But we must first suppose Isabella to have had a heart to lose, – consequently to have been a very different creature; and, in that case, she would have met with very different treatment.'

'It is very right that you should stand by your brother.'

'And if you would stand by *yours*, you would not be much distressed by the disappointment of Miss Thorpe. But your mind is warped by an innate principle of general integrity, and therefore not accessible to the cool reasonings of family partiality, or a desire of revenge.'

Catherine was complimented out of further bitterness. Frederick could not be unpardonably guilty, while Henry made himself so agreeable. She resolved on not answering Isabella's letter; and tried to think no more of it.

Chapter 28

SOON AFTER THIS, the General found himself obliged to go to London for a week; and he left Northanger earnestly regretting that any necessity should rob him even for an hour of Miss Morland's company, and anxiously recommending the study of her comfort and amusement to his children as their chief object in his absence. His departure gave Catherine the first experimental conviction that a loss may be sometimes a gain. The happiness with which their time now passed, every employment voluntary, every laugh indulged, every meal a scene of ease and good-humour, walking where they liked and when they liked, their hours, pleasures and fatigues at their own command, made her thoroughly sensible of the restraint which the General's presence had imposed, and most thankfully feel their present release from it. Such ease and such delights made her love the place and the people more and more every day; and had it not been for a dread of its soon becoming expedient to leave the one, and an apprehension of not being equally beloved by the other, she would at each moment of each day have been perfectly happy; but she was now in the fourth week of her visit; before the General came home, the fourth week would be turned, and perhaps it might seem an intrusion if she stayed much longer. This was a painful consideration whenever it occurred; and eager to get rid of such a weight on her mind, she very soon resolved to speak to Eleanor about it at once, propose going away, and be guided in her conduct by the manner in which her proposal might be taken.

Aware that if she gave herself much time, she might feel it difficult to bring forward so unpleasant a subject, she took the first opportunity of being suddenly alone with Eleanor, and of Eleanor's being in the middle of a speech about something very different, to start forth her obligation of going away very soon. Eleanor looked and declared herself much concerned. She had 'hoped for the pleasure of her company for a much longer time – had been misled (perhaps by her wishes) to suppose that a much longer visit had been promised – and could not but think that if Mr and Mrs Morland were aware of the pleasure it was to her to have her there, they would be too generous to hasten her return.' – Catherine explained. – 'Oh! as to *that*, papa and mamma were in no hurry at all. As long as she was happy, they would always be satisfied.'

'Then why, might she ask, in such a hurry herself to leave them?'

'Oh! because she had been there so long.'

'Nay, if you can use such a word, I can urge you no farther. If you think it long – '

'Oh! no, I do not indeed. For my own pleasure, I could stay with you as long again.' – And it was directly settled that, till she had, her leaving them was not even to be thought of. In having this cause of uneasiness so pleasantly removed, the force of the other was likewise weakened. The kindness, the earnestness of Eleanor's manner in pressing her to stay, and Henry's gratified look on being told that her stay was determined, were such sweet proofs of her importance with them, as left her only just so much solicitude as the human mind can never do comfortably without. She did – almost always – believe that Henry loved her, and quite always that his father and sister loved and even wished her to belong to them; and believing so far, her doubts and anxieties were merely sportive irritations.

Henry was not able to obey his father's injunction of remaining wholly at Northanger in attendance on the ladies, during his absence in London; the engagements of his curate at Woodston obliging him to leave them on Saturday for a couple of nights. His loss was not now what it had been while the General was at home; it lessened their gaiety, but did not ruin their comfort; and the two girls agreeing in occupation, and improving in intimacy, found themselves so well-sufficient for the time to themselves, that it was eleven o'clock, rather a late hour at the Abbey, before they quitted the supper-room on the day of Henry's departure. They had just reached the head of the stairs, when it seemed, as far as the thickness of the walls would allow them to judge, that a carriage was driving up to the door, and the next moment confirmed the idea by the loud noise of the house-bell. After the first perturbation of surprise had passed away, in a 'Good Heaven! what can be the matter?' it was quickly decided by Eleanor to be her eldest brother, whose arrival was often as sudden, if not quite so unseasonable, and accordingly she hurried down to welcome him.

Catherine walked on to her chamber, making up her mind as well as she could, to a further acquaintance with Captain Tilney, and comforting herself under the unpleasant impression his conduct had given her, and the persuasion of his being by far too fine a gentleman to approve of her, that at least they should not meet under such circumstances as would make their meeting materially painful. She trusted he would never speak of Miss Thorpe; and indeed, as he must by this time be ashamed of the part he had acted, there could be no danger of it; and as long as all mention of Bath scenes were avoided, she thought she could behave to him very civilly. In such considerations time passed away, and it was certainly in his favour that Eleanor should be so glad to see him, and have so much to say, for half an hour was almost gone since his arrival, and Eleanor did not come up.

At that moment Catherine thought she heard her step in the gallery, and listened for its continuance; but all was silent. Scarcely, however, had she convicted her fancy of error, when the noise of something moving close to her door made her start; it seemed as if someone was touching the very doorway – and in another moment a slight motion of the lock proved that some hand must be on it. She trembled a little at the idea of anyone's approaching so cautiously; but resolving not to be again overcome by trivial appearances of alarm, or misled by a raised imagination, she stepped quietly forward, and opened the door. Eleanor, and only Eleanor, stood there. Catherine's spirits however were tranquillised but for an instant, for Eleanor's cheeks were pale, and her manner greatly agitated. Though evidently intending to come in, it seemed an effort to enter the room, and a still greater to speak when there. Catherine, supposing some uneasiness on Captain Tilney's account, could only express her concern by silent attention; obliged her to be seated, rubbed her temples with lavender-water, and hung over her with affectionate solicitude. 'My dear Catherine, you must not – you must not indeed – ' were Eleanor's first connected words. 'I am quite well. This kindness distracts me – I cannot bear it – I come to you on such an errand!'

'Errand! – to me!'

'How shall I tell you! – Oh! how shall I tell you!'

A new idea now darted into Catherine's mind, and turning as pale as her friend, she exclaimed, ' 'Tis a messenger from Woodston!'

'You are mistaken, indeed,' returned Eleanor, looking at her most compassionately – 'it is no one from Woodston. It is my father himself.' Her voice faltered, and her eyes were turned to the ground as she mentioned his name. His unlooked-for return was enough in itself to make Catherine's heart sink, and for a few moments she hardly supposed there were anything worse to be told. She said nothing; and Eleanor endeavouring to collect herself and speak with firmness, but with eyes still cast down, soon went on. 'You are too good, I am sure, to think the worse of me for the part I am obliged to perform. I am indeed a most unwilling messenger. After what has so lately passed, so lately been settled between us – how joyfully, how thankfully on my side! – as to your continuing here as I hoped for many, many weeks longer, how can I tell you that your kindness is not to be accepted – and that the happiness your company has hitherto given us is to be repaid by – but I must not trust myself with words. My dear Catherine, we are to part. My father has recollected an engagement that takes our whole family away on Monday. We are going to Lord Longtown's, near Hereford, for a fortnight. Explanation and apology are equally impossible. I cannot attempt either.'

'My dear Eleanor,' cried Catherine, suppressing her feelings as well as she could, 'do not be so distressed. A second engagement must give way to a first. I am very, very sorry we are to part – so soon, and so suddenly too; but I am not offended, indeed I am not. I can finish my visit here you know at any time; or I hope you will come to me. Can you, when you return from this lord's, come to Fullerton?'

'It will not be in my power, Catherine.'

'Come when you can, then.' –

Eleanor made no answer; and Catherine's thoughts recurring to something more directly interesting, she added, thinking aloud, 'Monday – so soon as Monday; – and you *all* go. Well, I am certain of – I shall be able to take leave however. I need not go till just before you do, you know. Do not be distressed, Eleanor, I can go on Monday very well. My father and mother's having no notice of it is of very little consequence. The General will send a servant with me, I dare say, half the way – and then I shall soon be at Salisbury, and then I am only nine miles from home.'

'Ah, Catherine! were it settled so, it would be somewhat less intolerable, though in such common attentions you would have received but half what you ought. But – how can I tell you? – Tomorrow morning is fixed for your leaving us, and not even the hour is left to your choice; the very carriage is ordered, and will be here at seven o'clock, and no servant will be offered you.'

Catherine sat down, breathless and speechless. 'I could hardly believe my senses, when I heard it; – and no displeasure, no resentment that you can feel at this moment, however justly great, can be more than I myself – but I must not talk of what I felt. Oh! that I could suggest anything in extenuation! Good God! what will your father and mother say! After courting you from the protection of real friends to this – almost double distance from your home, to have you driven out of the house, without the considerations even of decent civility! Dear, dear Catherine, in being the bearer of such a message, I seem guilty myself of all its insult; yet, I trust you will acquit me, for you must have been long enough in this house to see that I am but a nominal mistress of it, that my real power is nothing.'

'Have I offended the General?' said Catherine in a faltering voice.

'Alas! for my feelings as a daughter, all that I know, all that I answer for is, that you can have given him no just cause of offence. He certainly is greatly, very greatly discomposed; I have seldom seen him more so. His temper is not happy, and something has now occurred to ruffle it in an uncommon degree; some disappointment, some vexation, which just at this moment seems important; but which I can hardly suppose you to have any concern in, for how is it possible?'

It was with pain that Catherine could speak at all; and it was only for Eleanor's sake that she attempted it. 'I am sure,' said she, 'I am very sorry if I have offended him. It was the last thing I would willingly have done. But do not be unhappy, Eleanor. An engagement you know must be kept. I am only sorry it was not recollected sooner, that I might have written home. But it is of very little consequence.'

'I hope, I earnestly hope that to your real safety it will be of none; but to everything else it is of the greatest consequence; to comfort, appearance, propriety, to your family, to the world. Were your friends, the Allens, still in Bath, you might go to them with comparative ease; a few hours would take you there; but a journey of seventy miles, to be taken post by you, at your age, alone, unattended!'

'Oh, the journey is nothing. Do not think about that. And if we are to part, a few hours sooner or later, you know, makes no difference. I can be ready by seven. Let me be called in time.' Eleanor saw that she wished to be alone; and believing it better for each that they should avoid any further conversation, now left her with 'I shall see you in the morning.'

Catherine's swelling heart needed relief. In Eleanor's presence friendship and pride had equally restrained her tears, but no sooner was she gone than they burst forth in torrents. Turned from the house, and in such a way! – Without any reason that could justify, any apology that could atone for the abruptness, the rudeness, nay, the insolence of it. Henry at a distance – not able even to bid him farewell. Every hope, every expectation from him suspended, at least, and who could say how long? – Who could say when they might meet again? – And all this by such a man as General Tilney, so polite, so well-bred, and heretofore so particularly fond of her! It was as incomprehensible as it was mortifying and grievous. From what it could arise, and where it would end, were considerations of equal perplexity and alarm. The manner in which it was done so grossly uncivil; hurrying her away without any reference to her own convenience, or allowing her even the appearance of choice as to the time or mode of her travelling; of two days, the earliest fixed on, and of that almost the earliest hour, as if resolved to have her gone before he was stirring in the morning, that he might not be obliged even to see her. What could all this mean but an intentional affront? By some means or other she must have had the misfortune to offend him. Eleanor had wished to spare her from so painful a notion but Catherine could not believe it possible that any injury or any misfortune could provoke such ill-will against a person not connected, or, at least, not supposed to be connected with it.

Heavily passed the night. Sleep, or repose that deserved the name of sleep, was out of the question. That room, in which her disturbed imagination had tormented her on her first arrival, was again the scene of agitated spirits and unquiet slumbers. Yet how different now the source of her inquietude from what it had been then – how mournfully superior in reality and substance! Her anxiety had foundation in fact, her fears in probability; and with a mind so occupied in the contemplation of actual and natural evil, the solitude of her situation, the darkness of her chamber, the antiquity of the building were felt and considered without the smallest emotion; and though the wind was high, and often produced strange and sudden noises throughout the house, she heard it all as she lay awake, hour after hour, without curiosity or terror.

Soon after six Eleanor entered her room, eager to show attention or give assistance where it was possible; but very little remained to be done. Catherine had not loitered; she was almost dressed, and her packing almost finished. The possibility of some conciliatory message from the General occurred to her as his daughter appeared. What so natural, as that anger should pass away and repentance succeed it? and she only wanted to know how far, after what had passed, an apology might properly be received by her. But the knowledge would have been useless here, it was not called for; neither clemency nor dignity was put to the trial – Eleanor brought no message. Very little passed between them on meeting; each found her greatest safety in silence, and few and trivial were the sentences exchanged while they remained upstairs, Catherine in busy agitation completing her dress, and Eleanor with more good-will than experience intent upon filling the trunk. When everything was done they left the room, Catherine lingering only half a minute behind her friend to throw a parting glance on every well-known cherished object, and went down to the breakfast-parlour, where breakfast was prepared. She tried to eat, as well to save herself from the pain of being urged, as to make her friend comfortable; but she had no appetite, and could not swallow many mouthfuls. The contrast between this and her last breakfast in that room, gave her fresh misery, and strengthened her distaste for everything before her. It was not four-and-twenty hours ago since they had met there to the same repast, but in circumstances how different! With what cheerful ease, what happy, though false security, had she then looked around her, enjoying everything present, and fearing little in future, beyond Henry's going to Woodston for a day! Happy, happy breakfast! for Henry had been there, Henry had sat by her and helped her. These reflections were long indulged undisturbed by any address from her companion, who sat as deep in thought as herself; and the appearance of the carriage was the first thing to startle and recall them to the present moment. Catherine's colour rose at the sight of it; and the indignity with which she was treated striking at that instant on her mind with peculiar force, made her for a short time sensible only of resentment. Eleanor seemed now impelled into resolution and speech.

'You *must* write to me, Catherine,' she cried, 'you *must* let me hear from you as soon as possible. Till I know you to be safe at home, I shall not have an hour's comfort. For *one* letter, at all risks, all hazards, I must entreat. Let me have the satisfaction of knowing that you are safe at Fullerton, and have found your family well, and then, till I can ask for your correspondence as I ought to do, I will not expect more. Direct to me at Lord Longtown's, and, I must ask it, under cover to Alice.'

'No, Eleanor, if you are not allowed to receive a letter from me, I am sure I had better not write. There can be no doubt of my getting home safe.'

Eleanor only replied, 'I cannot wonder at your feelings. I will not importune you. I will trust to your own kindness of heart when I am at a distance from you.' But this, with the look of sorrow accompanying it, was enough to melt Catherine's pride in a moment, and she instantly said, 'Oh, Eleanor, I *will* write to you indeed.'

There was yet another point which Miss Tilney was anxious to settle, though somewhat embarrassed in speaking of. It had occurred to her, that after so long an absence from home, Catherine might not be provided with money enough for the expenses of her journey, and, upon suggesting it to her with most affectionate offers of accommodation, it proved to be exactly the case. Catherine had never thought on the subject till that moment; but, upon examining her purse, was convinced that but for this kindness of her friend, she might have been turned from the house without even the means of getting home; and the distress in which she must have been thereby involved filling the minds of both, scarcely another word was said by either during the time of their remaining together. Short, however, was that time. The carriage was soon announced to be ready; and Catherine, instantly rising, a long and affectionate embrace supplied the place of language in bidding each other adieu; and, as they entered the hall, unable to leave the house without some mention of one whose name had not yet been spoken by either, she paused a moment, and with quivering lips just made it intelligible that she left 'her kind remembrance for her absent friend.' But with this approach to his name ended all possibility of restraining her feelings; and, hiding her face as well as she could with her handkerchief, she darted across the hall, jumped into the chaise, and in a moment was driven from the door.

Chapter 29

CATHERINE WAS too wretched to be fearful. The journey in itself had no terrors for her; and she began it without either dreading its length, or feeling its solitariness. Leaning back in one corner of the carriage, in a violent burst of tears, she was conveyed some miles beyond the walls of the Abbey before she raised her head; and the highest point of ground within the park was almost closed from her view before she was capable of turning her eyes towards it. Unfortunately, the road she now travelled was the same which only ten days ago she had so happily passed along in going to and from Woodston; and, for fourteen miles, every bitter feeling was rendered more severe by the review of objects on which she had first looked under impressions so different. Every mile, as it brought her nearer Woodston, added to her sufferings, and when within the distance of five, she passed the turning which led to it, and thought of Henry, so near, yet so unconscious, her grief and agitation were excessive.

The day which she had spent at that place had been one of the happiest of her life. It was there, it was on that day that the General had made use of such expressions with regard to Henry and herself, had so spoken and so looked as to give her the most positive conviction of his actually wishing their marriage. Yes, only ten days ago had he elated her by his pointed regard – had he even confused her by his too significant reference! And now – what had she done, or what had she omitted to do, to merit such a change?

The only offence against him of which she could accuse herself, had been such as was scarcely possible to reach his knowledge. Henry and her own heart only were privy to the shocking suspicions which she had so idly entertained; and equally safe did she believe her secret with each. Designedly, at least, Henry could not have betrayed her. If, indeed, by any strange mischance his father should have gained intelligence of what she had dared to think and look for, of her causeless fancies and injurious examinations, she could not wonder at any degree of his indignation. If aware of her having viewed him as a murderer, she could not wonder at his even turning her from his house. But a justification so full of torture to herself, she trusted would not be in his power.

Anxious as were all her conjectures on this point, it was not, however, the one on which she dwelt most. There was a thought yet nearer, a more prevailing, more impetuous concern. How Henry would think, and feel, and look, when he returned on the morrow to Northanger and heard of her being gone, was a question of force and interest to rise over every other, to be never ceasing, alternately irritating and sooth-ing; it sometimes suggested the dread of his calm acquiescence, and at others was answered by the sweetest confidence in his regret and resentment. To the General, of course, he would not dare to speak; but to Eleanor – what might he not say to Eleanor about her?

In this unceasing recurrence of doubts and inquiries, on any one article of which her mind was incapable of more than momentary repose, the hours passed away, and her journey advanced much faster than she looked for. The pressing anxieties of thought, which pre-vented her from noticing anything before her, when once beyond the neighbourhood of Woodston, saved her at the same time from watching her progress; and though no object on the road could engage a moment's attention, she found no stage of it tedious. From this, she was preserved too by another cause, by feeling no eagerness for her journey's conclusion; for to return in such a manner to Fullerton was almost to destroy the pleasure of a meeting with those she loved best, even after an absence such as hers – an eleven weeks absence. What had she to say that would not humble herself and pain her family; that would not increase her own grief by the confession of it, extend an useless resentment, and perhaps involve the innocent with the guilty in undistinguishing ill-will? She could never do justice to Henry and Eleanor's merit; she felt it too strongly for expression; and should a dislike be taken against them, should they be thought of unfavourably, on their father's account, it would cut her to the heart.

With these feelings, she rather dreaded than sought for the first view of that well-known spire which would announce her within twenty miles of home. Salisbury she had known to be her point on leaving Northanger; but after the first stage she had been indebted to the post-masters for the names of the places which were then to conduct her to it; so great had been her ignorance of her route. She met with nothing, however, to distress or frighten her. Her youth, civil manners and liberal pay, procured her all the attention that a traveller like herself could require; and stopping only to change horses, she travelled on for about eleven hours without accident or alarm, and between six and seven o'clock in the evening found herself entering Fullerton.

A heroine returning, at the close of her career, to her native village, in all the triumph of recovered reputation, and all the dignity of a countess, with a long train of noble relations in their several phaetons, and three waiting-maids in a travelling chaise-and-four, behind her, is an event on which the pen of the contriver may well delight to dwell; it gives credit to every conclusion, and the author must share in the glory she so liberally bestows. – But my affair is widely different; I bring back my heroine to her home in solitude and disgrace; and no sweet elation of spirits can lead me into minuteness. A heroine in a hack post-chaise, is such a blow upon sentiment, as no attempt at grandeur or pathos can withstand. Swiftly therefore shall her post-boy drive through the village, amid the gaze of Sunday groups, and speedy shall be her descent from it.

But, whatever might be the distress of Catherine's mind, as she thus advanced towards the Parsonage, and whatever the humiliation of her biographer in relating it, she was preparing enjoyment of no everyday nature for those to whom she went; first, in the appearance of her carriage – and secondly, in herself. The chaise of a traveller being a rare sight in Fullerton, the whole family were immediately at the window; and to have it stop at the sweep-gate was a pleasure to brighten every eye and occupy every fancy – a pleasure quite unlooked for by all but the two youngest children, a boy and girl of six and four years old, who expected a brother or sister in every carriage. Happy the glance that first distinguished Catherine! – Happy the voice that proclaimed the discovery! – But whether such happiness were the lawful property of George or Harriet could never be exactly understood.

Her father, mother, Sarah, George, and Harriet, all assembled at the door, to welcome her with affectionate eagerness, was a sight to awaken the best feelings of Catherine's heart; and in the embrace of each, as she stepped from the carriage, she found herself soothed beyond anything that she had believed possible. So surrounded, so caressed, she was even happy! In the joyfulness of family love everything for a short time was subdued, and the pleasure of seeing her, leaving them at first little leisure for calm curiosity, they were all seated round the tea-table, which Mrs Morland had hurried for the comfort of the poor traveller, whose pale and jaded looks soon caught her notice, before any inquiry so direct as to demand a positive answer was addressed to her.

Reluctantly, and with much hesitation, did she then begin what might perhaps, at the end of half an hour, be termed by the courtesy of her hearers, an explanation; but scarcely, within that time, could they at all discover the cause, or collect the particulars of her sudden return. They were far from being an irritable race; far from any quickness in catching, or bitterness in resenting affronts: – but here, when the whole was unfolded, was an insult not to be overlooked, nor, for the first half hour, to be easily pardoned. Without suffering any romantic alarm, in the consideration of their daughter's long and lonely journey, Mr and Mrs Morland could not but feel that it might have been productive of much unpleasantness to her; that it was what they could never have voluntarily suffered; and that, in forcing her on such a measure, General Tilney had acted neither honourably nor feelingly – neither as a gentleman nor as a parent. Why he had done it, what could have provoked him to such a breach of hospitality, and so suddenly turned all his partial regard for their daughter into actual ill-will, was a matter which they were at least as far from divining as Catherine herself; but it did not oppress them by any means so long; and, after a due course of useless conjecture, that, 'it was a strange business, and that he must be a very strange man,' grew enough for all their indignation and wonder; though Sarah indeed still indulged in the sweets of incomprehensibility, exclaiming and conjecturing with youthful ardour. – 'My dear, you give yourself a great deal of needless trouble,' said her mother at last; 'depend upon it, it is something not at all worth understanding.'

'I can allow for his wishing Catherine away, when he recollected this engagement,' said Sarah, 'but why not do it civilly?'

'I am sorry for the young people,' returned Mrs Morland; 'they must have a sad time of it; but as for anything else, it is no matter now;

Catherine is safe at home, and our comfort does not depend upon General Tilney.' Catherine sighed. 'Well,' continued her philosophic mother, 'I am glad I did not know of your journey at the time; but now it is all over perhaps there is no great harm done. It is always good for young people to be put upon exerting themselves; and you know, my dear Catherine, you always were a sad little scatter-brained creature; but now you must have been forced to have your wits about you, with so much changing of chaises and so forth; and I hope it will appear that you have not left anything behind you in any of the pockets.'

Catherine hoped so too, and tried to feel an interest in her own amendment, but her spirits were quite worn down; and, to be silent and alone becoming soon her only wish, she readily agreed to her mother's next counsel of going early to bed. Her parents seeing nothing in her ill-looks and agitation but the natural consequence of mortified feelings, and of the unusual exertion and fatigue of such a journey, parted from her without any doubt of their being soon slept away; and though, when they all met the next morning, her recovery was not equal to their hopes, they were still perfectly unsuspicious of there being any deeper evil. They never once thought of her heart, which, for the parents of a young lady of seventeen, just returned from her first excursion from home, was odd enough!

As soon as breakfast was over, she sat down to fulfil her promise to Miss Tilney, whose trust in the effect of time and distance on her friend's disposition was already justified, for already did Catherine reproach herself with having parted from Eleanor coldly; with having never enough valued her merits or kindness; and never enough commiserated her for what she had been yesterday left to endure. The strength of these feelings, however, was far from assisting her pen; and never had it been harder for her to write than in addressing Eleanor Tilney. To compose a letter which might at once do justice to her sentiments and her situation, convey gratitude without servile regret, be guarded without coldness, and honest without resentment – a letter which Eleanor might not be pained by the perusal of – and, above all, which she might not blush herself, if Henry should chance to see, was an undertaking to frighten away all her powers of performance; and, after long thought and much perplexity, to be very brief was all that she could determine on with any confidence of safety. The money therefore which Eleanor had advanced was enclosed with little more than grateful thanks, and the thousand good wishes of a most affectionate heart.

'This has been a strange acquaintance,' observed Mrs Morland, as the letter was finished; 'soon made and soon ended. – I am sorry it happens so, for Mrs Allen thought them very pretty kind of young people; and you were sadly out of luck too in your Isabella. Ah! poor James! Well, we must live and learn; and the next new friends you make I hope will be better worth keeping.'

Catherine coloured as she warmly answered, 'No friend can be better worth keeping than Eleanor.'

'If so, my dear, I dare say you will meet again some time or other; do not be uneasy. It is ten to one but you are thrown together again in the course of a few years; and then what a pleasure it will be!'

Mrs Morland was not happy in her attempt at consolation. The hope of meeting again in the course of a few years could only put into Catherine's head what might happen within that time to make a meeting dreadful to her. She could never forget Henry Tilney, or think of him with less tenderness than she did at that moment; but he might forget her; and in that case to meet! – Her eyes filled with tears as she pictured her acquaintance so renewed; and her mother, perceiving her comfortable suggestions to have had no good effect, proposed, as another expedient for restoring her spirits, that they should call on Mrs Allen.

The two houses were only a quarter of a mile apart; and, as they walked, Mrs Morland quickly dispatched all that she felt on the score of James's disappointment. 'We are sorry for him,' said she; 'but otherwise there is no harm done in the match going off; for it could not be a desirable thing to have him engaged to a girl whom we had not the smallest acquaintance with, and who was so entirely without fortune; and now, after such behaviour, we cannot think at all well of her. Just at present it comes hard to poor James; but that will not last for ever; and I dare say he will be a discreeter man all his life, for the foolishness of his first choice.'

This was just such a summary view of the affair as Catherine could listen to; another sentence might have endangered her complaisance, and made her reply less rational; for soon were all her thinking powers swallowed up in the reflection of her own change of feelings and spirits since last she had trodden that well-known road. It was not three months ago since, wild with joyful expectation, she had there run backwards and forwards some ten times a-day, with an heart light, gay, and independent; looking forward to pleasures untasted and unalloyed, and free from the apprehension of evil as from the knowledge of it. Three months ago had seen her all this; and now, how altered a being did she return!

She was received by the Allens with all the kindness which her unlooked-for appearance, acting on a steady affection, would naturally call forth; and great was their surprise, and warm their displeasure, on hearing how she had been treated, – though Mrs Morland's account of it was no inflated representation, no studied appeal to their passions. 'Catherine took us quite by surprise yesterday evening,' said she. 'She travelled all the way post by herself, and knew nothing of coming till Saturday night; for General Tilney, from some odd fancy or other, all of a sudden grew tired of having her there, and almost turned her out of the house. Very unfriendly, certainly; and he must be a very odd man; – but we are so glad to have her amongst us again! And it is a great comfort to find that she is not a poor helpless creature, but can shift very well for herself.'

Mr Allen expressed himself on the occasion with the reasonable resentment of a sensible friend; and Mrs Allen thought his expressions quite good enough to be immediately made use of again by herself. His wonder, his conjectures, and his explanations, became in succession hers, with the addition of this single remark – 'I really have not patience with the General' – to fill up every accidental pause. And, 'I really have not patience with the General,' was uttered twice after Mr Allen left the room, without any relaxation of anger, or any material digression of thought. A more considerable degree of wandering attended the third repetition; and, after completing the fourth, she immediately added, 'Only think, my dear, of my having got that frightful great rent in my best Mechlin[22] so charmingly mended, before I left Bath, that one can hardly see where it was. I must show it you some day or other. Bath is a nice place, Catherine, after all. I assure you I did not above half like coming away. Mrs Thorpe's being there was such a comfort to us, was not it? You know you and I were quite forlorn at first.'

'Yes, but *that* did not last long,' said Catherine, her eyes brightening at the recollection of what had first given spirit to her existence there.

'Very true: we soon met with Mrs Thorpe, and then we wanted for nothing. My dear, do not you think these silk gloves wear very well? I put them on new the first time of our going to the Lower Rooms, you know, and I have worn them a great deal since. Do you remember that evening?'

'Do I! Oh! perfectly.'

'It was very agreeable, was not it? Mr Tilney drank tea with us, and I always thought him a great addition, he is so very agreeable. I have a notion you danced with him, but am not quite sure. I remember I had my favourite gown on.'

Catherine could not answer; and, after a short trial of other subjects, Mrs Allen again returned to – 'I really have not patience with the General! Such an agreeable, worthy man as he seemed to be! I do not suppose, Mrs Morland, you ever saw a better-bred man in your life.

His lodgings were taken the very day after he left them, Catherine. But no wonder; Milsom Street you know.' –

As they walked home again, Mrs Morland endeavoured to impress on her daughter's mind the happiness of having such steady well-wishers as Mr and Mrs Allen, and the very little consideration which the neglect or unkindness of slight acquaintance like the Tilneys ought to have with her, while she could preserve the good opinion and affection of her earliest friends. There was a great deal of good sense in all this; but there are some situations of the human mind in which good sense has very little power; and Catherine's feelings contradicted almost every position her mother advanced. It was upon the behaviour of these very slight acquaintance that all her present happiness depended; and while Mrs Morland was successfully confirming her own opinions by the justness of her own representations, Catherine was silently reflecting that *now* Henry must have arrived at Northanger; *now* he must have heard of her departure; and *now*, perhaps, they were all setting off for Hereford.

Chapter 30

CATHERINE'S DISPOSITION was not naturally sedentary, nor had her habits been ever very industrious; but whatever might hitherto have been her defects of that sort, her mother could not but perceive them now to be greatly increased. She could neither sit still, nor employ herself for ten minutes together, walking round the garden and orchard again and again, as if nothing but motion was voluntary; and it seemed as if she could even walk about the house rather than remain fixed for any time in the parlour. Her loss of spirits was a yet greater alteration. In her rambling and her idleness she might only be a caricature of herself; but in her silence and sadness she was the very reverse of all that she had been before.

For two days Mrs Morland allowed it to pass even without a hint; but when a third night's rest had neither restored her cheerfulness, improved her in useful activity, nor given her a greater inclination for needle-work, she could no longer refrain from the gentle reproof of, 'My dear Catherine, I am afraid you are growing quite a fine lady. I do not know when poor Richard's cravats would be done, if he had no friend but you. Your head runs too much upon Bath; but there is a time for everything – a time for balls and plays, and a time for work. You have had a long run of amusement, and now you must try to be useful.'

Catherine took up her work directly, saying, in a dejected voice, that 'her head did not run upon Bath – much.'

'Then you are fretting about General Tilney, and that is very simple of you; for ten to one whether you ever see him again. You should never fret about trifles.' After a short silence – 'I hope, my Catherine, you are not getting out of humour with home because it is not so grand as Northanger. That would be turning your visit into an evil indeed. Wherever you are you should always be contented, but especially at home, because there you must spend the most of your time. I did not quite like, at breakfast, to hear you talk so much about the French-bread at Northanger.'

'I am sure I do not care about the bread. It is all the same to me what I eat.'

'There is a very clever Essay in one of the books upstairs upon much such a subject, about young girls that have been spoilt for home by great acquaintance – "The Mirror," I think. I will look it out for you some day or other, because I am sure it will do you good.'

Catherine said no more, and, with an endeavour to do right, applied to her work; but, after a few minutes, sunk again, without knowing it herself, into languor and listlessness, moving herself in her chair, from the irritation of weariness, much oftener than she moved her needle. – Mrs Morland watched the progress of this relapse; and seeing, in her daughter's absent and dissatisfied look, the full proof of that repining spirit to which she had now begun to attribute her want of cheerfulness, hastily left the room to fetch the book in question, anxious to lose no time in attacking so dreadful a malady. It was some time before she could find what she looked for; and other family matters occurring to detain her, a quarter of an hour had elapsed ere she returned downstairs with the volume from which so much was hoped. Her avocations above having shut out all noise but what she created herself, she knew not that a visitor had arrived within the last few minutes, till, on entering the room, the first object she beheld was a young man whom she had never seen before. With a look of much respect, he immediately rose, and being introduced to her by her conscious daughter as 'Mr Henry Tilney,' with the embarrassment of real sensibility began to apologise for his appearance there, acknowledging that after what had passed he had little right to expect a welcome at Fullerton, and stating his impatience to be assured of Miss Morland's having reached her home in safety, as the cause of his intrusion. He did not address himself to an uncandid judge or a resentful heart. Far from comprehending him or his sister in their father's misconduct, Mrs Morland had been always kindly disposed towards each, and instantly, pleased by his appearance, received him with the simple professions of unaffected benevolence; thanking him for such an attention to her daughter, assuring him that the friends of her children were always welcome there, and entreating him to say not another word of the past.

He was not ill inclined to obey this request, for, though his heart was greatly relieved by such unlooked-for mildness, it was not just at that moment in his power to say anything to the purpose. Returning in silence to his seat, therefore, he remained for some minutes most civilly answering all Mrs Morland's common remarks about the weather and roads. Catherine meanwhile, – the anxious, agitated, happy, feverish Catherine, – said not a word; but her glowing cheek and brightened eye made her mother trust that this good-natured visit would at least set her heart at ease for a time, and gladly therefore did she lay aside the first volume of the Mirror for a future hour.

Desirous of Mr Morland's assistance, as well in giving encouragement, as in finding conversation for her guest, whose embarrassment on his father's account she earnestly pitied, Mrs Morland had very early dispatched one of the children to summon him; but Mr Morland was from home – and being thus without any support, at the end of a quarter of an hour she had nothing to say. After a couple of minutes' unbroken silence, Henry, turning to Catherine for the first time since her mother's entrance, asked her, with sudden alacrity, if Mr and Mrs Allen were now at Fullerton? and on developing, from amidst all her perplexity of words in reply, the meaning, which one short syllable would have given, immediately expressed his intention of paying his respects to them, and, with a rising colour, asked her if she would have the goodness to show him the way. 'You may see the house from this window, sir,' was information on Sarah's side, which produced only a bow of acknowledgment from the gentleman, and a silencing nod from her mother; for Mrs Morland, thinking it probable, as a secondary consideration in his wish of waiting on their worthy neighbours, that he might have some explanation to give of his father's behaviour, which it must be more pleasant for him to communicate only to Catherine, would not on any account prevent her accompanying him. They began their walk, and Mrs Morland was not entirely mistaken in his object in wishing it. Some explanation on his father's account he had to give; but his first purpose was to explain himself, and before they reached Mr Allen's grounds he had done it so well, that Catherine did not think it could ever be repeated too often. She was assured of his affection; and that heart in return was solicited, which, perhaps, they pretty equally knew was already entirely his own; for, though Henry was now sincerely attached to her, though he felt and delighted in all the excellencies of her character and truly loved her society, I must confess that his affection originated in nothing better than gratitude, or, in other words, that a persuasion of her partiality for him had been the only cause of giving her a serious thought. It is a new circumstance in romance, I acknowledge, and dreadfully derogatory of an heroine's dignity; but if it be as new in common life, the credit of a wild imagination will at least be all my own.

A very short visit to Mrs Allen, in which Henry talked at random, without sense or connection, and Catherine, wrapt in the contemplation of her own unutterable happiness, scarcely opened her lips, dismissed them to the ecstasies of another tête-à-tête; and before it was suffered to close, she was enabled to judge how far he was sanctioned by parental authority in his present application. On his return from Woodston, two days before, he had been met near the Abbey by his impatient father, hastily informed in angry terms of Miss Morland's departure, and ordered to think of her no more.

Such was the permission upon which he had now offered her his hand. The affrighted Catherine, amidst all the terrors of expectation, as she listened to this account, could not but rejoice in the kind caution with which Henry had saved her from the necessity of a conscientious rejection, by engaging her faith before he mentioned the subject; and as he proceeded to give the particulars, and explain the motives of his father's conduct, her feelings soon hardened into even a triumphant delight. The General had had nothing to accuse her of, nothing to lay to her charge, but her being the involuntary, unconscious object of a deception which his pride could not pardon, and which a better pride would have been ashamed to own. She was guilty only of being less rich than he had supposed her to be. Under a mistaken persuasion of her possessions and claims, he had courted her acquaintance in Bath, solicited her company at Northanger, and designed her for his daughter in law. On discovering his error, to turn her from the house seemed the best, though to his feelings an inadequate proof of his resentment towards herself, and his contempt of her family.

John Thorpe had first misled him. The General, perceiving his son one night at the theatre to be paying considerable attention to Miss Morland, had accidentally inquired of Thorpe, if he knew more of her than her name. Thorpe, most happy to be on speaking terms with a man of General Tilney's importance, had been joyfully and proudly communicative; – and being at that time not only in daily expectation of Morland's engaging Isabella, but likewise pretty well resolved upon marrying Catherine himself, his vanity induced him to represent the family as yet more wealthy than his vanity and avarice had made him believe them. With whomsoever he was, or was likely to be connected, his own consequence always required that theirs should be great, and as his intimacy with any acquaintance grew, so regularly grew their fortune. The expectations of his friend Morland, therefore, from the first over-rated, had ever since his introduction to Isabella, been gradually increasing; and by merely adding twice as much for the grandeur of the moment, by doubling what he chose to think the amount of Mr Morland's preferment, trebling his private fortune, bestowing a rich aunt, and sinking half the children, he was able to represent the whole family to the General in a most respectable light. For Catherine, however, the peculiar object of the General's curiosity, and his own speculations, he had yet something more in reserve, and the ten or fifteen thousand pounds which her father could give her, would be a pretty addition to Mr Allen's estate. Her intimacy there had made him seriously determine on her being handsomely legacied hereafter; and to speak of her therefore as the almost acknowledged future heiress of Fullerton naturally followed. Upon such intelligence the General had proceeded; for never had it occurred to him to doubt its authority. Thorpe's interest in the family, by his sister's approaching connection with one of its members, and his own views on another, (circumstances of which he boasted with almost equal openness,) seemed sufficient vouchers for his truth; and to these were added the absolute facts of the Allens being wealthy and childless, of Miss Morland's being under their care, and – as soon as his acquaintance allowed him to judge – of their treating her with parental kindness. His resolution was soon formed. Already had he discerned a liking towards Miss Morland in the countenance of his son; and thankful for Mr Thorpe's communication, he almost instantly determined to spare no pains in weakening his boasted interest and ruining his dearest hopes. Catherine herself could not be more ignorant at the time of all this, than his own children. Henry and Eleanor, perceiving nothing in her situation likely to engage their father's particular respect, had seen with astonishment the sudden-ness, continuance and extent of his attention; and though latterly, from some hints which had accompanied an almost positive command to his son of doing everything in his power to attach her, Henry was convinced of his father's believing it to be an advantageous connection, it was not till the late explanation at Northanger that they had the smallest idea of the false calculations which had hurried him on. That they were false, the General had learnt from the very person who had suggested them, from Thorpe himself, whom he had chanced to meet again in town, and who, under the influence of exactly opposite feelings, irritated by Catherine's refusal, and yet more by the failure of a very recent endeavour to accomplish a reconciliation between Morland and Isabella, convinced that they were separated for ever, and spurning a friendship which could be no longer serviceable, hastened to contradict all that he had said before to the advantage of the Morlands; – confessed himself to have been totally mistaken in his opinion of their circumstances and character, misled by the rhodo-montade of his friend, to believe his father a man of substance and credit, whereas the transactions of the two or three last weeks proved him to be neither; for after coming eagerly forward on the first overture of a marriage between the families, with the most liberal proposals, he had, on being brought to the point by the shrewdness of the relator, been constrained to acknowledge himself incapable of giving the young people even a decent support. They were, in fact, a necessitous family; numerous too almost beyond example; by no means respected in their own neighbourhood, as he had lately had particular opportunities of discovering; aiming at a style of life which their fortune could not warrant; seeking to better themselves by wealthy connections; a forward, bragging, scheming race.

The terrified General pronounced the name of Allen with an inquiring look; and here too Thorpe had learnt his error. The Allens, he believed, had lived near them too long, and he knew the young man on whom the Fullerton estate must devolve. The General needed no more. Enraged with almost everybody in the world but himself, he set out the next day for the Abbey, where his performances have been seen.

I leave it to my reader's sagacity to determine how much of all this it was possible for Henry to communicate at this time to Catherine, how much of it he could have learnt from his father, in what points his own conjectures might assist him, and what portion must yet remain to be told in a letter from James. I have united for their ease what they must divide for mine. Catherine, at any rate, heard enough to feel, that in suspecting General Tilney of either murdering or shutting up his wife, she had scarcely sinned against his character, or magnified his cruelty.

Henry, in having such things to relate of his father, was almost as pitiable as in their first avowal to himself. He blushed for the narrow-minded counsel which he was obliged to expose. The conversation between them at Northanger had been of the most unfriendly kind. Henry's indignation on hearing how Catherine had been treated, on comprehending his father's views, and being ordered to acquiesce in them, had been open and bold. The General, accustomed on every ordinary occasion to give the law in his family, prepared for no reluctance but of feeling, no opposing desire that should dare to clothe itself in words, could ill brook the opposition of his son, steady as the sanction of reason and the dictate of conscience could make it. But, in such a cause, his anger, though it must shock, could not intimidate Henry, who was sustained in his purpose by a conviction of its justice. He felt himself bound as much in honour as in affection to Miss Morland, and believing that heart to be his own which he had been directed to gain, no unworthy retraction of a tacit consent, no reversing decree of unjustifiable anger, could shake his fidelity, or influence the resolutions it prompted.

He steadily refused to accompany his father into Herefordshire, an engagement formed almost at the moment, to promote the dismissal of Catherine, and as steadily declared his intention of offering her his hand. The General was furious in his anger, and they parted in dreadful disagreement. Henry, in an agitation of mind which many solitary hours were required to compose, had returned almost instantly to Woodston; and, on the afternoon of the following day, had begun his journey to Fullerton.

Chapter 31

MR AND MRS MORLAND'S surprise on being applied to by Mr Tilney, for their consent to his marrying their daughter, was, for a few minutes, considerable; it having never entered their heads to suspect an attachment on either side; but as nothing, after all, could be more natural than Catherine's being beloved, they soon learnt to consider it with only the happy agitation of gratified pride, and, as far as they alone were concerned, had not a single objection to start. His pleasing manners and good sense were self-evident recommendations; and having never heard evil of him, it was not their way to suppose any evil could be told. Good-will supplying the place of experience, his character needed no attestation. 'Catherine would make a sad heedless young house-keeper to be sure,' was her mother's foreboding remark; but quick was the consolation of there being nothing like practice.

There was but one obstacle, in short, to be mentioned; but till that one was removed, it must be impossible for them to sanction the engagement. Their tempers were mild, but their principles were steady, and while his parent so expressly forbad the connection, they could not allow themselves to encourage it. That the General should come forward to solicit the alliance, or that he should even very heartily approve it, they were not refined enough to make any parading stipulation; but the decent appearance of consent must be yielded, and that once obtained – and their own hearts made them trust that it could not be very long denied – their willing approbation was instantly to follow. His *consent* was all that they wished for. They were no more inclined than entitled to demand his *money*. Of a very considerable fortune, his son was, by marriage settlements, eventually secure; his present income was an income of independence and comfort, and under every pecuniary view, it was a match beyond the claims of their daughter.

The young people could not be surprised at a decision like this. They felt and they deplored – but they could not resent it; and they parted, endeavouring to hope that such a change in the General, as each believed almost impossible, might speedily take place, to unite them again in the fullness of privileged affection. Henry returned to what was now his only home, to watch over his young plantations, and extend his improvements for her sake, to whose share in them he looked anxiously forward; and Catherine remained at Fullerton to cry. Whether the torments of absence were softened by a clandestine correspondence, let us not inquire. Mr and Mrs Morland never did – they had been too kind to exact any promise; and whenever Catherine received a letter, as, at that time, happened pretty often, they always looked another way.

The anxiety, which in this state of their attachment must be the portion of Henry and Catherine, and of all who loved either, as to its final event, can hardly extend, I fear, to the bosom of my readers, who will see in the tell-tale compression of the pages before them, that we are all hastening together to perfect felicity. The means by which their early marriage was effected can be the only doubt; what probable circumstance could work upon a temper like the General's? The circumstance which chiefly availed, was the marriage of his daughter with a man of fortune and consequence, which took place in the course of the summer – an accession of dignity that threw him into a fit of good-humour, from which he did not recover till after Eleanor had obtained his forgiveness of Henry, and his permission for him 'to be a fool if he liked it!'

The marriage of Eleanor Tilney, her removal from all the evils of such a home as Northanger had been made by Henry's banishment, to the home of her choice and the man of her choice, is an event which I expect to give general satisfaction among all her acquaintance. My own joy on the occasion is very sincere. I know no one more entitled, by unpretending merit, or better prepared by habitual suffering, to receive and enjoy felicity. Her partiality for this gentleman was not of recent origin; and he had been long withheld only by inferiority of situation from addressing her. His unexpected accession to title and fortune had removed all his difficulties; and never had the General loved his daughter so well in all her hours of companionship, utility, and patient endurance, as when he first hailed her, 'Your Ladyship!' Her husband was really deserving of her; independent of his peerage, his wealth, and his attachment, being to a precision the most charming young man in the world. Any further definition of his merits must be unnecessary; the most charming young man in the world is instantly before the imagination of us all. Concerning the one in question therefore I have only to add – (aware that the rules of composition forbid the introduction of a character not connected with my fable) – that this was the very gentleman whose negligent servant left behind him that collection of washing-bills, resulting from a long visit at Northanger, by which my heroine was involved in one of her most alarming adventures.

The influence of the Viscount and Viscountess in their brother's behalf was assisted by that right understanding of Mr Morland's circumstances which, as soon as the General would allow himself to be informed, they were qualified to give. It taught him that he had been scarcely more misled by Thorpe's first boast of the family wealth, than by his subsequent malicious overthrow of it; that in no sense of the word were they necessitous or poor, and that Catherine would have three thousand pounds. This was so material an amendment of his late expectations, that it greatly contributed to smooth the descent of his pride; and by no means without its effect was the private intelligence, which he was at some pains to procure, that the Fullerton estate, being entirely at the disposal of its present proprietor, was consequently open to every greedy speculation.

On the strength of this, the General, soon after Eleanor's marriage, permitted his son to return to Northanger, and thence made him the bearer of his consent, very courteously worded in a page full of empty professions to Mr Morland. The event which it authorised soon followed: Henry and Catherine were married, the bells rang and everybody smiled; and, as this took place within a twelve-month from the first day of their meeting, it will not appear, after all the dreadful delays occasioned by the General's cruelty, that they were essentially hurt by it. To begin perfect happiness at the respective ages of twenty-six and eighteen, is to do pretty well; and professing myself moreover convinced, that the General's unjust interference, so far from being really injurious to their felicity, was perhaps rather conducive to it, by improving their knowledge of each other, and adding strength to their attachment, I leave it to be settled by whomsoever it may concern, whether the tendency of this work be altogether to recommend parental tyranny, or reward filial disobedience.

NOTES

1 A family joke. In a letter to her sister Cassandra in 1776, Jane Austen wrote, 'Mr Richard Harvey's match is to be put off until he has got a better Christian name, of which he has great hopes.'

2 The 'Beggar's Petition' by the Revd Thomas Moss (1769)

3 'The Hare and Many Friends' from Gay's Fables (1727)

4 Alexander Pope (1688–1744). Quotation from 'Elegy to the Memory of an Unfortunate Lady' (1717).

5 Thomas Gray (1716–71). Quotation from 'Elegy' (1751) (misquoted).

6 James Thompson (1700–48). Quotation from *The Seasons*. 'Spring' (1728) (misquoted).

7 William Shakespeare (1564–1616). Quotations taken from *Othello*, Act III, Scene iii, line 332 (misquoted); *Measure for Measure*, Act III, Scene i, line 79 (misquoted) and *Twelfth Night*, Act II, Scene iv, line 117.

8 This quotation remains unidentified.

9 Here meaning odd-looking people or objects.

10 *Cecelia* (1782) and *Camilla* (1796) were written by Fanny Burney. *Belinda*, (1786) was written by Maria Edgeworth.

11 Orange-red.

12 Both novels are by Ann Radcliffe: *The Mysteries of Udolpho* (1794) and *The Italian* (1797).

13 *Castle of Wolfenbach* written by Mrs Parsons (1793); *Clermont* by Regina Maria Roche (1798); *The Mysterious Warning*, again by Mrs Parsons (1796); *The Necromancer: or the Tale of the Black Forest* by Lawrence Flammenberg, translated by Peter Teuthold (1794); *The Midnight Bell* by Francis Latham (1798); *The Orphan of the Rhine* by

Mrs Sleath (1798); *Horrid Mysteries*, from the German of the Marquis of Grosse, by P. Will (1796).

14 *Sir Charles Grandison* (1753–4). A novel in seven volumes by Samuel Richardson (1689–1761).

15 *Tom Jones*. A novel published in 1749 by Henry Fielding (1707–54). *The Monk* (1796) by M. J. Lewis (1775–1818).

16 Embroidered.

17 Mull is plain muslin, jackonet is a heavier one.

18 Jane Austen is poking fun at John Thorpe here. Blaize Castle was relatively new, built only in the eighteenth century.

19 Johnson's *Dictionary* (1755) and Blair's *Lectures on Rhetoric* (1783).

20 A fireplace invented by Benjamin Thompson, Count Rumford (1753–1814).

21 A bed covered in cotton on which there are fancy figures.

22 Something which has been made of mechlin lace.

WORDSWORTH CLASSICS

General Editors: Marcus Clapham & Clive Reynard

JANE AUSTEN
Emma
Mansfield Park
Northanger Abbey
Persuasion
Pride and Prejudice
Sense and Sensibility

ARNOLD BENNETT
Anna of the Five Towns
The Old Wives' Tale

R. D. BLACKMORE
Lorna Doone

ANNE BRONTË
Agnes Grey
The Tenant of Wildfell Hall

CHARLOTTE BRONTË
Jane Eyre
The Professor
Shirley
Villette

EMILY BRONTË
Wuthering Heights

JOHN BUCHAN
Greenmantle
The Island of Sheep
John Macnab
Mr Standfast
The Three Hostages
The Thirty-Nine Steps

SAMUEL BUTLER
Erewhon
The Way of All Flesh

LEWIS CARROLL
Alice in Wonderland

CERVANTES
Don Quixote

ANTON CHEKHOV
Selected Stories

G. K. CHESTERTON
Father Brown:
Selected Stories
The Club of Queer Trades
The Man who was Thursday
The Napoleon of Notting Hill

ERSKINE CHILDERS
The Riddle of the Sands

JOHN CLELAND
Memoirs of a Woman of Pleasure: Fanny Hill

SELECTED BY
REX COLLINGS
Classic Victorian and Edwardian Ghost Stories

WILKIE COLLINS
The Moonstone
The Woman in White

JOSEPH CONRAD
Almayer's Folly
Heart of Darkness
Lord Jim
Nostromo
The Secret Agent
Selected Short Stories
Victory

J. FENIMORE COOPER
The Last of the Mohicans

STEPHEN CRANE
The Red Badge of Courage

THOMAS DE QUINCEY
Confessions of an English Opium Eater

DANIEL DEFOE
Moll Flanders
Robinson Crusoe

CHARLES DICKENS
Bleak House
Christmas Books
David Copperfield
Dombey and Son
Great Expectations
Hard Times
Little Dorrit
Martin Chuzzlewit
Nicholas Nickleby
Old Curiosity Shop
Oliver Twist
Our Mutual Friend
Pickwick Papers
A Tale of Two Cities

BENJAMIN DISRAELI
Sybil

THEODOR DOSTOEVSKY
Crime and Punishment
The Idiot

SIR ARTHUR CONAN DOYLE
The Adventures of Sherlock Holmes
The Case-Book of Sherlock Holmes
The Lost World & other stories
The Return of Sherlock Holmes
Sir Nigel
The White Company

GEORGE DU MAURIER
Trilby

ALEXANDRE DUMAS
The Three Musketeers

MARIA EDGEWORTH
Castle Rackrent

GEORGE ELIOT
Adam Bede
Daniel Deronda

WORDSWORTH CLASSICS

WORDSWORTH CLASSICS

THOMAS LOVE PEACOCK
*Headlong Hall &
Nightmare Abbey*

EDGAR ALLAN POE
*Tales of Mystery and
Imagination*

FREDERICK ROLFE
Hadrian the Seventh

SIR WALTER SCOTT
*Ivanhoe
Rob Roy*

WILLIAM SHAKESPEARE
*All's Well that Ends Well
Antony and Cleopatra
As You Like It
The Comedy of Errors
Coriolanus
Hamlet
Henry IV Part 1
Henry IV Part 2
Henry V
Julius Caesar
King John
King Lear
Love's Labours Lost
Macbeth
Measure for Measure
The Merchant of Venice
The Merry Wives of
Windsor
A Midsummer Night's
Dream
Much Ado About Nothing
Othello
Pericles
Richard II
Richard III
Romeo and Juliet
The Taming of the Shrew
The Tempest
Titus Andronicus
Troilus and Cressida*

*Twelfth Night
Two Gentlemen of
Verona
A Winter's Tale*

MARY SHELLEY
Frankenstein

TOBIAS SMOLLETT
Humphry Clinker

LAURENCE STERNE
*A Sentimental Journey
Tristram Shandy*

ROBERT LOUIS STEVENSON
*Dr Jekyll and Mr Hyde
The Master of Ballantrae
& Weir of Hermiston*

BRAM STOKER
Dracula

R. S. SURTEES
*Mr Sponge's
Sporting Tour*

JONATHAN SWIFT
Gulliver's Travels

W. M. THACKERAY
Vanity Fair

TOLSTOY
*Anna Karenina
War and Peace*

ANTHONY TROLLOPE
*Barchester Towers
Can You Forgive Her?
Dr Thorne
The Eustace Diamonds
Framley Parsonage
The Last Chronicle
of Barset
Phineas Finn
Phineas Redux
The Small House at
Allington
The Way We Live Now
The Warden*

IVAN SERGEYEVICH TURGENEV
Fathers and Sons

MARK TWAIN
*Tom Sawyer &
Huckleberry Finn*

JULES VERNE
*Around the World in
Eighty Days & Five
Weeks in a Balloon
Journey to the Centre
of the Earth
Twenty Thousand
Leagues Under the Sea*

VIRGIL
The Aeneid

VOLTAIRE
Candide

LEW WALLACE
Ben Hur

ISAAC WALTON
The Compleat Angler

EDITH WHARTON
The Age of Innocence

GILBERT WHITE
*The Natural History
of Selborne*

OSCAR WILDE
*Lord Arthur Savile's
Crime & other stories
The Picture of
Dorian Gray
The Plays*
IN TWO VOLUMES

VIRGINIA WOOLF
*Mrs Dalloway
Orlando
To the Lighthouse*

P. C. WREN
Beau Geste

Bhagavad Gita

DISTRIBUTION

AUSTRALIA & PAPUA NEW GUINEA
Peribo Pty Ltd
58 Beaumont Road, Mount Kuring-Gai
NSW 2080, Australia
Tel: (02) 457 0011 Fax: (02) 457 0022

CZECH REPUBLIC
Bohemian Ventures s r. o.,
Delnicka 13, 170 00 Prague 7
Tel: 042 2 877837 Fax: 042 2 801498

FRANCE
Copernicus Diffusion
81 Rue des Entrepreneurs, Paris 75015
Tel: 01 53 95 38 00 Fax: 01 53 95 38 01

GERMANY & AUSTRIA
Taschenbuch-Vertrieb
Ingeborg Blank GmbH
Lager und Buro Rohrmooser Str 1
85256 Vierkirchen/Pasenbach
Tel: 08139-8130/8184 Fax: 08139-8140

Tradis Verlag und Vertrieb GmbH (Bookshops)
Postfach 90 03 69, D-51113 Köln
Tel: 022 03 31059 Fax: 022 03 39340

GREAT BRITAIN
Wordsworth Editions Ltd
Cumberland House, Crib Street
Ware, Hertfordshire SG12 9ET
Tel: 01920 465167 Fax: 01920 462267

INDIA
Rupa & Co
Post Box No 7071,
7/16 Makhanlal Street, Ansari Road,
Daryaganj, New Delhi – 110 002
Tel: 3278586 Fax: (011) 3277294

IRELAND
Easons & Son Limited
Furry Park Industrial Estate
Santry 9, Eire
Tel: 003531 8733811 Fax: 003531 8733945

ISRAEL
Sole Agent —**Timmy Marketing Limited**
Israel Ben Zeev 12, Ramont Gimmel, Jerusalem
Tel: 972-2-5865266 Fax: 972-2-5860035
Sole Distributor – Sefer ve Sefel Ltd
Tel & Fax: 972-2-6248237

ITALY
Logos — Edizioni e distribuzione libri
Via Curtatona 5/J
41100 Modena, Italy
Tel: 059-418820/418821 Fax: 059-280123

NEW ZEALAND & FIJI
Allphy Book Distributors Ltd
4-6 Charles Street, Eden Terrace, Auckland,
Tel: (09) 3773096 Fax: (09) 3022770

MALAYSIA & BRUNEI
Vintrade SDN BHD
5 & 7 Lorong Datuk Sulaiman 7
Taman Tun Dr Ismail
60000 Kuala Lumpur, Malaysia
Tel: (603) 717 3333 Fax: (603) 719 2942

MALTA & GOZO
Agius & Agius Ltd
42A South Street, Valletta VLT 11
Tel: 234038 - 220347 Fax: 241175

PHILIPPINES
I J Sagun Enterprises
P O Box 4322 CPO Manila
2 Topaz Road, Greenheights Village,
Taytay, Rizal
Tel: 631 80 61 TO 66

SOUTH AFRICA
Chapter Book Agencies
Postnet Private bag X10016
Edenvale, 1610 Gauteng
South Africa
Tel: (++27) 11 425 5990
Fax: (++27) 11 425 5997

SLOVAK REPUBLIC
Slovak Ventures s r. o.,
Stefanikova 128, 949 01 Nitra
Tel/Fax: 042 87 525105/6/7

SPAIN
Ribera Libros, S.L.
Poligono Martiartu, Calle 1 - no 6
48480 Arrigorriaga, Vizcaya
Tel: 34 4 6713607 (Almacen)
       34 4 4418787 (Libreria)
Fax: 34 4 6713608 (Almacen)
       34 4 4418029 (Libreria)

UNITED STATES OF AMERICA
NTC/Contemporary Publishing Company
4225 West Touhy Avenue
Lincolnwood (Chicago)
Illinois 60646-4622
USA
Tel: (847) 679 5500 Fax: (847) 679 2494

DIRECT MAIL
Bibliophile Books
5 Thomas Road, London E14 7BN,
Tel: 0171-515 9222 Fax: 0171-538 4115
Order hotline 24 hours Tel: 0171-515 9555
Cash with order + £2.50 p&p (UK)